FEATHERING YOUR NEST

THE RETIREMENT PLANNER

FEATHERING YOUR NEST

THE RETIREMENT PLANNER

The IDS Financial Library

L I S A · B E R G E R

WORKMAN PUBLISHING, NEW YORK

To my retirement safety net, my sibs: Diane Stoner, Peter Berger, Cathy Gilson, and Donny Berger.

Copyright © 1993 by Lisa Berger

All rights reserved. No portion of this book may be reproduced—
mechanically, electronically, or by any other means, including photocopying—
without written permission of the publisher. Published simultaneously in Canada
by Thomas Allen & Son Limited

Library of Congress Cataloging-in-Publication Data
Berger, Lisa L.
Feathering your nest : the retirement planner / Lisa Berger.
p. cm.
Includes index.
ISBN 1-56305-296-2 (pbk.)
1. Retirement income—United States—Planning. 2. Finance, Personal—
United States. 3. Investments. I. Title.
HG179.B456 1993 332.024′01—dc20 92-50928
CIP

Cover and book illustrations: Rob Saunders

Workman books are available at special discounts when purchased in bulk for
premiums and sales promotions as well as for fund-raising or educational
use. Special editions or book excerpts can also be created to specification.
For details, contact the Special Sales Director at the address below.

Workman Publishing Company, Inc.
708 Broadway
New York, NY 10003

Manufactured in the United States of America

First printing June 1993
10 9 8 7 6 5 4

THANKS

Hundreds of people helped me with this book, offering information, explaining things, and giving encouragement. It couldn't have been done without my agent, Gail Ross, who knows how to take care of a writer. It couldn't have been as thorough without the editorial and research help of Ellen Drought, Lauren Chambliss, Pam Terrell, Arthur Jones, and Mark R. Bacon. It couldn't have been half as interesting without the library services and wise counsel of James Srodes, Srodes Global News Service. And, it couldn't have been finished without the attentiveness of my thoughtful editor, Suzanne Rafer.

A number of people were extremely generous with their time and provided technical expertise. Many thanks to Robert Albertson, CFP, Armstrong, Welch & Macintyre; Bronwyn Belling, American Association of Retired Persons; Donna Clements, William M. Mercer, Inc.; Carl Desmarias, CPA, O'Connor & Desmarias; Thomas Drought, attorney, Cook & Franke; Mary Malgoire, CFP, Malgoire Drucker, Inc.; Richard Sills, attorney, Sills & Brodsky; Michael Tievy, benefits consultant, Gorrelick, Tievy, and Associates; and Mary Jane Yarrington, senior policy analyst, National Committee to Preserve Social Security and Medicare.

IDS

Many people at IDS Financial Services helped with this book, providing ideas and information. Technical expertise on special areas of financial planning came from Ryan Larson and Larry Melin (annuities); Kurt Larson (bonds); Dennis Abrahamzon (estate planning); Jeff Witte (estate planning and Social Security); Tim Bechtold and Andy Warwick (insurance); Randy Boser (long-term care); Janet Sundeen (health insurance); Jan Holman and Jim Maher (mutual funds); Connie Ford (volunteerism); Bob Spector and Kitty Taylor (taxes); and Joane Anderson, Lisa Hoene, Mary Komornicka, Cathie Madden, and Tim Meehan (pension plans).

Special thanks to Dennis Gurtz, Lynn Nelson, and Vicki Lubben for their thorough reviews and helpful suggestions, and to Connie Fukuda for coordinating the IDS review effort.

CONTENTS

sion Watchdog • When It's Forced on You: Early Retirement • Decisions, Decisions: Does Pension Max Pay? • Women's Predicament • Know Your Rights

Your Home: A Nest Egg of Wood and Glass • Testing Distant Waters: Real Estate Away From Home • Life Insurance: Another Egg in Your Retirement Basket • Disability Income Insurance • The Ultimate Piggy Bank: Annuities

How Does Social Security Work? • How Much Can I Expect to Receive? • Go Early or Stay Late? • Limits on What You Earn • Family Considerations • When the Time Comes: How to Sign Up • Will Social Security Be Around When My Time Comes? • Other Benefits: Disability and Survivors • Medicare • Applying for Medicare • Doctors and Bills: How Medicare Works • Quality Concerns • Is Medigap Necessary?

Where There's a Will • Probate • Sidestepping Probate: Living Trusts • Living Wills and Beyond—Preparing for Health Care Crises • Durable Health-Care Power of Attorney • Talking to Your Family About Dying (Gulp) • Finding a Will, Trust, or Estate Attorney • Funeral Planning • Estate Planning • "Put Your Money in Trust" • State Taxes

Don't Turn Your Back on the IRS • Know the Language, Know the Land • Plot Your Progress • Pinpoint Where Taxes Can Hurt You • The Deduction Game • An Assault on All Fronts: State and Local Taxes • Taxes and Living Abroad

Introduction

A PRIMER FOR YOU AND ME

This book is for all of us who have sidestepped around the notion of retirement. It was not written for the financially sophisticated individual who knows the ins and outs of 401(k)s, retirement locales, and tax treatment of lump sum distributions. Instead, it's for readers who have awakened to the fact that fulfilling dreams for the future requires making plans today.

As the title indicates, this is a planner containing information an intelligent beginner needs in order to learn about retirement. Throughout, it poses common questions and offers short answers for quick reference. However, retirement is never simple, and so the more complete answers form the bulk of the chapters.

Writing this primer has been an eye-opening experience for me, akin to learning a foreign language. As I picked up the vocabulary and ideas, I discovered new ways of thinking, new customs, and a new culture. Now, I'm virtually bilingual, but it wasn't easy!

RETIREMENT: A PERSONAL EXPERIENCE

When I started to write this book, I objected to the word "retirement" because it sounded dated. It raised pictures of an older generation—Air Stream elderlies who winter in Tucson or couples living on an inadequate pension from the husband's job of 40 years. This wasn't the scenario for *my* retirement.

In truth, I hadn't given much thought to retirement, although I'm fortysomething and should have. I've always assumed that I would gradually taper off work, move to a perfect desert climate, do a little adventure traveling, and acquire a terrific second serve. Talk about living in a dream world.

Not that my dream is beyond reach. But it is woefully lacking in one essential: financial reality. How am I going to finance this picture of paradise, this life of excursions to the Red Sea spaced comfortably between weeks on the tennis court?

I had always assumed that planning for retirement was more about accepting growing old than managing money. While I was slowly coming to grips with hints of arthritic joints and creeping farsightedness, I had been ignoring my money's health and future. Sure, I have an IRA, a self-employment pension plan, and a few investments, but my contributions have been erratic at best. The years have ticked by, and I have been treating money as if I were a 20-year-old, spending instead of saving.

I have lots of company. Although a large bloc of wage earners are saving for retirement (63 percent, according to surveys), most don't save enough. My problem, and maybe yours, is that I've been assuming that Social Security and my paltry IRA would carry the load. In fact, polls show that whereas 60 percent of people aged 45 to 65 believe Social Security and pensions will be their major sources of income after retirement, in truth they provide just 35 percent of the average individual's retirement income.

A trust company executive interviewed by *Fortune* magazine said it best: "People imagine someone else is saving for them— the company, government, their parents. They don't realize that if they don't take responsibility, no one else will."

The Lesson of the Early Saver

As I learned more about retirement and the necessity for smart saving, I was struck with the realization that time was a-wasting. A powerful piece of arithmetic drove the point home for me, and it may startle you too. If an 18-year-old puts $2,000 into a retirement plan every year until she's 26 and then stops saving, she'll have as much money at age 65 as someone who starts saving when she is 35 and keeps adding every year until age 65. That's the shocking beauty of saving early and letting the dollars compound.

I can't turn back my clock to 18, but I can take to heart the lesson of the math: It's never too soon to start planning and saving for retirement.

Another fact I'd been ignoring in my fantasies about senior scuba diving was that I've been stashing money in the wrong places. Every year or so, I have been casually dumping savings for retirement into conservative accounts—bonds, money market funds, treasury bills—then forgetting about it. This is a questionable investment strategy even when interest rates are high, but when rates plunged into low single digits, my ignorance and inattention really cost me. My retirement nest egg was earning about 5 percent on a good day! At this rate, I wouldn't be able to afford a new diving mask.

My stock investments haven't been any more thoughtfully made. Over the years I've acquired a collection of cats and dogs—a few blue chips, some depressed stocks on the verge of a turnaround, some shares of a start-up biotech firm, a mutual fund specializing in Pacific Basin companies. Stock market swings, not any long-term investment strategy, determined when I'd buy and sell. Consequently, I missed out on the gains that come from sticking with a particular stock or fund through its high and low cycles.

This was a hard lesson to swallow because I pride myself on being a savvy investor. I've been writing about money, investing, and personal finance for fifteen years, and can debate the pros and cons of the most arcane instruments with any money manager. But investment smarts are not the same as retirement planning smarts. I could avoid getting killed in a bear market and pocket profits in a bull market, but I didn't know how to plan for twenty years from now.

When it comes to retirement planning, we have to look at everything from a different angle. Accept the bitter truth that we're going to get old and enjoy the sweet truth that we're probably going to have long, fairly healthy lifetimes. Devising an investment strategy for buying a home next year or for putting the kids through four years of college is not the same as planning in order to live money-worry-free for decades of retirement.

Investing for retirement is like three-dimensional chess. On one level are all the time considerations: how long retirement will last, rates of return over the years, and annual inflation rates. On the second level are all the financial considerations: savings, IRAs, pension plans, annuities, funds, taxes, and more. And on the third level are the personal considerations: where to live, what to do, health outlook, and family medical history.

Clearly, retirement planning is going to be a great deal more complicated than choosing between a three-month bond and a three-year note.

LIVING INTO OUR EIGHTIES

The new complexity about retirement planning for people like us is that we'll probably live well into our eighties and need money for a good 20 years after our last day on the job. Professional planners, in estimating clients' financial needs, routinely assume they'll live into their nineties! Naturally, I hope I'm blessed with longevity genes, but I had never considered the ramifications of such a long life.

How much money I'm going to need requires serious thinking and projections. Not only do I have to consider my lifestyle—where to live, how much travel, what I do, leisure-time expenses—but I also have to add in an element over which I have no control, namely inflation. Even if my retirement goal is based on a modest lifestyle and an annual income at 70 percent of what I'm making now, inflation is going to balloon what I need into astronomical six-figure territory. With inflation marching along at about 4 percent, in 20 years every retirement dollar will be worth about 45 cents.

Given the length of time—20 years until retirement and another 20 in retirement—including inflation in my calculations has become as essential as knowing where I'm going to live.

WHAT WE CAN COUNT ON

L ike many people, I have no company pension; in my case because I'm self-employed. Frankly, it's a blessing in disguise because then we have to invest in our own plans and savings, and not rely on an employer to fund our pensions. Not much is secure or guaranteed in this world, and that's especially true for company pension plans. In recent years, the percentage of employees covered by pensions has been dropping steadily (it's now down to 43 percent) as companies discontinue plans, go bankrupt, or reorganize their plans into offerings with minimum guarantees. People depending solely on their employer providing a comfortable cushion for their senior years may well find themselves on a thin mat.

I don't mean to be an alarmist, but I'm a belt-and-suspenders kind of person. If you're like me, the current trend in company pension plans would compel you to build a personal retirement plan even if you worked for the most solvent,

most generous employer.

Another piece of this harsh reality is putting Social Security in its proper place, which isn't going to be on Easy Street. While I'm reasonably sure that payments won't be radically cut in the decades ahead, natural caution prevents me from assuming they'll blossom. Social Security provides about 23 percent of retirees' income today (for those with a retirement income of at least $20,000), so we should figure on a similar portion in coming years. We're going to get a green check every month, but we shouldn't count on it to live on. Ultimately, the bulk of retirement income for many of us will come from personal savings and investments.

MONEY ISN'T EVERYTHING

U nderpinning everything is how good your health will be. I won't be able to win the national 65s in singles and you won't be able to chase your dreams if our bodies are falling apart.

Good health, like financial planning, requires thinking ahead. Just as today's investments will determine how much money we'll have in 20 years, what we eat and how much we exercise today will affect how well we function years down the road. And, say experts, the right diet and exercise can actually slow down the ailments that come with aging. So, retirement planning has to include learning about nutrition, about the ways behavior affects the aging process, and about the steps we can take to keep ourselves healthy.

RETIREMENT PLANNING: A WAY OF LIFE

This primer is as much about planning for retirement as about living through it. Planning can begin as early as your twenties, and it shouldn't be put off any later than your forties. But some people do, and then play catch-up into their fifties. And people on the doorstep of sixtysomething, staring retirement in the face, need to spend more time than ever before preparing to implement all their plans. As a result, this book is for a wide spectrum of readers. Some of the information is useful for those of you with 30 years or so to plot your strategies, and other sections, like those on medical care and retirement locales, are for those of you who are closing in on the experience.

In the course of writing this book, I've come to believe that the word "experience" doesn't capture retirement. I look at my father, who is in his mid-seventies, starting a new business, traveling around the world, playing tennis three times a week, and getting married again, and I hope that my senior years will mirror his.

"The great thing about getting older," a philosopher once said, "is that you don't lose all the other ages you've been." I intend to use all my youthful years to make sure that my retirement years are just as fulfilling, and just as much fun. So should you!

Chapter 1

MAPPING YOUR FINANCIAL FUTURE

Think of retirement as a foreign place you've never visited, which may be warm and comfortable or cold and rough. You know it's likely you will be traveling to this place. Whether early or late, you'll retire at some point in your working life. It's as inevitable as airfare hikes. But what you find when you arrive in this unexplored land all depends on your packing and preparation. You need a vision of what your retirement will look like and a map for getting there.

"People want to control their own destinies. So we don't talk about retirement per se much any more. Instead, we talk about financial independence."

—John Bowen, financial planner, *as quoted in* U.S. News and World Report

This mapping is more than simply saving without thought, which can easily be ineffective if you haven't a clear picture of what you're saving for and how much you'll need.

YOUR RETIREMENT MAP

Mapping out a retirement plan is particularly complicated for today's baby boomers and middle-agers because they face financial pressures other generations have not. For instance, many people in their forties are caught between supporting kids in college and providing financial help to aging parents, and so have been dubbed the "Sandwich Generation." This squeeze forces many to postpone preparing for retirement until family members are taken care of.

Another strain on retirement planning has been the erosion of many company pension plans. Traditionally, working people, probably including your parents, labored for decades for a single company, contributed to a pension plan, and on retirement began receiving regular checks for the same amount every month. Their retirement plan was a defined-benefit plan, which meant that their employer guaranteed their benefits and this promise was backed by the government.

But, like typewriters shoved aside for word processors, such plans are now being discarded and replaced by what are called defined-contribution plans. During the mid-1980s, the number of companies switching to these plans more than doubled to 13.4 million. Unlike their predecessor, these plans aren't government guaranteed and their monthly payout depends on how an employer invests pension contributions. They may

Q I'm 39 years old, work in an office, and pretty much spend the $32,000 a year I earn. How can I save for retirement?

A The easy answer is to rearrange your budget and squeeze savings from it. But getting a handle on spending is never easy or simple. Finding retirement dollars requires examining your entire financial picture.

produce a healthy return on contributions paid in or they may not, so they're less secure and more risky.

> *"People imagine someone else is saving for them— the company, the government, or their parents. They don't realize that if they don't take the responsibility, no one else will."*
>
> —*Loraine Tsavaris, trust company senior vice president, as quoted in* Fortune

An unsettling development in the retirement landscape has been the collapse of some pension plans. Between 1988 and 1991, at least 30,000 companies distributed whatever was in their pensions, then shut them down. Worse yet, pension insurance companies are going under, leaving employers and employees with severely depleted retirement accounts.

The upshot for retirement mappers is that you can't count on your company pension plan to feather your retirement nest entirely. You have to pull from other sources and plot your journey carefully, anticipating possible detours along the way.

Further complicating your arrangements is the likelihood that your retirement won't follow the route it did for your parents. The traditional pattern of leaving your job at age 65, never to work again, and then pursuing a life of leisure is fading fast. You may decide to slip out early at 55 and start your own business; you may be firmly committed to never quitting work; you may retire for a few years, then seek a new line of work; or you may plan to gradually diminish your work life through your sixties and seventies. These possible combinations of retirement, semi-retirement, part-time work, returning to work, and nonleisure

> *Forty-six percent of pre-retirees said they plan to work part time in retirement in order to supplement their income; 49 percent said they will work during retirement in order to keep themselves busy.*
>
> *IDS/ The Daniel Yankelovich Group Retirement Survey*

"Another big issue these days is multiple marriages. When you divorce, half your net worth is cut off, and you start all over again. Wives often fear that they won't get any of the pension benefits. So when you're planning, you have to make room for a lot of contingencies."

—Mary Merrill, *financial planner, as quoted in* U.S. News and World Report

pursuits erase the usual notions about financing retirement.

Just as your retirement may veer from the out-at-65 path, so too may your needs. You may be single or widowed, supporting a handicapped child, or planning to share the rest of your life with someone you're not married to. Or, you may have had a long military career that provides housing and health benefits for life. Another possibility is the specter of a costly chronic illness plaguing your retirement. Thus, you need a retirement map that fits your personal circumstances, and reflects your individuality.

MAPPING MECHANICS

Sketch your retirement map in pencil and keep it flexible. Your plan should be a living, breathing document that will change as you age and as unpredictable events, windfalls, and setbacks shape your life.

The mapping exercise will go most smoothly if your financial records are accurate and up-to-date. This book will show you what to do with these records, but it's up to you to keep the documents organized and current.

Make your mapping a collaborative effort. Don't try to do this alone—you'll need the ideas and advice of family members. A family conference is a good idea. Depending on where you are in your life, sit down with your adult children, parents, siblings, or other relatives who may play a part in your retirement, and talk about what you want and where you're going.

Raise the hard questions: Do you really want to live close to your children? Do you want to travel constantly, unfettered by family? What about inheritance—how much do you hope to leave for your children, or how much do you expect from your parents? Do you want to continue to live in the family home after the kids move out? Though these topics may be touchy, they need to be aired.

THREE KEY DECISIONS

Your route toward retirement is going to be steered by three key decisions that are essential to your planning. Even though it's likely you'll change your mind as time goes on, you still need to make firm assumptions. Here's what you should decide:

• What kind of lifestyle do you want after retirement?
• When do you want to retire?
• Do you want to move when you retire?

"I want to be a rich old lady. It's a lot easier to be poor when you're young than when you're in your seventies," says a 47-year-old woman who's saving 15 percent of her income and driving a 5-year-old car.

—*As quoted in* Fortune

Each of these decisions has financial and nonfinancial ramifications that bounce off each other. Of course, the interrelationships of these decisions make the process all the more complicated. But if your plans are done properly, the personal and financial aspects of retirement will fit together neatly, like properly assembled jigsaw puzzle pieces.

First, focus on these personal lifestyle decisions. This is why you're planning your retirement—so you can afford the life you want. Once you've thought out your goals, you can move on to the financial considerations.

HOW WILL YOU SPEND YOUR NEW LIFE?

Think about your retirement life—what you're going to do with days, weeks, months, and years of free time. As you're musing, toy with dormant dreams and ambitions, entertain ideas of new pursuits and interests, throw out a host of "what ifs." Leave no curiosity or fantasy unexplored. Consider everything.

If you have a serious hobby (wine collecting, competitive bowling, photography), can you take it to a new level of accomplishment? Are there parts of the world you've always wanted to know—not just visit—but to stay in for a prolonged period? Do you enjoy academics? Would you like to earn a new degree, acquire a foreign language, read philosophy, study American literature, know more French history?

Revive any youthful fantasies. Do you want to write a novel? Restore antique cars? Become an actor? Design a beach house? Work in the theater?

WHEN CAN YOU RETIRE?

The question "When to retire?" perplexes lots of people, especially those who want to get out early but don't know if they have enough resources. Clearly, early retirement raises more uncertainties and requires more planning.

Successful early retirement (before age 60) hinges on a strong sense of purpose and adequate financial resources. While the financial requirement is obvious, you might overlook the personal.

Early retirement can have a marked effect on your self-image, especially if your identity is wrapped up in your work. For some working people, careers or company affiliations define who

they are. It's inherent in the American work ethic that people typically judge themselves, and others, by what they produce, be it memos or machines. So the early retiree who is still healthy and able may need an enterprise or purpose to anchor to.

Q *I've been working since age 22, like my job, the people I work with, and don't ever want to retire. I figure many of my generation feel the same way. What are the chances I'll never retire?*

A *Not overwhelming. You may enjoy the working life now and think you never want to retire, but most people still retire around age 65. Today about 83 percent of men and 92 percent of women over age 65 have retired.*

WHAT ARE YOUR PRIORITIES?

Planning for retirement entails rearranging priorities. These questions will highlight your priorities and the areas where you don't want to make compromises.

1. How important is a house with space for spreading out and entertaining?

2. Would you be willing to eat out less to save money?

3. How important is a new car every three years?

4. Would you be content to forego vacations or trips some years?

5. How important is it to dress well and fashionably?

6. Can you eliminate some of your "premium" purchases, such as premium beer, ice cream, or pet food?

Early retirement is often unsatisfactory for people whose main network of friends and relationships revolves around work. People who relish the daily connections of the workplace may feel adrift and uneasy with early retirement.

Early retirement can be fulfilling for people who use it as an entrée into a new activity or a whole new life. However, early retirement will fail if it's just an escape from a boring or unsatisfying work life. Retirement breaks loose something like 2,000 hours of free time every year, so you should have stimulating plans for this time.

Of course, early retirement requires ample financial resources—sufficient income for those extra years when you're not eligible for pension benefits or Social Security. With the average life expectancy over 75, early retirees should figure on enough to last at least 25 years.

Making early retirement even more costly is the consideration that, contrary to popular belief, your living expenses may not decline upon retirement. Often people who retire in their fifties

EARLY RETIREMENT FACTS

• According to the U.S. Department of Labor, labor force participation figures—one measure of early retirement trends show some people leaving work earlier and earlier. In 1970, 83 percent of men aged 55 to 64 were working. By 1989 that figure had fallen to just over 67 percent.

• More middle-aged people are getting out sooner. In 1970, 94 percent of men 45 to 54 years old were in the work force. In 1992, 91 percent of men 45 to 54 were working.

• Almost 50 percent of all working men, and 60 percent of working women, opt to receive Social Security at the earliest age possible (62).

• Studies indicate that earnings are the most important factor in determining whether workers retire before age 65.

devote themselves to expensive projects, activities, and travel.

No one knows for certain how much you will need for retirement, and planners use different yardsticks. But they can give you a workable estimate. Some say you'll need 60 percent of your current income, others say 80 percent —and that 20 percent spread can make a sizable difference when estimating what you'll need. If your gross income is now $50,000 a year, your goal may be a retirement income of $30,000 (60 percent) or $40,000 (80 percent). As the table on page 20 shows, savings that generate $30,000 a year are noticeably smaller than savings that generate $40,000 yearly.

You'll also need a large enough retirement fund to withstand shrinkage. Think of your retirement finances as a snowball rolling downhill. It grows as you save and invest year after year. Early retirement not only stops this snowball from rolling, but begins the melting process sooner. In short, your money has fewer years to compound.

An important financial boundary line separates the early retiree from other retirees: The early bird has a much smaller pool of potential income sources. No one can collect Social Security retirement benefits until at least age 62, and then the amount is less than what you'll receive if you wait until 65. The same situation crops up with private pension plans, like IRAs and Keoghs. If you take money out before you're 59½, you may well owe a 10 percent tax. Payments from a company pension may also suffer from early withdrawal, as some employer plans impose penalties for early withdrawal.

Another possibility is that your employer's contribution may be based on a salary average and if your salary's about to go up, leaving early would shortchange you. The time for early retirement may well be your peak earning years, when you could be making hefty contributions to your retirement fund.

This situation throws the income burden on personal savings and investments. To retire early, this is the place to focus your attention.

The table on page 20 shows the income produced by nest eggs of various sizes.

WHERE DO YOU WANT TO LIVE?

Answering this question raises issues of both housing and geography. In thinking about housing,

FINANCIAL AVERAGES	
Family Income	Average Net Worth
$10,000–19,999:	$63,100
$20,000–29,999:	$89,600
$30,000–49,999:	$150,200
$50,000 and more:	$586,700

Federal Reserve Bulletin

Q I've lived in the Midwest all my life, and think I'd like to retire near the ocean. Is this just a pipe dream or can I actually do something now to make it happen?

A Millions of others have retired along sunny shores—why not you? But choose your sandy beach carefully, because for a variety of not always obvious reasons, some coastal states (like Delaware) are cheaper to live in than others (like Oregon).

consider whether you want to stay in your current place and how convenient it will be as you grow older. You don't want to spend your retirement mowing, weeding, or painting (unless you *enjoy* doing these).

Give your home a retirement survey: Is it designed with lots of stairs and cupboards that require footstools or have awkward configurations that require much bending and twisting? People outgrow their homes gradually, slowly realizing that the small inconveniences are unacceptable. Now is the time to catalogue the pluses and minuses of your home, and to evaluate whether it's the best place to settle into retirement.

Your housing decision may depend on real estate values and prices. If your home is not paid off, can you afford the mortgage and property taxes on your retirement income? If you own the home free and clear, have you thought about selling it, moving to a less expensive place, and using the leftover money to supplement your retirement fund? Are you prepared to treat your home as a financial resource, or do your emotional attachments to it make it unlikely you would ever sell or move?

Next consider geography—immediate surroundings and distant lands. In the immediate surroundings, examine your home's location in relation to friends, family, shopping, recreation, medical care, churches, and cultural institutions. When working, you move about daily, creating a network of personal and professional relationships. After retirement your travel patterns may shrink, so glance about to see what's within reach. If you've lived in a suburban home and always commuted, for instance, retirement may isolate you from friends or from needed services. Or if you've always lived in a city and near your job, you may prefer to abandon working-world congestion.

> "Personally, I want to die in an airport, briefcase in hand, mission accomplished."
>
> —Maggie Kuhn, leader of the Gray Panthers, as quoted in Age Wave, by Ken Dychtwald

People's jobs often determine where they live, and if this is true for you, ask yourself where you'd like to live when you're not tied down by the job.

People who have moved often know one of the truisms of modern living: moving a short distance is as much hassle as a long move. Regardless of whether you're going 2 or 2,000 miles, moving requires packing, sorting, address changes, and adjustments to new neighbors.

Let your mind wander to places you might like to live, and draw up a list of considerations.

Moving

This list will help you evaluate your present locale and any new regions you're eyeing.

- Location (close to shopping, services, family, friends)
- Neighborhood qualities (noise, traffic, crime, easy access, good neighbors)
- Transportation (public rapid transit, taxis, proximity to train stations, airports, and interstates)
- Housing conditions and amenities (garden, balcony, pool, low maintenance, few stairs)
- Climate
- Size (large? small?)
- Unique features (e.g., university town, on the coast, near major ski area)

Costs of housing and living will,

naturally, influence your decision, but don't let cost be the final criterion. You can make almost any place economical if you're willing to arrange priorities, make trade-offs, and juggle fixed and flexible expenses.

Some living expenses offer little leeway—you have little control over state and local taxes (sales, income, real estate, personal property, death taxes), medical care, insurance premiums, and loan payments.

Other expenses are more elastic. These are housing, food and clothing, furnishings, entertainment and cultural activities, recreation, hobbies, and travel.

The key to managing fixed and flexible expenses is setting priorities. If locale is most important to you and you've chosen an expensive place to live, then you make concessions on your daily lifestyle. However, if you must live in a particular kind of home, then you compromise on location or travel.

Who Will You Live With?

Don't overlook personal relationships in your retirement planning. If you're married, consider the odds that you and your spouse will be together and healthy into your senior years. Is one of you planning to retire while the other works? Is there a divorce in the

Q I recently inherited $50,000 from my parents. If I put this into a retirement account for 15 years, will I be able to live off it?

A You need a financial planner to help with this question. For a ballpark figure, he or she might estimate that the money will grow at 7 percent a year, meaning your windfall would total $137,951. Then the planner would factor in inflation, your living expenses, and other income to help you decide if you'll have enough.

WHAT AMERICANS OWN

Here are the percentages of Americans who own various assets.

Asset	All Households	Age 35–44	Age 45–54	Age 55–64
Home	64%	67%	74%	78%
IRA/Keogh	24	27	36	42
Stocks/Mutual funds	22	23	25	27
Passbook savings/CDs	73	72	74	75
Bonds/Money market acct.	9	8	10	12
Rental property	9	9	13	12
Motor vehicle	86	90	91	90
Equity in business/profession	12	16	18	16

U.S. Department of Commerce, Bureau of the Census

works? Weigh the likelihood that you will need a nest egg large enough to support both of you or yourself without the help of a spouse.

While two-thirds of all older (65 plus) people live in a family situation, many people spend at least a couple of years living alone. At age 65, 41 percent of all women and 16 percent of all men live alone, and by age 75, 50 percent of all women and 18 percent of all men live alone.

Unmarried couples and singles also need to mull over relationships, weighing whom, if anyone, they will want to live with. And if you're single and contemplating moving, consider how easily you make friends. A single person with a tight network of supportive friends and family nearby may think twice about moving away. Entertain the possibility of communal living—gathering a group of friends or family to share a large house.

HOW MUCH DO YOU NEED?

This table shows what size nest egg you need to retire at a particular age with a certain level of income, figuring you'll live to age 91.

The figures in the "Savings" column represent the nest eggs. Assume these "eggs" are sitting in an investment account earning a 7 percent annual rate of return and assume a 4 percent annual rate of inflation. The "Age" columns show the combined total you would get annually from the corresponding nest egg plus Social Security if you begin withdrawing at that age. However, if you begin withdrawing income at age 50 or 55, all the money is coming from your nest egg. Social Security won't kick in until you're 62. So if you want to retire at age 62 with an annual income of around $31,000, you'll need a $400,000 nest egg, as well as maximum Social Security benefits.

	ANNUAL INCOME			
Savings	Age 50	Age 55	Age 62	Age 65
$ 100,000	$10,721	$12,820	$15,547	$18,653
200,000	15,024	17,430	20,774	24,250
300,000	19,328	22,039	26,001	29,847
400,000	23,631	26,648	31,228	35,444
500,000	27,934	31,258	36,455	41,042
600,000	32,238	35,867	41,683	46,639
700,000	36,541	40,477	46,910	52,236
800,000	40,845	45,086	52,137	57,833
900,000	45,148	49,696	57,364	63,431
1,000,000	49,452	54,305	62,591	69,028

Westbrook Financial Advisers, Inc., Watchung, NJ

OTHER RETIREMENT FACTS

• The "official" retirement age of 65 was first decreed in Germany in 1883 by Otto Von Bismarck. To weaken the attractions of growing socialism, he introduced a spate of social security and labor laws and established 65 as the age when people had to retire to receive a state pension.

• Among people aged 60 to 64, about 85 percent feel positive about retirement and 33 percent feel "extremely positive," according to a survey of 400 pre-retirees.

• The biggest concern about retirement among people aged 45 to 64, according to the same survey, is how inflation will affect them. The next largest concern is health care costs.

There's a reason most people retire at age 65: It's the time when everything comes together—people are usually healthy and active enough to do whatever they like, and retirement benefits begin to flow.

Late retirees, on the other hand, may be the most fortunate, particularly if they relish their work and have the energy and health to keep pushing. Even people who postpone retirement not out of choice but for financial ne-

HOW MUCH DEBT IS TOO MUCH?

• Paying more than 10 percent of your after-tax income for debts and loans, not including mortgage.

• Mortgage payments that are more than 30 percent of your gross income.

• Drawing from savings for daily expenses.

• Paying the minimum due, or less, on monthly bills.

• Not knowing how much you owe.

• Creditors are sending repeated notices or threatening or actually initiating legal action.

• Having credit denied.

A RETIREMENT TIMELINE

Here's a schedule of financial and legal events that will start you thinking about when you might want to retire.

Age 25: Begin working for company that may offer a retirement plan.

Age 35: Income, savings, and investments warrant help of a financial planner to organize.

Age 45: A retirement plan in place and beginning to grow.

Age 55: You can withdraw from certain pension plans (Keogh, 401[k], 403[b], profit sharing) without tax penalty or having to annuitize if you quit, lose your job, or retire. You can sell your house and not owe taxes on a capital gain of up to $125,000. The minimum age for many senior communities.

Age 59½: You can withdraw a lump sum from certain pension plans—IRA, Keogh, 401(k)—without tax penalty.

Age 60: You qualify for senior discounts from motels and movies, and are eligible for senior programs such as Elderhostel, an international program for travel and study.

Age 62: You can begin receiving Social Security, but the amount will be less than if you wait until age 65.

Age 65: Social Security recipients are automatically enrolled in

Medicare hospital insurance program. If you're not receiving Social Security, you're eligible but must apply for Medicare coverage.

Age 65 years, 2 months: Social Security begins for people born in 1938. (Legal changes have extended the age at which people begin receiving Social Security payments.)

Age 65 years, 4 months: Social Security begins for people born in 1939.

Age 65 years, 6 months: Social Security begins for people born in 1940.

Age 65 years, 8 months: Social Security begins for people born in 1941.

Age 65 years, 10 months: Social Security begins for people born in 1942.

Age 66: Social Security begins for people born between 1943 and 1954. (See Chapter 5 for the entire Social Security payout schedule.)

Age 70: Increased Social Security benefits (if they're just starting); personal income does not reduce Social Security benefits.

Age 70 years, 6 months: By April 1 in the year after reaching 70½, you must begin withdrawing from private plans (IRA, Keogh) or pay penalty taxes.

cessity often find their lives enriched by their jobs.

The beauty of late retirement is that it allows time for savings and pension plans to build up. For instance, Social Security payments, when they are postponed until age 70, reach their highest possible level. Personal pension plans and savings have more time to accumulate as contributions from work continue to come in. In addition, the typical late retiree—someone in his or her seventies—has erased the usual financial obligations that so often strain a retirement fund. Mortgages are paid off, college educations complete, parents in need of support no longer around.

DISCOVER YOUR FINANCIAL PROFILE

For a full-color picture of your retirement life, you need a detailed financial profile of yourself today. This will be a full-length rendering of all your assets and liabilities, and it will show how money moves through your life (cash flow) and how you manage it.

Based on your profile, you can begin to determine how much in savings, investments, pension benefits, and Social Security you're going to need when you retire.

COMPUTE YOUR NET WORTH

"Net Worth" is an intimidating term because it's often associated with only the wealthy—the world of trust funds, large investment portfolios, and palatial homes. In truth, everyone has a net worth. This is the sum total of your possessions, whether they are cash, real estate, a savings account, furniture, a beer bottle collection, a closet full of shoes, or whatever.

When you know your net worth, you know the size of the building blocks that will form the foundation of your retirement. Calculating the depth of this foundation now, before you retire, enables you to add layers if necessary.

Figuring your net worth requires adding up all your assets, then subtracting your liabilities; the resulting figure is your net worth. Keep in mind that your net worth changes every day as markets rise and fall, so what you're aiming for is a snapshot of your finances. Don't worry about

SOURCES OF RETIREMENT INCOME

These percentages are for incomes over $20,000.

- Social Security and formal retirement plans: 40%
  - Personal earnings: 24%
  - Investments: 34%

Changing Times

changing values; just pick a date, such as last January 1, and put a value on each asset as of that date. If you're married, draw three columns on your net worth statement, showing your items, your spouse's, and those owned jointly.

Add Up Current Assets

Not everyone has the same assets, but the following are common. Value each at its immediate cash value—not the purchase price, but how much you would get if the asset were sold on your selected date. A couple of phone calls to auction houses or merchants who trade in your valuables (e.g., Oriental rugs, antique glass) should elicit a reasonable estimate of cash value. Avoid putting a high value on personal property because the chances are probably slim that you'll want to sell it, and a lofty estimate will skew your net worth.

1. Cash on hand: Include hidden emergency cash in a lockbox at the office or in a safe-deposit box. Don't forget unused traveler's checks.

2. Checking accounts

3. Savings accounts

4. Money market accounts

5. Certificates of deposit

6. IRA account

7. Keogh account

8. Company pension: Ask your employer for a summary annual report and an individual statement of benefits.

9. Employee savings plan

10. Life insurance cash value: The amount your policy would pay if cashed out immediately (its "cash surrender value"), not its face value or annuity value.

11. Annuities: Estimate immediate cash value. If it pays out only on retirement, put down zero. (In this case, it will be entered in your cash flow statement.)

12. Stocks: Use an old newspaper (available at libraries) for stock prices as of your selected date.

A Gallup poll of 1,000 baby boomers reveals that almost nine out of ten have begun planning for retirement. About 74 percent had begun initial retirement planning, 26 percent have IRAs, and 20 percent have a savings plan.

Best's Review

13. Bonds: Use the same method as with stocks.

14. Treasury bonds, bills, or notes: Immediate cash value, including losses for cashing in early.

15. Mutual funds: Use the same method as with stocks.

16. Partnerships, trust income: To value a partnership, consult with other partners as to how much they would pay for your share.

17. Home: Record current market value less 10 percent for the cost of selling.

18. Other real estate: Second home, raw land, time-share vacation home.

19. Vehicles: Cars, boats, snowmobiles.

20. Valuable personal property: Jewelry, valuable furnishings, computers, gold and silver.

21. Collectibles: Professionally appraised value of stamps, coins, art, baseball cards.

22. Receivables: Cash or other items of value people owe you.

23. Deferred income: Money immediately due from your employer or from an installment sale.

Add Up Current Liabilities

These are debts and obligations, most of which are easily ascertained. The only unknown may be taxes on capital gains or on income outside a salaried job.

1. Home mortgage: Unpaid principal balance.

2. Taxes owed: Local, state, federal, property.

3. Loans: Home equity, auto, education, personal.

4. Credit card balances

5. Unpaid household expenses: utility bills, repair or renovation expenses.

6. Margin account balances: What you owe a brokerage firm on a margin account.

7. Insurance premiums (only if overdue).

8. Alimony (only if overdue).

9. Medical bills (only if overdue).

Figure the Difference

Your net worth is the difference between the sum of your assets and the sum of your liabilities. People usually have more assets than liabilities. If you have more liabilities, you have a negative net worth.

A small, or even negative, net worth is cause for concern but not panic, unless you plan to retire soon. When liabilities overwhelm assets it means you have spent more than you've earned. You may be logging large credit card bills, carrying a hefty mortgage, or have little savings. If your net worth is small or negative, pinpoint your financial weak spots. Since it's hard to save when liabilities are high, it's often most sensible to consider which debts can be most easily reduced. Reducing credit card bills, for example, will not only increase your net worth, but will help free up money for savings as you spend less each month on interest.

Your net worth is a snapshot as of the date you selected, and it will change, sometimes unpredictably, as you age. An inheritance windfall, chronic illness, change of careers, divorce—a host of events can and probably will alter your

Q *I have been living in my house for years, but I don't own it—I rent. In figuring my net worth, does the house have any value on the asset side?*

A *No, unless you made a damage deposit that will be returned to you when you move out. That money goes into your asset column.*

financial picture. Consequently, your net worth must be regularly updated. Promise yourself to recalculate your net worth every year.

MANAGING CASH FLOW AND BUILDING NET WORTH

Your net worth rises and falls depending on saving and spending habits—how well you manage the flow of cash day to day eventually determines your net worth. The better you manage your cash and control your expenses, the more savings you salt away and the larger your net worth. Understanding your current cash flow is also useful for projecting future cash flow for retirement.

To prepare a cash flow statement, draw up a list of income and expenses, and record average monthly and annual expenses for each. Here are the categories:

Income
- Wages and salary
- Self-employment
- Dividends, interest, rents, fees, royalties
- Child support, alimony
- Social Security, pension, annuity (currently received)
- Profits from investments (stocks, partnerships)
- Tax refunds

Total Monthly Income:_____

Total Annual Income:_____

Expenses
- Housing: mortgage/rent
- Utilities: gas or oil, electric, water, trash removal, telephone, cable TV
- Maintenance: repairs, condo fees, yard upkeep
- Home insurance
- Real estate taxes
- State and federal income taxes; FICA (Social Security)
- Local taxes
- Transportation: personal auto gas, maintenance, insurance, car payments; public transportation expenses
- Groceries: food, liquor, tobacco, household supplies
- Meals out
- Clothing
- Cleaning, laundry, personal care (haircuts, manicures)
- Recreation: club dues, sporting equipment, and fees (i.e., court, green, chair lifts)
- Medical: health insurance, doctor, dentist
- Pets: special food, veterinarian
- Leisure: movies, cultural events, books, magazines, hobbies
- Vacation: travel, accommodations
- School fees, tuition, day care
- Gifts, charitable contributions
- Insurance premiums
- Miscellaneous (alimony, child support, personal business)

Total Monthly Expenses:_____

Total Annual Expenses:_____

THE NEST EGG: ESTABLISH A GOAL

Once you have a firm grip on your current finances, you can estimate how much you'll need at retirement.

There's no telling *exactly* how much money you're going to need in retirement—there are too many variables, especially if you're decades away. But this doesn't mean you throw up your hands and do nothing. You need a financial goal, even though the number may fluctuate. Over the years, you may earn more, you may earn less, but this offers a starting point.

To establish a goal, determine your financial base—using either the total of your current annual expenses or a percentage—anywhere from 60 to 100 percent—of your current after-tax annual income. Your place in this broad range depends on your present lifestyle, and how it might change when you retire. If you envision eventually cutting back on daily expenses, use a lower percentage. But if you're spending all that you earn, and have no plans to give it up, figure on a higher percentage. And if you're uncertain, play it safe and plan to need a substantial percentage of your current income. This base figure then must be adjusted for time-sensitive variables. These are inflation, investment rates of return, and the number of years your money has to grow. The resulting amount is your goal—how much you want to receive every year, before taxes, during your retirement.

Don't assume taxes on your income in retirement will be less than today. Your tax bill will depend on how much you earn from Social Security and other sources, and whether you accept your pension in a lump sum or as an annuity.

THE CALCULATIONS

No. 1. Current income multiplied by .60 to 1.00:

No. 2. Current annual expenses (total):

No. 3. Years to retirement:

No. 4. Inflation effect (Estimate what you think annual inflation will average over the years until you reach retirement. FYI: Inflation in 1991 was 2.8 percent; in 1992 it was 2.9 percent.):

No. 5. Multiply your annual retirement expenses (no. 1 or 2) by the figure in the table on page 30 that represents the number of years until you retire and your estimate of the inflation rate. For a 40-year-old woman earning $35,000 a year who plans to retire at 65 and estimates inflation will run 4 percent a year, the calculations are:

35,000 × .80 = $28,000
28,000 × 2.67 = $74,760

The final figure is your income goal—the amount you need to receive each year of retirement. Remember that this figure is a first estimate and it's going to change with your income and inflation, so you'll adjust it each year when you review your retirement plan.

At first glance this number may look awesome, but don't be discouraged. As daunting as it may seem, you already have acquired portions of your retirement nest egg; you're not starting from scratch. You'll receive Social Security, maybe retirement benefits from an employer pension plan, and it's possible you have a personal savings and/or a private pension plan, such as an IRA or Keogh.

Financial planners call this arrangement for how people will be supported in their retirement the

INFLATION EFFECT

Here's how inflation may affect your money. For example, if you have $1,000 and believe inflation over the next 5 years will be 3%, multiply $1,000 x 1.16. The total, $1,160, is what you will pay 5 years from now for something worth $1,000 today.

Years to Retirement	3%	4%	5%	6%
5	1.16	1.22	1.28	1.34
10	1.34	1.48	1.63	1.79
15	1.56	1.80	2.08	2.40
20	1.81	2.19	2.65	3.21
25	2.09	2.67	3.39	4.29
30	2.43	3.24	4.32	5.74

"three-legged stool." In theory, retirees will be supported more or less equally by each leg of the stool. But times are changing, and you may well have more than three sources of income (you may come into an inheritance) or less than three (no company pension). And very possibly, the legs on your retirement stool will be of varying lengths, or value.

SOCIAL SECURITY, MORE OR LESS

Any American who has worked for at least 10 years and paid the FICA (Federal Insurance Contributions Act) tax is eligible to receive money from Social Security. Nonworking spouses and spouses of eligible workers who have died also get Social Security retirement benefits. You can elect to begin receiving reduced payments when you're 62; you can wait until age 65; or you can postpone payments until age 70. The longer you wait to receive benefits, the more you will get.

The amount you pocket depends on your earnings when employed (which determine how much you contribute to FICA) and on when you start receiving pay-

ments. On average, Social Security replaces 40 percent of the wages a working person earned before retirement, and if you have a nonworking spouse, you'll receive close to 60 percent.

These are averages, however, and if your average annual income is relatively low (e.g, $10,000), Social Security may top 90 percent of your wages. On the other hand, higher wage-earners (e.g., $52,000) may take away as little as 19 percent of their earnings from Social Security.

A 65-year-old retiree today would receive a minimum of $456 and a maximum of $975 a month, but if you're years away from retirement, there's no way to tell exactly how much you will get. Also, Social Security is periodically given a cost-of-living adjustment (COLA) based on the unpredictable Consumer Price Index, and this will affect your benefits. (Social Security will tell you how much you've contributed to date if you submit a Personal Earnings and Benefit Estimate form, available from the Social Security Administration at 800/772-1213.) For planning purposes, use an average figure now; as you approach retirement, you can replace it with a figure that more accurately states

ESTIMATED ANNUAL SOCIAL SECURITY BENEFITS— SINGLE RETIREE AT NORMAL RETIREMENT AGE (65)

Retirement Year	Average	Maximum
2000	$13,669	$19,802
2005	18,333	27,529
2010	22,483	34,792
2015	28,833	45,532
2020	39,786	63,034
2025	48,506	76,909
2030	60,594	96,072

your benefits. (Chapter 5 contains a table on Social Security benefits for all income ranges.)

ESTIMATING YOUR PENSION INCOME

An estimated 44 percent of all full-time employees are covered by a corporate retirement plan and most other workers—government employees, self-employed, employees of nonprofit organizations—have some type of private pension plan.

Employers offer an assortment of pension plans, which are usually distinguished by how much the employee and the employer contribute and how benefits are paid out (e.g., lump sum, monthly increments, increasing amounts). Employer plans include defined-benefit plans, supplementary employee retirement plans, and defined-contribution plans. The latter include profit-sharing plans, employee stock ownership plans (ESOPS), savings plans, and 401(k) plans.

For a general idea of how much your employer pension plan will pay, use one of these estimates: a percentage, say around 50 percent, of your past year's salary, or a percentage of earnings per year.

(Pension experts sometimes use a third method, called an integrated formula, that takes into consideration how much an employee will receive from Social Security. It's a complicated formula employers use to figure their pension liabilities, and is explained in Chapter 5.)

The salary percentage is easy to figure: if you made $40,000 last year, count on your employer's pension paying you about $20,000 a year.

With percentage of earnings per year, multiply the number of years you've been an employee (or plan to be) times 1.5 percent (pension experts use between 1 and 2 percent, depending on the company plan) of your salary. If you're an 18-year employee making $45,000, here's the calculation: 18 × (.015 × 45,000) = $12,150. This is your annual pension.

If your employer is the military, or the state or federal government, you can generally count on even more. Military pensions offer 40 to 50 percent (the lower figure if you joined after August 1986) of pay after 20 years and can go up to 75

RETIREMENT ACCOUNTS

The following are the average percentages of certain income and age groups who have established individual retirement accounts, Keoghs, and/or employer-sponsored pensions.

Family income $20,000–29,999:	34.4 percent
Family income $30,000–49,999:	44.9 percent
Family income $50,000 and above:	69.2 percent
Family head age 35–55:	44 percent
Family head age 45–54:	45.5 percent
Family head age 55–64:	42.6 percent

Federal Reserve Bulletin

RETIRING FROM A GOVERNMENT JOB

If you've worked for the civil service more than five years, your retirement income is a percentage of the three-year average of your highest income years.

Years service	Multiply 3-year average highest income by this %	Years service	Multiply 3-year average highest income by this %
5	7.5	23	42.25
6	9.25	24	44.25
7	11.0	25	46.25
8	12.75	26	48.25
9	14.5	27	50.25
10	16.25	28	52.25
11	18.25	29	54.25
12	20.25	30	56.25
13	22.25	31	58.25
14	24.25	32	60.25
15	26.25	33	62.25
16	28.25	34	64.25
17	30.25	35	66.25
18	32.25	36	68.25
19	34.25	37	70.25
20	36.25	38	72.25
21	38.25	39	74.25
22	40.25	40	76.25

Department of Labor, Bureau of Labor Statistics

percent. U.S. government workers with 30 years receive, on average, about 56 percent of their final salary; employees of small municipalities may not receive as much. Civil service employees can estimate their pension by averaging their three highest salaries and multiplying this figure by a percentage that corresponds to the number of years employed. See the table on page 34.

TOTALING PERSONAL PENSION PLANS, SAVINGS, AND INVESTMENTS

What you end up with on retirement day depends to a large extent on how much you save and how skillfully you invest.

The most common personal re-

tirement plan is an Individual Retirement Account, in which you can invest up to $2,000 a year. You can establish a Spousal IRA and contribute up to $2,250 a year to it and your IRA combined if your mate doesn't work. The table below shows how much an annual $2,000 contribution will produce if left untouched at rates of return of 5, 7.5, and 10 percent (For more about IRAs, see page 159.)

There are a multitude of places to stash your retirement savings: mutual funds, money market and other funds, stocks, bonds, certificates of deposit, real estate, annuities, even foreign investments. The difference among all these is their level of risk, their return or yield, and their tax features. The next chapter explores these sav-

IRA TABLE

Years Established	5%	7.5%	10%
5	$ 11,604	$ 12,488	$ 13,431
10	26,413	30,416	35,062
15	45,315	56,154	69,899
20	69,438	93,105	126,005
25	100,227	146,152	216,363

Q I'm 39 and years away from retirement, so it's hard for me to know how much of my current income I'm going to need. What do the experts recommend?

A They tend toward the higher side, suggesting a minimum of 70 percent and close to 80 percent of your current income for comfort.

THE GRAND TOTAL

Now add up the retirement income (either monthly or annual) you can depend on:

- Social Security:
- Employer pension plan:
- Personal savings/investments:

If you're like most people, you'll find a sizable gap between your retirement goal and how much you can count on at this point. The next step, obviously, is to bridge the gap between where you are and where you want to be.

DON'T TRAVEL ALONE: GET PROFESSIONAL HELP

You may be tempted to map out a retirement plan alone, and the arguments for going solo can sound reasonable: it will cost less, you avoid the hassle of finding expert advice, and you don't have to share financial confidences with a stranger.

Consumers are naturally, and at times justifiably, skeptical of the financial planning profession. It's a young field that blossomed during the 1970s when insurance com-

ings and investment vehicles; for planning purposes think of them only in terms of return. Put another way, make an educated guess (keep it conservative) as to how much they'll grow each year.

To be sure, it's difficult to predict how much you'll be saving or investing. But give it a stab, and again make it conservative. Use the table below to pinpoint how your savings and investments will grow.

panies figured they could expand their offerings by wrapping a financial plan around various policies. Initially, financial planning was a sales tool, a vehicle that justified the purchase of select products. Today, financial planning has grown into a multifaceted specialty. It's not necessarily appropriate for all financial decisions. Tax matters or real estate questions are better left to specialists, for example. But to draw up a full-scale map for your retirement years, a financial planner may be helpful, if not essential.

When it comes to money matters, most people don't feel informed or experienced enough to make every decision alone. Money management is a complicated field; there's no disgrace in needing guidance. People nearing retirement who have done little planning, or investors who suspect their retirement savings may be too small, are prime candidates for planners.

HOW YOUR $1,000 WILL GROW

This is how $1,000 will grow if compounded annually. Round your savings and investments to the nearest one thousand. Multiply the return figure—after substituting a decimal point for the comma—by the number of thousands. For example, if you save $4,000 for 5 years at 6 percent growth, the calculation is: $4,000 × 1.338 = $5,352.

Years	6%	8%	10%
5	$1,338	$1,469	$ 1,610
10	1,790	2,158	2,594
15	2,396	3,172	4,177
20	3,207	4,660	6,727
25	4,292	6,848	10,835

> *"The primary role of a financial planner is to give advice, not to manage your money."*
>
> The Renaissance Years, *by Robert Veninga*

Regardless of the type of planner you choose, he or she should help you avoid costly errors or omissions, save you money in taxes, and help you choose smarter investments. Furthermore, a planner will encourage you to consider parts of your financial life that you may have been avoiding or overlooking, such as the soundness of your company pension plan. A planner will also urge you to organize your thinking and financial records. Moreover, he or she will help you implement the plans you have made.

VARIETIES OF PLANNERS

Anyone can use the label "Financial Planner," for the title is largely unregulated. Planners differ not only in their professional education and experience but also in what they emphasize in their financial plans. Thus a broker/dealer acting as a financial planner may stress long-term investment vehicles, whereas an attorney preparing a plan may focus on trusts and wills. Various professional associations impose credential requirements, standards of practice, and codes of ethics, but membership in these groups is purely voluntary.

Investment Advisers

Most financial planners are investment advisers. Investment advisers are a broad class of professionals that can also include stockbrokers, accountants, and money managers (also known as investment counselors or investment brokers). To be called an Investment Adviser, a person (or firm) must register with the Securities and Exchange Commission, a formality that requires completing forms about education, experience, and current practice, and pay a one-time $150 fee. Many states also require some type of registration. There are about 17,000 investment advisers, and their numbers are growing steadily.

An investment adviser may be an individual operating out of a home office or an employee of a gigantic pension fund management company. Some of the national brokerage firms and private financial management companies offer financial planning. In short, the title Investment Adviser doesn't tell a consumer much about what the individual does—you have to look further to other professional labels to get a sense of their orientation and the type of advice they're offering.

This group is largely compensated through commissions, a sales charge attached to a particular investment product, although some money managers and investment advisers receive a percentage of the assets under management. With a $250,000 retirement plan (savings, investments, insurance—all the more-or-less liquid assets), a typical 1.5 percent annual asset management fee totals $3,750.

Accountants as Planners

Certified Public Accountants (CPAs) can take courses on financial planning from the American Institute of Certified Public Accountants (AICPA) and receive a special designation, ''Accredited

Personal Financial Specialist,'' from the association.

Requirements for this title include being a CPA (a state-licensed tag with rigorous qualifications), 250 hours of experience in planning, passing an exam, and submitting six references from clients and co-workers. The APFS is a rare bird; there are about 300,000 CPAs in the country, of whom only about 600 have earned the APFS label.

Accountants who aren't CPAs and use the title ''PA'' (public accountant, or occasionally licensed public accountant or LPA), are also licensed by individual states but the requirements are less strict. A PA can, of course, offer financial planning. And if an accountant gives specific investment advice, he or she has to be registered with the Securities and Exchange Commission (SEC) as an investment adviser.

Accountants who prepare retirement plans often consult other financial advisers—brokers or insurance agents, for instance—to recommend investments and implement a plan. Because they're accountants and not professional investment advisers (they rarely register with the SEC as investment advisers), their advice tends

WHAT THE INITIALS MEAN

ADV	Investment adviser form filed with SEC
AICPA	American Institute of Certified Public Accountants
APFS	Accredited Personal Financial Specialist
CFA	Chartered Financial Analyst
CFP	Certified Financial Planner
ChFC	Chartered Financial Consultant
CLU	Chartered Life Underwriter
CPA	Certified Public Accountant
CPCU	Chartered Property/Casualty Underwriter
IAFP	International Association for Financial Planning
IBCFP	International Board of Standards and Practices for Certified Financial Planners
ICFP	Institute of Certified Financial Planners
JD	Juris Doctor (a doctor of law)
LLB	Bachelor of Law
MBA	Master of Business Administration
NASD	National Association of Securities Dealers
NAPFA	National Association of Personal Financial Advisers
PA	Public Accountant
PhD	Doctor of Philosophy
SEC	Securities and Exchange Commission

to be aimed more at tax moves. They may suggest generic savings plans or investments, or how a nest egg should be diversified, without recommending specific funds or companies.

Generally, certified public accountants charge a flat fee or work on an hourly basis. Their rates tend to be higher—$100 to $350 an hour—than those charged by less credentialed planners. However, an accountant may offer a "segmented financial plan," which is a plan for a single situation such as retirement, and usually costs less than a comprehensive plan. (For information about CPAs who offer planning and informational brochures, call 800/862-4272.)

Lawyers

Lawyers occasionally do retirement planning in conjunction with tax or estate planning. Law firms with trust departments (sometimes called an "in-house fiduciary prac-tice") typically serve wealthy individuals (net worth exceeding $500,000). Most often, consumers who use a lawyer have a substantial retirement nest egg and want advice on keeping the estate intact for the next generation. Estate lawyers are most helpful for people nearing retirement who are less concerned about investing and saving than they are about capital preservation. If investments, insurance, and tax accounting are needed, the lawyer often recommends or coordinates with other advisers.

If you're considering using a lawyer for retirement planning, make sure the individual has experience in the field and working

---

WATCHING INVESTMENT ADVISERS

The Investment Advisers Act of 1940 requires advisers to register with the SEC and authorizes the agency to monitor their activities and impose fines and civil penalties in cases of fraud, misrepresentation, or violations of securities laws. One of the Act's main purposes is to curtail certain conflicts-of-interest. However, the SEC has too few examiners to watch advisers closely, and according to its chairman, small advisers are inspected only about once every 30 years, unless there's obvious trouble. In 1990, the SEC considered 304 cases against investment advisers, then filed 20 administrative proceedings and 11 lawsuits.

relationships with other advisers who can fill in the gaps and help you to implement the plan. While the legal profession does not recognize financial planning as an official specialty for lawyers, it does sanction estate planning. A good sign of an experienced estate lawyer is membership in the American College of Trust and Estate Counsel, a national organization with state chapters, or in the American Bar Association subgroup Real Property, Probate and Trust. Some states offer certification for estate lawyers; ask a prospective lawyer if he or she is certified.

Lawyers usually charge hourly fees, so you need an idea of how much time will be required to prepare a plan, as well as any additional charges by other advisers.

Insurance Agents

Insurance agents are the original financial planners, and while most are primarily salespeople, some have acquired specialized financial experience and knowledge. Experienced agents usually have the credential CLU (Chartered Life Underwriter), ChFC (Chartered Financial Consultant), or CPCU (Chartered Property/Casualty Underwriter). These are designations given by a private association called The American College. Insurance agents are also licensed by individual states, which regulate and monitor their activities. To check whether any legal complaints have been made against an agent, contact your state insurance commission (usually headquartered in the state capital as a state government listing under Insurance Commissioner, Commissioner of Insurance, or Director of Insurance). Also, verify membership in good standing in the national insurance organizations, such as the National Association of Life Underwriters (1922 F Street, NW, Washington, DC 20006, 202/331-6000) and the American Council of Life Insurance (1001 Pennsylvania Avenue, NW, Washington, DC 20004, 202/624-2000), which has corporate members.

Whether the agent works for a company or is independent, the fee is generally a commission on products sold. Depending on the kind of insurance you purchase, commissions are 35 to 55 percent of the first year's premium. An important point to remember is that commissions are based on premiums, not on the value of the policy. An ethical insurance agent

CHECKING OUT A PLANNER

Some state and federal offices monitor and regulate financial professionals. While some agencies are vigilant, strong enforcers and offer revealing reports, others may be simply depositories for information, sending to inquirers copies of forms filed by the subject without evaluation.

Securities and Exchange Commission (450 Fifth Street, NW, Washington, DC 20549). The Office of Filings, Information and Consumer Services (202/272-7440) will tell you whether someone is a registered adviser and if any violations have been filed against him. Copies of Form ADV are available from SEC Publications (202/272-7461). Violations filings are available from the SEC Public Reference Branch (202/272-7450). Additional information is available for a fee from the Office of Disclosures (800/638-8241).

National Association of Securities Dealers (1735 K Street, NW, Washington, DC 20006, 800/289-9999). The NASD maintains files on stockbrokers, which include reports of any disciplinary actions. Information submitted by the broker is filed into the Central Registration Depository (CRD) and is available to consumers through state securities agencies. Call the NASD to learn if your broker has ever been disciplined by the NASD, federal or state regulators, or in criminal court.

North American Securities Administrators Association (555 New Jersey Avenue, NW, Suite 750, Washington, DC 20002, 202/737-0900). This association of state enforcement officers and special agents fields complaints about and monitors legal action against brokers, dealers, and investment advisers. For information about individuals, it will refer you to a state securities office (see state listings in the appendix).

should not steer you toward the policies and annuities that pay the highest commissions; ask about individual commissions and the pros and cons for each recommendation.

Banker or Trust Officer

A growing number of trust departments of banks will provide financial planning. Their strong areas tend to be investment advice and estate planning. Traditionally, bank trust departments have catered to individuals with large sums of money they want sheltered from taxes and preserved for beneficiaries. But deregulation has loosened restrictions on what banks can do, and they offer a growing array of related services, such as brokerage accounts (stocks and funds) and managing Keoghs and IRAs.

Bankers or trust officers may be well versed in managing investments and establishing trust funds, but as pure investment advisers, they tend to be conservative and recommend vehicles that show only modest returns. As financial planners, their track record depends in part on the expertise of other advisers they consult and in part on their personal training in

financial planning. In scrutinizing a banker or trust officer as a financial planner, ask exactly who will prepare the plan and what resources he or she will tap into. Some institutions that claim to offer financial planning simply prepare fill-in-the-blanks computer printouts.

The credentials of an individual banker depend on the individual; the profession imposes none. So while you may be able to verify

Q The woman who does my taxes every year has offered to prepare a financial plan that I can use for retirement. How do I know if it's any good?

A Odds are it'll be strong on tax planning and short in other areas. It should cover all facets of your financial life, and considerations about your personal life—does it?

designations such as CFA or CPA, there is nothing you can do to check banking credentials. Nevertheless, you can inquire about the solvency of the bank. Contact the Federal Deposit Insurance Corporation Consumer Hot Line (800/ 934-3342) and the Consumer and Community Affairs Division of the Federal Reserve System (20th and C Streets, NW, Washington, DC 20551, 202/452-2631).

The cost of planning by a banker or trust officer is usually a combination of a flat fee for the plan and commissions or percentages charged on the investments under management.

FINDING A FINANCIAL PLANNER

Begin your search by collecting names of planners, but avoid scanning the Yellow Pages (too many names, too many unknowns). Instead canvas friends and business acquaintances. Ask your lawyer, accountant, or tax preparer for recommendations. Perhaps your employer has worked with a planner (some companies offer employees financial counseling as a benefit). If no one knows or can recommend a plan-

ner, ask for names of accountants, estate attorneys, or brokers who can give you a couple of names. Lists of planners active in your area are also available from the various professional associations (see the credentials section, below). Another source of names are local newspapers or magazines that quote financial planners. Planners that reporters cite as sources are usually knowledgeable and up-to-date on trends or changes in the profession.

PARE YOUR LIST

Next, pare your list of planners by refining your requirements. Call the names, explain that you're shopping for a planner, and ask each to send you a description of his services and information on his professional background. This need not be a lengthy conversation; explain that right now you're simply collecting information. This process may be tedious and time-consuming. But finding the right planner is critical to your financial health. Commit yourself to spending at least as much time locating a planner as you would shopping for a new car.

For starters, you want a planner

PLANNER BACKGROUND

Planners sitting for the Certified Financial Planner examination come from these backgrounds:

Financial planning:	39%
Stock or securities brokerage:	19%
Insurance:	13%
Accounting:	14%
Banking:	12%
Other:	2%

International Board of Standards and Practices for CFP Inc.

who has at least three years' experience in *retirement* planning. A planner may try to claim experience in an earlier and somewhat similar job, such as being a stockbroker, or insist that retirement considerations are parts of every plan. Don't compromise on this requirement.

Your ideal planner should have experience preparing plans for people like yourself—similar age, profession, and income. A person's retirement planning needs vary according to his or her age and lifestyle, so avoid someone who may fashion a one-size-fits-all plan. Be aware that some planners specialize in certain types of clients, for example teachers, wealthy individuals (net worth over $1 million), or people 45 and older. You want someone who can anticipate the special kinds of situations you face, and who can propose solutions that have succeeded with clients like you.

KNOW THE CREDENTIALS

A planner should have credible educational and professional credentials. For starters, you want someone with a college degree in business or a related field (accounting, finance, economics) and an indication of having studied financial planning under the auspices of a professional organization. There are five active financial planning groups, each a little different. One of these calls itself a "college," but it's not an accredited four-year academic institution; it's a professional trade association that offers education.

• The International Association for Financial Planning (IAFP) is an educational association of about 15,000 members who pay a $195 fee to join. The IAFP maintains a "Registry of Financial Planning Practitioners," a directory of approximately 875 members who have met certain standards. These standards include possessing an academic degree and/or a financial planning educational designation (e.g., CFP), at least three years' experience as a financial planner, passing a basic knowledge exam, submission of the names of five client references, maintaining continuing education, registering with the SEC and applicable state securities agencies, and agreeing to abide by a code of ethics. Registry planners are practiced and knowledgeable, yet their membership is no guarantee of competence and honesty. These things you must

check for yourself. (Copies of the Registry and other IAFP publications—*A Consumer Guide to Financial Independence* and *The Registry Consumer Guide to Comprehensive Financial Planning*—are available free from IAFP, Two Concourse Parkway, Suite 800, Atlanta, GA 30328; 404/395-1605.)

About 450,000 people in the United States call themselves "Financial Planner."

Consumer Federation of America

• The Institute of Certified Financial Planners (ICFP) is an association whose approximately 7,000 members have earned the designation Certified Financial Planner (CFP). To use the initials CFP, a member must have at least one year's experience, adhere to the group's code of ethics, maintain a certain number of hours of continuing education, and pass an examination administered by the association's educational arm, the International Board of Standards and Practices for Certified Financial Planners—IBCFP. (For information about ICFP planners and copies of ICFP publications—*Se-*

FINANCIAL FLIMFLAMS

Fraud and trickery are not uncommon when the subject is money. Since financial advisers and planners are loosely monitored, consumers have to be wary. Here are some telltale signs to be alert to:

- Advisers who steer you toward investments in which they own or control more than a 5 percent interest. These may be limited partnerships and tax shelters involved in real estate, energy, or mining.
- Requests that you give money to an adviser personally. Do not give money to an individual; make your check out to the employing company or brokerage firm.
- Advisers who discourage you from seeking a second opinion on a recommended investment.
- Planners who charge "timing fees," on top of normal switching fees, for notifying clients about the best time to move money from one mutual fund to another. Such fees are considered unethical.
- Advisers who, purportedly for the sake of convenience, insist on obtaining power of attorney over your assets and investments. This enables them to buy, sell, and transfer your money without your knowledge, a situation ripe for fraud.

lecting a Qualified Financial Planning Professional: Twelve Questions to Consider and *Avoiding Investment and Financial Scams: Seeking Full Disclosure Is the Key*—write or call 7600 E. Eastman Avenue, Suite 301, Den-ver, CO 80231; 800/282-PLAN.)

- The National Association of Personal Financial Advisors (NAPFA) is an organization of planners who work on a fee-only basis, receiving no commissions on any of the investments they recommend. NAPFA members are full-time financial planners, and are prohibited from owning more than a 5 percent interest in any company or organization that will benefit from their recommendations. (For a list of NAPFA planners and copies of the booklets *Why Fee-Only Planning?* and *Financial Planner Interview: How to Choose a Financial Planner,* write or call 1130 Lake Cook Road, Suite 105, Buffalo Grove, IL, 60089; 708/537-7722.)

• The Personal Financial Planning Division of the American Institute of Certified Public Accountants. For a list of Accredited Personal Financial Specialist planners and a copy of the booklet, *Do I Need Personal Financial Planning?* call or write 1211 Avenue of the Americas, New York, NY 10036; 800/862-4272.

• The American College serves as the training school for the insurance industry and offers financial planning credentials. It's also the home of the American Society of Chartered Life Underwriters and Chartered Financial Consultants, who receive the designation CLU and ChFC. (270 Bryn Mawr Avenue, Bryn Mawr, PA 19010; 215/526-1490.

FIND OUT THE COST

A planner should clearly disclose how he or she is paid—usually either commission or fees or a combination of the two. Upwards of 90 percent of planners work on commission, but many planners have added a layer of fees to their commissions, thus creating a third category of payment structure. When talking about fees, make sure you clearly understand the arrangement. Here are the fundamentals:

Commission only: The planner receives a percentage of the investments you purchase as part of a retirement plan. The fee is a sales commission on every mutual fund, annuity, limited partnership, or other investment you buy. Obviously, this kind of fee has the potential for conflict of interest, with a planner making recommendations in order to increase a fee rather than assemble the best retirement package. Yet, commission planners insist that they are objective, and that this type of compensation is fair as long as a client knows about it. Furthermore, commission planners argue sometimes that this fee structure costs less than a flat-fee arrangement. With a commission-only planner, ask about the commission on *each* investment you make and find out whether these amounts are negotiable.

Fee-only: The planner receives a flat fee calculated either on an hourly basis (hourly rates around $100) for the complete plan (the typical charge is $3,000) or as a percentage of the assets invested or managed. Fee-only planners insist their method of payment makes them objective and their recommendations unbiased. However, some people feel it's inconvenient to work with planners who do not offer products necessary for implementing their plan.

Fee-offset: The planner charges a single fee for the financial plan, then reduces this amount by commissions from investments purchased through the planner.

Fee/Commission combination (sometimes called "fee-based"): The planner charges a fixed fee for consultation and drafting a plan (typically $500 to $3,000), and if he or she implements it and purchases investments, receives a commission on these.

Salary: The planner is employed and paid a salary by a financial institution, such as an insurance company, bank, or brokerage firm.

Some people use the way a planner is compensated as a litmus test for making their choice, believing that a planner who works only on an hourly rate or a planner who receives commissions costs less. But full disclosure is a better indication of competence and ethics than the payment structure. Avoid any planner who's vague or confusing about compensation or who refuses to discuss fees until you have signed as a client. Legitimate planners find it perfectly acceptable that you quiz them about their fees.

A Sampling of Costs

What you wind up paying depends on the type of planner, the size of your retirement fund, what you do with your money (life insurance? mutual funds? stocks? annuities?), and how often you consult your planner.

Keeping in mind all these variables, this is a sampling of the costs associated with setting up a comprehensive financial plan:

• Planner hourly fees: $75 to $250 per hour for a minimum of 10 to 15 hours.
• Fee-only planner's management cost: 1.5 percent to 10 per-

cent of money invested plus fees for discount broker and low-load mutual funds.

• A flat-fee plan: $1,000 to $10,000, plus 0.5 percent to 3 percent of assets under management.

• Commission on cash-value life insurance: 50 percent to 100 percent of first year's payment.

• Commission on limited partnership: 8 percent to 10 percent.

• Fee-and-commission plan, or fee-offset: $500 to $3,000 for the plan or $100 per hour, plus commission on investments from 3.5 percent to 10 percent.

• Plan prepared by a CPA (not a comprehensive plan): $400 to $500.

• Salaried planners with a brokerage house may charge $200 to $2,000 for a computerized plan plus product commissions.

INTERVIEW THE BEST CANDIDATES

Once you've eliminated the unsuitable or unqualified, apply further stipulations to the remaining planners. With the names of three or four top candidates in hand, arrange to talk with them in person. Yes, this may be inconvenient and a hassle, but your financial future may be at stake; the time and trouble are worth it.

Initial consultations to interview the planner should be free, even with planners who work for hourly fees. If a highly recommended planner insists on charging for this first session (some have blanket policies about charging for first consultations to weed out window shoppers or those looking for free advice), insist that the fee be applied to the total cost of the plan, if you decide to hire him or her.

Start your interview by asking the planner what information and documents he or she wants, how long it takes to prepare a plan, and who implements it. While you're on the topic, ask to see plans prepared for other clients. (The planner may have to mail these to you after removing the client's name). This sample plan will give you an idea of what this planner emphasizes, for instance minimizing estate taxes or maximizing high-yield investments. Make sure you'll be working directly with the planner, not with a less experienced assistant or associate.

Ask the planner how often he or she thinks your plan should be reviewed; if the answer is infrequently or never, move on to the next planner. For your own peace of mind, commit yourself to reviewing it annually *and* whenever there is a major change in tax laws, your life (marriage, divorce, death of close relative), or your finances.

Another question for a prospective planner is whether he or she will put your arrangement into a written agreement specifying the cost of the plan, who prepares and reviews it (and how often), how it's to be implemented, and any costs associated with implementation.

Ask a planner for the names and phone numbers of three clients whose circumstances and planning needs are similar to yours. (Your planner may have to give these to you later, after he's gotten permission from the references to release their names.)

In addition, ask the average size of the planner's accounts and whether the majority of the clients are individuals or companies. You don't want a planner more experienced drawing up corporate pension plans than plans for individual retirees.

Find out what criteria or research he or she uses to make decisions. If the planner is recommending investments such as limited partnerships, ask if he's performed "due diligence," that is, a thorough review of the investment sponsor's background, performance, and intended use of the funds. Planners associated with securities firms, insurance companies, or mutual fund groups should be open and clear about their business relationships. They should tell you up front whom they work for.

Finally, ask if he or she consults other professionals, such as accountants or lawyers, for specialized information. It's reassuring to know your planner is covering all your financial bases.

You may disagree with a planner's recommendations. Find out if a planner offers alternatives to suggestions or objects to your obtaining a second opinion about an investment idea. You want the freedom to consult other experts about your plan while maintaining a continuing relationship with a planner.

Be wary if a planner wants control over your assets. Don't sign with a planner who wants freedom to buy and sell for you without your permission (referred to as "investment discretion") under the guise of convenience. No one should have access to your money (or your investments) other than yourself or a designated relative. Despite how little you may know about money management and investing, retain the final decision on financial moves.

Conflicts of interest arise when planners have financial interests in the companies or investment vehicles they recommend. Occasionally you encounter a planner who is a major stockholder in a small company, or a general partner in a limited partnership or a real estate investment trust. This doesn't occur often, but if it does, it spells trouble because inevitably the planner's financial interests become more important than yours.

Here are two unbreakable rules: Avoid planners who recommend investments that they own or control, and don't allow any final money decisions to be made by anyone other than yourself or someone known and close to you.

Before hiring a planner, you should check with state and federal agencies to see if any legal or criminal actions have been filed against him or her. State attornies general or securities commissioners are normally responsible for monitoring financial advisers; they field complaints, launch investigations, and issue indictments, and will tell inquirers if an adviser is registered with the state, and if any enforcement action has been taken or is pending.

The Securities and Exchange Commission also registers investment advisers. To be registered, an adviser completes a form (called Form ADV) about his professional background and employers, and submits this with $150. Exempt from registration are advisers with fewer than 15 clients, advisers who don't provide specific advice on securities, and advisers who are registered broker/dealers. Copies of an adviser's Form ADV can be obtained from the SEC or the individual, but keep in mind the information came from the adviser himself. Ask to see Part II of Form ADV, which an adviser is required to show to anyone who pays for investment advice; should an adviser hedge or refuse on this request, pack up your papers and find someone else.

For a thorough background check on a planner, ask to see a resume or biography, and randomly select items to verify, such as college degrees or work experience. You can also contact the local Better Business Bureau to inquire about any complaints.

At the end of the interview, after you've amassed reams of information, apply one final test: your instincts. Chemistry and personal reactions are good indicators of how well you'll work with someone. Your planner is going to learn everything about your personal finances, so you must feel comfortable and respect him or her. Think about the questions the planner asked. A smart, seasoned planner inquires about your retirement goals, what you have already done to plan for retirement, your spouse's plans and opinions, and your risk-comfort level. Dwelling on the size of your assets or the extent of your insurance coverage suggests that the planner is more interested in what you can do for him than vice versa.

Finally, don't be intimidated by planners who speak in unfathomable jargon or refuse to explain complicated ideas. You don't want a planner who can't communicate or who regards clients as ignorant children. Be firm on this point. Walk away from any plan-

WHAT DOCUMENTS YOUR PLANNER WANTS TO SEE

- Will, trust agreements
- Loan agreements (mortgage, personal, vehicle)
- Employment contract
- Employment benefit plan manual, benefit plan annual statement
- Annual statements for IRA, Keogh, 401(k), profit sharing, brokerage accounts
- State and federal tax returns (four years)
- Paycheck stubs (two pay periods)
- Social Security payment record (if you have it)
- Credit card statements (last two)
- Asset appraisals
- Insurance policies (life, disability, health, other), annual statement on life insurance policy
- Business partnership papers, business sale/purchase agreement

ner who talks over your head or implies you're too uninformed to manage your money.

HOW PLANNERS WORK

A planner generally starts by asking you to complete an extensive questionnaire requesting specifics (with dates and amounts) about your finances: assets, investments, savings, pension plans, salary, other income, debts, insurance, and spending patterns. In short, statements of your net worth and cash flow. The planner will also want to review documents, such as mortgages, wills, and employment contracts.

You'll probably meet at least twice with your retirement planner, first to talk about your financial profile, expectations, and retirement needs. At the initial meeting, you and the planner will discuss your retirement goals and risk-tolerance level. At the second meeting, the planner will have collected your completed forms, and analyzed, synthesized, and probably squeezed your particulars through a computer, to produce a map for reaching your short-term and long-term goals. The planner may also have recommendations

for meeting these goals. However, if the planner doesn't name specific investments, he or she will likely put you in touch with a broker/dealer or investment adviser who'll be able to make them.

More likely, your planner will suggest specific funds, types of stocks or bonds, kinds of insurance policies or annuities, high-yield instruments, or tax shelters. If your planner is a licensed broker/dealer or affiliated with one, he will execute your plan. Otherwise, you use your own broker or one the planner recommends.

WHAT A RETIREMENT PLAN LOOKS LIKE

What follows are examples of retirement plans from three financial planners. The plans are summaries taken from actual client plans—complete plans are long and complex—and include the individual planners' different assumptions about inflation and lifetimes. They're not models and you shouldn't expect yours to look like them, but they'll give you an idea of what to expect in details and recommendations from financial planners.

SIX COMMON MISTAKES IN RETIREMENT PLANNING

1. *The Scarlett O'Hara mentality:* I'll worry about it tomorrow. Putting off planning until age 45 or later.

2. *Trusting in government.* Overestimating how much Social Security and an employer's pension will contribute to retirement income. In a survey of 400 people aged 45 to 64, about 59 percent said they expect to rely primarily on Social Security or pension benefits when they retire. However, according to the U.S. Department of Treasury, these two sources combined will account for just 35 percent of the average retiree's income, although others think it will be as high as 40 percent.

3. *What Me? Retire?* Believing you'll work until you drop. Healthy 40- and 50-year olds often declare they'll never retire completely, but statistics show that most people don't work much beyond age 65.

4. *Impatience.* Not giving savings and investments time to grow, and instead moving money around seeking higher, and riskier, returns. These people forget the Rule of 72, which illustrates how soon your money doubles: Divide any annual interest rate into 72 to determine the number of years before the money doubles. If you're earning 8 percent, divide that into 72 to arrive at 9 years. In 9 years, you'll have twice what you started with.

5. *Neglecting personal decisions.* Questions about what you'll do, where you'll live, and with whom are shoved aside. As well as having money, it's equally important in retirement to have a purpose to your day, something to look forward to, and someone to share it with.

6. *Assuming living expenses will drop.* Depending on your lifestyle, where you plan to live, and what you plan to do, retirement may easily cost as much as your working life.

PLAN FOR LARRY AND CATHY

Personal Data

Larry and Cathy, both 38, are just beginning to think about retirement planning. They live in southern California and have three children—twin girls aged six and a boy aged eight. Larry is a manager with a large aerospace corporation and Cathy works for an association of health clubs. Larry has a 401(k) retirement plan, which he contributes to every year.

About 62 percent of baby boomers are "concerned about outliving their retirement savings," compared with 52 percent of the general population.

International Association for Financial Planning

Larry enjoys work and plans to keep at it until his late sixties; Cathy will retire when he does. They have no plans to move when they retire and don't expect living expenses to drop appreciably when they stop working.

Financial Data

Larry's gross salary: $55,000
Cathy's gross salary: $30,000
Family after-tax income:
$70,000
Annual expenses: $52,000
Savings and retirement fund
(qualified tax-exempt): $65,000

Retirement Plans and Assumptions

Larry's age at retirement: 68
Life expectancy for planning
purposes: 95
Retirement period: 27 years
Inflation over the period: 5%
Family's annual discretionary income (difference between after-tax income and annual expenses): $18,000
Larry's annual investment in 401(k): $8,000
Annual growth of 401(k): 10%

Retirement Goals:

Larry's retirement fund at age 68 (the growth of his 401[k]):
$2,450 x 160
Personal savings: $1,600,000
Annual *after-tax* income needed in year 2022 (adjusted for inflation): $224,000

Annual withdrawals (after tax) from Larry's retirement fund: $181,140

Expected annual Social Security benefits (in 3% inflated dollars after tax): $43,000

Planner's Recommendations

Cathy and Larry appear to be well prepared for retirement. However, because neither has a pension plan (other than Larry's 401[k]), they will need to save all their discretionary cash ($18,000 a year) and hope they can increase their income to save even more.

Except for $43,000 in Social Security benefits, they are personally responsible for everything. While they will have enough money in the first year of retirement, by the tenth year, with 5 percent inflation, they will need to supplement the $181,140 (after-tax) withdrawal from Larry's 401(k) and Social Security with more than $183,000 of personal funds. If they save $18,000 a year for 30 years and earn 6.5 percent (after tax), they will have about $1,600,000 at retirement in personal investments. By delaying retirement until age 68, they have a chance, even though they have three chil-

dren to put through college.

Cathy and Larry need to keep saving everything they can and to make sure they maximize tax-deductible retirement contributions. Retirement contributions should be invested in pure growth at this stage of their retirement lives, and allocated this way:

- Large cap U.S. stocks (companies with sizeable assets and capital): 50%
- Small cap U.S. stocks: 20%
- International stocks: 30%

The assumed 10 percent returns are not easy to obtain, but over time this portfolio should do better. In 25 to 30 years, the portion of equities could be reduced to around 70 percent, but growth is important even in retirement.

Other savings should be more conservatively invested. Because of their relatively high tax bracket, their investments should be allocated:

- Short, intermediate, and long-term municipal bond funds: 50 to 60%
- U.S. stocks, international stocks, U.S. real estate (REITs or limited partnerships): 30 to 40%
- Cash for emergencies: 10%

As assets accumulate, fixed and variable annuities could be used in place of the bond and stock funds. The tax deferral of those vehicles will pay off if held for at least 10 years. These personal assets will need to do triple duty: emergency funds, education funds, and finally retirement income. (Source: Dennis M. Gurtz, CPA, CFA, Dennis M. Gurtz Associates/IDS)

PLAN FOR DIANE

Personal Data

Diane is single, 46, lives in Illinois and likes to travel. She works for the government and hopes to retire early. While she has inherited money from her parents and plans to use this money as her retirement nest egg, she would also like to remodel her home and help pay for the education of her two nephews. Her retirement questions revolve around how much travel she can afford, what she can spend on remodeling and tuition, and how early she can retire.

Financial Data

Diane's annual salary: $ 50,358
Income from
  investments: 20,594

Total gross income: $ 70,952
Annual expenses
  (includes taxes): 53,465
Investment assets
  (appreciated
  inheritance): 469,084
Current asset
  allocation:
  Cash equivalents 30%
  Stocks and stock
  funds 28%
  Bonds and bond
  funds 39%
  Other 3%

Retirement Plan Assumptions

Diane's age at
  retirement: 57 years
Life expectancy (for
  planning): 92 years
Inflation over the
  period: 3%
Before-tax return on
  retirement
  investments: 9%
Before-tax return on
  other investments: 7.66%
After-tax return on
  other investments: 5.64%
Annual nursing care
  expenses (beginning
  in year 2030): $40,000
Annual contributions to
  pension: 5,975

Retirement Goals (Status at age 57)

Value of personal investments:	$649,821
Value of pension investments:	56,904
Personal investment income:	30,058
Annual living expenses:	52,603

Retirement Goals (Status at age 67)

Value of personal investments:	$641,945
Value of pension investments:	134,711
Personal investment income:	28,208
Social Security income:	14,292
Pension income:	49,220
Annual living expenses:	80,756

Recommendations

Retirement at age 57 is feasible, but note that there is a long period between 57 and 64 when Diane will not only need all investment income but also will draw down $22,000 to $35,000 of principal each year (because her pension plan doesn't begin to pay out until age 65). Correct management of investments during this time is critical. Retirement at age 50 is not possible unless long-term investment returns stayed at 10.5 percent and other goals (home remodeling, nephews' education) were forfeited. Retirement at age 65, given assumptions about savings and return, means complete financial security and even wealth in Diane's later years. (Source: Mary A. Malgoire, MBA, CFP, Malgoire Drucker, Inc.)

PLAN FOR PETER AND LEE

Personal Data

Peter and Lee are 55 and 54, live and work on the East Coast, and have four children. Peter is a doctor and Lee has never worked for compensation outside the home. Peter has set up a profit-sharing Keogh at work and has been making significant contributions to it since it was established. Their mutual passion is sailing and when Peter retires around age 65, they would like to move to a warm location on the water in either Florida or the Caribbean. They don't expect any change in their cash flow needs in retirement.

Financial Data

Peter's gross salary:	$150,000
Total family income (including income from rental properties and investments):	165,000
Family after-tax income:	130,000
Annual expenses:	90,000
Retirement savings (qualified tax-exempt):	400,000
Rental property ($50,000 equity) and other investments:	200,000

Retirement Plans and Assumptions

Peter's age at retirement:	65
Life expectancy (for planning):	95
Retirement period:	30 years
Inflation over period:	5%
Family's annual discretionary income:	$40,000
Peter's annual investment in Keogh:	26,800
Annual growth of Keogh:	10%

Annual appreciation of equity in rental property:	5%
Other investment growth (annual after tax): ·	8.5%
Cash flow needs in retirement same as today:	$90,000

Retirement Goals

Family retirement fund at age 65 (qualified):	$1,464,620
Annual after-tax income needed in year 2002 (adjusted for inflation):	146,600
Value of rental property/other investments at age 65:	430,593
Social Security payments (annual, after tax, beginning age 65):	21,600
Annual withdrawals from Peter's retirement fund (after tax):	87,200
Annual withdrawals from other investments (after tax):	37,800

PLAN FOR A LONG LIFE

Here are the average retirement life spans:

Retirement Age	Individual	Couple
55	28 years	34 years
60	24	30
65	20	25
70	16	21
75	12	16

Recommendations

Because Peter and Lee are within 10 years of retirement, they must try to put a larger percentage of discretionary income into their retirement plan (two-thirds versus one-half when they were younger). In addition, while 10 years is an adequate time to manage the risk of a volatile stock market, they must be cautious as retirement nears and they begin to need to make withdrawals. Since they plan to relocate upon retirement, they should plan to use the equity from their present home (taking the one-time $125,000 tax-free exclusion) to buy a new home with the smallest mortgage feasible.

Current asset allocation for growth should be:

- Cash or cash equivalents: 10%
- Equities: 50%
- Bonds or fixed income: 25%
- Real estate: 15%

After 10 years in retirement, this should be gradually adjusted to:

- Cash: 10%
- Equities: 35%
- Fixed income: 45%
- Real estate: 10%

Also, near retirement they should sell their rental property and add the projected equity to their retirement nest egg. (Source: Robert L. Albertson, CFP, Armstrong, Welch & Macintyre, Inc.)

Chapter 2

INVESTING TODAY FOR A COMFORTABLE TOMORROW

Everyone is an investor of some sort, even if you simply store the coin collection passed down to you from your grandmother. Investors generally fall into one of three categories, and you'll probably recognize yourself in one of these.

The "Money Is Fun" type. These people like to learn about investing, monitor holdings, enjoy the subtleties of fractions and percentages. They read the *Wall Street Journal* for entertainment,

> *"The secret to making money over time is being invested and staying there, not chasing the market."*
>
> —*Chief investment officer, U.S. Trust, as quoted in* Fortune

track the stock market weekly if not daily, and have a pretty good idea of what the prime rate is. They scrutinize every purchase, make their own decisions, and confidently slide in and out of investments. These people are a small minority.

The "Once-a-Year, Whether It Needs It or Not" type. These people are basically bored by or uninterested in investing but know they need to pay more attention. So, once a year—around tax time, December 31, or when tuition checks are due—they engage in a flurry of investment activity. They call their stockbroker or accountant and make decisions, but then lose interest. Their resolution fades, and their money languishes wherever they put it last. Most people fall into this category.

The "Wake Me When It's Over" type. These are people who dislike the subject of investing, and will do *anything* not to deal with it. They're uncomfortable with figures and frustrated with the complexities of choosing an investment. Their eyes glaze over when the subject comes to money markets, rates of return, or asset allocation. Their investment style consists largely of finding someone else to take charge—spouse, financial planner, friendly stockbroker, anyone who shows a modicum of interest and ability. They want to hand their money to someone trustworthy and smart, and

Q My brother's a stockbroker and over the years I've bought stocks—some blue chips, some stocks of new biotech companies he says will take off—and a couple of mutual funds. Is this the kind of investing that will prepare me for retirement?

A No, no, no. This kind of investing lacks purpose. You need to step back and figure out what you want your money to do—grow? produce income? help lower taxes?—then methodically allocate portions of your investment money for different purposes, which is called asset allocation.

never make another decision until retirement. Thus, how their investments do depends on the expertise of the current surrogate investor—and on luck. Like the second investment type, this category has lots of followers.

UPDATE YOUR INVESTMENT STYLE

If you fall into either of the latter two categories, you need to update your investment style. You can't afford not to, and thinking about retirement is a useful start. A definite goal in mind—a dollars-and-cents target and a timetable, even a rough one—will add determination and immediacy to your investment decisions. Also helpful are some general principles that even the most bewildered or reluctant investor can absorb. Remember these investment principles while you are managing your money, and your investment performance will reflect your new-and-improved investment style.

Investing Is Simpler Than Brain Surgery, and Easier to Learn. The subject of investing is routinely overcomplicated, so investors are easily intimidated by it. Professionals wrap it in jargon, and successful practitioners are treated as icons. Sure, in its advanced state investing can be enormously complex. But most of us never reach that point. Managing your money wisely does not depend on a degree in economics or decades on Wall Street. The bulk of it is rooted in common sense and elementary information.

Use It or Lose It. Money languishing in a savings account will never amount to much. Inflation, and ultimately taxes, will wear it down to virtually nothing. It must be invested, and those investments must be reviewed regularly as the money climate and individual circumstances change.

Patience *Is* a Virtue. Once you've invested your money, you have to give it time to grow. The standard investment vehicles—stocks, bonds, funds—require a minimum of three years before they can be fairly judged. Of course, some of your investments will do better than others. But resist bailing out for at least a couple of years.

WHY YOU NEED INVESTMENT SKILLS

Social Security and employer pensions—money you have little control over—will make up about 40 percent of your retirement income; the rest depends on you. Upwards of 60 percent will have to come from your savings and investments. Exactly how much money that will be depends on how well, and how wisely, you invest.

You're also going to need investment skills far into your retirement years. Few people enter retirement and immediately begin withdrawing from their nest eggs and have enough to last their entire lives. Long lifetimes and decades of retirement mean that even in the full bloom of retirement, you must think about where to invest your money. In order to support you, your retirement fund must continue to grow as you touch 70 and older. Remember, odds are that if you turn 65, you'll live long into your eighties. So, basic investment skills are even more essential to retirement than knowing a good travel agent!

Knowing how to invest depends largely on information. There are few absolutes in investing (''cut your losses and let profits run,'' comes to mind). With much of investing based on predicting economic scenarios, no investing technique or piece of advice is infallible. Ultimately, smart investing comes down to having lots of information (considering a number of possibilities and choices) and knowing the likelihood of something happening. And sometimes even this is not enough.

As a retirement planner you are in a better position than an all-purpose investor. You have a specific goal, and you have time. Your investing doesn't have to generate profits immediately. Whether you've got a few years or 20 years, this time allows your investments to grow into serious money.

AN INVESTMENT STRATEGY FOR RETIREMENT

Everyone's investment strategy is a little different, hinging on when you begin dipping into your investments and the rate at which you draw them down. A person in his early fifties who will be retiring soon to work part-time at a new venture may need far more than someone who won't quit until his late sixties and has a substantial company pension.

Your investment strategy should have an underlying goal—not simply a dollar target but guidelines for how and when this money will be used. Investors should consider how to balance growth and income. Growth investments are known for long-term accumulation though their year-to-year increases may be erratic and unpredictable, while income investments add to your assets at a steady percentage, albeit not a large one, every year. In practice, most investors opt for a combination of growth and income with one predominating. People usually have an idea of how much growth or income they need, with expectations pegged to what they know of prevailing interest rates, inflation rates, and annual returns from various categories of stocks and funds.

For instance, in early 1993, three-month Treasury bills were paying 2.9 percent, while 10-year notes were paying about 7 percent. The Dow Jones Industrial Average for the preceding 12 months had increased 3 percent. Of course, these figures change daily but they indicate trends and boundaries. They become even more meaningful, and helpful to an investment strategy, when viewed in perspective. This brings you back to information—knowing where rates have been and the direction they're pointing.

Another element in an investment strategy is the question of access or liquidity. How easily can you get to the cash in your investments? Investors need to divide their money into categories of liquidity. Cash that might be needed for immediate, unexpected emergencies should never be locked up in penalty-heavy accounts. By contrast, money that is intended for nothing other than distant retirement can be locked up for years to come—particularly if that illiquidity comes hand in hand with a higher rate of return.

MEASURING YOUR COMFORT LEVELS: RISK AND SAFETY

How you feel about risking your money, and the other side of the equation—how safe it must be —will drive many of your investment decisions. The risk-comfort spectrum extends from Very Conservative (you don't want to risk losing one dollar regardless of how little your money earns) to Very Aggressive (you're willing to risk most of your money for the possibility that it will grow enormously). Most investors' tolerance for risk is not black or white; they fall somewhere in the gray middle, preferring a mixture of safe-but-slow growing invest-

THE RECORD SO FAR

This table shows how common stocks, long-term government bonds, and the consumer price index (i.e., inflation) have grown over the past 20 years. Keep these figures in mind when forming expectations for your investments.

	Common Stocks: Total Yearly Returns (Dividends Reinvested)*	Long-Term Government Bonds: Yearly Total Returns	Change in the Consumer Price Index (Annual Rate of Inflation)**
1972	19%	6%	3%
1973	−15%	−1%	9%
1974	−26%	4%	12%
1975	37%	9%	7%
1976	24%	1%	5%
1977	−7%	−1%	7%
1978	7%	−1%	9%
1979	18%	−1%	13%
1980	32%	−4%	12%
1981	−4%	1%	9%
1982	21%	40%	4%
1983	23%	1%	4%
1984	6%	15%	4%
1985	32%	31%	4%
1986	18%	24%	1%
1987	5%	−2%	4%
1988	17%	10%	4%
1989	31%	16%	5%
1990	−3%	6%	6%
1991	31%	19%	3%
1992	7.7%	8%	3%

* Based on Standard & Poor's Composite Index of 500 stocks. Data from Ibbotson Associates, Chicago.
**Based on the Consumer Price Indexes for All Urban Consumers. Data from *The Business One Irwin Business and Investment Almanac, 1992,* and Ibbotson Associates, Chicago.

ments and high-risk, high-potential investments.

Think of risk and safety as a monetary seesaw. When the seesaw is at rest and level, risk and safety are equal. However, when the risk end rises, the thrill (and the possibility you'll fall off) also goes up and safety hits a low. But when the safety end rises, the risk level dips. Investments are like this: a few raise you to the high end of the seesaw, others rest at the quiet, no-thrill, no-spill end, and many occupy the middle ground, offering a little promise and a little security.

"Now the stock market is the only game in town for people like me. I'm just not going to accept a four percent CD. And there's no way I'm going to lock up my money in a seven percent U.S. Treasury bond or a six percent municipal bond for ten years."

—*69-year-old widow, as quoted in the* Wall Street Journal

Your investment strategy should match your risk-comfort level. This quiz will help give you an idea of how much risk you can tolerate.

HOW MUCH RISK CAN YOU HANDLE?

1. Two weeks after buying 100 shares of $20 stock, the price leaps up to over $30. You decide to:

   a. Buy more stock—it's obviously a winner.

   b. Sell your stock and take your profits.

   c. Sell half your stock to recoup some cost and hold on to the remainder.

   d. Do nothing and wait for it to advance further.

2. You win $300 in an office football pool. You:

   a. Spend it on groceries.

   b. Try to boost your good fortune further and purchase lottery tickets.

   c. Put it in a money market fund.

   d. Put it in your brokerage account to buy stock.

3. On days when the stock market takes big jumps, you:

   a. Wish you owned more stock but do nothing.

b. Call your broker and ask for recommendations.

c. Feel glad you're not in the market, being whipsawed by its gyrations.

d. Pay little attention to how it moves.

4. You're planning a Caribbean vacation and can either lock in a fixed room-and-meals rate of $150 per day or book standby and pay anywhere from $100 to $300 per day. You:

    a. Grab the fixed-rate deal.

    b. Talk to friends who have been there about the availability of last-minute accommodations.

    c. Book standby and also arrange vacation insurance because you're leery of the tour operator.

    d. Take your chances with stand-by.

5. The owner of your apartment building is converting the units to condos. Tenants like you can buy their apartments for $75,000 or sell their option for $15,000. On the open market, units have recently sold for close to $100,000 and their price seems to be going up. For financing, you'll have to borrow the down payment and carry mortgage and condo fees higher than your present rent. You:

    a. Buy your apartment.

    b. Buy your apartment and look around to buy another.

    c. Sell the option and arrange to rent the apartment yourself.

    d. Sell the option and move out because you think the conversion will attract couples with small children.

6. You have been working for three years for a privately owned management consulting firm that has been growing strongly. As a senior executive, you are offered the option of purchasing up to 2 percent of company stock—2,000 shares at $10 a share. Although the company is private, its majority owner has successfully, and lucratively, sold three other businesses, and intends to sell this one eventually. You decide to:

    a. Purchase all the shares you can and tell the owner you would invest more if allowed.

    b. Purchase all the shares.

    c. Purchase half the shares.

    d. Purchase only a token number of shares.

7. You go to Atlantic City for the first time, walk through the gambling hall, then pick a game. You choose:

    a. Quarter slot machines.

    b. $5 minimum-bet roulette.

    c. Dollar slot machines.

    d. $25 minimum-bet blackjack.

8. For a friend's birthday, you want to take him to a special, memorable restaurant. However, your friend lives in a city you don't know, so to find this restaurant, you:

    a. Read restaurant reviews appearing in the local newspapers.

    b. Ask co-workers if they know of a suitable restaurant.

    c. Call the only other person you know in this distant city, who eats out a lot but only recently moved there.

    d. Visit the city one evening before your special dinner to check out restaurants and their menus.

9. The expression that best describes your lifestyle is:

    a. No guts, no glory.

    b. Just do it!

    c. Look before you leap.

    d. All good things comes to those who wait.

10. Your attitude toward money is best described as:

    a. A dollar saved is a dollar earned.

    b. You've got to spend money to make money.

    c. Cash and carry only.

    d. Wherever possible, use other people's money.

Score your answers:

1: a-4, b-1, c-3, d-2

2: a-1, b-4, c-2, d-3

3: a-3, b-4, c-2, d-1

4: a-2, b-3, c-1, d-4

5: a-3, b-4, c-2, d-1

6: a-4, b-3, c-2, d-1

7: a-1, b-3, c-2, d-4

8: a-2, b-3, c-4, d-1

9: a-4, b-3, c-2, d-1

10: a-2, b-3, c-1, d-4

What Your Score Means

• 10–17 points: You're a conservative investor. You don't like to take chances with your money, even though you won't reap big profits.

• 18–25 points: A semi-conservative investor, someone who sticks with safe investing most of the time but will take a small chance given enough information.

• 24–32 points: A semi-aggressive investor. You're willing to take chances with your money, ready to risk it if you think the odds of it earning more are in your favor.

• 33–40 points: An aggressive investor. You look for every opportunity to make your money grow, even though the odds may be long. The aggressive investor thinks of money as a tool for making more money, not to be tucked away to grow slowly and safely.

> *"The near-complete failure of gold to protect against a loss in the purchasing power of the dollar must cast grave doubt on the ability of the ordinary investor to protect himself against inflation by putting his money in 'things.'"*
>
> The Intelligent Investor, *by Benjamin Graham*

Although people's tolerance for risk temporarily rises or falls with their sense of financial well-being, confidence in the future, and investment experience, over the long run it's fairly constant. Knowing your risk-tolerance level will help you make investment decisions that give you both peace of mind and a feeling of success and progress. The conservative inves-

tor who goes against his instincts and invests heavily in, for instance, biotech start-ups, may have many sleepless nights regardless of how well the stock does. And the aggressive investor whose money is largely in U.S. Treasury bonds will be discontent regardless of how safe his money is.

ALLOCATING RISK IN YOUR INVESTMENT DECISIONS

The notion of balancing investments to manage risk is called asset allocation. The idea is simple: diversify your investments, spread them out among investments that offer varying degrees of risk and whose economic fortunes are in opposition. So while one investment may rise substantially, another may dip, then vice versa. But as the years tick by, the entire investment portfolio will show a reasonable gain.

With the help of an investment adviser or financial planner, you'll decide how to allocate your retirement investments. This decision should be based on your risk tolerance, investment objectives, age and job prospects, liquidity needs, amount of investments, tax bracket, and whether the assets are in a tax-qualified account.

The following are examples of asset allocations, to give you an idea of how investments can be spread out. The people in these scenarios plan to retire by age 65, or earlier depending on their investments, and are putting at least 10 percent of their pre-tax income into their retirement savings.

YOUNG, AGGRESSIVE ALLOCATION

A working couple in their thirties with many investment years ahead and eager for growth may choose a relatively aggressive strategy for their retirement fund. Asset allocation for such a strategy would be:

• Blue chip growth funds or stocks for steady, moderate growth: 30%

• Small-company growth funds or stocks for somewhat unpredictable growth that may be stellar or slow: 20%

• Tax-exempt bond funds or bonds for better-than-average interest rates: 20%

• Other (e.g., more growth funds, international equities, partnerships, venture capital): 20%

Q I work too hard for my money to risk losing it, so I put it in savings bonds where it won't be eaten away by a drop in the market or falling real estate prices. Is it possible I'm too conservative?

A Very definitely, and being too conservative is a mistake many investors make. Think about investing for the long haul—10, 20 years. You need to put your money where it will grow, and over the decades the stock market, despite crashes and setbacks, has outpaced virtually every other investment.

• Cash/money market account for relatively low interest rates but offering immediate access for emergencies or three months of daily expenses: 10%

MIDDLE-AGED, MODERATE ALLOCATION

A person in her mid-forties who already has accumulated some assets may want a fairly even mixture of safety to preserve what she has combined with aggressiveness to outstep the effects of inflation. Asset allocation for such a strategy would be:

• Blue chip growth funds or stocks for steady, reliable growth: 40%
• Small-company growth funds or stocks, or international stocks: 10%
• High-yield bond funds or municipal bonds: 30%
• Cash/money market account for emergencies or three months' spending: 10%
• Other (e.g., real estate, partnerships): 10%

LATER LIFE, CONSERVATIVE ALLOCATION

A working couple in their late fifties, hoping to retire at 65 or earlier, has accumulated considerable assets in pension and retirement accounts. Their objective is to create enough income to re-place their working salaries and also to keep some investments in growth instruments for future income. Their asset allocation would be:

• Blue chip stock funds or stocks: 40%
• High-yield fixed-income bonds or municipal bonds: 40%
• Cash/money market account: 10%
• Real estate: 5%
• Other (e.g. partnerships, growth funds, international stocks): 5%

In measuring the mix for your investments and allocating your assets, ask yourself these questions. The answers will suggest whether it's a good investment, you need more information, or you should stay away.

1. Is the investment's annual return guaranteed, estimated, or highly variable, and does it meet your expectations?

2. What are the chances you can lose the entire investment amount and is the potential profitability worth this risk?

3. Are any of the investment's tax consequences—immediate and/or future—known and acceptable to you?

RISK, RETURN, AND LIQUIDITY: A RANKING OF INVESTMENTS

	Risk*	Return**	Liquidity†
Passbook savings	low	low	high
CD	low	low	medium
Money market acct.	low	low	high
U.S. Savings Bonds	low	low	medium
T-notes	low	medium	medium
T-bills	low	medium	medium
Treasury bonds	low	medium	low
Municipals	low	medium	low
Corporate bonds	low	medium	low
Stock funds	medium	high	high
Bond funds	low	medium	high
Common stock	high	high	high
Preferred stock	medium	medium	high

* Risk: Likelihood of losing principal.
**Return: Likelihood of earning returns well over rate of inflation.
† Liquidity: How readily you can turn the investment into cash without losing principal or paying a penalty.

4. Do you know enough about how this investment earns money? If it underperforms for a number of years, can you switch to an alternative without a major penalty?

5. How liquid is your investment? What kind of fees or penalties are charged if you must get at your money immediately? Can you do without the money if it's locked up for years?

6. Are your investments diversified enough to withstand various market gyrations?

INVESTOR PROFILES

Here's a comparison of two groups of share owners—baby boomers (aged 35–44) and seniors (over age 65)—showing what percentage of each group fits into certain categories.

	Baby Boomer	Senior
Male	63%	65%
Employed	94%	17%
Completed college	33%	18%
Married	73%	55%
Widowed	2%	23%
One-person household	14%	39%
Median age	40	71
Household income	$48,100	$29,600
Portfolio value	$ 7,500	$45,800
First entered market last year	9%	0.9%
Willing to take substantial/moderate risks	44%	13%
Have IRA/Keogh	46%	47%
Own NYSE stock	62%	81%
Own OTC stock	25%	23%
Own mutual fund	65%	64%
Own one stock only	36%	23%
Use full-service broker only	58%	64%
Use discount broker only	27%	13%
Use both full-service and discount brokers	15%	23%

Shareholder Ownership 1990, New York Stock Exchange, Inc.

WHERE TO PUT YOUR MONEY

The menu of investment choices grows daily. Professional investors and financial institutions continue to devise ways to attract money. Like exotic flower growers, they're constantly creating variations, hybrids, and new species of financial greenery. For an investor, the new offshoots sometimes offer better deals, sometimes not. But if you're familiar with the garden-variety offerings, you can better judge whether the latest species is worthwhile or an old bouquet in a new pot.

Investments fall into broad categories depending on their yield, annual return, safety, riskiness, and liquidity. So the descriptions that follow are based on different objectives.

STOCKS: INVESTMENTS FOR GROWTH AND APPRECIATION

These investments should make up the heart of most retirement accounts because of their record for steady, better-than-inflation growth and relative safety. This is particularly true when purchased as long-term investments; over the short run (less than three years), their growth may be erratic and appreciation negligible. But give them time and the results are usually profitable.

COMMON STOCK

When a company incorporates, it creates shares of stock and assigns each share an arbitrary value ("par value"). Each share represents a fraction of the company's ownership, and when these pieces are sold to the general public, the company becomes publicly owned, with each shareholder owning a percentage of the corporation. What people pay for each share depends on supply and demand. This ownership gives a stockholder the right to vote at stockholders meetings (most people don't attend and so sign a proxy form) and receive dividends, if the company pays them (not all do). This partial ownership is also called "equity," and stocks are also called "equities."

Companies sometimes create more than one type of stock. For instance, it may offer a Class A and Class B stock, with more voting rights given to Class A stockholders. Some companies issue preferred stock, which gives the holder preferential treatment, that is, fixed and higher dividends and, if the company is ever liquidated and assets distributed, preference over common stockholders.

Another variation is "convertible preferred" stock, which costs more than common and gives a stockholder the right to convert shares at a later date into a certain number of shares of common. Exactly how many shares of common depends on the stock's "conversion ratio." For example, if you own 100 convertible preferreds with a three-to-one ratio, you may eventually turn them into 300 shares. Investors like convertible preferred because they usually pay a higher dividend and they don't fluctuate in price as much as common stock. The cherry on the sundae is that you can convert to common stock when its price has run up, so you get a bit of the gain.

But all this goodness is not risk-free. Depending upon the dividend, the per-share price of the converted common shares of convertible preferred is usually more than for common, the dividend or yield is less than that of other high-

WHEN DIVIDENDS COUNT: KNOW YOUR DIVIDEND DATES

Declaration date: The day the board of directors meets and declares it will pay a quarterly dividend.

Payment date: The day the company mails out dividend checks (usually 10 to 30 days after the declaration date).

Record date: The day an investor has to be officially on the corporate books as a stockholder.

Ex-dividend date: Because it takes five business days to transfer stock on the corporate books, a stock's price is reduced by the amount of the dividend five days before the record date. An investor purchasing stock on the ex-dividend date or later has missed the cutoff to receive the company's upcoming dividend payment.

HOW GOOD IS GOLD?

Gold should be, at best, only a small part of your retirement investments. No more than 5 percent, experts recommend. Why? Because gold's traditional allure as a sure thing in times of trouble—when interest rates zoom upward, international crises erupt, or financial markets tumble—has vanished. Over the past decade, only the 500-plus point tumble in the stock market produced a spike in gold prices, and they soon returned to their $300 to $400 per ounce level. You can't count on gold as a cushion for tough times, only as a temporary soft spot.

There are a number of ways to invest in gold, but beware—the field is peppered with scams. Don't buy any over the phone, through the mail, or from anyone you don't know and trust. Don't invest in any nonpublicly traded companies. Your investment options are:

- Stocks of publicly traded gold mining companies
- Gold certificates
- Gold bullion
- Gold coins

yield investments, and the stock price can go down as easily as up.

A GARDEN OF COMMON STOCKS

It's not enough to know the varieties of common stock. They're also clumped together by how they perform, industry grouping, size, or unique characteristic, such as when they went public. The equity portion of your retirement portfolio, if it includes individual stocks (an alternative is stock mutual funds, which are explained later), should contain a mixture of these stocks. It's impossible to predict which type is going to do well, but a balanced sampling will help protect your portfolio from being weighted down by poor performers. This raises an obvious question: what's the best mixture? Answering this gets into the realm of crystal ball gazing. No one knows for sure, despite what professional investors, brokers, or financial planners may tell you.

The right mix for you depends, as with asset allocation, on your age, retirement expectations, and needs. Some stocks are known to gain steadily over the long haul while others produce immediate income, and still others skyrocket or plunge unpredictably. And many stocks act in a variety of roles, sometimes growing, sometimes falling into cycles, sometimes stagnating for years and then suddenly reviving. They're presented here according to how risky they're considered and how much income they produce.

Low Risk, Low Income

Value stocks: These are priced relatively cheaply compared with the overall market because their business is in a downturn or unpopular. Their unpopularity may also be attributable to a company's weak performance or to general economic trends. Despite their financial hard times, they may be sound companies and their fortunes may improve. And the value stocks that do turn around and beef up their earnings, and begin to pay dividends, advance into the low-risk, high-income category.

Low Risk, Moderate Income

Blue chips: These companies have long histories of rising earnings, steady dividends, sound finances, and established brands or reputations, although there's no official "blue chip" designation. They're market leaders—corporations such as AT&T, General Electric, and Philip Morris—with healthy earnings growth and a modest but not insubstantial dividend.

A subspecies of the blue chip are "franchise" stocks, companies with a dominant market share: by dint of their marketing power, they "own" the franchise. Don't get confused—these aren't franchise companies. They're corporations, such as Coca Cola Co. and H&R Block, that are known for doing well in tough economic times. However, they're also frequently expensive—selling for many times their earnings records.

Low Risk, High Income

High-yield stocks: Most publicly traded stocks (but not all) pay dividends, and many of those with steady, predictable cash flows are committed to paying dividends that beat the interest you'd receive from a strong savings account. The best known of these stocks are utility companies. Unlike some other high-yield securities, their payments tend to be dependable and many retirees use them as a source of regular income. There are no guarantees, however, that any company paying a high yield today will pay it tomorrow. Dividends can be reduced, and sometimes companies in desperate need to raise cash by selling stock promise high dividends, then can't sustain the payments. In recent years at least 30 utilities cut or eliminated their dividends. Preferred stock also pays yields that at times compete with other interest investments; common stocks that pay high yields are known as equity-income stocks. As investments for appreciation, however, high-yield stocks usually don't gain much in value over the years. People buy them for the dividends, not for long-term growth.

Moderate Risk, Low Income

Growth stocks: These stocks have records of consistent, steady sales and earnings growth, which usu-

STOCK YIELDS

This is a list of average yields, in December, on the more than 1,700 stocks in the NYSE Composite Index.

1981	6.7%
1982	5.2
1983	4.4
1984	4.5
1985	3.6
1986	3.4
1987	3.4
1988	3.6
1989	3.2
1990	3.7
1991	2.4
1992	3.0

Fact Book for the Year 1991, New York Stock Exchange, Inc.

ally outpaces the market in general and the rate of inflation. While they may be buffeted by industry slowdowns or cyclical events, they're usually not thrown off by economic downturns. On the other hand, they don't post dramatic, unexpected increases in their earnings.

High Risk, Low Income

Small-company growth stocks, sometimes referred to as "small cap" stocks (as in capitalization, as in the total value of their outstanding shares). These usually have a market value under $100 million (yup, that's small) but a history of around 12 percent annual growth. They have a reputation for growing faster than the economy and other companies in their industry, but their mercurial growth makes them riskier (they can stumble as quickly as soar). While not household names like the blue chips, these can have established reputations in their industry.

High Risk, High Income

Distressed stocks (aka "turnaround stocks" or "bottom fishing"): These are distant cousins of value stocks—"distant" because their financial condition is much more precarious. In fact, the company may be in bankruptcy or on the brink of it. Some professional investors specialize in these stocks, and watch them carefully on the chance the company may be another Chrysler, one of the more famous phoenix-like turnarounds. Investors (usually steely-nerved pros) buy the stock or bonds of companies in bankruptcy, or about to emerge from bankruptcy after reorganization, on the gamble that the reconfig-

---

PROMISING INDUSTRIES IN 1993

- Education (e.g. textbook publishing)
- Transportation (e.g. railroads)
- Metals (e.g. copper)
- Software (e.g. automation software)
- Health Care (e.g. HMOs)
- Transaction processing (e.g. credit card verification)

Fortune magazine

THE ULTIMATE BLUE CHIPS

These are the companies in the Dow Jones Industrial Average as of December 1992:

Allied-Signal	Eastman Kodak	J.P. Morgan
Aluminum Co. of America	Exxon	Philip Morris
American Express	General Electric	Procter & Gamble
AT&T	General Motors	Sears
Bethlehem Steel	Goodyear	Texaco
Boeing	IBM	Union Carbide
Caterpillar	International Paper	United Technologies
Chevron	McDonald's	Westinghouse
Coca-Cola	Merck	Woolworth
Disney	Minnesota Mining and Manufacturing	
Du Pont		

ured company will survive, and thrive. For instance, when Federated Department Stores (owner of Bloomingdale's and Jordan Marsh, among others) came out of bankruptcy in early 1992, bottom fishers snapped up its stock. In the week it emerged from Chapter 11, the stock went from $12 a share to $17.

Cyclical stocks: These rise and fall with economic news, such as changes in interest rates, consumer spending, or energy prices.

They'll have a string of good years, a string of flat or bad years, and so on. Industries famous for being whipsawed by economic cycles are auto manufacturers, airlines, heavy machinery, and steel. Other companies move up and down because of specific economic events as opposed to the general climate. When interest and mortgage rates fall, construction and housing companies prosper. Unlike growth stocks, cyclicals don't march on a steady upward slope—they advance over hill and dale. They're not recommended for long-term holding, and investors have to be prepared to sell when they're doing well.

Trash or Treasures

The saying, "One man's trash is another man's treasure," certainly can be applied to investments. The

three groups of stocks here don't fall neatly into any single risk/income category and have to be judged really on a company-by-company basis.

Penny stocks: These are usually valued at less than a dollar and "thinly" traded (meaning not many change hands in a given day). Their prices are not listed in newspapers but are quoted in

AVOIDING SCAMS

State and federal securities enforcement agencies offer these tips for avoiding scams:

- Don't deal with unfamiliar securities firms—only those you know and trust.
- Beware of securities offered over the telephone by strangers, or unknown securities traded on foreign exchanges.
- Don't listen to high-pressure sales talk.
- Beware of promises of spectacular profits.
- Don't buy on tips and rumors.
- Don't invest in anything that requires an immediate decision and immediate payment.
- Don't give out your credit card number for "identification" or "verification." Use it only for actual purchases.
- Beware of any "completely risk-free" investment.
- Avoid any broker or salesperson who won't provide information in writing.

"pink sheets," a listing of trading information on small securities circulated among brokers. As investments, they're often over-rated and overtouted, if not outright fraudulent. So many abuses have surrounded the selling of penny stocks, notably high-pressure phone tactics by salespeople working out of boiler rooms, that the SEC has imposed a rule requiring salespeople to obtain written consent from investors for their purchase.

New issues ("initial public offerings—IPOs"): These are rarely recommended for safe investing for obvious reasons: they have no track record and their future is a coin toss. Professionals who make money with them often don't hold on for long, taking profits after an early and often temporary run-up. Pros have lots to choose from. In October 1992, a record 65 companies went public. Inexperienced investors often get caught up in IPOs fads and the flurry of media attention and market speculation that can accompany new issues. The latest IPO frenzy swirled around new issues of biotechnology stocks; in the 1980s it was high-tech start-ups.

Foreign stocks: A number of foreign companies are traded on

Q I've heard that mutual funds are a smart investment, especially for the long run, but I'm concerned about locking up my money. How hard is it for me to take money out, and will I lose a bundle?

A It's very easy to withdraw money from a mutual fund —simply call your broker and ask to sell whatever you need. Whether you'll take a hit financially depends on the net asset value the day you sell and whether your broker collects a commission at the time of sale.

American stock exchanges, but instead of stock, their trading currency is called an American Depository Receipt (ADR). However, they act like stocks selling at per share prices. About 110 foreign issues are listed on the New York Stock Exchange, with about half coming from Europe (mainly the U.K.). Foreign stocks have become such a staple in American markets that you may already own some and not know it. Actively traded foreign stocks include Matsushita Electric (Japan), Benetton (Italian), and SmithKline Beecham (British). Foreign stocks hold special appeal to investors because they are also affected by currency fluctuations as well as the stock market.

MASTERING STOCK FUNDS

Mutual funds are one of the best ways for investors to profit from the long-term growth of securities and to avoid costly errors in picking individual stocks. These funds—collections of anywhere from 30 to 300 separate stocks or bonds managed by an investment company—enable you to diversify your holdings into dozens of companies without necessarily investing huge sums of money. With mutual funds, your investment performance isn't dependent on the fortunes of a small group of stocks. But like a stock, you earn money through the appreciation in the value of your fund shares, dividends, and payouts of capital gains (money made on the sale of individual stocks).

For retirement planning, mutual funds are hard to beat. With many designed to perform over the long haul, they're tailor-made for investors who don't want to constantly make decisions or worry about their money. Most financial planners say mutual funds should be the bedrock of any retirement plan, and typically recommend that people in their early thirties should invest as much as 80 percent of their retirement money in mutual funds. Even retirees, they advise, should keep a sizable portion of their money in mutual funds, although these funds should be geared more to income than growth.

To invest in mutual funds, you purchase shares of the fund either through a stockbroker, financial planner, or insurance agent, or directly from the fund company. (Most funds have a $250 to $2,000 minimum.) What you pay per share is called the "offer price" and this amount includes sales commissions (loads) and fees. The value of a mutual fund share is called the "net asset value" and is figured daily, according to how the fund's holdings are doing. Most funds are "open-ended," meaning they always accept new investors. Less common are "closed-end" funds (see below).

As a mutual fund shareholder, you usually receive a payout at least once a year. This money may be a capital gains distribution—profits from the sale of individual stocks. You may also get dividends (sometimes called an income distribution) from the fund's collection of stocks. Investors can either pocket this money, or reinvest it in the fund.

Investors who own funds that are part of a larger family—a company that manages many separate funds—often have the option of easy switching among funds. Usually you can move your money between funds by simply telephoning the fund company (many have 800 numbers). However, you may pay a fee and the fund company may limit the number of times a year you can switch.

Closed-End Funds: These are a distant cousin of the mutual fund. While they, too, consist of a portfolio of stocks, the funds are "closed," meaning they offer a

---

MUTUAL FUND FACTS
(AS OF THE END OF 1992)

- Number of mutual funds: 3,833
- Number of mutual fund accounts: 68 million
- Main reason people invest in them: "Funds are more diversified"
- Financial goals of mutual fund investors (most to least important):
    1. Retirement
    2. More money now
    3. Children's education
    4. Major purchases
    5. Providing inheritance

Investment Company Institute

fixed number of shares that never changes. The value of a share of a closed-end fund rises or falls with investor supply and demand. In contrast, mutual fund prices go up and down with the value of the individual stocks owned by the fund. Closed-end funds trade on an exchange (usually the New York) and usually sell at either a premium (when investor demand bids up the price of the limited number of shares) or a discount to the value of the fund.

WHAT MUTUAL FUNDS COST

Mutual funds charge investors fees and sales commissions. Some are imposed when you buy or sell your shares; others are annual charges that investors don't pay directly but are taken from the fund and reflected in their value. Here's a rundown of the charges you may pay:

• Sales commissions on purchase (called "loads"). Load funds charge a maximum of between 4.5 and 8.5 percent of your initial investment. Some funds charge low loads of 1 to 3 percent or no load at all. In most cases, the more you invest, the lower the load.

• Fees when you sell. Funds that don't charge an up-front load may charge an exit fee if you sell your shares within a certain time, usually between one to six years. Called a "back-end load" or "contingent deferred sales charge," this may be a percentage of the original purchase amount or of the proceeds you take out; it usually declines over time. Another type of rear load is a redemption fee, which may be imposed anytime shares are sold and be either a flat dollar amount or a percentage of what you redeem.

• Annual advisory fees (for the fund management company) range from 0.5 to 1 percent of the fund's assets, and affect the value of your shares. You don't pay this fee directly.

• The "12b-1" fee (named after an SEC rule) ranges from 0.25 to 1.25 percent of the fund's assets. It's imposed to cover marketing expenses for the fund and affects the value of your shares. You don't pay this fee directly.

SELECTING A MUTUAL FUND

Selecting a fund (or preferably funds) depends on what you expect of your money. Mutual funds

KEEPING TRACK OF YOUR MUTUAL FUND

Here's how to understand the symbols used in newspaper listings.

First column: Abbreviated fund name. Some funds appear under a major listing for the fund family. Symbols beside the name:

"p": fund charges a 12b-1 fee.

"f": fund's reported price for the previous day.

"t": fund charges a redemption fee and a 12b-1 fee.

"r": fund charges a redemption fee.

Second column: NAV—net asset value per share. Sometimes called the bid price. What you would receive if you sold your shares.

Third column: Offering price. Sometimes called the buy or ask price. What you would pay per share if buying. Includes sales charge or load. If "NL" appears, fund charges no load and purchase price is same as net asset value.

Fourth column: Change. How much in dollars and cents the share price changed on the previous trading day.

specialize in various groups of companies, and each performs differently. Here are the broad groupings and conventional wisdom about their prospects.

• Aggressive growth (stocks of young, emerging companies): The aim is not immediate income but maximum capital gains.

• Growth (stocks of established, known companies): The aim is long-term capital gains rather than dividends.

• Total return (growth and income funds, equity income funds, "balanced" funds): The aim is twofold: to pay solid dividends for steady income and to show long-term capital gains.

• Income (utility funds, corporate and government bond funds, municipal bond funds): The aim is immediate income with little or no long-term growth.

• International (outside the U.S.) funds, global (anywhere in the world) funds, or international money market funds: The aim is both immediate and long-term growth, not income.

A fifth category is a miscellaneous grouping of very specialized funds. These include:

• Index funds. These invest in stocks that mirror the performance of a specific index, such as the Value Line Composite Index or Standard & Poor's 500. One attraction: management fees are lower because there are few decisions to be made about what to buy.

• Socially conscious or social values funds. These invest in stocks of companies known for political or environmental advocacy. One such fund for example, doesn't purchase stocks of companies operating in South Africa.

• Sector funds. These invest in stocks of companies in a single industry, such as health and biotechnology, energy, aerospace, new technologies, or financial services.

FINDING A MUTUAL FUND

Investors can choose from among more than 3,000 active mutual funds. A *Directory of Mutual Funds* detailing investment goals, size, minimum investment, and fees is available for $5 from the Investment Company Institute, 1600 M Street, NW, Suite 600, Washington, DC 20036.

• Gold and precious metals funds. These invest in companies that operate gold, silver, or platinum mines.

HOW'S YOUR FUND DOING?

You can follow the value of your mutual fund shares as you can any publicly traded stock, for they're reported daily in newspapers. The figure you zero in on is the "NAV"—net asset value—because it indicates how much you would receive for your shares if you sold them today (minus any back-end loads).

Annual performance figures are in the fund's prospectus (see below), but are not easy to convert to a percentage return. Add "dividends from net investment income" plus "distributions from net realized gains" plus (or minus) "net realized and unrealized gains [losses] on securities," and divide by the "net asset value" at the end of the previous period. This information should be in a table found within the first five pages of the prospectus.

Another way is to find your fund in the annual mutual fund review issue of one of the national business publications *(Barron's, Fortune, Forbes, U.S. News and World Report, Money, Kiplinger's Personal Finance Magazine, Financial World)*; these usually come out every January or February. Some of these ratings are better for comparing funds than obtaining a precise measure of their performance because they don't include adjustments for loads and fees. Read the footnotes carefully to learn how they arrive at their numbers or rankings.

Total annual return figures for mutual funds assume that you reinvested all capital gains and dividends. So if you withdrew or put in any money, published annual returns don't accurately reflect *your* gains. To figure your annual return, calculate each of the following:

Step 1

1. NAV of all your shares (beginning of year): $_____

2. Income (dividends, capital gains, sales) received: $_____

3. New money invested: $_____

4. NAV of all your shares (end of year): $_____

Step 2

Figure your net investment over the year by subtracting income received (number 2) from new money invested (number 3). In these calculations, use numbers that reflect total amounts (which may include loads and fees).

Step 3

Subtract the net investment from the end-of-year net asset value (number 4), then divide by the beginning-of-year net asset value (number 1). Convert this into a percentage by subtracting 1 and moving the decimal two places to the right.

Working the Steps

Here's an example of how to use the steps: On January 1 this year, you owned 210 shares of the Big Dreams Fund, whose shares had a net asset value of $20.50. During the year, you received a distribution of $80 and you bought 10 more shares costing $240 (including load). On December 31 of this year, you owned 220 shares that had a net asset value of $25.75. (The number of shares you own changes constantly because of dividends and distribution. When in doubt, just call the fund. They can also give you the total current value.) Figure your return:

Step 1

1. NAV of all your shares (beginning of year): $4,305
2. Income (dividends, capital gains, sales) received: $80
3. New money invested: $240
4. NAV of all your shares (end of year): $5,665

Step 2

New money invested:	$240
Income:	− 80
Net invested:	160

Step 3

End-of-year net asset value:	$5,665
Net investment	− 160
Total:	5,505

Divide 5,505 by NAV (begin): $5,505 ÷ 4,305 =	1.279
Convert to percentage (subtract 1, move decimal over two places):	28%

SCAN THE PROSPECTUS

One of the best sources of information about a fund is its prospectus, which is mailed to fund investors and discloses relevant facts about the fund's managers, finances, and investments. It's an intimidating document—lots of dense type and legal language—but worth deciphering. Scan it for this information:

• **Fund name and date:** Some companies issue one prospectus for a group of funds, but it will clearly show in tables and text which information applies to all and which to individual funds. Make sure you have the most re-

Q I own a number of funds in a mutual fund family, which allows me to switch between funds a couple of times a year. This sounds like a good way to follow the best gainers. Is it?

A Not really, because each time you go out of one fund and into another (in fact selling and buying), you're creating a tax event and you may also be racking up transaction costs. Leave market timing to the pros.

cent prospectus; funds must issue them every year.

• **Investment objective:** Does the fund's objective (e.g., buying low-priced, distressed stocks for long-term capital gains) match yours? Review the fund's investment portfolio to see if its holdings are consistent with its objectives. Keep in mind, however, that its objectives are goals, not guarantees. Mutual funds, even those composed of government securities, can't promise a guaranteed yield or minimum share value.

• **Fees:** All fees, front-end and back-end, must be disclosed; they usually appear in the "Summary of Fund Expenses" and "Per Share Data" at the beginning. How do these fees compare with similar funds? How much do the fees affect your yield and annual return?

• **Risk:** The prospectus describes its level of risk by stating the quality of its investments, for instance "investment grade" with AAA or Aa ratings or "lower quality" with BBB ratings, and the proportion of its investments that is in each risk category.

TIPS FOR INVESTING

Instead of putting all your money into one fund, diversify. Aim to own at least five different funds so that a portion of your investments does well in any kind of market.

Every January, mutual funds post annual results, and it'll be a temptation to jump into the hottest fund, the one reporting the biggest gains. Resist that temptation, and instead focus on performance figures for the past five and ten years. These are much better indicators of future performance, although still no guarantee. The departure of a fund manager or an extraordinary event (like the bankruptcy of a large holding) can shatter a fund's track record.

Try to give your mutual fund three to five years before judging its performance, and don't try to time the market; mutual funds aren't for traders but for long-term holders. Invest steadily and regularly, not as the market moves from week to week. If your fund logs truly dismal results for four quarters in a row, consider moving your money to another.

A simple way to improve returns is to reinvest dividends and capital gains back into a fund by buying more shares. Presumably, as the fund price gradually rises, so too do your holdings. (This tactic also works for individual stocks.) Buying shares this way is also a little cheaper than the normal route because you don't pay commissions. The actual process of reinvesting is simple: you sign a form from the company authorizing the use of your dividends this way. Then instead of a check you receive a statement from the fund company telling you how many additional shares (or fractions of shares) your dividends have bought.

Dividend reinvesting has two negatives: One, if the share value does not rise steadily, you're investing in a stagnant or losing fund. The second is one of record keeping: when you sell your shares, you need to know for tax purposes what you originally paid, and gained or lost. All those fractions of shares you've bought along the way are a nightmare to compute into gains or losses! (But relief is on the way—more and more fund families are providing this information to investors.)

Another investment tactic is dollar-cost averaging. This method funnels money into a fund or stock gradually, thus averaging out the cost over time. Say your goal is to own 500 shares of Biobonanza Fund. Rather than buy them all today at $30 a share, which may be the top of the market, you buy shares at regular monthly or quarterly intervals regardless of whether the price is rising or falling. Your final cost for the shares is the average price over the acquisition period. If the share price rises during this time, you've gained; if the price dips, you acquire shares at a lower cost.

For dollar-cost averaging to make sense, you must believe in the long haul—this isn't for speculators going for quick gains.

Some investors use dollar-cost averaging only with mutual funds, because many mutual fund companies don't charge extra commissions for each purchase. Buying individual stocks every month through a broker could run up commission costs.

BONDS AWAY

When you buy stock, you purchase a tiny piece of a company. When you buy corporate bonds, you lend the company the price of the bond. In return for your loan, which the company promises to pay back by a certain date, the company agrees to pay you interest. It's this interest that attracts investors. Of course, the amount of interest depends on the company's finances (how much it needs the money), when it plans to pay it back, and the general economy (competing interest rates). And the value of your bond—its market price—rises and falls with general interest rates. When general interest rates are rising, bond

Q: I hear people at work talking about buying "OTC" stocks, and I don't know what they mean.

A: It's only a small mystery. OTC stands for "over-the-counter," which refers to the market that sells the stock; in this case it's the National Association of Securities Dealers Automated Quotations system (also called NASDAQ). The other big markets are the New York Stock Exchange (the "big board") and the American Stock Exchange (the "Amex" or the "curb exchange").

values fall because the interest they're paying is less than prevailing rates. Conversely, when general interest rates fall, bond prices move upward as their interest rates become more attractive.

This steady interest or regular income has made bonds a favorite among retirees. But bonds aren't the gentle, predictable investment they once were. Like the other money markets, they have been rocked and rolled by the era of takeovers and leveraged buyouts, by ricocheting interest rates and recessions. Today, the bond market—once the sleepy backwater of Wall Street—can be as mercurial as the hottest biotech stock.

Companies aren't the only institutions that issue bonds. The U.S. government, government agencies, and local governments sell bonds, too.

Investing in bonds is, in part, a numbers game. Bonds can be reduced to an assortment of figures, each providing a piece of a puzzle. And when you have all the numbers, you have a complete picture. Math phobics have a problem with bonds, but little calculation is involved. It's more a matter of filling in the blanks than bringing out the calculator. Your assessment of a bond can be reduced to five figures, which will tell you what you need to make a decision.

1. Coupon yield: The declared percentage paid of a bond's face value. A $1,000 bond with a 10 percent coupon yield pays $100 a year. This figure never changes, even when the bond price does.

2. Coupon rate: The fixed dollar amount you receive. On the bond above, it's $100, and it, too, never changes.

3. Current yield: The price of a bond rises and falls in its lifetime. If the market value of a $1,000 bond dips to $900, and its coupon rate is $100, the current yield is a bit over 11 percent ($100 \div 900$).

4. Maturity date: The year the issuing company promises to pay off its loans (buy back its bonds) at face value. Bonds are often classified according to their date to maturity: short-terms expire within 1 year, intermediates in 5 to 10 years, and long-terms expire out to 30 years.

5. Yield to maturity: This figure applies to a bond held to maturity and bought after it's issued when its market price is higher or lower than its face value. This amount is the yield over the years until it matures and figured in with the gain or loss on the purchase price.

CORPORATE BONDS

Corporate bonds come in all shapes and sizes, depending on the collateral behind them. (Remember, these are loans.)

READING THE BOND PAGE

Bond prices are reported daily in newspapers. These listings are full of information, though you need to decipher the abbreviations. For example, this was a listing in the Wall Street Journal *for bonds issued by Atlantic Richfield Co.*

Bonds	Cur Yld.	Vol.	Close	Net Chg.
ARich 8⅝ 00	8.5	8	101¼	+¼
ARich 10⅜ 95	9.3	20	111¾	+¾

What the numbers mean: 8⅝ and 10⅜ are the coupon rates. The next figures are the maturity dates: 00 is 2000 and 95 is 1995. The current yields—8.5 percent and 9.3 percent—indicate that the bonds are selling for a premium. That is, their closing prices—$1,012.50 and $1,117.50—are higher than their face value, which is always $1,000. Volume tells the number of bonds traded the preceding day.

U.S. Government agency bonds are quoted in 32nds. Thus a 99.24 quote means 99²⁴⁄₃₂ or 99.75.

- Bonds backed by company buildings or property are *mortgage bonds.*
- Bonds backed by securities the company owns are *collateral bonds.*
- Bonds backed by a company's equipment are *equipment trust bonds.*
- Bonds backed by the company's reputation—its good faith and credit rating—are *debentures.*
- Bonds that can be transferred into a company's common stock are *convertible bonds.*

Fortunately, individual investors don't have to worry about judging how solid and safe a corporate bond's collateral might be. A number of companies specialize in judging and rating the credit-

BOND RATING COMPANIES

Rating Company	Credit Rating Scale (Highest to Lowest)
Moody's Investors Service	Aaa–C
Standard & Poor's	AAA–D
Fitch Investor Service	AAA–D

worthiness of individual bonds. Moody's Investors Service, Standard & Poor's, and Fitch Investor Service evaluate bonds and rate them on a lettered scale. Moody's top rating is Aaa; S&P's is AAA. The next level is double-A, and a poor rating (meaning risky) is double-B and below. If S&P rates a bond "C," the company may stop paying interest; a "D" rating means the company is in default and not paying interest.

Corporate bonds with a BB (or Ba) rating or lower are considered "junk bonds." To sell bonds with such low ratings, the company must offer investors some inducement. In exchange for purchasing these wobbly investments, the company offers head-turning interest rates. These are yields many points above what better-quality bonds or high-yield instruments promise. Junk bonds are not for

the faint-hearted, or the retirement investor. But a bond's rating is not the only ingredient to be evaluated.

Exactly when a company intends to buy back its bonds raises another element in these intricate investments. Despite the published maturity date, a corporation may change its mind and pay off its loans early. In the language of bond traders, it may "call" its bonds before maturity. Companies do this when prevailing interest rates drop below what they're paying on bonds. Rather than pay investors more interest than they have to, companies call their bonds and issue new ones at lower rates. So investors have to give up the bonds paying above-market interest rates. It's like a homeowner refinancing when mortgage rates drop. Some bond issuers, to reassure investors, stipulate they will not call a bond for at least a certain number of years, such as five or ten, after it's issued. It's worth asking about when buying a bond.

LOCAL GOVERNMENT: MUNIS

Government bonds come in an assortment of flavors and shapes. Municipal bonds ("munis") are issued by state and local government agencies (e.g. housing authority, water board, highway department, airport authority, utility, hospital). They're in a special class by themselves because their interest is exempt from federal income tax. Better yet, in most states their payments are also exempt from state and local taxes if the investor is a resident taxpayer. They're the only bond with this feature, and so gain in popularity as people's tax rates rise.

Of course, this special feature means that municipal bonds pay a lower yield than corporate bonds. Investors comparing them have to size up pre-tax and after-tax yields to decide whether a muni is more attractive. Generally, they work best for people in the 28 percent or higher federal bracket or residents confronting high state and local income taxes. Investors also have to be wary of munis that are "callable"—that can be paid off before their maturity date. If your muni is callable, you're not locked in to a set yield.

There are two types of municipal bonds: general obligation (GO) bonds and revenue bonds. The GO bonds are backed by taxes. The issuing authority's ability to impose and collect taxes ensures that it will make its bond payments. Revenue bonds are backed by revenue generated by the project for which the bonds were issued, such as a highway, airport, or hospital. From an investor's vantage point, the GO bonds tend to be safer.

A word of caution about munis: they're not fail-safe. Stories of municipalities or issuing authorities going broke were once big news, but no longer. The largest muni default ever was that of the Washington Public Power Supply System (remember WHOOPS?). Today, stories about school authorities, highway projects, and housing construction projects going broke are not uncommon. To avoid a shaky project, investors watch a muni's rating and shy away from anything below an A rating. Quality is important with munis.

U.S. GOVERNMENT BONDS (NOTES AND BILLS)

Bonds from the federal government come in four varieties: U.S. Treasury bills, U.S. Savings Bonds, U.S. Treasury notes, and U.S. Treasury bonds. (Technically, any government IOU that lasts longer than a year is a bond. If it expires in less than a year, it's a bill.) All U.S. securities are very marketable—you can buy and sell them easily, and you don't have to keep them until their expiration date. The interest you earn on any U.S. Treasury debt is exempt from state and local taxes, although you'll owe federal income taxes.

U.S. Treasury bills run for 3 months, 6 months, or 12 months, and the minimum denomination is $10,000. T-bills aren't sold with a stated interest rate. Instead, the government sells them at a discount—at less than their face value. When they come due, the bill holder receives the face value, so the difference between the discount price paid and the face value received represents the interest paid. For instance, you might pay $9,565 for a six-month T-bill; in six months you pocket $10,000, earning $435 or 4.5 percent (9 percent annual).

U.S. Savings Bonds are either Series EE or Series HH, and one leads to the other. The original maturity of Series EE bonds is 12 years, and like T-bills, they're sold at a discount to their face value—in this case 50 percent. But the difference between the discount price and what you receive when you redeem them "floats," or moves with the market. To be more exact, the interest rate floats so that it equals 85 percent of the interest rate paid by U.S. Treasury five-year notes. You have to keep your U.S. Savings Bond at least five years to earn this interest—if you cash it in sooner, your return will suffer. Series EE bonds come in denominations from $50 to $10,000 and can be bought from banks, savings and loans, and through payroll deduction. Regardless of where you purchase it, there's no commission for buying or redeeming.

The only way to buy Series HH bonds is by cashing in at least $500 worth of Series EE bonds. Series HH bonds are a little heftier than their smaller sibling—the minimum denomination is $500 and they mature in ten years. You pay face value for them and their interest (which is paid out twice a year) is fixed when they're issued.

Investors usually roll into Series HH bonds to defer taxes on interest earned from Series EE. The IRS allows investors to roll over interest earned on Series EE into Series HH and not pay taxes until a bond's maturity date. The bonds are exempt from state and local taxes, but you do have to pay federal taxes on interest payments.

U.S. Treasury notes and **U.S. Treasury bonds** work identically except for their maturity dates. T-notes are medium-term bonds that expire in one to ten years; Treasury bonds (simply "Treasuries") run for ten to 30 years. They're "auctioned" by the government in large quantities to brokerage and investment firms who buy them in big blocks. Individual investors purchase them either through a broker or directly from the U.S. Treasury (see below). The minimum denomination is $1,000, and like corporate bonds, their current yield (not to be confused with their coupon yield, which is pegged at a certain percentage when issued) and price change daily as they're bought and sold on the open market.

Government IOUs stand out from corporate bonds because they're not callable—the government can't decide to pay off its bonds early and avoid paying the interest rate it promised. If you buy T-notes or Treasuries, you can lock in an interest rate for the lifetime of the debt. However, in return for this security and the safety of investing in government securities, your interest rate will be a little lower than corporate bond returns.

T-bills, T-notes, and Treasuries cost next to nothing to invest in. You can buy them directly (and automatically reinvest or roll over your money) from the U.S. Treasury through a program called "Treasury Direct." It's offered through regional branches of the Federal Reserve Board (call 202/874-4000 for a list of branches and investing information) and imposes no commission. If you buy them indirectly—through a broker, bank, or employer, for instance—you'll pay a small commission, about $50.

GINNIE MAE AND HER RELATIVES

Other government agencies besides the U.S. Treasury sell IOUs and the most popular of these are "Ginnie Maes," short for securities issued by the Gov-

A RANKING OF BONDS

This chart will give you an idea of how the yields of corporate and government bonds compare. It shows the total return (interest plus appreciation) in 1992.

Type	Yield
Corporate (long-term)	9.39%
Municipals	10.80%
Treasury bonds (30-year)	8.05%
Treasury notes (5-year)	7.19%
Treasury bills (1-year)	4.67%

Ibbotson Associates, Chicago

ernment National Mortgage Association. This association pools fixed-rate home mortgages that are insured by the Veterans Administration and the Federal Housing Administration. The government backing makes these ultra-safe investments—little chance of the backer going out of business! (If an individual homeowner defaults, the government, not Ginnie Mae investors, swallows the loss.) But the government *guarantees* only the original investment, not the interest, although, of course, it makes every effort to pay interest and normally does.

When you invest in a Ginnie Mae, you're buying a piece of this mortgage pool, owning part of thousands of people's mortgages. So, you receive monthly payments of interest and principal from these thousands of homeowners. (They're also called "pass-through certificates" because they pass along to investors payments from homeowners.) But your investment income isn't predictable or fixed because homeowners may pay off mortgages early, especially when interest rates are falling and they can refinance at a lower rate. When this happens, investors are also paid off early and their Ginnie Mae expires. If you decide to invest in another Ginnie Mae at this time, your return will most likely be less than what you were originally receiving.

Ginnie Maes are sold in $25,000 units and subsequent $5,000 units, and their initial maturity extends 15 to 30 years, unless they're paid off early. Prepayments can shrink their lifetime dramatically and, depending on whether you paid more or less than their face value, hurt or boost your yield. (If you're confused, flip back to the basic bond section, which explains how what you pay affects a bond's yield.) Experts say investors should figure a seven to ten year lifetime on a Ginnie Mae. To compensate for this element of uncertainty, Ginnie Maes pay higher interest rates than U.S. Treasury bonds. And unlike government bonds, their payments are subject to state taxes.

You can't buy Ginnie Maes directly from the government; you must use a broker/dealer. Depending on its yield, you pay a discount (less than $100 per unit if the yield is low) or a premium (more than $100 if the yield is high) over par value. Commissions on Ginnie Maes are not broken out; they're computed as part of the quoted price. A common commission is 1 to 6 percent of your investment.

Fannie Mae and **Freddie Mac,** both government sponsored, are siblings of Ginnie Mae. The Federal National Mortgage Association (Fannie Mae) and Federal Home Loan Mortgage Corporation (Freddie Mac) also pool mortgages. But these are conventional home mortgages, making them a little less safe than the Ginnie Mae pools, which are composed of guaranteed home mortgages.

Fannie Mae and Freddie Mac bonds pass through to investors principal and interest payments from homeowners' payments. The difference between the two crops up when homeowners skip payments. Freddie Mac investors are guaranteed interest and principal payments every month. Fannie Mae investors are guaranteed only interest; principal may come later. The compensation for this added pinch of risk with Fannie Maes? You guessed it—a fraction-higher yield.

Fannie Mae or Freddie Mac certificates are bought through financial institutions, not from the government, and come in $10,000 denominations and $5,000 increments. You can get them for less by purchasing them through a mutual fund. Or, if you believe in a strong home mortgage market but prefer stocks, you can buy the Fannie Mae common stock on the New York Stock Exchange.

Sallie Mae, a cousin in this government family, offers bonds issued by the Student Loan Marketing Association. Composed of student loans and backed by Sallie Mae assets, they're protected against default by the U.S. Department of Education and rated AAA. Sold in units of about $10,000, their yields are about a third of a point more than Treasury bills and interest is exempt from state and local taxes. Investors, who like the idea of investing in the student loan business but prefer stock, can buy Sallie Mae common stock, which is traded on the New York Stock Exchange.

A new member of the government-backed family is **Connie Lee,** securities pooled by the College Construction Loan Insurance Association. It underwrites college construction loans, especially for schools that don't have fat endowments. Investors wanting to take advantage of Connie Lee's insurance and the bond's Standard & Poor's AAA rating can purchase construction bonds issued by the

educational institution that's borrowing the money. These can be bought through normal channels—financial institutions and broker/dealers.

THE LATEST OFFSPRING: CMOS

Collateralized Mortgage Obligations (CMOs) are a relatively new species of mortgage-backed securities. (In a previous life, CMOs were known as REMICs, real estate mortgage investment trusts—formally conduits, informally trusts—and were available only to institutions.) CMOs generally consist of pools of bonds from Ginnie, Fannie, and Freddie but can be issued by other agencies. They're one step removed from actual mortgage-backed bonds and so are not government-guaranteed. Their appeal is that the pooling of bonds allows them to offer a variety of maturity dates, two to twenty years, and steady if unpredictable interest payments.

Each CMO is unique, with a different mix of underlying securities, yields, and payment schedules. They have no fixed maturities because prepayments on mortgages can be made anytime.

As a result, investors don't know how long they will continue to pay out. CMOs come with many different expected maturities (referred to as "tranches"), depending on their prepayment schedule (fast to slow) and yield. The fast tranche has the shortest maturity, paying interest and principal within two to three years, and the lowest yield.

CMOs are a real stew of varieties of mortgages, yields, and payment schedules—so probably the best way for novices to invest is through a mutual fund. Though you'll pay more in fees, you have the comfort of letting a professional money manager figure out the payments and risks.

Professionals advise investors interested in CMOs to ask their stockbrokers to give them a "scenario analysis," which plots out the yield and prepayment risks of a particular CMO.

ZEROS CAN AMOUNT TO SOMETHING

A "zero-coupon" bond is any bond sold at a discount—less than its face value—and paying off all its interest at maturity when redeemed for its full face value. For example, a five-year 6 percent bond (they all come in $1,000 denominations) would sell for $792.09 and pay $1,000 when it matures in five years. It's called zero coupon because you don't redeem a coupon every six months to receive interest—interest accumulates until maturity. Zeros are issued by corporations, the U.S. government (e.g., Series EE), government agencies, and state and local governments. Their maturity dates extend from six months to 30 years, and investors should plan on holding them until maturity. Bailing out early (they're traded on the market) may cut into their yield (if interest rates have risen) or capture a gain (if rates have fallen).

Zeros are simple and convenient: buy one, tuck it away, and on maturity receive exactly the interest you bargained for. Interest is automatically reinvested, and grows, rather than being paid out periodically. Small investors don't have the hassle and expense of reinvesting or making a new investment decision. Yet, their convenience also has a price, and their yield tends to be less than other types of bonds. The commission on zeros is frequently 1 percent of face value, but since they're bought at discount, this commission may be a sizable percentage of the amount actually paid.

Another drawback is taxes: the interest they accumulate is taxable every year, even though you don't see any cash until the maturity date. You can avoid this problem by buying tax-exempt, municipal zeros or by placing them in a tax-deferred account, like an IRA.

Sophisticated investors have created a high-yield hybrid of Treasury zero-coupon bonds called STRIPS ("separate trading of registered interest and principal of securities"). Investors with a lump sum (say, $500,000 from a pension plan payout) can buy $1,000 pieces of Treasuries with fixed interest rates and staggered maturity dates. As these STRIPS expire, they produce a steady income flow in retirement, like an annuity (see page 217), and avoid the risk of an annuity company defaulting. On the other hand, brokers charge commissions for STRIPS, unlike Treasuries, and you'll owe taxes on the interest. Dubbed a "do-it-yourself annuity," STRIPS are for the savvy investor who has a large sum to draw down over 20 years of retirement.

Q Bonds don't make any sense to me. I know they're traded like stocks, but whenever stocks go down, bond prices seem to go up. What gives?

A Think of a bond as an IOU from a company that promises to pay back the amount you lent it (the price of the bond) at some later date. In the meantime, it also promises to pay interest on the amount you lent it. If this interest is higher than what stocks are returning to investors, then people will sell their stocks and buy the higher-yielding bonds. If the interest bonds pay is less than what stocks are producing, then investors sell their bonds and buy stocks.

INVESTING IN BONDS

Before proceeding with bond investments, remember to:

• Weigh the law of opposites when assessing the attractions of a bond. As the market price of the bond rises, its current yield falls; when the price falls, its current yield rises.

• Stagger your maturity dates, a technique called "laddering." Bond maturities run from a couple of years up to 30 years. Near-term rates are lower but you have the freedom to reinvest your money at prevailing rates. Those with the longer maturity dates pay higher interest, but you're locked into that rate. If you want to take out your money to earn a higher rate elsewhere, you probably will have to sell your bond at a loss.

• Bonds are sold in large chunks —$1,000 and $5,000 minimums are typical. Broker commissions on Treasury bonds and bills, and on short-term corporate bonds, are low: $25 to $50 for a $5,000 investment. Long-term corporate bonds and municipals generate higher commissions, in the realm of 0.5 to 6 percent of the amount invested. While investors pay commissions separately in Treasury purchases, commissions for munis and some bonds are not broken out but calculated into the value of the investment, which is "marked up."

BOND FUNDS

The price of individual bonds, some with a $25,000 minimum, can make it costly to invest in a variety of them. Enter bond funds. Just as equity mutual funds consist of a collection of common stocks, bond mutual funds are a collection of a particular type of bond.

They're an easy and less costly way to invest in income securities. Also, they're tradable, and so cashing out before maturity doesn't necessarily mean taking a loss. In fact, they don't have maturity dates because their managers are constantly rolling over the bonds' many maturity dates. How much or how little you earn will depend on what's in the fund, the direction of interest rates, and your timing. Your money is completely accessible and some funds even offer the option of taking money out by simply writing a check.

With a bond, you receive interest checks twice a year, and must decide how to use that money. Bond funds have automatic reinvestment features. A bond guarantees to pay you its face value on a certain date as well as interest along the way. A bond fund is more speculative: for sure, you'll earn interest but instead of a face value, you own a share of the fund. That share price can go up or go down, just like the price of a stock.

Bond funds may cost more than individual bonds. You'll pay a commission or load on your purchase, and an annual management fee. However, because they are buying in $1 million blocks, you get the benefit of lower transaction costs, as well as diversification and professional management. Like stock mutual funds, bond funds come in various shapes and sizes.

Short-term: Government or corporate bonds that pay about 1 percent more than money market funds. They fluctuate little in value because they're invested in securities with one year maturities.

Long-term: These offer more attractive yields, but the value of the individual shares will drop precipitously during periods when rates rise (or gain when rates fall).

Muni funds: Some muni bond funds are composed of issues from different state agencies; others concentrate on one state. The earnings from a single-state fund are tax-free to resident investors, but multi-state funds may create a state tax bill for investors. Any state tax due is deductible on your federal return. Another feature of muni funds is default insurance. Investors nervous about the solvency of a muni can buy insurance for their muni bond funds. If the bond issuer defaults, the insurance company pays the interest and dividends. The cost of this insurance will cut a bit into your yield —around 0.25 percent.

Mortgage-backed: These funds pool mortgage-backed securities (Ginnie Mae, Freddie Mac, Fannie Mae) and offer a relatively low-risk, moderate-yield investment.

Corporate: These may be a hodgepodge of sorts, composed of top-rated corporate bonds, as well as a smattering of BBB-rated corporates to boost the yield and government issues to add security.

Government: These bond funds invest in U.S. Treasury bills, notes, and bonds, pay a steady income, but are not totally risk-free. If interest rates rise, the value of individual shares is likely to drop.

"**Government Plus**": These are composed of government bonds with fund managers boosting yields through option writing. These pay wondrously high yields, but their total returns are much lower because their fat dividend checks eat into the capital and so the share price drops.

Unit trusts: Sometimes considered a form of bond fund, these are a bit different. Unit trusts are a bundle of securities (corporate bonds, munis, Ginnie Maes, even common stock) sold in $1,000 pieces and promising steady, high-yield returns. They have a specific expiration date, when all interest and gains are distributed, and their semi-annual (or monthly or quarterly) payout may be erratic because the holdings mature at various times. Investors sometimes receive just interest and at other times, when bonds mature, interest and principal.

BASICS ABOUT INVESTING IN BOND FUNDS

When considering bond funds, keep in mind the following:

• Stick with top-quality bonds for retirement investing. Some bond funds have an official Stan-

GOVERNMENT BOND BASICS

Type	Denominations	Maturity at Issuance
Series EE	$50 to $10,000	12 years
Series HH	$500 to $10,000	10 years
T-bills	$10,000 to $1 million	13 to 52 weeks
T-notes	$1,000 to $1 million	1 to 10 years
T-bonds	$500 to $1 million	5 to 35 years
Ginnie Mae	$25,000	10 to 30 years
Fannie Mae	$10,000 ($5,000 after)	2 to 25 years
Freddie Mac	$10,000 to $500,000	1 to 9 months

dard & Poor's rating. The top rating is AAAf ("f" for fund). However, some funds do not have an S&P rating (only because they haven't paid for one) even though their portfolios may be composed of trouble-free government issues. Corporate bond funds aren't as safe as government issues, but their yields are higher. "Safe" for corporate bond funds is BBB or better.

• When interest rates are rising, short-term bond funds make more sense. ("Short-term" here means maturities under one year). Otherwise, you're investing in bonds whose value is slipping as rates rise.

• Know a fund's total return (the interest plus the appreciation in the fund's share price), not only its current yield. Investors grabbing funds with high current yields may be disappointed at the total return. And don't forget to calculate any taxes on your investment.

• Bond funds are handy if you want access to your money. You can buy and sell them like any security.

• Commission fees or sales loads on bond funds should be low. While some mutual fund companies sell no-load funds, they all charge annual fees anywhere from 0.25 percent to over 2 percent.

• Consider the added value of convenience features associated with bond funds, such as check writing, minimum deposit and balance requirements, and telephone account transfer services.

REAL ESTATE INVESTMENT TRUSTS (REITs)

These are professionally managed funds that own property such as office buildings, apartments, shopping centers, and nursing homes. You invest in them by buying a REIT's stock, which is traded on the major exchanges.

REITs offer a relatively inexpensive way for individuals to invest in real estate—just the cost of the stock. (A couple of mutual funds also specialize in REITs). Like all stocks, the price reflects the value of the group's assets, in this case real estate holdings, as well as investor opinion, so REIT prices jump up and down with the rest of the stock market.

REITs make money for investors in a couple of ways. Their properties generate a steady stream of cash from rent payments and this flows almost entirely to shareholders. In fact, they're legally required to pay out a minimum 95 percent of taxable income every year, which is why REIT dividends easily outpace other types of stocks. Often their rates rival, even outpace, high-yield utilities. REITs also cash in when they sell their properties, presumably at a profit, and funnel the capital gains to investors. The high yields REITs pay also help push up the value of the stock, creating a double benefit for shareholders. As a REIT increases its dividends, it becomes more desirable and so the price of its stock moves upward.

Investing in a REIT sidesteps one of the biggest drawbacks of real estate investing—an inability to take out your money anytime. In a REIT, your investment isn't tied up for years; you can buy or sell stock any day. However, REITs do share real estate's most characteristic feature: the roller-coaster ride of boom-and-bust prices. When property values sink, whether from a glut of office space, a stagnant home mortgage market, or savings and loans defaults, REITs suffer.

REITs tend to specialize in particular kinds of real estate, concentrating their holdings in, for instance, health care facilities, strip malls, or large apartment buildings. Many REITs also stick to particular regions of the country and their narrow focus typically makes them more sensitive than broadly based investments to the fortunes of individual business sectors and local economies.

"Investors tend to think they are buying real estate when they buy REITs. But in fact, they are investing in the operating company."

— *Robert Frank, REIT analyst,*
Financial World

There are about 200 REITs traded on the major markets (NYSE, AMEX, NASDAQ) and they come in three basic flavors: equity, mortgage, and hybrid. Equity REITs invest in tangible property—they buy it, manage it, develop it, sell it. Mortgage REITs are more financiers than property managers. They hold the mortgages, like a bank or savings and loan, and don't actively manage property. As a result, they're less a real estate investment and more a play on financing rates. When interest rates fall, their price climbs, so they're riskier but pay a somewhat higher dividend. Hybrid REITs combine the equity and mortgage approaches, owning and managing property as well as financing purchases.

In addition to these main three, two other varieties have cropped up: CMO (collateralized mortgage obligations) REITs and FREITs (finite life-equity REITs). The CMO REITs are pools of collateralized mortgages (see page 104 to refresh your memory on CMOs) and are super-sensitive to interest rates, which can rapidly launch or torpedo their stock price. Only

investors with strong stomachs need apply.

FREITs buy and sell properties with time-limited mortgages, generally 5 to 15 years. They have a set portfolio, which they usually don't add to, and at the end of their time they dissolve. Their short life-span can work against them, making them operate more like a limited partnership with not enough time for the properties to appreciate. If their fixed portfolio of properties doesn't do well in the appointed period, investors are out of luck.

Investors should concentrate on quality REITs, and the best indi-

THE REIT RECORD

These are figures for the preceding 12 months, as of February 1991 and 1992.

Annualized dividend yields (January 1993):	7.5%
Annualized dividend yields (1992):	8.92%
Annualized dividend yields (1991):	9.89%
Total returns (January 1993):	13.69%
Total returns (1992):	19.80%
Total returns (1991):	− 0.23%

National Association of Real Estate Investment Trusts, Inc.

cator of this is financial strength. Debt that totals less than 50 percent of the REIT's market value (individual share price multiplied by number of shares outstanding) is a good sign. Also, examine the source of the cash flow; it should be generated by operations, not one-time sales or borrowing.

A steady history of growing dividends is another vital sign. Yet, investors should beware of a REIT paying a dividend three or four points above the going rates of 30-year Treasuries. An elevated yield can signal trouble in the stock and possibly a future dividend cut. (It may be a sign of a desperate need for investors and new money.)

Quality REITs are usually established funds, not newcomers; they have at least a three-year history. Brand-new REITs have no track record or proven management, and their offering prices often settle at a lower level because the start-up expenses have artificially jacked them up. So experienced investors eyeing a new REIT often wait for the price to quiet down before buying in.

The quality of a REIT's managers is a crucial element, but harder for an individual investor to assess. Managers who are stockholders in the company are a good sign. REITs that are "self-administered" have managers who are employees, thus eliminating an added layer of fees and profiting from managers who have a stake in the trust's performance.

Over the long haul, professional investors estimate that REITs produce around a 12 percent annual return. They do well when their holdings are well managed and produce strong yields.

REAL ESTATE LIMITED PARTNERSHIPS (RELPs)

In these partnerships, individual investors buy units (usually the minimum is $5,000 to $10,000) in a company that buys and manages various kinds of property, often specializing in particular types—apartments, oil and gas wells, commercial buildings, shopping centers, warehouses. A RELP has a finite lifetime—generally 8 to 12 years—and over the course of this life, investors may receive some income from rental properties. But the principal investment and any profit is tied up until the properties are sold. In other words, it's like most real estate investments—you have to let your money sit for a number of years before it grows, so it's not for people who want access to their money.

RELPs are sold by brokerage houses, financial planners, and insurance agents and tend to pay handsome commissions to salespeople. An 8 percent load plus other up-front fees that frequently reach 20 percent of an investment are not unusual.

RELPS had their heyday in the early 1980s when the Economic Recovery Tax Act set them up as a solid tax shelter. But when Congress shut down the shelter in 1986, RELPs had only their properties to prop them up. Since then, they have been promoted solely as a real estate investment, a hedge against inflation, and a safe bet on appreciation. But you probably know what happened to real estate in the late 80s. As property values plummeted, lots of individuals as well as retirement funds lost money in RELPs. Between 1980 and 1990, investors put $44 billion into RELPs and lost $10 billion.

Investors may have a hard time learning exactly how their RELP is faring. If it isn't traded on a secondary market (which reflects only its immediate value, not necessarily long-term prospects), the only places to turn are partnership documents and financial state-

ments. One yardstick is the formula that fixes the value of an investment at ten times the partnership's annual net distributed earnings. Unfortunately, scanning a RELP's listing of properties doesn't tell an investor much either—assessing property values is the domain of professionals.

When a RELP turns bad, an investor's first thought is getting out. There is a small secondary market for selling RELP units. One possibility is to ask a broker to list your units on the National Partnership Exchange (Napex), a computerized directory. If you find a buyer within seven days and the transaction goes over $10,000, each of you will owe a 2 percent commission. Sales under that amount carry fees of up to $200. Remember, though, that prices paid for a RELP on a secondary market are routinely one-third or less of its original value. So getting out early usually means taking a stinging loss. It can also bring on a sizable tax bill. Most RELPs offer tax shelters—deductible losses for your taxes. But when you sell your RELP, these losses may come back to haunt you. The IRS may consider your losses, depending on their size, a tax gain and bill you accordingly.

Some RELPs are designed for safety and conservative investing. Called "triple net lease" RELPs, they buy completed buildings for cash and lease them to tenants who are responsible for the property taxes, maintenance, and insurance (hence, "triple net"). The RELP collects the rent, which it passes on to investors, creating a steady return. The biggest hazard with this variety of RELP is losing a tenant and having to carry a vacant building for months. But if all goes according to schedule, a triple net RELP begins to sell its properties between 7 and 12 years, showing investors capital appreciation profits.

A spin-off of a RELP is the "roll-up"—a collection of partnerships rolled into one entity, which may be a master limited partnership (MLP) or REIT. The roll-up is then listed and sold on a stock exchange, making it a more liquid investment, but you may well pay several times its value.

If you've owned a RELP for years and it hasn't gone anywhere, don't be surprised to receive a notice from the general partners announcing that they are structuring into a roll-up and going public. Good news? It depends. When a limited partnership is headed toward roll-up territory, the general partners have to inform investors (in a thick document called an exchange offer), and 51 percent of the partners must approve the change.

"Investors sign on for an eight-year cruise, discover it's become a 30-year cruise, and they can't change the skipper."

—Money manager, on people
learning their RELP is becoming a
roll-up, Business Week

The big reason for voting "yes" is that a roll-up is a much more accessible investment than a RELP. On the downside, most roll-ups have declined in value since first going public and their track record is discouraging. By the end of 1991, reports *Financial World* magazine, the average share value of a roll-up was about one-quarter what it was when the roll-up initially restructured. This still held true at the end of 1992.

Two culprits are responsible: the inherent structure of roll-ups and the real estate woes of the 1980s. Limited partnerships are designed with a specific lifetime and a schedule for selling properties. But roll-ups run indefinitely with no timetable for sales and profit-taking. Taking profits can be postponed indefinitely while the roll-up struggles with sagging real estate prices and cumbersome finance charges.

THE LANGUAGE OF INVESTING

As you compose your retirement portfolio, you'll talk to professionals who know more than you about strategies and techniques for investing. That's their business; they should know more. But sometimes they wrap their ideas and reasons in Wall Street jargon, and you need a dictionary to decipher what they're saying. Here are some commonly used terms that you may hear from your broker or investment adviser:

Bulls and **bears:** These stock market symbols represent the two directions stocks can move. If a stock or entire market is moving down and losing value, it's called bearish or a bear market. (This use of "bear" supposedly originated with a fable about traders who sold the skins of bears before they were trapped. Such traders, who were betting on a falling market, were called "bear-skin jobbers.") Upward movement and a gain in value is called bullish, or bull market.

Contrarian: This investor makes decisions that are contrary to the opinions of Wall Street and the general movement of the market. This approach sounds simple and obvious but requires discipline and confidence. When everyone is yelling, "Buy, buy!" this investor is insisting, "Sell, sell." This investor keeps his money in cash or bonds when the stock market is taking off; buys stocks of unglamorous, out-of-favor companies; and looks for undervalued, ignored stocks. The "buy" signs a contrarian looks for are low price/ earnings ratios (keep reading for an explanation of this term). The converse of this strategy is the maxim followed by some professionals: "Never fight the tape." This means, buy when the market looks positive. (The tape is the electronic reporting system, which was once a paper ticker tape, indicating stock prices throughout the trading day.)

Fundamentals: These are the economic basics of a company, and for one school of investors,

INVESTMENT NEWSLETTERS

There are literally hundreds of investment newsletters offering education and advice. Some carry general information, whereas others are in-depth publications that follow every conceivable financial specialty. They're issued weekly, biweekly, sometimes monthly. Most publishers will send potential subscribers sample issues. Here's a sampling of useful newsletters for retirement planning:

- *100 Highest Yields* (P.O. Box 088888, North Palm Beach, FL 33408; $98 per year).
- *Donoghue's MoneyLetter: Guide to Mutual Fund Profits* (Box 8008, Holliston, MA 01746; $109 per year).
- *The Retirement Letter* (7811 Montrose Rd., Potomac, MD 20854; $87 per year).
- *The Hulbert Financial Digest* (316 Commerce St., Alexandria, VA 22314; $135 per year). Tracks the performance of investment newsletters.
- *Market Logic* (3471 North Federal Highway, Fort Lauderdale, FL 33306; $95 per year).
- *Dick Davis Digest* (P.O. Box 9547, Fort Lauderdale, FL 33310; $140 per year). Summaries of information and recommendations from 400 investment newsletters.
- *The Mutual Fund Strategist* (P.O. Box 446, Burlington, VT 05402; $149 per year).

the most important factors affecting the value of a stock. The fundamentals include multiyear trends in sales, earnings, price/earnings ratio, market or competitive position, assets-to-liabilities ratio, return on equity, dividends, and book value.

Price/earnings ratio (called "PE" or "multiple"): a measure of a stock's value that compares its market price to its annual earnings. Stated as a single number, it's arrived at by dividing the per-share market price (e.g., $30) by its reported per-share annual earnings (e.g., $2). (This PE is 15.) The higher the ratio, the more in demand, and more expensive, the stock. Some professionals advise investors to stay away from high PE stocks on the theory the price will eventually tumble, and to look for stocks with lower-than-average ratios. Here is a list of the average PE in the final quarter of the year for all stocks in the New York Stock Exchange Composite Index: 1986: 16.1; 1987: 15.5; 1988: 12.7; 1989: 15; 1990: 14.8; 1991: 25.8; 1992: 22.7.

Random walk: This theory holds that a stock's past performance—price movement and volume traded—cannot be used to predict how it will do tomorrow. Its path is random. Opponents of this theory believe in technical indicators.

Technical indicators: Some professionals believe that national economic trends and stock market trading patterns are the best indicators of how an individual stock will do. These indicators are the direction and momentum of the entire market ("tape action"), market volume (how many shares are being traded—200 million a day is heavy), individual stock price trend, volume traded, and volatility. Some technicians are also "chartists"—they map the highs and lows of a stock over time, looking for patterns that tell them to buy or sell.

THE COST OF INVESTING: COMMISSIONS

Commissions are a fact of investment life, and while they shouldn't be the determining factor in your investment decisions, you should know how they affect your return. Every time you buy or sell stocks, bonds, and many funds, you pay a commission to the company that executes the trade.

Financial service firms set their own commission rates. Before 1975, commissions were regulated and uniform; today they're competitive and negotiable. By and large, commissions fall into three ranges depending on the type of brokerage firm: full-service, discount, and deep-discount.

Full-service brokerage firms charge on the basis of the dollar value of your investment or, for large volume or active traders, on the number of shares. Investors generating more than a single $500 commission or $1,000 a year in commissions may be able to negotiate a discount. Most brokerages have minimum commissions of $20 to $50.

Commissions charged by discount brokers and deep-discount brokers are 50 to 75 percent less than what full-service brokers charge. On top of commissions, these firms charge a service or processing fee for administering your account—mailing confirmations, annual reports, company proxies, dividend checks, and storing your stock certificates. When a broker retains possession of your certificates, legally they are kept under the brokerage firm's name—its "street name." Most investors use this arrangement; the risks of the broker losing or absconding with your certificates are virtually nil. If you don't trade often, you may be charged an annual "inactivity" fee of $50 or more.

BRANDS OF BROKERS

Full-service, discount, and deep-discount stockbrokers differ in the kind and level of service, as well as commissions and fees. Virtually each type trades stocks, funds (loaded and no-load), government bonds, munis, corporate bonds, and options. While they cater to slightly different investors, they're always eager for new clients. You decide which broker to use; you don't have to be a high roller to call on any of them.

FULL-SERVICE BROKERS

Full-service brokerages can be large national companies, mid-sized regional firms, and small, specialized "boutique" firms. As the name implies, what they share in common is soup-to-nuts service: They buy and sell recommendations; do research on individual stocks; issue regular progress reports on how your holdings are doing; and provide a smorgasbord of other offerings, such as retirement planning and cash management. One of their newest dishes is the "wrap" account. For a yearly fee equal to a percentage of your assets (usually between 1 and 3 percent), the broker places your holdings in the hands of a professional money manager.

What distinguishes full-service brokers from the others (which also offer these services but price them individually) is the broker-client relationship.

If you use a full-service broker, you'll talk to the same person every time you trade, have a question, or need information. On first meeting, the smart broker will ask about your investment objectives, how much you want to put in the market, review what you might already own, and explain how he or she works. Don't be confused if your broker's title is not "stockbroker." More likely he's an account executive, financial counselor, retail broker, or registered representative.

Your brokerage account can be either a cash or a margin account. With a cash account, you establish credit by providing a bank reference or depositing money with the broker. When the broker buys a stock for you, he sends you an invoice which you must pay within five days.

Using a margin account is like operating on credit. You pay only

Q I went into one of the big brokerage firms, asked to talk with a broker, and was handed over to a young woman who's obviously a new broker. How do I know if she, or any broker for that matter, is any good?

A Here are a few questions to help you judge a broker: Are her recommendations consistent with your financial goals? Does her advice sound reasonable and make sense? (For instance, no grandiose promises about takeover profits.) Does she follow up on your requests for information and trade confirmations?

a portion of the purchase price of a stock (as little as 50 percent on the initial purchase) and borrow the rest from the brokerage firm.

Naturally, the broker charges interest on this loan. Active and optimistic traders use margin accounts, betting their stock price will rise, and they can use the brokerage's money to earn a profit. The danger of margin investing appears when a stock's price goes down. In this case, the investor must maintain a balance in margin payment equal to at least 25 percent of the stock value. Should a stock plunge, the margin player can lose the total original cost of the stock plus interest charges. If you're aiming to accumulate money you need for retirement and a broker suggests establishing a margin account, walk away.

Another turnoff is the discretionary account that gives a broker authority to make trades for your account without notifying you first. (Wrap accounts include discretionary trades, but these are by professional money managers, not simply brokers.) Reasons a broker might propose for this authority—speedier execution of trades, difficulty reaching you—make little sense. Beware. The only acceptable reason for such an account would be unusual circumstances —you're leaving the country and want your broker to sell all your stocks while you're gone.

"An estimated 75 percent of U.S. investors keep their shares in street name and get financial reports and dividends forwarded to them by their brokers."

Wall Street Journal

When you call your broker to place an order (or he calls you with a recommendation to buy or sell), he'll give you as much information, research, and psychological hand-holding as you need. This is where full-service brokers distinguish themselves: knowing clients and their investment goals, and providing explanations and research to back up their ideas. If a broker suggests buying a particular stock, bond, or fund, he should answer all your questions and send you relevant research. The usual sources of information on an investment are Standard & Poor's tear sheets (single-page summaries); *Value Line* reports; and a company's annual reports, quarterly statements, prospectus, and 10K report, which it files with the SEC.

Full-service brokers should also explain all the mechanics and

COMPARING COMMISSIONS

The average cost of a $3,000 trade—100 shares at $30:

Full-service broker:	$80
Discount broker:	$48
Deep-discount broker:	$33

choices in making an investment. For instance, a "limit order" means making a decision to buy a stock at a price up to a certain limit. This way, an investor won't buy a stock whose price skyrocketed out of range that particular day. Another trading wrinkle is the "good 'til canceled (GTC)" order, meaning an order to buy at a certain price in up to 30 days or until you personally cancel the order. Investors use this method when they want to buy a stock at a price lower than the current price but don't want to be constantly watching for it to reach the target price.

You can also impose a "stop-loss" order, which instructs your broker to sell stock if it dips to a certain price. This way, you automatically limit your losses. None of these investing tactics affects commissions. While all types of brokerages offer these options, your full-service broker should advise you on when to use them.

A full-service broker's advice and recommendations may be no better than your own ideas. Stockbrokers are also employees, and their firms also buy and sell securities. Many brokerage firms "underwrite" securities, meaning that they promise the issuing company to sell its stock. (When you buy a stock that your broker's firm is an under-writer for, this fact is noted on the confirmation slip.) Thus your broker's recommendations may be influenced by the firm's underwritings.

Another potential problem is a tendency to make frequent "buy" recommendations and only a rare "sell" recommendation. You may get plenty of advice about when and what to purchase, but have to decide on your own about when to sell. Be wary of a string of "buy" signals from your broker. Ask about good times to sell.

Less common, but not unheard of, is a broker who pushes a client to make numerous trades in order to generate fat commissions. This excessive trading, called "churning," is illegal and can cause a broker to lose his license. (This is one of the significant hazards of giving a broker discretionary authority.)

"You have to be aggressive picking your broker. Investors tend to be much too shy and afraid of asking questions and questioning the broker's judgement."

—*Stephen Diamond, Securities Administrator, Maine, as quoted in* USA Today

---

Most brokers know that if their clients don't make money, they'll lose customers. Nevertheless, with a full-service broker working on commission, there is always the possibility of conflict of interest. Brokers have been known to promote high-commission invest-ments, like fully loaded mutual funds, limited partnerships, and options to boost their returns. Be alert to the broker who seems more salesperson than investment adviser.

DISCOUNT BROKERS

Discount brokers are to full-service brokers as cafeterias are to restaurants with tuxedoed waiters. With a discount broker, you deal with an institution that offers a menu of investment services, each with a specific price tag; with a full-service broker, you deal with an individual ("Hello, my name is Bob and I'll be your broker for the next few years") who offers a fixed-price meal.

Discount brokerage companies don't provide free research, recommendations, advice to clients, or individual account monitoring; nor do they actively promote certain stocks, bonds, or funds. Commissions cover the cost of processing transactions—period. A discount broker may offer as many services as a full-service broker, but for an additional fee.

Discounters, like their full-service brethren, confirm trades in writing, send out regular account reports, hold securities in their

INVESTING WITH YOUR PC

*You can use your personal computer to monitor your invest-
ments, collect information, and plan your retirement goals.
Most of these programs are geared toward money management
and investment tracking, with only a portion devoted to retirement planning. But they're useful in making money decisions
today that will affect your retirement. Most run on an IBM or
Apple system and require a certain amount of memory and a
hard drive. Some need an internal modem for on-line data retrieval. Make sure a program is compatible with your computer.*

CompuServ: An on-line service that provides stock quotes and other
current investment data. (Price: $29.99 for software, $7.95 per month.
Produced by CompuServe, Inc.)

Dow Jones News Retrieval: On-line service for market quotes, data
bases, investment information. (Price: $29.95 for connection, per min-
ute charge varies according to time of day. Produced by Dow Jones,
Inc.)

Individual Investors Guide to Computerized Investing: An on-
line service and data base on stocks, bonds, and funds. (Price: $23.
Produced by American Association of Individual Investors.)

Managing Your Money (with Andrew Tobias): For record keeping
and budgeting. No financial planning component, but does track investments as long as you enter the data. No modem required. (Price:
$36.49. Produced by MECA Ventures.)

Prodigy: An on-line service for stock quotes and investment information. (Price: $34.99 for software, $14.95 per month. Produced by Prodigy Information Services.)

Quicken: For budgeting, checking, money management, and tracking investments. (Price: $41.99 Produced by Intuit.)

Smart Investor: Offers information, research, even executes trades. On-line service with Prodigy. (Price: $69.99 for software and $9.95 per month. Produced by Reality Technologies with *Money* Magazine.)

T. Rowe Price Retirement Planning Kit: For retirement planning and record keeping. Calculates personal financial holdings and goals. Includes information on T. Rowe Price funds. (Price: $15. Produced by T. Rowe Price.)

Value/Screen II: An on-line service that provides current data on market prices. (Price: $281 per year. Produced by Value Line Publishing.)

Wealthbuilder: Requires inputting your personal financial data to produce a financial plan that includes retirement goals. Makes investment suggestions. Updated data can be purchased regularly. (Price: $109.99. Produced by Reality Technologies.)

Wealthstarter: A simpler version of Wealthbuilder. For financial planning and investing beginners. Does not include recommendations on asset allocation or investment selection. (Price: $24.99. Produced by Reality Technologies.)

PICKING A BROKER

When shopping for a full-service stockbroker, make sure to explore these areas:

- Are the broker's recommendations consistent with your comfort level and investment objectives?
- Is the broker careful and methodical: Do you receive confirmation slips soon after your trade and account statements monthly? If you ask for a report, do you receive it within a reasonable amount of time? Does he execute your orders without error?
- How often does your broker call you with a "hot takeover candidate" or a distressed company "about to turn around?" Is your broker more salesperson than investment adviser?
- What's the broker's track record? How have his or her investment recommendations performed over past years? (He may not have a complete performance record in writing but should tell you how well his accounts have done.)
- Will the broker provide references—names of clients you can talk to?

street name, and give market quotes over the phone. A special feature with many discounters is 24-hour telephone service (trades made during off-hours are executed the next working day).

Discount brokers are for people comfortable making their own investment decisions, investors who have a sense of when to buy, sell, or switch, and who take the initiative. They stay current on economic and business trends, know the pros and cons of various investments, and come up with their own ideas of which stocks, bonds, and funds to buy.

Many investors use both full-service and discount brokers. To execute their own ideas, they call up the discount house. If unsure or in need of research, they call on a full-service broker. For fairness' sake, when an investment idea comes from the full-service house, the trade should be executed through that broker. Some investors are known to have accounts at half a dozen brokerages, utilizing brokers' individual areas of experience and success.

If discount brokers are cafeterias, deep-discount brokers are sidewalk vendors. You get immediate, no-frills fare at the lowest price on the block. Depending on the broker and the size of the trade, fees may be half a discount broker's. Also, they may not trade mutual funds, some kinds of bonds, limited partnerships, annuities, or certificates of deposit. Their specialty is cheap and efficient execution of trades. They usually have a limited number of branch offices, keep their staffs to a minimum, and don't maintain an in-house research department.

In short, deep discounters are for active stock traders, not investors looking for one-stop shopping in an assortment of investments, and maybe a little advice.

REGULATING BROKERS

Anyone selling securities has to be registered with one of the stock exchanges (New York Stock Exchange, American Stock Exchange) and/or the National Association of Securities Dealers (NASD). Although these groups are self-regulatory organizations (meaning nongovernmental and run by their members), they are closely watched by the Securities and Exchange Commission.

Moreover, they possess some enforcement muscle. They handle complaints and can take serious disciplinary action, including revoking a broker's license. Typical client complaints include slow payment of checks or delivery of securities, errors in executing trades, high-pressure sales tactics, and failing to transfer accounts.

WHAT IF A BROKER GOES OUT OF BUSINESS?

Brokerage firms that are registered with the SEC are also members of the Securities Investor Protection Corporation (SIPC). If a member firm goes out of business, SIPC guarantees investors' claims up to $500,000 per individual, including $100,000 for cash claims. It doesn't guarantee coverage of trading losses—only money lost by a brokerage house's liquidation.

PLACES FOR PARKING CASH

There will be times in your investment life when you need to park cash—a place where it can sit safely, in no danger of losing value other than through inflation, and where you can pull it out with ease when you decide where to invest it. In return for this safe haven, you forego the prospect of your money growing. At best, it will produce a modest yield.

A word about interest rates: the difference among various places to park your money is often no more than 0.5 percent. But some people devote enormous time and effort to finding marginally higher rates and occasionally jump into questionable arrangements simply for the sake of an added 0.75 percent. In choosing where to park your money, look beyond interest rates. Consider these features:

• How easily and immediately can you withdraw your money? Is there a time element involved?

Any early-withdrawal penalties?

• How safe is your money? Is it federally insured?

• What fees are charged for the account? What is the minimum deposit?

• How is the interest calculated —compounded monthly, quarterly, yearly? Compounding makes a difference in later years, not immediately. After six years, $1,000 in an account earning eight percent compounded monthly would be worth $1,613. Compounded annually it would be $1,587.

Some of the U.S. Government securities already discussed (T-bills and notes) can be good short-term places to park your cash. Here are a few others.

MONEY MARKET FUNDS

These are a type of mutual fund offered by brokerage firms, insurance companies, and mutual fund groups. Their managers invest in short-term government and corporate paper, and their interest rates are generally higher than money market accounts offered by banks but a little lower than short-term bond funds. The yield and safety of money funds vary a little depending on what they invest in —U.S. Government securities, tax-exempt bonds, or a general mix of short-term notes from corporations, government, and financial institutions.

"In our culture, the feeling used to be that you could leave your money anywhere. We're undergoing a re-evaluation of that. People are saying that banking transactions are like others. You've got to know where your money's going."

—Research director, Veribanc, Inc.,
as quoted in the Chicago Tribune

Money fund interest rates are variable, not fixed, and if rates are dropping, money market funds respond accordingly. When you buy money market funds, you purchase shares at usually $1 face value, which rarely varies, and receive regular interest payments. Minimum deposits are usually $1,000. Fees charged for your account are tiny: Managers charge the fund less than 1 percent of total assets and individual investors may have to pay a per-check fee.

While your money market fund deposit is not government-insured and it could drop in value (very unlikely), so far no money market fund has failed.

MONEY MARKET ACCOUNTS

These are available at banks in the form of a savings account paying an interest rate that floats but exceeds a passbook savings account. You can usually withdraw money anytime simply by writing a check, although the bank may have a limit on how many withdrawals you can make per month. And if your account drops too low, you may be charged a fee. Money in these accounts is safe, and insured by the federal government up to $100,000.

CERTIFICATES OF DEPOSIT

These are issued by banks, savings and loans, and credit unions, offering a fixed interest rate for a set period of time, such as six months, a year, two years, or longer. The longer the time, the higher the interest, and generally their rates are higher than those for money market accounts. Brokers also offer CDs, which they purchase from banks. If the CD is issued by a bank, your principal up to $100,000 is insured by the Federal Deposit Insurance Corporation (FDIC).

Most institutions charge a penalty if you withdraw early—as much as six months interest. However, CDs purchased through brokers may not have early withdrawal penalties but their downside is that they probably pay a flat interest rate, not a compounded one. Of course, the best rate is for "jumbo" CDs—units over $100,000. These pay as much as a percentage point more.

If you're shopping for CDs, find out whether you can withdraw interest occasionally or whether it must be reinvested. Also ask at what intervals the interest is compounded.

Some financial institutions offer savings instruments called "subordinated capital notes" that look like CDs but are not. They may offer interest rates a notch above what CDs promise, but your money is not completely safe. The big difference is that these notes are not federally insured (if the institution goes bankrupt, the government won't make good on your deposit). Furthermore, these notes are callable, meaning the institution can pay them off anytime and investors are left having to find a new place to park their money. Or, they may not be redeemable until maturity.

Chapter 3

GETTING YOUR DUCKS IN LINE: PERSONAL SAVINGS AND PENSION PLANS

Saving is easier said than done, as everyone knows. Two-thirds of Americans have no savings other than their pension plans and the equity in their homes, says an economist at Stanford University. Some economists maintain that our poor saving record has more to do with demographics than with spending habits. If they're right, this pattern may change as the population ages and more people enter their peak savings years.

"The lifecycle saving theory suggests that a high share of household income will be saved in a country that has a large fraction of its population in the high-saving years from 45 to 64," declares Stephen Meyer, a vice-president of the Federal Reserve. He notes that the high-saving age group in the United States will increase from its present 18.5 percent of the population to 28 percent in the next 20 years.

But even as you move into your

best saving years, finding and holding on to those extra dollars for retirement will take discipline and creative thinking.

SAVING: THE MORE IT HURTS, THE BETTER IT FEELS

Starting in your thirties, say financial experts, you should save at least 10 percent of your pretax income. Yup. 10 percent. Before taxes. If you postpone saving, that number inches upward. Wait until your fifties and to reach the same retirement goal (usually assumed to be 60 to 80 percent of your current income), you must sock away upwards of 20 percent. The message is clear—save early and save often. Or, remember EMILY: Early Money Is Like Yeast—it makes dough grow.

The secret of successful saving is contained in the miracle of compounding. This is a relatively simple mathematical phenomenon that begins slowly, then accelerates in a way that multiplies your savings to wonderful new heights. If today you put $1,000 into a long-term investment paying 8 percent, that money in five years will be worth $1,470. Not much, you complain. However, keep it in that account and in ten years, you'll have more than doubled your money to $2,160. It's not quite in the league of loaves and fishes, but the results are still astounding.

But compounding does nothing if there's no money to compound. Like flossing your teeth or eating less fat, saving should become second nature. It can even become a satisfying routine as you watch your bank account pile up. Savers have devised all sorts of gimmicks to force themselves into tucking money away regularly.

• They deposit money in iron-fisted accounts that allow early withdrawals only with hefty penalty payments.
• They tell employers to deposit portions of paychecks in savings plans before they see them.
• They instruct brokers or fund managers to reinvest dividends and any capital distributions.
• They cut back on "walking around" money that dribbles away in gourmet take-out food or impulsive shoe purchases. In the same vein, they pare down the number of credit cards they carry. By eliminating easy cash and forcing themselves to spend more thoughtfully, they save the nickels and dimes that add up.

THE MIRACLE OF COMPOUNDING

Here's what happens to $1,000 in an account earning 8 percent a year, compounded annually.

End of Year	Amount	End of Year	Amount
1	$1,080	11	$2,332
2	1,166	12	2,518
3	1,259	13	2,720
4	1,360	14	2,937
5	1,469	15	3,172
6	1,587	16	3,426
7	1,714	17	3,700
8	1,851	18	3,996
9	1,999	19	4,316
10	2,159	20	4,661

• They avoid using easy, yet expensive money, like revolving charge accounts, running credit card balances, and high-interest loans.

THE CREDIT CARD SINKHOLE

Credit cards may well be the biggest hazard to steadfast saving. They're like a huge sinkhole into which consumers toss millions of dollars every year. Don't believe it? Think taxes, vacations, and rising health insurance are bigger threats? Here are the facts: Two-thirds of all credit card holders carry a balance forward from month to month, and the average person owes $2,474 in credit card debt, which generates $465 in annual interest charges. This is expensive money. The average credit card interest rate is about 18.4 percent, compared with home-equity loans, which are running between 7 and 8 percent.

The obvious solution to this gash in your wallet is to either cut up your credit cards (not likely) or pay off your balance every month. But that, too, may be impossible, although you should make an Olympian effort to pay off as big a chunk as possible. There's another way to stem the bleeding: lower your monthly interest charge, which determines the size of the monthly balance.

It's not as hard as it may sound: You want a credit card that charges the lowest interest possible, and odds are it's not the card you're holding now. First, find out what your present card charges. Today that means anywhere between 10 and 22 percent. Big span, and in terms of interest, big bucks.

To locate a financial institution that offers lower rates (credit cards are issued by individual institutions; there's no single company that issues Mastercard or Visa cards), check a couple of sources. The *Wall Street Journal* (first week of the month) and *Money* magazine (monthly) publish lists of institutions offering low-rate credit cards. You also may find low rates offered by your savings and loan, alumni association, or professional organization.

In shopping for a lower-rate card, remember to factor in any annual fee. Also consider how much "float time" the card allows —this is the period between the date you make a purchase and the date that interest charges kick in. It's usually between 30 and 60 days, and for people stretching out their payments, this time definitely translates into money.

True, not everyone can qualify for a low-rate credit card. Institutions prefer people with solid

Q I'm in debt and my wages may be garnisheed. Can my creditors collect from my pension?

A Nope. It's illegal for your pension benefits to be garnisheed unless they're being paid out to you already. However, you may be able to take money from your pension to pay your creditors.

PAYING OFF YOUR BANK CARD SAVES BUNDLES

Paying off your monthly balance on a credit card that charges 18.5 percent can produce an annual return of 28 percent, explains the Bankcard Holders of America.

"Suppose you invested $100 and made 28 percent interest (an impossibility, but just pretend). You would earn $28 in one year. If you're in a 33 percent tax bracket, your taxes would be $9.24 and your net return $18.48.

"If you use that $100 to pay off a credit card charging 18.5 percent, you're using after-tax dollars. Over a year, you would save $18.48 interest (equal to 18.48 percent) you don't have to pay the credit card company. So paying off your credit card produces an 18.48 percent return, which in dollars and cents is the equivalent of the 28 percent return."

credit histories and/or regular, sizable balances. And not all low-rate cards are bargains. The annual fee may wipe out whatever you save on interest. Some cards are what's called "secured cards." Usually aimed at high-risk customers, they are expensive: You have to maintain a minimum amount (for example, $500 or $1,000) with the institution and that money may earn less than what you can earn elsewhere.

Another less-than-terrific deal are cards with enticing low rates that are just introductory. After the hoopla and advertising push, the institution jacks the rate up. Institutions can raise rates whenever they like, as long as they give 15 days notice.

When you do get a handle on your credit card expenses, make an equally concerted effort to hold on to what you've saved.

SMART SAVING

In looking for a place to stash your savings, keep in mind these words to save by:

• Practice sophisticated saving. Gone are the days when you could open a passbook savings account

EIGHT WAYS TO BOOST YOUR SAVINGS

1. Beef Up Interest Rates: Redistribute money you have in an interest-bearing account, for instance a money market fund or a NOW account, into other equally safe but higher yielding accounts, such as utility stocks and mortgage-backed securities.

2. Don't Pay for Services That Are Free: Your regular routine of getting and spending probably includes paying for services that are offered elsewhere for free or for less. Look into credit cards with lower annual dues, free checking accounts, free rental car insurance when you use a credit card.

3. Grab Those Discounts: Membership organizations like the American Automobile Association, American Association of Retired Persons, and American Express card confer special discounts, such as lower rates on car rentals, hotel rooms, prescription drugs, health club fees, and restaurant meals.

4. Don't Let Money Languish in Your Checking Account: Even a NOW account isn't as profitable as a money market account or mutual fund with checking features that pays over 3 percent. Keep only enough

at the bank where you have a checking account, and leave it at that. For one thing, the country has shrunk—savings institutions from coast to coast are as close as your telephone. And the passbook savings account has been replaced by a cornucopia of savings offerings, including certificates of deposit, money market accounts, NOW accounts, and a rich variety of mutual funds. Don't be constrained either by geography or by traditional saving patterns.

• Nothing is forever. No matter where you put your money, you can't assume it will always be safe and earning what's promised. Check on your savings account every year, and if the institution or

in your bank checking account to cover relatively small, regular payments. Move the rest to higher ground.

5. Pay Off Those Credit Card Bills: The routine 18 percent interest many credit cards and department stores charge can eat into your savings like an infestation of carpenter bees. Pay off the bills every month, even if it means borrowing elsewhere (at lower rates).

6. Pare Down Insurance Premiums: Your premiums are partially determined by the deductible. Go for the highest—you won't be able to make those $100 claims, but you will save in lower premiums.

7. Be a Smart Shopper: Big-ticket purchases like televisions, VCRs, and refrigerators are often sold with pricey service contracts that can add 10 percent to your tab. Live dangerously and save your money —odds are the item won't break down and is probably under a manufacturer's warranty anyhow.

8. Don't Spend That Tax Refund: Many people use tax refunds as a kind of vacation plan or Christmas fund. Instead, earmark that money for a savings account.

your rate of return looks shaky, consider moving your money.

• Convenience is critical. If saving is a nuisance, requiring a special trip to a savings and loan or digging out account numbers for complicated forms, the money may never make it to the bank. Make saving as easy and convenient as taking out the garbage.

FROM PENNIES TO DOLLARS AND SENSE

Saving is a habit, and the more automatic it becomes, the more successful you'll be. The best savers not only earmark part of their paycheck but also refrain from those small, daily outlays that nibble into weekly budgets, and sabotage savings goals.

To see if you've got the savings bug, take this quiz.

1. How often do you pay in cash?
- **a.** All the time
- **b.** Most of the time
- **c.** Half the time
- **d.** Rarely

2. How often do you make instant gratification purchases, like the latest high-tech tennis racquet?
- **a.** Rarely
- **b.** Every couple of months
- **c.** Probably once a month
- **d.** Weekly

3. Do you regularly feed a piggy bank with loose change?
- **a.** Yes, daily
- **b.** Every week or so
- **c.** When I remember
- **d.** I don't own a piggy bank

4. Do you buy household items in bulk at reduced prices or purchase discount brands?
- **a.** Always
- **b.** Most of the time
- **c.** When I remember
- **d.** Rarely

5. Have you drawn up a budget and do you follow it?
- **a.** Yes, and yes
- **b.** Yes, and sometimes
- **c.** Yes, and no
- **d.** No and no

6. You're given $200 for your birthday. What do you do with it?
- **a.** Save it all
- **b.** Save $150, spend $50
- **c.** Save half, spend half
- **d.** Spend it all

7. How often do you use your ATM card?
- **a.** Only when I get my paycheck
- **b.** Once a week
- **c.** Mondays and Fridays
- **d.** Almost daily

8. How often do you use discount services, such as off-peak telephone hours, self-service gas, generic drugs, and coupons?
- **a.** Always
- **b.** Most of the time
- **c.** When I remember
- **d.** I usually don't remember

Score it: $a = 4$, $b = 3$, $c = 2$, $d = 1$.

If you scored 32–28, you're a Natural Saver; 27–24, you're a Budding Saver; 23–16, you're a Sometime Saver; less than 16, you need to develop saving instincts.

NO-SWEAT SAVING: EMPLOYER PENSION PLANS

One of the easiest saving schemes is offered by employers—company pension plans are a relatively painless way to sock away sizable sums. In 1991, about 43 percent of all workers participated in some type of company pension plan, and employers are constantly devising new benefit menus. To get the most satisfying meal, you need to know what goes into each dish. Here's a rundown on company-sponsored retirement plans.

WHERE DO YOU STAND?

While retirement plans make a job more attractive and people more eager to work for a company, your employer is not required by law to offer you a pension plan. Many companies, particularly small service businesses, don't. Furthermore, some pension plans don't include all employees—part-timers or people in certain positions may not be able to join a company plan. So your first step is to find out if your employer has a pension plan. (If not, don't panic. More later about plans you can devise for yourself.)

Once you've established that your company has a plan, and you're eligible to participate, find out about "vesting," which refers to how long you must work to receive benefits. When you're fully vested, you don't lose your benefits if you quit or retire early. The usual length of time is three to five years, and companies usually use one of three methods to determine when an employee vests:

• "Cliff vesting" promises full benefits after five years.
• "Graded vesting" guarantees a percentage of an employee's benefits (e.g., 20 percent) in a few years (e.g., five or seven) and the remainder some, but no more than ten, years later.
• "Top-heavy" vesting happens when most of a plan's benefits (60 percent) are going to top executives. When a plan reaches "top-heavy" status, all employees become vested, either 100 percent after three years or 20 percent after two years employment, then 20 percent for each year after, with total vesting at six years.

Employees also become fully vested if they reach normal retirement age, generally 65, die, or are disabled, or if a pension plan is terminated.

Information about vesting as well as the management of your

plan is readily obtainable. Employers are required by law (the Employee Retirement Income Security Act—ERISA) to report to

ARE YOU IN A CREDIT CRUNCH?

A glance at your bank account reveals how your savings plan is progressing, but sometimes the signs of a credit crunch are less clear. While most people at some point struggle to pay monthly bills or juggle payment schedules, other consumers are way over their head in debt. Here are the signs of a credit crisis, according to Citibank, a large issuer of Mastercards and Visa cards. If you're experiencing two or more of these, you probably have a serious spending problem.

- Your monthly payments to creditors equal more than 20 percent over what you take home every month, after subtracting mortgage or rent payments.
- You're using savings to pay daily expenses.
- You're using cash advances from credit cards to pay for daily expenses or other creditors.
- You pay the minimum due, or less, on your monthly bills. You're often late paying bills.
- You're receiving calls or letters from creditors about overdue bills.
- You argue with family members about money problems.
- You're working overtime or at a second job to keep up with your spending.
- You're denied credit.
- Creditors are suing you or garnisheeing your wages.

"Coping with a Credit Crisis," Citibank Mastercard and Visa

pension plan participants how the plan operates and the precise benefits due each employee. This report is called a Summary Plan Description and although the law doesn't mandate the exact form of an SPD, it must be understandable to the average employee. It should describe your plan, how you become eligible, how your benefits are figured, and how you can lose your rights to benefits.

In addition to the SPD, you can ask your employer for an annual report on the plan's finances—investments, assets and liabilities, loans, distributions—and a statement of your accumulated benefits (Form 5500 or 5500-C if your plan has fewer than 100 participants). You're legally entitled to all these facts, and if your employer balks at providing them, contact the U.S. Department of Labor, Pension and Welfare Benefit Programs, Division of Technical Assistance and Inquiries, Room N-5658, 200 Constitution Avenue, NW, Washington, DC 20210; 202/ 219-8771.

Company pension plans fit into one of two drawers: defined-benefit plans and defined-contribution plans. Ever since pensions were first offered in this country (by the American Express Company in 1875), defined-benefit plans have been more common. In the 1980s, about 80 percent of pensions were defined benefits. But lately the pension climate has changed, and defined-contribution plans are now filling the sky.

THE INNER WORKINGS OF DEFINED BENEFITS

While the name "defined-benefit" plan doesn't exactly trip lightly from the tongue, it aptly describes what this pension offers: a stated and guaranteed amount of money, or benefit, upon retirement. The amounts paid are usually established by a formula that takes into account your earnings, years of service, and age at retirement. This kind of plan is normally completely funded by the employer; employees usually don't contribute to it.

The science of determining exactly how much an employee will receive in benefits fills volumes of pension manuals. Pension benefit experts have sculpted entire careers on figuring what employees will get.

The "career-average" formula uses a percentage of the average of your salary over all your years of employment—often in the

Q I started contributing to the company pension plan as soon as I was hired, but I left the company before I was vested. Do I lose what I put into the plan?

A No, you get your money back plus what it has earned, but not what your employer put in. Every employee is vested to receive his own contributions.

range of 1 to 5 percent. So, for example, a paralegal employed by a law firm for 25 years and whose average annual salary is $31,000 would receive an annual pension on retirement of $15,500 (2% × 31,000 × 25). (Sometimes the percentage is a fixed portion of an employee's annual pay.)

The "final-pay" formula works like the career-average formula but uses an employee's average earnings over his or her last three or five years of work (early retirees who forego raises in their final years lose out).

Some employers take a different tack, paying employees (often union members) a fixed amount for every year of service. With the "flat-benefits" formula, all employees receive the same pension, regardless of their earnings. Occasionally employers will tier their flat-rate plans, paying amounts that vary according to job classification. A moving and storage company, for instance, may offer a plan that gives all vested employees $300 a month; or it may tier the payments with hourly workers receiving $300 per month and salaried employees $400 per month.

Employers putting together a defined-benefit plan may also stir in other figures. Social Security payments may be used to reduce individual benefits. This is called "integration" or "permitted disparity." While recent laws limit its use, it is still common practice.

If you are faced with integration, make sure your employer is not using an inflated amount for your anticipated Social Security payments. Consumer organizations such as the National Senior Citizens Law Center recommend

HOW DEFINED BENEFITS ARE FIGURED

Companies that offer a defined-benefits plan can calculate benefits a couple of ways. Here's the percentage of employees of medium and large private companies according to how their benefits are figured.

Method of Determining Payment	Percent of Employees
Flat dollar amount	41%
Dollar amount per years of service	25%
Total benefit, including supplemental payment, equals flat dollar amount	30%
Total benefit, including supplemental payment, per year of service	4%

1988 Employee Benefits Survey, U.S. Department of Labor

that employees faced with "permitted disparity" submit their Social Security earnings and benefits records to employers to make sure they calculate correctly. The Center also points out that cost-of-living increases in Social Security benefits after you retire can't be used to further offset your company pension payments.

By and large, defined-benefit plans don't include adjustments for increases in the cost of living. A company promises you amounts in current dollars, and that's what you'll pocket 20 years from now. Even the occasional company that does allow for the effects of inflation usually won't make that promise in writing but will boost payments only periodically depending on profits.

Your pension, if you're married, also pays out to your spouse. Employers are legally bound to offer to pay your pension in a "Qualified Joint and Survivor Annuity," meaning that after you die, your spouse receives at least 50 percent of what you were getting.

HOW'S YOUR PLAN DOING?

Here are the fifteen largest underfunded defined-benefit plans in 1992, according to the Pension Benefit Guaranty Corporation. The PBGC says that these plans are not necessarily at immediate risk but that should they go under, it may not be able to cover all the losses.

TOP 15 COMPANIES WITH UNDERFUNDED PENSIONS

Company	Funding Ratio*
New Valley Corp.	49%
Loews Corp.	49%
Sharon Steel Corp.	53%
Laclade Steel	55%
Carter Hawley Hale	56%
Chrysler Corp.	58%
American National Can	58%
Borg-Warner	59%
Bridgestone-Firestone	59%
Rockwell International	59%
Anchor Glass	60%
National Intergroup	60%
TWA	63%
Occidental Petroleum Corp.	65%
ACF Industries	66%

*Ratio indicates percentage of pension plan that is funded.

Since this coverage extends the number of years benefits are paid, it reduces the annual amount you receive before you die. You can elect not to continue benefits to your spouse, but to waive this right, your spouse has to sign a written release.

There are limits on a defined-benefit plan: a maximum amount an employer can drop into a pension fund and can pay a retiree each year. The cap set by the government on benefits in 1993 is $115,641 (at age 65) or 100 percent of pay, if less. That number is adjusted regularly for inflation and is significantly reduced, in most cases, for retirees under 65.

Although a defined-benefit plan isn't forever—it can be terminated —it does have a guardian angel in the form of the federal Pension Benefits Guarantee Corporation, which insures benefits if a plan goes belly-up.

The likelihood of your defined-benefit plan being shut down is in the realm of "Not Likely, But Not Impossible." Companies can pull the plug on their plans for a number of reasons: underfunding, overfunding, or a change in corporate strategy. If a plan ceases because the company's in financial trouble and the plan's under-

funded (meaning the company has not put away enough or its investments haven't performed as expected), the PBGC steps in.

The government promises to cover monthly benefit payments up to $2,250 (at age 65), but anything you're owed over that, you can kiss good-bye. Of course, if your employer goes out of business but the pension is fully funded, your money is protected. The pension plan is held in trust and usually not included in the assets used to pay off creditors.

Closing down an overfunded or a reasonably solvent plan forces employees into another position— deciding what happens to their money. In the recent years, companies with plump pension funds (funds so well invested that they've earned more than is owed plan members) have opted to pay off employees and use the surplus for growth, acquisitions, or reducing other debts.

If a distressed company shuts down its plan and the PBGC moves in, employees get their pension in a lump sum or in a lifetime annuity (starting at age 65) based on benefits earned at the time the plan folded. (Employees who opt for an annuity face another potential hazard if the annuity company is financially shaky. Should the annuity company get in trouble, as happened with the monumental Executive Life, pensioners are in serious jeopardy.)

When an employee leaves a company, the defined-benefit plan doesn't go along with you. It's not "portable," as the experts call it; you're removed from the plan and must begin anew with the next employer. What about your benefits? If you aren't vested, you're owed nothing. But, if you quit and are vested, your salary-based benefits are frozen at the level they were when you left and remain there until you claim them at retirement or sooner if they're available. For job-hoppers, this may well mean collecting a scattering of tiny pension payments.

Defined-benefit plans are not designed for the upwardly mobile: They're tailored for the employee who sticks with a company for 30 or 40 years. As a result, defined-benefit plans are dwindling from the workplace as quickly as rotary phones and manual typewriters. Over the past decade, the number of employees in defined-benefit plans has inched up 2 percent while employees enrolling in other types of plans has surged by 200 percent.

Retirement dollars have been flooding into the alternative employer pension plan: defined-contribution plans. Even employees already enlisted in a defined-benefit plan are directing some of their savings toward the other. According to the Labor Department, 41 percent of defined-benefit participants are also stashing away retirement money in other kinds of plans.

IF YOU WORK FOR THE GOVERNMENT

Government workers—whether they drive a school bus, pursue cases as an assistant district attorney, deliver mail, or write laws in a state capitol—usually have defined-benefit pension plans that are collectively negotiated. Yet, these plans differ from the off-the-shelf defined-benefit plans of private employees. In ways, they're more generous and in ways they're tighter. Here's how the government employees' retirement kitty differs:

• Employees are often required to contribute to their plans—a percentage of earnings (e.g., 5 percent) in *after-tax* dollars.

WHAT IF YOUR PENSION PLAN FOLDS?

The government agency responsible for monitoring pension plans is the Labor Department's Pension and Welfare Benefits Administration, which has about 300 investigators watching approximately 870,000 private pension funds.

The Pension Benefit Guaranty Corporation, another agency of the federal government, insures the benefits of company-sponsored defined-benefit plans up to $27,000 a year per employee. That currently encompasses about 40 million employees. However, the PBGC doesn't insure or guarantee money in defined-contribution plans.

Pension plans that employers have replaced with annuities are not guaranteed by the PBGC. Typically this happens when a company terminates its pension plan and, instead of distributing the money to vested employees, deposits the funds into annuities. But if the annuity goes belly-up, there goes the pension money. (See Chapter 4 for what happens with failed annuities.)

If your company declares that it's canceling the pension plan and putting the money into annuities, you may have the option of taking your pension out in a lump sum. Definitely consider this option, especially if the insurance company issuing the annuity has less than sterling ratings.

• Employees can pocket their full pensions early, frequently after 30 years of service, regardless of their age.

• Benefits are usually computed by finding the average of the three highest-earning years and multiplying that by a percentage (e.g., 2 percent) times years of service.

• Few plans are integrated, or offset by Social Security.

• Plans are automatically adjusted for inflation (called the COLA adjustment).

• Disability immediately opens the door to plan benefits; no waiting for retirement age.

WHAT TO EXPECT FROM YOUR PENSION

You're part of a defined-benefit plan and may retire at age 55 or 65. Here's the percentage of your annual salary that your pension plan will cover for various lengths of service, according to the Bureau of Labor Statistics.

Retirement Age and Final Annual Salary	Years in Plan				
Age 55	10	15	20	25	30
$15,000	7.6%	11.1%	15.6%	19%	25.3%
20,000	7.2	10.5	14.4	17.6	22.7
25,000	7	10	13.7	16.8	21.4
35,000	6.7	9.8	13.4	16.6	20.6
45,000	6.7	9.9	13.3	16.6	20.5
55,000	6.8	10	13.5	16.8	20.6
Age 65	10	15	20	25	30
$15,000	12.7%	18.6%	24.1%	29.2%	34.4%
20,000	11.6	16.9	21.9	26.4	30.9
25,000	11.2	16	20.6	25.1	29.4
35,000	10.6	15.4	20.1	24.6	28.9
45,000	10.5	15.4	20	24.7	29
55,000	10.6	15.5	20.3	25	29.3

Monthly Labor Review

IF YOU WEAR A UNIFORM

When it comes to pensions, the Military Retirement System has a deservedly four-star reputation. Plan members don't have to contribute to it and can bail out with lifetime benefits after 20 years of service. Furthermore, the benefits are adjusted for inflation. Military personnel who joined before 1986 and retire after 20 years get 50 percent of their base pay for the three highest-paying years; if they hang around longer than 20 years, they can reap up to 75 percent. Men and women who joined after 1986 get 40 percent at 20 years and up to 75 percent for 30 years.

THE INNER WORKINGS OF DEFINED-CONTRIBUTION PLANS

About the only thing these plans have in common with defined benefits is they're both designed for retirement. Otherwise, they're as related as the Grand Canyon and Grand Marnier.

Think of defined-contribution plans as a savings account you have with your employer. Generally, you and your employer regularly contribute a certain amount.

"Since 1988, some 30,000 firms have walked away from traditional pensions, often leaving workers with lump-sum payouts far smaller than what they would have received if their plans had survived."

Money

When you retire, the size of that savings account depends on how much was put in and how well the pension money was invested. The account may have grown in leaps and bounds, or barely kept up with inflation. Although some defined-contribution plans are funded only by an employee or only by the employer, the contributions are often mutual.

When retirement arrives, the employee can receive a lifetime annuity, payments over a period of years, or a single check. In the event you leave your employer before retirement, your vested defined-contribution money goes with you and can continue to grow, if you put it in another plan.

Employers offer a long roster of defined-contribution plans, which vary according to the corporate structure and the nature of the contributions. The main contenders are the 401(k), and its sibling 403(b) for nonprofit and educational institutions; profit-sharing plans; money-purchase pension plans; employee stock ownership plans (ESOPs); and thrift plans.

It's All in the Numbers: 401(k) and 403(b)

These plans have become as much a fixture in corporate America as the paid vacation. A survey of large companies by the benefits experts, Hewitt Associates, reveals that 95 percent offer some type of 401(k). Furthermore, about two-thirds of big-company employees join these plans. And for good reason. In one neat package, they wrap together a small raise, tax deferral, and retirement savings. The 403(b) plans are similar to the 401(k) in that they're tax-deferred retirement plans, but they're designed for employees of certain nonprofit organizations (charitable groups with a 501[c] [3] tax status), public schools, colleges, hospitals, churches, and social welfare agencies.

An employee with a 401(k) earmarks a certain amount of pay every month, which is taken from pre-tax earnings; usually this money is matched in some fashion by the employer. The employer's contribution is akin to a raise, even though the employee can't touch it for the time being, which is why the 401(k) is sometimes referred to as a "cash or deferred compensation arrangement." (You may also hear them called "salary reduction plans" because money siphoned into the plan reduces what an employee takes home every month. But salary is not really reduced, it's just diverted.) In most 403(b) plans, employers usually don't add a

YOU'RE IN CHARGE

"The shift to defined contributions has forced employees to take more responsibility for retirement. They have discretion as to how to invest the money and must make substantive decisions about their own financial futures."

—Bill Miner, *The Wyatt Company,* as quoted in the Chicago Tribune

COME ON, YOU CAN DO BETTER

The average employee in a 401(k) in 1990 put away only 4.9 percent of salary into the plan, down from 5.2 percent the year before, according to a survey by MassMutual Pension Management.

financial sweetener, although some nonprofits have begun to match funds.

Vesting in a 401(k) usually comes after five years, but the 403(b) effectively imposes no vesting limit—employees have immediate access to any employer contributions, undoubtedly one reason few employers contribute to their plans.

At retirement time (or when an employee leaves a company), the 401(k) coughs up all the contributions plus what it's earned over the years. Usually, this money is taken out in a lump sum (creating a blistering tax bill), although five-year or ten-year income averaging —if you're eligible—can soften

the blow. Or, of course, you can roll it over into an IRA. (Alas, recipients of payouts from a 403[b] aren't allowed to average income, but they, too, can roll their money into an IRA and defer taxes.)

The 401(k) does have certain curbs—employees can't tuck away limitless amounts of money. In 1993, employee contributions (before taxes) to a 401(k) were topped at $8,994, a ceiling that's raised yearly by inflation. Employees can sock away more—the lesser of $30,000 a year or 25 percent of their compensation—they just can't put off paying taxes on anything over the $8,994 limit. And employers can't make contributions that will top the $30,000 or 25 percent limit. Employer contributions are usually a percentage (50 percent is common) of the amount an employee sets aside.

The nonprofit laborer can put up to 25 percent of pre-tax salary, but no more than $9,500, in a 403(b).

Since 1987, federal employees have been able to contribute to their Thrift Savings Plan (TSP). The rules are basically the same as for 401(k) plans. TSP participants (newer employees) also enjoy a generous money matching program from Uncle Sam.

What can make or break these plans as retirement savings vehicles is how the money is invested. Most employers offer plan members at least three diverse investments (not counting company stock), allowing them to move money between investments at least quarterly, and to spread their money among investments. Many plans offer an array of investment outlets with an assortment of funds. Savers can then divvy up their money among company stock, stock and bond funds, and interest-sensitive funds, such as money markets and guaranteed investment contracts (GICs).

Chances are that a portion of your 401(k) money is in GICs—fixed-interest-bearing notes issued by insurance companies and occasionally by banks. This is especially likely if you indicated to your employer that you were interested in steady interest growth for your money. A recent survey of 80 large employers indicates that about 50 percent of defined contributions are invested in GICs.

Money in GICs isn't completely guaranteed—only the interest is guaranteed. GICs usually run for three to five years, at which time the investment manager rolls the

money into another one that will pay maybe a little higher, may be a little lower, rate. A different animal with the same stripes is the BIC (bank investment contract), which is managed by banks and has the added appeal of federal insurance behind the deposits. As a result, BICs tend to pay a little less interest than GICs.

"If you are investing your money for the long haul, the record is unequivocal. Assuming five percent inflation, fixed-income assets will return about eight percent per year, while the stock market will average a return of 12 percent a year."

—*Michael K. Evans, economist, as quoted in* GQ

While GICs might dominate the 401(k) investment horizon right now, financial planners recommend that relatively young employees (say, under 50) not be too conservative with their retirement dollars and direct some to equity funds. Over the decades until you retire, insist legions of professional investors, the stock market will outperform all other models.

But there's an exception to this assertion: an employer's own stock. An employee shouldn't tie up an entire nest egg in his employer's stock, even if it's healthy, solvent, and promises an exciting future. The reason? Too many valuable eggs in one basket. The soundest approach is to spread your savings among equity and fixed-interest funds.

Regardless of where you aim your 401(k) or 403(b) money, it isn't stuck there forever. Most plans allow participants to shift their money between funds. But *you* have to decide when to switch. Employers and plan managers avoid getting involved in the business of recommending where people should stash their nest eggs.

Under certain conditions you can even pull your money out of these plans and not get hit with a 10 percent early distribution penalty. The IRS says you can take out your money penalty-free if:

• You have a "qualifying" medical disability; in other words, if the IRS thinks your condition is serious enough.
• You have to make payments

under a qualified domestic relations court order; for example, payments to a spouse, ex-spouse, or child.

• You have to pay for medical care costs over 7.5 percent of your gross income.

• Your plan has "excess contributions" or "excess deferrals"—money paid in over the amount the company is allowed to shelter.

• You're over 55 and are "separated from service," that is, left your job (only 403[b] participants).

Short of withdrawing your money, your 401(k) might allow borrowing. If the company allows it, employees can borrow up to half their account value (up to a maximum of $50,000) and pay it

Among employees with a 401(k) plan who leave a company before retirement, only 13 percent roll the money into another tax-deferred savings account. Everyone else spends it— 34 percent use it for immediate purchases and 30 percent use it to pay off debts.

Employee Benefit Research Institute

back at current rates over five years. You can also borrow from a 403(b) if it's invested in a tax-deferred annuity and the custodian or carrier allows it; if the money's in a mutual fund, you cannot. The rules for borrowing are the same as for other company pension plans.

When you leave a company before retirement, you take your 401(k) money with you and face a choice: either roll it into another retirement plan, like an IRA, or spend it. Should you be part of a 403(b) tax-deferred annuity plan, you have other options: Keep your money with your former employer

How Big a Lump?

This table shows average lump sums from savings and thrift plans paid to employees, according to a Bureau of Labor Statistics survey of 109,000 companies and benefits for 32 million employees. The sums are the result of an average 10 percent annual growth and are for employees who have been in a plan from ten to 30 years and who earn $15,000 to $55,000 a year. The sums assume midpoint contributions (shown in the table on page 157) by employees and employers.

Annual Earnings	Years in Plan				
	10	15	20	25	30
$15,000	13,159	21,146	30,395	41,598	56,531
20,000	17,552	28,224	40,581	55,526	75,480
25,000	21,946	35,283	50,744	69,465	94,396
35,000	30,399	48,883	70,330	96,254	130,872
45,000	37,814	60,800	87,463	119,725	162,803
55,000	45,252	72,770	104,684	143,317	194,896

Monthly Labor Review

or take it along to the new job, should that employer offer a similar plan. In any case, if you're like the millions of savers who don't roll over this money, you will owe ordinary taxes (and possibly a 10 percent penalty tax) on it, plus your retirement account will be back to zero. In your next job you'll have to begin saving all over again. (More later about ways to roll over.)

Plain Vanilla: Thrift Plans

If your company benefits experts use the term "savings and thrift plan," your untrained ear may assume they're talking about a 401(k). Close, but not quite. They're similar, except for one broad curve in the road. The amount you contribute to your savings plan each month can come out of your pre-tax earnings, making it a 401(k), and even from your after-tax earnings, at which point it becomes a simple thrift plan. Your employer may or may not match your savings, which are invested in your name.

Employers who do kick in a share may add a percentage of what you save or a flat dollar amount. And they may beef up their contribution as your number of years on the job grows. On rare occasions an employer will figure its contribution based on profits.

The cap on what you and your boss can put into a savings plan is 25 percent of your salary or $30,000, whichever is less. If you're also part of a defined-benefits plan, your total benefit cap drops. As with other defined-contribution plans, your savings plan money can be invested in stock, bond, and balanced funds as well as in fixed-income instruments like GICs.

SLICE OF THE PIE: PROFIT-SHARING PLANS

In addition to formal retirement plans, employers often supplement workers' paychecks, and retirement ambitions, with profit-sharing plans. The Bureau of Labor Statistics reports that almost one-fifth of employees of medium and large companies are profit-sharers.

Profit-sharing plans come in three forms: cash, deferred, and combination. The cash plan pays employees a portion of its profits (which can be figured a number of ways) in cash or stock. This arrangement is a straight bonus, not really a retirement plan, so often these companies also offer defined-benefit plans.

The deferred plan also pays in cash or stock according to company profits, but the payment is deposited into individual employee accounts and can't be touched until retirement, disability, or sometimes if the employee leaves the firm. Of course, the combo plate includes immediate cash or stock and deferred profit sharing. Of the three, the better retirement arrangements are the deferred and combo plans because taxes are postponed until you actually pocket the cash or stock. However, should your employer get into financial difficulty, your deferred benefits could be at risk. Unlike pension plans and 401(k)s, deferred compensation is not protected from the company's creditors nor insured by the PBGC.

"By the time you reach retirement age, every dollar you saved at age 25 will have earned ten times what every dollar you saved at 45 earned."

—*Michael K. Evans, economist, as quoted in* GQ

THE LARGEST ESOPs

These are the 20 largest ESOPs in the country (by number of employees), as reported by the National Center for Employee Ownership.

Kroger
J.C. Penney
McDonnell Douglas
Rockwell International
Publix Supermarkets
Carter Hawley Hale
Grumman
HealthTrust
FMC Corp.
Coldwell Banker
Hallmark Cards
Dynacorp
Lowe's Companies
Avis
America West Airlines
EPIC Healthcare Group
Science Applications
Ruddick
Parsons
Price Chopper

FEW FABLES HERE: ESOPS

One of the best-known profit-sharing plans is the Employee Stock Ownership Plan (ESOP), which bestows *only* a company's own stock but not for immediate trading or selling. While ESOPs can form a rich retirement plan, they serve a number of other purposes—incentives for employees, a source of additional financing for a company, and a vehicle for lowering corporate taxes. (ESOPs were splattered with mud during the 1980s when a few companies formed them to fend off hostile takeovers, but most companies don't use them this way.) For this primer, I've focused on the retirement features.

Basically, an ESOP is a trust fund that parcels out company stock to employees. The stock is kept in an employee's name and distributed when the employee leaves or retires. An ESOP can be "leveraged" or "unleveraged," depending on how it gets its cache of company stock. A leveraged

---

HOW DO YOU STACK UP?

Here is the range of annual amounts employees and employers in medium and large companies contributed to savings and thrift plans—401(k)—in 1989.

AVERAGE PAY	EMPLOYEE CONTRIBUTION			EMPLOYER CONTRIBUTION		
	Min.	Midpt.	Max.	Min.	Midpt.	Max.
$15,000	188	1,126	2,064	124	468	494
20,000	249	1,498	2,746	165	622	657
25,000	310	1,869	3,429	205	774	816
35,000	433	2,610	4,787	286	1,075	1,134
45,000	555	3,336	6,116	365	1,375	1,450
55,000	678	4,004	7,330	445	1,674	1,765

Monthly Labor Review

ESOP borrows money to purchase stock from a company, and this loan is repaid by the company. The company's loan payments thus represent its contribution to the plan. (It's not as complicated as it sounds if you think of an ESOP as a separate entity, not a company program.) Or, a company can create an ESOP trust fund, and periodically give it money to purchase stock or stock to purchase stock; in this case, it's an unleveraged ESOP.

Through an ESOP, an employer may either occasionally give employees stock as a bonus, make the contribution part of a continuing program, or sell them shares. With most companies, an ESOP is

---

"You're really asking for trouble using ESOPs as a substitute pension plan. They're not insured, they're not funded, they're not anything, and if an employer goes sour, the employee loses his job and his retirement income."

—*Michael S. Gordon, attorney who helped draft pension legislation, as quoted in the* **Wall Street Journal**

---

not the main pension plan, but an added benefit. The National Center for Employee Ownership, a research organization that tracks ESOPs, reports that there are about 10,000 active ESOPs and that the vast majority are in privately held companies.

Like other retirement plans, ESOPs must follow a host of rules about vesting (within five to seven years), who's eligible to participate (plans can't discriminate in favor of high-paid employees), how the funds are invested (at least 51 percent in company stock), and how the benefits are distributed.

ESOPs create a unique situation for employees because retirement money is tied up in securities that may not be readily tradable. To make this money available for someone on the brink of retirement, an ESOP has a couple of provisions for cashing in stock. Employees who are at least 55 and have been in an ESOP for at least ten years are allowed to convert at least 25 percent of their account out of company stock into other investments. At age 60 you're allowed to pull out 50 percent of your company stock. Employees holding ESOP stock that is not publicly traded must be allowed to sell their stock back to the company at a fair market value, and some ESOPs establish a floor or minimum price at which they promise to buy stock from employees. (Stock of privately held firms has to be independently appraised every year.)

All this talk of share values raises a nagging concern: how smart is an ESOP as a retirement plan? As your sole source of retirement money, an ESOP is risky. The company stock can sour and lose much of its value, or worse yet, the company can go bankrupt. Although these events sound extreme, employees who once belonged to the ESOPs of Pan Am and the brokerage firm Thomson McKinnon know from experience that they're not impossible.

An ESOP is a way to participate in your employer's bright future, but it works best when it's an additive to your basic benefits blend.

CONSTRUCTING YOUR OWN PENSION PLAN

As a working person, you can construct a personal pension plan regardless of what your employer offers, a plan you can carry with you wherever you work. And if you work for yourself, you have a host of possibilities. The retirement plan available to everyone is the Individual Retirement Account, which has lost some of its luster in recent years but still is a safe, warm place for your retirement dollars to grow.

To refresh your memory, an IRA is a retirement fund that you set up with a maximum annual contribution of $2,000 ($2,250 for

> **Q** *I owe alimony and child support to my ex-wife. Can the court tap into my pension for that money?*
>
> **A** *Yes it can, by issuing a Qualified Domestic Relations Order, which authorizes your pension plan administrator to make payments from your pension to whomever the court designates.*

a Spousal IRA), which grows unencumbered by taxes until you withdraw the money. In the good old days, your IRA contribution was tax-deductible, reducing your taxable income. Today, that gem of a deduction has disappeared for many people—only people not participating in a company retirement plan or who make less than a certain amount can slice their entire IRA contribution from their taxable income. This prohibition also applies to spouses—if your husband has a company plan and you file taxes jointly, you can't deduct for an IRA. You can deduct the full amount if your adjusted gross income is under $25,000 ($40,000 for couples). If you earn between $25,000 and $35,000, your deduction diminishes (take off $10 for every $50 over $25,000) until it vanishes entirely at $35,000. Couples lose their deduction at $50,000.

You're in charge of your IRA money, deciding where to invest, when to move out of one investment into another, and ultimately, when and how to withdraw your money. Of course, if you remove money before age 59½, you'll pay a 10 percent penalty, and by law you *must* start extracting money by age 70½. You really get clob-bered if you don't start taking out money by age 70½—a 50 percent penalty on the minimum amount you should withdraw *plus* regular income taxes. Nevertheless, the decisions are still yours. No employer or company dictates your "retirement age" or decides whether you should accept an annuity or a lump sum. Sounds great, but this control also means you're responsible for your IRA fund blossoming or languishing.

"One of the major reasons why private pensions do not play a larger role in providing retirement income is that they generally are not adjusted for inflation."

—Rep. William J. Hughes,
Chairman, Subcommittee on
Retirement Income and Employment

Money watchers report that about two-thirds of all IRA money is deposited in fixed-income funds such as money markets. They also point out that while these funds have been averaging gains around 5 percent, stock funds have consistently scored higher returns. In short, they say that an investment with a guaranteed yield has no place in an IRA for anyone under age 55. You can't put your money into collectibles such as coins, art, precious metals or antiques, but other than that, you can deposit your IRA in virtually any type of investment with a brokerage firm, bank, savings and loan, credit union, insurance company, or financial services company. (Naturally you wouldn't put your money into a tax-free municipal bond fund because IRA earnings *are* free of taxes.)

The big question for many people is whether to keep contributing to an IRA even if they don't qualify for the tax deduction. The answer is that maintaining an IRA clearly makes sense for someone already contributing maximum amounts to other retirement plans. After all, your money does accumulate tax-free until withdrawal.

IRAs should not be treated as simple, safe plans that you set up and forget—they need to be watched and tended. Although you shouldn't be chasing invest-

CAN YOU DEDUCT YOUR IRA?

The extent to which you can deduct your IRA contributions depends on your adjusted gross income (AGI) and whether you file taxes as an individual or as a married couple. Here are limits:

Filing Status	AGI	Deductibility
Single	$0–$25,000	Full
Single	$25,000–$34,999	Partial
Single	$35,000 and above	None
Married	$0–$40,000	Full
Married	$40,001–$49,999	Partial
Married	$50,000 and above	None

ments that promise fractionally higher returns, consider switching your money if your earnings consistently lag behind the market. Remember, too, that your IRA is not completely untouchable until 59½. There is a way to skirt the early-withdrawal penalty. It's found in Section 72(t) of the tax code and works like this: You can begin taking out money at any age if your annual withdrawals represent a series of equal payments over your life expectancy. To devise a successful, and acceptable-to-IRS, withdrawal schedule, get the help of a bank or another financial institution.

Once you start taking your series of equal payments, you have to stick with it for five years or until you hit 59½, whichever comes later. As you go along, you'll owe taxes only on the portion of your withdrawal that represents deductible contributions and earnings. Such calculations are how an accountant earns her keep.

ROLLOVER IRA

This may sound like a command to your dog, but it's really a special event in the life of a retirement plan—moving money from

an employer plan into an individual IRA in order to avoid taxes. You can roll money over into your IRA for many reasons: You leave your job, retire, your employer is ending its pension plan, or you've become disabled. (However, if you don't transfer it directly into a recognized (by the Internal Revenue Service) IRA, your employer is going to hold on to 20 percent of it to cover withholding taxes.)

As with your initial IRA, you decide how to invest a rollover IRA. However, you don't have to move the entire amount, and what you don't put into the rollover will be taxed.

If you don't roll your money into another retirement account, presto, the tax man cometh. You'll pay ordinary income taxes and a 10 percent penalty if you're under 59½. (The ins and outs of other pension rollovers are tackled in Chapter 7, "Dodging Taxes in Retirement.")

Usually in January, when the President and Congress begin squabbling over the budget, or in April, when taxpayers realize how much they have to pony up, the subject of changing IRA rules arises. Ever since the 1986 Tax Reform Act eliminated the $2,000 deduction for most IRA contributors, politicians have been toying with proposals for reinstating some type of deduction or giving people penalty-free access to IRAs. All this talk makes for lively debate and certainly perks up the ears of most wage-earners. But don't bank on the IRA of yesteryear returning.

YOU HAVE A SAVIOR IN THE SEP-IRA

This retirement plan, the Simplified Employee Pension, is designed for the self-employed and is basically an IRA with expanded capacity. A souped-up IRA, so to speak. You're still in charge and you have more maneuvering room with this pension plan. If you have any self-employment income, you can have a SEP. All you needed to qualify in 1992 was $374 in income.

Even though SEP-IRAs are designed for the self-employed, employers can create a SEP-IRA for individual employees. Small businesses that can't afford a full-scale pension plan often establish SEP-IRAs for their employees. The disadvantage of a SEP from an employer's point of view is that contributed money is vested immediately and is controlled by the employee.

As with the IRA, you (or your employer) establish a SEP account with a financial institution and make annual contributions to the plan. Your timetable for putting

---

WHERE YOU PUT YOUR IRA MONEY

About $650 billion is deposited in IRA accounts in these institutions:

Banks, savings and loans, credit unions:	39%
Mutual funds:	26%
Brokerages:	24%
Insurance companies:	11%

Investment Company Institute

DOUBLE YOUR MONEY

A 35-year-old executive with $50,000 in a company retirement plan leaves her job and doesn't roll over her savings. She pays the taxes and penalty, and invests the remainder in an account earning 8 percent. When she's 59, she'll have $123,754. If she had rolled the $50,000 over into a tax-deferred retirement plan, she would have had $245,285 at age 59.

away money is downright leisurely —for the previous tax year, you have until April 15 to open an account and put away money.

With a SEP-IRA, you can tuck away a fair amount, although there is a limit: 15 percent of an employer's payroll or if you're self-employed, 15 percent of your net earnings up to $30,000. Since the 15 percent includes half of your self-employment tax and is computed after you have subtracted

your SEP contribution, it really comes to about 13 percent of your taxable business income. When contributions come from an employer, they're limited to 15 percent of all eligible employees' compensation or about 13 percent of your paycheck.

The money you put into a SEP-IRA is tax-deductible—you pay no income taxes on it until withdrawal time. The money your plan earns is also free from taxation, again until you take it out.

As with other "self-directed" retirement plans, you can invest your money in CDs, mutual funds, stocks, bonds, or other vehicles.

The paperwork on this pension is a breeze compared with other plans. You fill out one form and that's it. No annual filings, no reports to the IRS, no songs and dances whenever you want to change your investment. And, you don't have to contribute every year to keep the plan open and operating. When you do make payments, there is no minimum, only a maximum.

At the magic age of 59½, you may start withdrawing SEP-IRA money. As with the whole family of personal retirement plans— IRAs, SEPs and Keoghs—you get hit with a 10 percent penalty tax if you take out money before you're 59½. You can get around this rule only if you have a disabling injury; make a series of equal periodic withdrawals (explained earlier); need medical care; or, of course, you die and the money goes into your estate.

For those who dutifully wait until the magic age, there's no getting around taxes on the amount you take out. This raises a small catch: Lump sum withdrawals from this plan can't be taxed using five or ten-year forward income-averaging. Your tax bill will be due immediately. But, if you receive your money in installments or annuities, you're taxed only on what you pocket each year.

A SPORTING INVESTMENT: KEOGHS

Keoghs are to IRAs as sports cars are to the family station wagon. While more complicated and demanding in terms of cost and upkeep, Keoghs, which are tax deductible, have the potential of delivering a more exciting retirement. And, like a Lotus or Lamborghini, they're not for everyone—Keoghs are for the self-employed, which may mean a

farmer in Kansas or a doctor in Kentucky. And should you happen to have employees, they have to be included in the plan.

Anyone can establish a Keogh, as long as you have self-employment income, whether from freelancing articles for your profession's journal or selling herb wreaths through a local craft shop. You can set up a Keogh even if you have a retirement plan at work.

WHAT'S A KEOGH?

The word "Keogh" comes from Eugene J. Keogh, a congressman from New York who authored the 1962 tax retirement act for the self-employed.

You have a choice when you establish a Keogh: You can make it a flexible plan with limited contributions or an unbending plan that accepts larger contributions. The first option, called a profit-sharing plan, lets you contribute anything between zero and 15 percent of your taxable business income (as explained above, in practice this figures to 13.043 percent). One year you can put away nothing, and the next you can stash away the max. This is the better choice if you're not sure about your earnings and the exact amount you'll be able to save from year to year.

The second option, called a money-purchasing plan, demands that you contribute a certain amount every year, but it allows you to contribute more each year than with profit sharing. You figure how much—up to 25 percent of taxable business income (20 percent, after adding self-employment tax and subtracting what you plan to contribute to the Keogh) to a maximum $30,000. Then you *must* put in that amount every year, or your plan loses its IRS blessing.

Bear in mind that these two options are not mutually exclusive: Your Keogh can encompass both. You can earmark a modest percentage of your income for a money-purchase plan and also shove dough into a profit-sharing plan. Feeding two plans enables you to put away as much as possible while avoiding sizable required contributions. Money fed into employees' plans also side steps taxes, and employees can make after-tax contributions.

Keoghs, like the SEP-IRA, accept contributions for the past tax year up to April 15. However, the plan must be in place with a financial institution before the end of the tax year.

With you making the decision about how much to put into each, these are obviously defined-contribution plans. There's also such a critter as a personal defined-benefits plan, but you need professional help to establish one. The fees charged for setting up and managing this plan can run into the thousands, and your investments have to meet the requirements of ERISA (the Employee Retirement Income Security Act). That's the bad news. The good news is that you can shelter a lot of money this way—annual benefits equal to the lesser of 100 percent of your average compensation for the highest three consecutive years or $108,963.

Your professional adviser can help you figure how much you want to contribute. (To refresh your memory: With defined benefits you focus on how much you want to receive; with defined contributions, you focus on how much to put in.) Usually, these defined-benefit plans are for the well-heeled, self-employed individual who wants to shelter lots and needs an immediate, substantial pension plan.

At age 59½, when you start taking money from your Keogh, you'll owe taxes on what you receive, not only on its accumulated earnings. Subject to a number of qualifications, if you take out a lump sum distribution, you may be eligible to average the income over five or ten years. Talk to your tax expert.

Q *What does "qualified" mean when talking about a retirement plan?*

A *This refers to its tax status with the IRS. "Qualified" means the retirement plan is designed to be exempt from certain taxes as its investments grow and until withdrawal. Money in nonqualified plans is not sheltered from taxes.*

FROM ONE POCKET TO ANOTHER: BORROWING FROM YOUR PENSION

It may be tempting at times, especially when you read those huge benefit numbers in your plan's annual report, to raid your pension plan to buy a house, pay college bills, or take a great vacation. Well, forget it. Though the money is definitely yours, only a personal tragedy such as serious hardship, death, or disability will break it loose before the appointed time.

You may be able to borrow from your company pension, however, but only if your situation meets the strict requirements of the Employee Retirement Income Security Act. Your loan can be no more than the greater of $10,000 or half of your accrued benefits, but at most $50,000, and the plan may insist on a minimum to your loan request, for instance, $1,000. You have to repay the loan within five years, unless it's for your primary residence, in which case you have more time to repay. The interest you'll be charged will be competitive with market rates. You can't borrow at all from a SEP, IRA, or Keogh.

WHERE TO GO FOR HELP

The following free publications can help with your pension questions.

- *How to File a Claim for Your Benefits*
- *Reporting and Disclosure Guide for Employee Benefit Plans*
- *Guide to Summary Plan Description Requirements*
- *Often-Asked Questions About Employee Retirement Benefits*
- *What You Should Know About the Pension Law*

All of the above are available from the U.S. Department of Labor, Pension and Welfare Benefits Administration, Public Disclosure Room N-5507, 200 Constitution Avenue, NW, Washington, DC 20210; 202/219-8771.

- *A Guide to Understanding Your Pension Plan.* Available from the American Association of Retired Persons, 601 E Street, NW, Washington, DC 20049.
- *Retirement Plans for the Self-Employed,* IRS Publication 550. Available from IRS Forms Distribution Centers.
- *Pension and Annuity Income,* IRS Publication 575. Available from IRS Forms Distribution Centers.
- *A Lay Person's Guide to Private Employer-Sponsored Health and Pension Benefits After Retirement.* Available from the National Senior Citizens Law Center, Suite 700, 1815 H Street, NW, Washington, DC 20006; 202/887-5280.
- *Fundamentals of Employee Benefit Programs.* Available from the Employee Benefit Research Institute, 2121 K Street, NW, Washington, DC 20037; 202/659-0670.

BE YOUR OWN PENSION WATCHDOG

Employers are required to give you a yearly financial summary of your pension plan, showing where your money is invested and how well these investments are doing. For a close look at your pension, you need to request in writing from your employer a government Form 5500. This will tell you about any changes in managers, conflicts of interest, or loans to relatives of plan trustees, all of which signal trouble. One line of Form 5500 even asks managers whether they've committed fraud.

In studying your pension plan summary, look at its holdings. Assets in defined-benefit plans should equal at least 60 percent of liabilities; otherwise it may be on thin ice. Cause for concern among assets is lots of junk bonds (bonds rated below investment grade and paying high returns).

Another area for scrutiny is plan management. Large corporate pension plans are usually managed by professional benefits experts devoted full-time to monitoring how funds are invested and disbursed. Expert managers know the ins and outs of investing retirement funds as well as the federal regulations that spell out how they should be handled. However, at many small companies, pension plans are frequently tended to by company employees, like the chief financial officer or the human resources director, whose full-time responsibilities lie elsewhere.

Bright yellow warning signs are plan managers who earn commissions on investments sold to the plan (a definite conflict of interest) and loans to trustees, or relatives of trustees, at favorable rates.

WHEN IT'S FORCED ON YOU: EARLY RETIREMENT

Many corners of corporate America have restructured in the past decade, a process of paring down and shuffling that has thrown legions of employees into early retirement. For some, the offer for early retirement arrives soon after their fiftieth birthday. Often, employees are given just a few weeks to decide whether to accept various early retirement enticements.

SUSPICIONS, SUSPICIONS

If your employer won't provide detailed information about your pension plan, call the Labor Department's Division of Technical Assistance and Inquiries (202/219-8771). If you have a complaint or suspect your plan's managers are involved in illegal activities, such as kickbacks, embezzlement, or extortion, call the Pension and Welfare Benefits Administration (202/219-8776).

The employees most vulnerable to shady dealings with their pension plans are the millions of workers in plans that have fewer than 100 participants. These plans don't have to be audited by independent CPAs, file their financial results with the government only every three years, and worse yet, are often managed by company owners and executives. The 401(k) is particularly defenseless because it's not watched by the Pension Benefit Guaranty Corporation. The biggest dangers: embezzlement and illegal loans from the plan. If you suspect a rip-off, contact a regional office of the Pension and Welfare Benefits Administration (see Appendix B).

Usually, these trimmings strengthen your pension plan in one of several ways.

Of course, your firm can simply hand you a lump sum that can be either spent immediately or put toward retirement. But another way the company may directly build up your pension plan is to give you credit for more years of service than you actually accumulated and to artificially add to your age the same amount of years.

Let's say, for instance, your firm offers a defined-benefits pension starting at age 65. It calculates the benefits by multiplying an average of your last three years pay by the number of years you have been employed. Then, that figure is multiplied by 2 percent. If you were to retire at age 60 with 20 years of service and an average income of $50,000, your pension would work out to $20,000 a year —and you wouldn't start receiving it for another five years. But by adding five years to both age and years of service, you would receive $25,000 immediately.

That's a pretty powerful inducement to leave your desk and blotter behind five years sooner than you may have planned.

But early retirement extras aren't all gravy. Employees who refuse early retirement and continue to work may well receive annual salary raises that will boost their pension calculation. Even more basic, if you're part of a defined-contribution plan, your employer continues to contribute to your pension fund, and this keeps growing until normal retirement time. Early retirement cuts short the final years of growth, a time when funds show the biggest gains (remember compounding?).

An employee confronted with an early retirement option should run the numbers: what happens to your pension if you stay and what happens if you take the enticements and leave? A common scenario is the 55-year-old employee whose early retirement package totals $200,000 in a defined-contribution plan. This would yield about $20,000 annually from a lifetime annuity. However, if the employee stays put for ten years and the plan grows at a steady 7 percent, then it virtually doubles to $400,000. The resulting annual annuity would more than double because you would be ten years older.

"The annual defined-contribution pension for a retiree who has been earning $15,000 a year averaged 19 percent of income or $2,850 a year. Under a defined-benefit plan, the average pension for the same retiree would have been $4,200 a year, or 28 percent of salary. Similar differences continue until annual salary surpassed $100,000."

Nation's Business

Alas, many employees don't have a choice about whether to accept early retirement, which sometimes is more a shove than an offer. However, knowing how forced early retirement may eat into your plan, despite the added inducements, can put you in a stronger position to bargain for tastier sweeteners. You may be able to negotiate a fatter severance, if you can show how your pension is hurt by your untimely departure.

DECISIONS, DECISIONS: DOES PENSION MAX PAY?

Employees on the eve of retirement may encounter the quandary about "pension max." Should they or shouldn't they? Pension max (full name: pension maximization proposal) involves deciding whether to accept a single-life pension and buy an annuity, or to buy a simple joint-and-survivor pension. The decision involves weighing a list of trade-offs. Here are the facts.

A single-life pension consists of maximum monthly payments to an employee until his or her death. A spouse receives nothing. The joint-and-survivor arrangement calls for lower monthly joint payments (normally 10 to 20 percent less) that extend beyond the death of the employee through the spouse's lifetime. When the re-

tiree dies, the benefits a surviving spouse receives are reduced to about half.

The idea with pension max is to create your own survivor plan that is less costly and pays more to the remaining spouse. A pensioner can opt for the single-life pension, and use part of the money to purchase life insurance for a mate to use when the pension participant dies, and presumably the life insurance could fund a larger survivor payment than a joint-and-survivor plan.

Sounds reasonable, but the arrangement has pitfalls. Whether pension max is advisable for you depends on a couple of things. First, your pension. Add a gold star if payments, either single-life or joint-and-survivor, include cost-of-living adjustments. Pension max computations frequently omit the impact of COLAs, and inflation will surely eat into payouts over the years. On the other hand, consider the age and health of your spouse. If he or she is in poor health and not likely to survive you, accepting lower payments under a joint-and-survivor plan doesn't make sense.

Second, the life insurance. Enter a black mark if the cost of the life insurance is more than the *after-tax* difference between single-life payments and joint-and-survivor payments. The computation of the amount of the life insurance required can be very complicated. However, assuming the amount required is $100,000, if the cost is a monthly premium of $570 and the gap between the two pension arrangements is $350 a month, then the life insurance loses ground.

To make the pension max decision, you need to ask these questions—the numbers will point out the answer.

Q When Congress abolished mandatory retirement through the amendments to the Age Discrimination in Employment Act, did it apply to everybody?

A No. Certain groups of employees, including college professors, can still have a mandatory retirement age.

- How much less are monthly payments for joint-and-survivor plans than single-life? Does either include a cost-of-living adjustment, and what percent?
- When the primary participant dies and payments go to the surviving spouse, what fraction are payments of the original pension?
- What size annuity would be comparable to the monthly payments a spouse would receive with joint-and-survivor? What are the monthly premiums for this coverage?
- What will be your taxes on pension income versus annuity income?

WOMEN'S PREDICAMENT

It's an ugly fact of life in America that working women don't fare as well as men in the realm of pension benefits. Social Security payments aren't designed for the two-income family, homemakers, divorced women, single mothers, or women who must change jobs frequently because of family demands. In addition, women's lower wages translate into lower Social Security and private pension payments. And, the infamous "widow's gap" in the Social Security law declares that a widow may receive no benefits until age 60, regardless of her husband's age.

The pensions that do trickle down to widows or divorced women typically don't equal what men receive. The raw truth is that women often spend many of their earning years taking care of children and the elderly, and when they do work at paying jobs, often they are paid less than men. Also women live longer; combine these factors and they add up to smaller pensions.

Although it would be nice to correct the inequities of laws and wages, that's a long-term agenda.

In 1970, women received 70 percent of the Social Security benefits men received; by 1989, that percentage had grown to just 73 percent. In 1974, women's average private pension income was 73 percent of men's; by 1987, that ratio had plummeted to 58 percent.

USA Today

For now, women have to take steps to secure and protect their current or prospective pensions.

Women: Talk with your husband about his retirement plan and survivor benefits. Understand that when you waive your survivor benefits in order to receive larger benefits when he retires, you risk losing all benefits should he die before you. The same is often true with lifetime annuity benefits—without the joint-and-survivor clause, the money stops when the primary participant dies.

Women going through divorce after a long marriage need to talk with their lawyer about including the husband's retirement benefits as part of the settlement package. Many state courts, backed up by federal pension law, can compel a man to divvy up benefits as part of the marital property.

The bottom line for many women is that they shouldn't count on Social Security or a company pension to cushion their retirement. Given the possibility that you've changed jobs repeatedly over the years, worked for small, service companies, worked part-time, or started and stopped working, your company pension— if you have one—may not amount to much. The smartest course for

Q *I'm living with someone. We're not married, but we plan to be together for the rest of our lives. If he dies, can I get any of his pension benefits?*

A *While it depends on the specifics of his employer's plan, experts say they know of no pension plans in the country that allow retirement benefits to be paid to surviving nonmarried partners.*

any woman is to build up a personal retirement savings. At a minimum, this should entail her own IRA; a Keogh, or a SEP-IRA if she has self-employment income; and a tax-deferred thrift plan.

For help and information on company and spouse's benefits due you, these are useful booklets: *Your Pension Rights at Divorce*

(Pension Rights Center, 918 16th Street, NW, Washington, DC 20006) and *A Woman's Guide to Pension Rights* (American Association of Retired Persons, 601 E Street, NW, Washington, DC 20049).

KNOW YOUR RIGHTS

When it comes to making laws, Capitol Hill tinkers with pension laws, year in and year out, more than any other area of legislation. For working folks, this means what was true about your benefits yesterday may not hold true today. Here's a summary of the major pension laws and the ways they affect your benefits.

Employment Retirement Income Security Act of 1974 (ERISA)

1. Establishes individual rights covering vesting and participation.

2. Increases incentives for Keoghs and IRAs for employees not covered by a company pension.

3. Imposes rules about investing for plan managers.

4. Imposes funding requirements.

5. Establishes the Pension Benefits Guaranty Corporation.

6. Establishes ESOPs as an employee benefit.

Multiemployer Pension Plan Amendments Act of 1980

1. Establishes financial requirements for companies that withdraw from multiemployer pension plans.

2. Provides government insurance for certain plans in financial trouble.

Tax Equity and Fiscal Responsibility Act of 1982 (TEFRA)

1. Requires pension plans for high-paid employees in small companies to also provide benefits for lower-paid employees, such as

---

PENSION POVERTY

In 1989, the median income of elderly women was $7,655—58 percent that of elderly men ($13,107).

Aging America, Trends and Projections, U.S. Senate Special Committee on Aging, 1991 Edition

---

secretaries, and paralegals.

2. Changes Keogh contribution limits.

Retirement Equity Act of 1984 (REA)

1. Increases pension protection for widows and divorced spouses.

2. Lowers minimum ages for vesting.

3. Eases rules about how breaks-in-service affect pension eligibility.

Single Employer Pension Plan Amendments Act of 1986

Strengthens federal insurance for pension plans that terminate in 1986 or after.

Tax Reform Act of 1986

1. Shortens vesting period.

2. Increases minimum pension coverage.

3. Limits integration of pensions with Social Security payments.

4. Limits salary contributions to 401(k)s.

5. Limits contributions to IRAs by people covered by an employer plan and earning over certain amounts.

6. Imposes tax on lump-sum distributions to people under age 59½.

7. Creates Simplified Employee Pension salary reduction option for employees of small companies.

Omnibus Budget Reconciliation Act of 1986

1. Continues benefit accruals for employees working beyond age 65.

2. Prohibits plans from setting maximum age limits that exclude older workers from joining a pension plan.

Pension Protection Act (part of Omnibus Budget Reconciliation Act of 1987)

1. Establishes new funding limits for defined-benefit plans.

2. Increases premiums paid by pension plans into the Pension Benefit Guaranty Corporation.

Technical and Miscellaneous Revenue Act of 1988

Tightens rules for companies on funding.

Revenue Reconciliation Act of 1989

1. Tightens rules on terminating plans.

2. Imposes penalties for companies that overstate pension liabilities in order to increase their tax deductions.

3. Requires deferred compensation to be included in figuring total compensation and Social Security wage base.

Omnibus Budget Reconciliation Act of 1990

1. Increases taxes on plans that pay out excess funds.

2. Increases insurance premiums paid to PBGC.

3. Extends Social Security to state and local government employees not part of an employee retirement plan.

Older Workers Benefit Protection Act of 1990

1. Extends protection of the Age Discrimination in Employment Act to employee benefits.

2. Sets minimum standards for waiving rights in early retirement.

Chapter 4

ADDING TO YOUR PERSONAL WEALTH

E ven if you haven't invested dollar one in a retirement plan, you probably own assets that eventually will feather your retirement nest. These assets work double time: You use and enjoy them today while they gain in value as retirement approaches. These are often assets you live with for years: home, real estate, life insurance, and annuities.

A home, for instance, not only offers shelter but can produce tax advantages and income. If you don't own a home, there are other real estate possibilities. Likewise, life insurance and annuities have tax-saving features and income-producing qualities. So in piecing together your retirement plan, you always include these quiet wealth-builders.

"The best investment on earth is earth."

—Louis Glickman, professional investor

YOUR HOME: A NEST EGG OF WOOD AND GLASS

If you own a home, it usually is your most valuable asset and a resource that can help fund your retirement. What part it plays depends on your individual situation: the value of your house, the size of your investment in it, your lifestyle, your choice of retirement location. There are a number of ways to parlay your home into a retirement investment:

1. Take accumulated equity out of your home and put it elsewhere, where it may grow better and faster (and perhaps tax-free).

2. Find alternative financing to reduce what you currently pay for your housing.

3. Downsize your real estate investment with a different home. In other words, if you sell your present home and purchase a home for less than what you receive, you can put the difference into other investments.

4. Improve the value and size of current real estate holdings for more appreciation.

But, before tapping into your home real estate investment, realize it's more than a roof over your head. Your emotional attachment to your current home, and your feelings about where and how you want to live in the future, will

Q I've always rented (now it's a two-bedroom apartment), but I'm saving up to buy a house. Since I probably won't have enough money for another couple of years, should I put my house savings into a less expensive real estate investment, such as a limited partnership?

A No, a home should be your first priority. But there may be ways to get into one sooner than you think. Talk to a real estate broker about minimum deposit properties (5 percent down), graduated payment mortgages, and distressed or foreclosed homes.

color your real estate investment decisions. The degree to which you view your home with the same critical eye as, say, a mutual fund, will determine how much it contributes to your retirement.

To turn vague feelings into strong opinions that will influence your decisions, ask yourself these questions:

• How happy or content am I with my present home?

• Do I think I'm living in the area I'll be living in when I retire?

• Do I think of my home primarily as an investment or as a place to live? (For an honest answer, ask yourself how you'd feel if the market value of your home dropped well below what you paid for it. Or the converse: Is your home always for sale, given the right price?)

• How do I feel about moving and adjusting to new surroundings?

• Do I put much time and effort into improving my home? Do I enjoy renovating or refurbishing?

PAYING FOR YOUR DREAM

If you're many years from actually retiring, the home you live in now may not be the place you occupy at retirement, so start thinking about steering your housing dollars into retirement funds. What follows are explanations of ways to take money out of your home or ways to pay less for housing. You have many choices, and as one expert has noted, there will be more tomorrow. "The mortgage market changes virtually from day to day, so you can wait a few weeks and, if you haven't committed suicide in the meantime, try again, even with the same lenders," advises real estate writer William G. Connolly.

REFINANCING: CAN YOU AFFORD TO LOWER YOUR COSTS?

Refinancing looks like a no-brainer. Who wouldn't like to pay off an existing mortgage and get another one at a lower rate? For example, a homeowner holding an 11 percent, 30-year $100,000 mortgage can refinance by obtaining, usually from another lender, a 9 percent mortgage. Pay off the old mortgage, and monthly payments drop by $148.

But as the saying goes, you have to spend money to save money. So it is with refinancing; the transaction involves more than simply trading in your old mort-

> *"Regular mortgages are pretty well standardized, so the buyer knows what he's getting. With the seconds, there are so many more variables—on interest rates, fees, service charges, unusual payment schedules —there's just a lot of things that the buyer has to be aware of."*
>
> —Richard DeMong, author of study for Consumer Bankers Association, as quoted in the Boston Globe

gage for a new model. It's similar to taking out a brand-new loan, and paying again all the costs associated with that loan. So in deciding whether to refinance, you need to compare costs and benefits.

Begin with the cost of shedding your current loan: Check whether your mortgage agreement includes a prepayment penalty. That is, if you pay the loan off early, will you pay an extra fee?

Most refinancing expenses arise from the cost of acquiring the new loan. Just as you did when you first bought your home, you'll pay closing costs, such as application and loan processing, title insur-

ance, attorney's fees, and appraisal fees. The specifics of closing costs vary. Standard expenses include a loan origination fee and financing points (one point equals 1 percent of your mortgage). These points, unlike those attached to your original loan, are not immediately tax-deductible but are deducted over the life of your new financing. Some costs may be waived; if you have a lot of equity in your home, you may not need mortgage (default) insurance. Using the new 9 percent, $100,000 mortgage mentioned above, recouping the 5 percent closing costs ($5,000) will take almost three years.

Your lender will tell you what costs are being charged, which may be waived, and the total transaction cost. Lenders may differ on their costs, so it's worth shopping around not only for rates but also for low closing costs.

Traditional real estate wisdom applies the "Two-Two-Two" rule to refinancing decisions: If you've lived in your house at least two years, the new rate is at least two percentage points below your current rate, and you plan to stay in the house at least another two years, refinancing probably makes sense.

But don't apply the rule slavishly. Refinancing may be smart in other circumstances. For instance, if rates plunge a year after your mortgage terms were set, you don't want to wait a year and risk them rebounding. And a drop of less than 2 percent may still make refinancing attractive if you're planning to live in the house for many years. Over the long haul, refinancing to lower a rate by 1.5 percent can be profitable.

When refinancing, you can also look for a shorter pay period, say fifteen years instead of thirty. Although this switch will usually bump up your monthly payments, it reduces the overall cost of your loan. And by paying off your loan early, you build up more equity in your home, which can be tapped into later. Also, you can begin retirement with no burdensome mortgage hanging over your head.

REFINANCING: DOES IT PAY?

Payments and savings on a $100,000 mortgage refinanced to 8 percent.

Current Rate (%)	Current Monthly Payment	Monthly Savings @ 8%	Annual Savings @ 8%
9.0	$ 805	$ 71	$ 852
9.5	841	107	1,284
10.0	878	144	1,728
10.5	915	181	2,172
11.0	952	218	2,616
11.5	990	256	3,072
12.0	1,029	295	3,540
12.5	1,067	333	3,996
13.0	1,106	372	4,464

Mortgage Bankers Association of America

Refinancing may be used to take out equity from your home, particularly a home whose value has registered rewarding gains. For example, if the value of your house has risen from the original purchase price of $150,000 to $200,000, and you hold a $100,000 mortgage, your equity is $100,000. Generally lenders limit refinancing to 75 percent of the current market value of your home. So the more your home has appreciated, the more you can take out through refinancing. But if market values have dropped since you bought, 75 percent of the current value may not replace your present mortgage.

By arranging for a *larger* mortgage, in essence borrowing from your house, you pocket the money that represents the increase in the value of the house. This money can be applied to other investments—markets or funds you think will grow more than real estate. And, your new interest payments will be tax-deductible, but only to a point. (Generally, you can deduct an amount equal to the current balance of the original loan you took out when you purchased the house ["acquisition indebtedness"], plus improvements, plus $100,000.)

THE UPS AND DOWNS OF ARMS

An ARM (adjustable-rate mortgage, also called a variable mortgage) is a home loan with an interest rate that changes every one, three, five, or seven years. Generally, ARM rates follow the two-six formula: they can't move more than two percentage points per adjustment period and no more than six percentage points in their lifetime. (The rate on a conventional fixed-rate 30-year mortgage never moves.) Lenders adjust ARM rates in line with a standard interest-sensitive measurement, such as one-year Treasury bills, the 11th District Cost of Funds Rate (a West Coast index), the prime rate, or the London Interbank Offering Rate (called LIBOR).

ARMs appeal to the home investor and risk-taker. At the outset, the rate is usually lower than conventional rates, an attraction even though a borrower has to live with the chance that the rate will climb. Buyers who expect to move within a few years, before the ARM can take off, like this kind of mortgage.

But sometimes even a buyer planning to put down roots may find an ARM appealing. Real estate professionals maintain that they're preferable to fixed-rate mortgages when they're about three points lower. This is called the spread, and the wider the spread, the more attractive the ARM. However, you have to beware of lenders who offer enticingly, yet artificially low rates, then bump them up after the first year.

Your ARM agreement sets forth the terms of the loan, and you should be sure your lender follows the agreement to the letter. This compliance normally includes adequately notifying you when rates are dropping as well as rising; maintaining a fixed spread between your rate and that of the financial instrument to which it's pegged, such as the T-bill; using the stated index when adjusting the rate; adhering to the agreed-upon date for adjusting the rate; and following the correct rounding

---

KEEP AN EYE ON YOUR VARIABLE RATE

Banks routinely make mistakes in calculating what borrowers must pay on their variable mortgages, according to economist Michael K. Evans. Bankers' most common errors:

1. Bank raises your interest rate by more than the limit stipulated in your mortgage agreement.

2. Bank does not lower your interest rate when relevant market instrument rate drops.

3. Bank alters the spread between the market instrument rate and your loan even though the agreement fixes the spread.

4. Bank ties your interest rate to the wrong market instrument, confusing for instance T-bills with T-notes.

5. Bank rounds up your interest rate to the nearest $\frac{1}{8}$ point. Over years, this rounding costs.

6. Bank computer miscalculates your monthly payments.

GQ

procedures, not just rounding *up*, but rounding to the closer figure.

While some ARMs are adjusted yearly, you can arrange for a "Three-One" rate. Your interest, instead of being adjusted after the first year, runs unchanged for another two years, so your first adjustment comes at three years. Then rates are adjusted yearly. Of course, you pay a slightly higher rate, maybe 0.75 percent, for this option.

A "convertible ARM" gives a borrower the option of turning an ARM loan into a fixed rate anytime between the second and fifth years. For this privilege, the borrower pays a higher rate than for a nonconvertible ARM.

You may encounter a kind of ARM called a "stable" loan, which combines features of an ARM and a fixed-rate mortgage. With this loan, a portion of the loan principal is borrowed at a fixed rate and a portion is adjustable. The borrower chooses the particular blend for the two rates —for example, 50/50 fixed and adjustable, or 75/25 fixed and adjustable. Which ARM you go for depends on your assessment of the direction and pace of interest rates, plus plans you may have for moving or staying, plus your per-sonal financial situation.

With any ARM, borrowers need to be alert. Financial experts and federal agencies have found that lenders make errors in calculating ARM rates in about 30 percent of the estimated 12 million outstanding ARMs.

GRADUATED-PAYMENT MORTGAGE (GPM): FOR THE YOUNG AND OPTIMISTIC

A graduated-payment mortgage is largely designed for the young and optimistic, allowing them to pay the lowest available rates in the early years of a mortgage, then assume heavier interest charges as their income improves. A GPM works in reverse order of a conventional loan: interest charges start low, then rise on an agreed timetable. Over the life of the mortgage, interest will be about one-half percentage point higher than a fixed rate. The lower-than-market entry rate of GPMs attracts many first-time buyers.

BALLOON MORTGAGES: MORE THAN HOT AIR

Balloon mortgages, which are fixed-rate, short-term loans with a kicker (or balloon) at the end of the period, are for people expecting to trade up into a more valuable home.

At the beginning of a balloon mortgage, rates are usually at least one-half point less than those for 30-year fixed loans. Balloons usually extend for five to seven years, at which time the entire amount is due—all principal and interest. The loan is either paid off entirely or the lender refinances. If a homeowner with a balloon mortgage decides not to sell and stay put, he's gambling on finding a new mortgage at a similar or lower rate. Some lenders will extend the financing at current rates, but others won't.

Balloon mortgages come in two sizes: "7/23" and "5/25." They offer a fixed rate for seven or five years, then if payments are up-to-date, an extension at the then current market rates for 23 or 25 years. However, if market rates are way above the original rate— more than 5 percent—the lender doesn't have to extend the loan at the original terms; you have to reapply and the loan must be rewritten.

People taking out balloon mortgages usually intend to sell the house and pay off the balloon while the low rate prevails.

Sounds like a clever scenario. But as investors have discovered, real estate often defies logical predictions. Real estate markets tumble with little warning and houses can't be sold. An owner may also find herself in a jam if interest rates rise quickly, making refinancing a costly venture. Worse trouble may crop up for someone on the verge of retirement whose balloon has come due but who can't qualify for a new, similar-sized mortgage because of lower income. For this reason, experts warn buyers on the edge of retirement to avoid balloons unless they have liquid assets available to pay them off if necessary.

REVERSE MORTGAGES

As the name says, these mortgages reverse the normal flow of money in a home loan. They're also called "home-equity conversion" mortgages. A lender makes periodic payments to a homeowner in amounts based on the house's value, prevailing interest rates, appreciation, and the owner's age. Aimed at homeowners in need of cash who don't want to move, reverse mortgages allow them to cash in their home's equity without selling or giving up the family homestead. It's a loan based on the value of a house that's eventually paid off in cash or with proceeds from selling the house, when the seller either moves or dies.

How many years a lender pays depends on the particulars of the mortgage. It may be a certain number of years, or until you move out, or as long as you're in the house and until you die. When the time comes, you pay off the loan, usually by selling the house; or should you die, your estate sells the house and pays the loan. You'll owe both the principal amount and the interest that's been charged during the life of the loan. (They're sometimes called "rising-debt" loans because the amount you owe increases as interest compounds.)

The money you receive from the lender may come to you for the rest of your life (called a "tenure reverse mortgage") or for a set time, typically between 5 and 20 years (a "term" reverse mortgage). Another possibility is a loan that's a line of credit, with the homeowner taking out money as needed. And lenders may combine offerings—a tenure or term mortgage plus a line of credit. The amount you receive depends on the equity in your home, your age, interest rates, and loan fees. The older the homeowner (thus fewer years for payments to be made) and the more valuable the home, the larger the cash advance.

Your reverse mortgage is secured by a lien on your property, so when your house is sold or transferred (such as given to children), the loan *must* be repaid. But the loan is a "nonrecourse" loan, meaning the lender has no other recourse than the home to obtain payment—no going after other assets or heirs.

Not all reverse mortgages are alike. Lenders differ in when they make payments, which may be monthly, intermittently through a line of credit, or all at once in a lump sum. They also differ in how long they pay (fixed term or as long as you're in the house). Some loans are available from commercial lenders, some through state or local government agencies.

Reverse mortgages through private lenders sometimes can be lender-insured. With a government-insured loan, the homeowner continues to receive payments if the lending institution defaults. The insurance also benefits the lender, for if a homeowner outlives the value of the loan, the

HOW A REVERSE MORTGAGE WORKS

Marion Goodfellow bought her home in 1952 for $12,000 and today it's worth $200,000. At age 78, she arranged for a reverse mortgage through the Connecticut Housing Finance Agency (a number of state and local agencies have home equity conversion programs). She will receive a payment every month for the next 10 years. In the first year, she will get $555 a month. This amount will increase 3 percent every year, bringing her last year's monthly payments to $724. If her home appreciates substantially during the 10 years, the payment period may be extended. Regardless, she is not required to make any repayment as long as she lives in her home.

Options for Elderly Homeowners, U.S. Department of Housing and Urban Development

government covers the continuing payments. Thus insured loans can run indefinitely. In contrast, uninsured loans last for a fixed number of years—they must be repaid on a date the homeowner and lender agree on. The advantage of uninsured loans is that they pay larger advances, impose fewer charges, and generally have no risk premium (see below). But they also raise the possibility of a homeowner having to repay the loan while trying to stay in the home.

Lender-insured reverse mortgages (or Federal Housing Administration–insured) pay as long as the borrower stays in the house. (What's insured is that you don't have to sell and move out until you want to.) Repayment isn't required until you die, or decide to sell and move. However, if you move out for twelve months, even if you plan to return, the lender can call the loan.

Like other kinds of home financing, reverse mortgages aren't free. In fact, they're quite expensive, and homeowners may end up paying fees equal to a third or even half of their home's value. These mortgages carry origination fees, application fees, closing costs, and interest charges. Although interest rates may rise (increasing what you owe the lender), you don't receive any more money. Also,

WHAT A REVERSE MORTGAGE PAYS

These are monthly payments to a single borrower with a lender-insured reverse mortgage:

Home Value	Age	Monthly Amount
$ 80,000	70	$ 272
	75	359
	80	467
	85	597
$100,000	70	$ 340
	75	450
	80	585
	85	747
$120,000	70	$ 409
	75	540
	80	703
	85	897
$140,000	70	$ 478
	75	631
	80	820
	85	1,046
$200,000	70	$ 684
	75	903
	80	1,174
	85	1,494

American Association of Retired Persons

transaction fees called "risk premiums" can add 2 to 7 percent of the loan, and they're either paid up front or financed.

Reverse mortgages are not for all homeowners. Younger homeowners, even people in their sixties, may receive relatively small checks compared with septuagenarians. Also, people who don't stay in their house for years will find the mortgages expensive. Since the hefty fees are charged up front, years are needed to make the loan worthwhile.

In addition, lenders eventually liquidate what is many people's last remaining valuable asset. And should the terms of the loan require an elderly homeowner to move, this can be traumatic and financially devastating. For many, reverse mortgages should be a last resort. In fact, recognizing the serious ramifications of a reverse mortgage, the government requires borrowers of FHA-insured money to first meet with a loan counselor to explore alternatives.

TRADING DOWN

Trading down—selling the family homestead for a more modest, less costly abode—has a long and honorable history. But trading is not the prerogative of only the about-to-retire. Anyone can trade down, and in certain circumstances it may be a smart move. However, don't make this decision on your own—talk to your accountant and real estate broker about the tax spins and other pertinent factors.

The success of trading down as an investment decision, as opposed to a lifestyle move, depends on timing. In itself, trading down simply nets you cash. And the gains from trading down can be enhanced if pending retirement isn't forcing you into selling and you have the luxury of timing your sale. With time on your side, you can be on the lookout for those periods when real estate values spike. But to avoid getting clipped by having to buy a smaller place during the same spike, you may have to rent for months, perhaps years, until prices ease off.

You can also use trading down to generate income. You act as your buyer's lender, letting him make monthly mortgage payments to you rather than a lending institution. Buyers often like this arrangement because sellers usually charge rates a tad lower than commercial lenders. The buyer secures relatively cheap money and

WHO'S INTERESTED?

"The strongest interest in reverse mortgages comes from 62-year-old married men. Yet the typical borrower is a 76-year-old single woman," reports The New York Times. *It goes on to say, "What this indicates is that many couples initially hope that income from a reverse mortgage will help finance an early retirement. In fact, because the monthly income is based on life expectancy, they quickly realize that tapping the equity so early is not a viable option because their loan advances will be too low."*

For more information on home equity conversion loans, write for a free copy of the AARP booklet Home Made Money, Consumer's Guide to Home Equity Conversion *and for a state-by-state list of lenders to:*

AARP Home Equity Information Center, 601 E Street, NW, Washington, DC 20049.

you earn a respectable return on your home equity.

If you do offer seller financing, insist on a reasonable down payment. A buyer in financial difficulty will be more reluctant to walk away from a purchase in which he's made a sizable investment. Furthermore, if the buyer does default and you take the house back, you want to cover your costs and any repairs.

It is most important to screen your buyer carefully to make sure he or she is financially qualified before agreeing to finance the sale. Check financial statements, tax returns, credit ratings, sources of income. Ask your accountant for a reading on them. Scrutinize this person as carefully as you would a potential business partner. You don't want the major headaches of a buyer who can't make monthly payments and continues to occupy your old home. Having to evict someone, then arranging to sell the place again, is more trouble than you ever want.

HOME EQUITY LOANS

Remember the second mortgages that people used to take out to add on a new kitchen or a second bedroom for the kids? Well, they're now called "home equity loans," and they're used not only for home improvements but also to start new business ventures and pay medical bills. Or to plump up a retirement fund.

The popularity of home equity loans has jumped since 1986, when Congress declared that tax deductions for most consumer loans were being phased out, with the notable exception of home equity loans. (Tax deductions, that is, for loans up to $100,000.)

A home equity loan can be either a lump sum payment or a line of credit that you tap into when you want. The maximum amount of the loan is generally figured at 75 percent of the assessed value of a home minus any existing mortgage. The lender may also factor in any other debts, income, and credit history. If you own a $175,000 home and have a $90,000 mortgage, your maximum home equity loan is $41,250, assuming you've no credit or income problems ($175,000 × .75 − $90,000 = $41,250).

If your home equity loan is a line of credit, it may run for a fixed number of years or be renewable after a certain period. Interest on these loans usually rises and falls in lockstep with the prime rate. Your rate won't be prime but a set number of percentage points over it and most likely it will have a cap over which it cannot rise. Lenders have been known to freeze lines of credit if interest rates rise above what they can charge. This is

Q I've owned my home for about 10 years, and it's now worth a lot more than I paid. When I retire, won't I be able to live off this equity?

A Yes, if the equity is enough (which is hard to tell now, not knowing what real estate values will be when you retire) and if you can afford to move. Given the uncertainties of home values, don't count on your home being your primary source of retirement money.

worth asking the lender about. Also find out how often rates can be adjusted—monthly? every six months? By and large, interest rates on home equity loans are a little lower than those on conventional loans because the default rate is so low for them.

Your home equity line of credit is typically available simply by writing a check using a checkbook supplied by the lender. Some lenders insist on a minimum amount for writing a check and, of course, the maximum is your total line of credit.

A home equity loan that pays a single sum usually charges fixed interest. You make regular payments just as you would for a conventional home mortgage.

The fees for a home equity loan are like those of other home-based financing plans: application fee, appraisal fee, up-front points, and closing costs (attorney fees, title search, insurance, recording, preparation, and filing). A credit line may also impose a small fee for each transaction. These fees aren't chicken feed, so you should be sure the sum you borrow justifies them.

There are a number of ways you can repay this loan: a varying monthly payment representing a fraction of the interest and principal; a varying monthly payment representing interest only, with principal repaid in a single payment at the end; or a set amount every month. This is negotiable among lenders, and it's worth shopping for the arrangement most suitable for you.

Your repayment timetable is usually broken into two phases: the active line-of-credit phase, which can run for years, and the second half, when you stop borrowing and start making serious repayments.

Think of home equity credit lines as a high-rolling cousin of credit cards, with the allure of access to a sizable amount of money, tax-deductible interest, and all the dangers of overuse and deep debt.

Avoiding a Home Equity Rip-Off

Home equity loans have become so popular and commonplace that they've spawned a rash of scams. Itinerant salesmen offering to repair roofs or foundations, lay new driveways, install satellite dishes, and perform other varieties of home improvements are duping homeowners into signing contracts that are home equity loans in disguise.

The rip-off works like this: A homeowner signs what he or she thinks is a regular contract but is really a loan application secured by his or her home for exorbitant interest rates. The bogus contractor makes a faint effort to do the construction or repair work (it often goes unfinished or is very substandard), then grabs the entire home equity loan or line of credit you unknowingly applied for and disappears. The homeowner is left with a shoddy repair job and a lender demanding payments on the home equity loan.

> *"Whether it's credit cards or other types of installment loans, people know they're there and they worry about it. A home equity loan is very convenient, but at the same time doesn't put the pressure on people. Then when you go to retire, the money's not there."*
>
> —*Wayne Chertow, financial planner, as quoted in the* Chicago Tribune

While this scam is just the latest ploy of the fly-by-night home contractor, the home equity loan spin makes it particularly menacing. If you think you've been duped into signing an unwanted home equity loan and less than three days have passed, you can cancel the agreement, call off the repair work, and receive all the money back. If more than three days have passed and you feel you are the victim of fraud or misrepresentation, talk to an attorney (legal experts associated with the National Consumer Law Center are familiar with home equity scams) and your state consumer affairs or attorney general's office.

MORTGAGE HELP FROM THE GOVERNMENT

Two government agencies—the Federal Housing Administration (FHA) and the Veterans Administration (VA)—offer mortgage help through commercial lenders. These mortgages are aimed at first-time buyers of modestly priced homes. The government doesn't actually lend money —home buyers apply to a commercial lender, and if they qualify, the government gives its guarantee to the lender that the loan will be repaid. The government's guarantee makes the mortgage a very-low-risk loan, and so the lender charges rates lower than those normally applied to mortgages.

Borrowers apply for a government-guaranteed loan through normal channels to an FHA- or VA-approved lender. To qualify for an FHA loan, a house has to be modestly priced for the area (valued at 95 percent of the median home value). The FHA tops reverse equity loans at a maximum $124,875. They require a small down payment and up-front loan origination and insurance fees.

For a VA loan, you need to be active in the military, a veteran, or an unmarried surviving spouse. This loan doesn't necessarily require a down payment and the charges are lower than conventional rates.

TESTING DISTANT WATERS: REAL ESTATE AWAY FROM HOME

TIMESHARING

As a real estate investment, timesharing has little to recommend it. Yet, it can play a small role in your retirement future if you use it to test an area where you might want to live full-time.

Timesharing involves purchasing a week or two every year at a vacation resort. You buy a piece of an apartment or home, usually furnished and situated in a resort community, and own the right to use it every year at a designated time. Frequently, the timeshare resort is affiliated with other such resorts and owners can trade their weeks for times at these other places. In short, a timeshare is a guaranteed vacation at the same place (or a similar one) and same time every year.

The cost of a timeshare of course varies with the resort, but on average shares run around $8,500 (plus annual maintenance fees). Much of this money, however, goes into sales and marketing overhead, not the value of the unit. One of the biggest problems with the timeshare as an investment is its poor turnover prospects. Timeshare units have a history of being hard to sell, and their values rarely reach, let alone exceed, the original purchase price.

Nevertheless, the well-publicized woes of the timeshare business and the surplus of units for sale has produced bargains for sharp shoppers. While timeshare properties are studded with land mines—title hassles, financially troubled developers, inadequate resort management, extra maintenance and upkeep expenses—they may be worth tiptoeing through for a place that gives you a low-cost, long-term look at a prospective retirement home. But forget it as an investment.

A SECOND HOME/RENTAL PROPERTY

A decisive, financially smart way to test distant waters is a second home. A second home is a practical route to discover whether that beach community or mountain village you love in August would make a pleasant place to live when you retire. Visitors tend to experience a place through the rose-colored glasses of vacation-time fun. But the community that lures you with balmy breezes in June may turn out to be inaccessible by automobile in December. Only by actually living there, even for a few weeks or months of the year, can you really get to know a place, warts and all. (Chapter 9 gives suggestions for finding and evaluating a retirement locale.)

The economics of buying a second home may also make it inviting. While you'll pay a slightly higher interest rate and larger down payment for your second property, especially if you plan to rent it out for a portion of the year, the mortgage interest can be tax-deductible. If you use the house more than 10 percent of the number of days it's rented plus 14, you can still write off your interest payments and real estate taxes. So, if you rent it for 90 days, you must live in the house at least 24 days in order to deduct the mortgage interest. (Here's the calculation: 10 percent of 90 = 9, plus 1 day. Then add 14.)

Living in your second home part-time and renting it at other times can be a very advantageous arrangement. The place can generate a positive cash flow, giving you income, and if you actively manage it, depreciation can shelter it from taxes (up to losses of $25,000 per year, assuming your annual adjusted gross income is under $100,000).

Don't count on the house making you rich, though. The real estate market is too quirky to promise rising values. Many people have been burned by the pipe dream of a valuable property tomorrow while paying onerous finance charges today.

Real estate experts say the best properties are those "handyman specials" that seem barely habitable. What looks like a bottomless sinkhole may cost less in repairs than originally thought, making its low sale price very attractive. For example, extreme foundation cracks, major roof holes, or even faulty electrical wiring can be fixed, depending on the house and where it is, for thousands of dollars less than expected. Admittedly this may be somewhat of a stretch, but many have done it successfully.

If you're thinking about buying a second home and rental property, weigh the investment factors first. Consider the cost of purchase, financing, and maintenance, and the potential income from renting it. Look for something you can actively manage (this doesn't mean you fix leaky faucets; finding a tenant and collecting the rent is sufficient) so you can get the full tax deduction. Anticipate rental headaches (finding a plumber to fix that leaky faucet) and realize that the quality of your tenants can make or break your investment.

RAW LAND

Who hasn't fantasized about buying a couple of acres in a favorite spot with dreams of someday building a home and retiring on the parcel?

It's a lovely fantasy—but watch out. As an investment, raw land has claimed multitudes of victims. Typically, investors misjudge the attractions of their few wooded acres or stretch of beach. The promised shopping center nearby never happens, the interstate over the hill is never built, and investors never recoup their purchase prices.

However, if you're buying with the sincere intention of eventually moving onto your property, first consider the ramifications. Are you prepared to be rooted to this one place during your retirement? What if you're working at a job, part-time or otherwise, somewhere else? What if you want to attend school somewhere else? What about traveling?

You may want to try out the area first by renting a home so you can assess the community, the amenities, the services, and even your prospects for finding work or starting a business. Renting will introduce you to the local real estate market—agents, lending institutions, appraisers—so you can fully understand land values and building costs. While the area may change by the time you want to move, knowing the local real estate climate may keep you from paying too much or buying the wrong parcel. If you're hoping to build a place, check out the zoning restrictions—a town with historic districts might restrict building.

LIFE INSURANCE: ANOTHER EGG IN YOUR RETIREMENT BASKET

The main purpose of life insurance, as you are probably aware, is to provide money to family and dependents when you die. That's the simple part. But life insurance has evolved to do far more than provide financial comfort for survivors.

Some people want their dollars to do more than just wait for the Grim Reaper. So their life insurance fund assumes the added function of an investment that can grow untouched by taxes. Thus life insurance wears two hats: It

Q I've been reading that there are lots of real estate foreclosures available because people can no longer afford the big mortgages. How do I find out about these places?

A Begin with the real estate section of your local newspaper for listings of auctions. Contact the Resolution Trust Corporation, the government agency that's handling all the failed S&L properties, for lists of homes in your region for sale (801 17th Street, NW, Suite 200, Washington, DC 20434; 202/416-4200). Also, find a real estate broker familiar with area banks that hold foreclosures.

delivers death benefits and acts like a tax-deferred investment.

Many consumers find the subject of life insurance unfathomably complicated. For good reason. The terms surrounding it are worthy of a Pentagon double-speak award. But the vocabulary is just the outer layer—the clothing, as it were. Underneath it all, life insurance offers death benefits, and frequently savings (investing, if you prefer).

TERM INSURANCE

Life insurance in the solitary role of providing only death benefits is called term insurance. You buy coverage for a certain number of years (a "term"). If you die while the insurance is in effect, the money is paid to whomever you designate. You can't tap into the money you've paid during the term and if you die after that, no one receives anything.

Contrary to what you may believe about insurance products, term insurance is clear and straightforward. Virtually every facet of term coverage is fixed and doesn't waver unless you change it. You decide how long coverage should last, whether one or many years; if you opt for a short time,

such as one year, you may well be able to renew it.

During your term, you pay premiums based on the amount of your coverage and the period you've signed up for. Typically, a health exam will be required for just the first year, but not if you renew. At renewal time, you may also have the choice of converting term coverage to another type. If you're over 50, "convertible term" is worth considering.

Term insurance is the least costly of all varieties of life insurance because it doesn't have a savings element. However, as you

LIFE INSURANCE FACTS

- More than 80 percent of the U.S. population has life insurance coverage.
- $74.3 billion is paid out every year on premiums.
- Every year 2.9 million people receive death benefits.
- Americans spend 5 percent of their disposable income on life insurance policies.

age, the premiums march upward. Some companies don't even offer term to people over 70, since by that time the premiums are inordinately expensive.

Monthly premiums will vary with insurance companies because they use different assumptions about mortality and expenses. If you want term coverage, it's worth shopping around for a policy. For instance, annual premiums for a 45-year-old man buying yearly renewable term insurance for $250,000 varies among 10 companies from $400 to $1,000. A 45-year-old woman paying for the same policy from the same companies encounters premiums from $350 to $900 (sorry, fellas, but women pay less because they live longer).

Term coverage is available through agents, the mail, and from "premium quote services." These services act as brokers between individuals and insurance companies, collecting premium rates from many carriers and selling policies to consumers over the phone, usually for a fee. If you want to sign up for one of the quoted policies, you can go through the quote service, which picks up the agent fee. Quote services focus mainly on price comparison, however,

and consumers should consider other factors, such as the quality of the company, when choosing an insurance company (more on this later).

"Slightly more than half of all full-time employees in medium and large private establishments . . . have employer-provided life insurance protection while working."

Monthly Labor Review

Term insurance is generally considered best for people in their twenties and thirties who have small children and want to protect their families from financial disaster. Figuring how much term insurance you need depends on a policyholder's income and dependents' needs, such a mortgage, debts, or looming college tuition payments. For people in their sixties whose children are grown and educated, mortgages are almost paid off, and retirement plans are in place, term coverage may not be the best choice.

The common wisdom for many years has been that term coverage

Q *I'm married, in my forties, and have a secure job in a hospital. My husband and I don't have any children and each of us makes a good wage. Do I need life insurance?*

A *True, life insurance is usually protection in case the main wage-earner dies and young children need support. But people also buy it to ensure payment of debts or funeral expenses, to leave an inheritance to a loved one, and for their own added peace of mind.*

is preferable to coverage that includes a savings plan. Consumer watchdogs have advised people who want a savings vehicle as well as death benefits to buy term and invest separately, pointing out that insurance policies as investments perform only so-so. For many

years, this was largely true. But today, consumers will find a number of insurance-plus-savings policies that perform admirably.

CASH-VALUE INSURANCE: A SAFETY NET WORTH SOMETHING

Insurance that promises not only to pay death benefits but to save or invest part of your premiums falls under the large umbrella of cash-value coverage. And since there are a slew of ways insurance companies can handle the cash portion of a policy, there are numerous types of policies. You've most likely heard the names: whole life, universal life, variable life, variable universal life.

The Whole Enchilada: Whole Life

Whole life, also known as straight life or permanent life, does what its name implies: it continues for your entire life. And because policyholders pay over a long, indefinite period, the policy takes on the additional role of savings account.

What complicates whole life for people is not the death benefits, but the savings part. The variations on whole life largely revolve around the rate at which this money accumulates and what happens to it. Policyholders have lots of choices as to the kind of return they want: Low but guaranteed? Market-sensitive and not guaranteed? (These choices also render these policies "participating." When the premiums and benefits are set, as with term coverage, it's called "nonparticipating.")

And there are choices to make about what happens to excess returns on your money: Does it go back to the policyholder as dividends? Does it go into the benefits coverage to increase it? Is it credited to premiums so they are reduced?

With traditional whole life, you sign up for a certain level of coverage and your premium is the same every year. As your premiums accumulate and compound, your policy develops a cash value, which you can withdraw as a loan, as well as a death-benefit value. According to an AARP survey, after 10 years of paying premiums on an ordinary whole life policy, each $1 paid contains $.65 cash value ($.71 for women). But in the policy's early years, it has little cash value because of commissions and expenses. Part of your premium goes for commissions and expenses; part for death insur-

ance coverage; and part into cash or savings.

When you buy a whole life policy, the agent will tell you the *projected* growth rate for the cash portion, although this figure is just an estimate, not a promise. Typically, there's a guaranteed minimum return (somewhere in the ballpark of 5 percent) with the possibility that the money may do better. Usually the growth rate is on a par with conservative, interest-sensitive returns, such as those

A BIT OF INSURANCE TRIVIA

The word "policy" comes from the Italian "polizza," meaning a written and folded document. Mediterranean traders in the Middle Ages insured their cargos, recording this insurance on long, folded papers. When the idea for insurance first appeared in England around 1720, the word "policy" came with it.

DID YOU KNOW?

The first life insurer in the United States was the Corporation for the Relief of Poor and Distressed Presbyterian Ministers and for the Poor and Distressed Widows and Children of Presbyterian Ministers, established in 1759.

from corporate bonds. An agent who suggests returns are better than prevailing money market rates may be pushing too hard for a sale. Remember that projected returns beyond the guarantees, called policy illustrations, are sales tools to help you understand how the policy works; they are not predictions for what you'll earn.

During the lifetime of your policy, you can borrow against its cash value for your retirement, to pay back loans, whatever. As the cash value of your policy grows, you decide how to apply the money. Your policy may pay dividends (earnings on your cash value plus insurance company earnings) that you can add to your

death benefits so that they increase. Alternatively, you can use the money to offset and reduce premium payments, or you can take a cash payment.

When you pay your premiums (monthly, bimonthly, annually, or one lump sum) and how your money grows (at a guaranteed rate, at interest-market rates, at stock-market rates) distinguish the types of whole life policies.

Modified life is whole life coverage with premiums that are not the same every year but are modified to be less in early years and larger later. *Limited payment* whole life offers coverage for an entire life but premium payments are made for a limited number of years. Since payments are made for only 15 or 20 years, instead of a lifetime, they are higher than with straight whole life. *Single premium* whole life consists of one large payment for complete coverage. People typically opt for this type of coverage when they have a lump sum to invest.

Universal Life: First in Flexibility

Universal life is cash-value insurance that offers a long menu of choices and flexibility. Opting for universal life is like fixing a meal from a buffet—a little of this, a little of that, and pretty soon you have dinner. You decide how much you want to pay, and adjust your selections accordingly.

With universal life, the policyholder decides on the size of the premiums, payment schedule, and size of death benefits. Once you set your targets, the carrier tells you how many years you must pay to reach them. Or, you can declare your payment schedule, death benefits, and how long you want to pay, and the carrier determines the size of premium needed to meet those goals. You can change the mix as you go along, adjusting the coverage level and how long it should be in force, the timetable for paying premiums, and the portion of your policy that goes toward cash value.

The returns on these policies are hard to figure. The cash value moves along the same path as interest-sensitive instruments such as money market funds, but a policyholder who varies premium payments may have a hard time plotting exactly how much the policy's earning.

Universal life's best feature is its flexibility—you're in the driver's seat in determining the premiums, payment schedule, and benefits. Furthermore, the cash portion accumulates tax-free and you may be able to borrow from it for a tax-free loan. But the price of that flexibility is uncertainty over

WHAT HAPPENS TO YOUR LIFE INSURANCE PREMIUMS

Here's where insurance companies invest policyholders' money:

Bonds (mostly high-grade bonds):	60%
Stocks:	5%
Commercial mortgages:	21%
Cash and short-term investments:	12%
Real estate:	2%

American Council on Life Insurance

how much your cash value grows and will be worth.

A spin-off of universal life is *excess interest whole life*. Its premiums and death benefits are set at fixed amounts while the cash value floats with rates similar to market-sensitive instruments. This float makes it something of a gamble on interest rates—if they go up, your cash earns a better return and you have excess earnings. However, if rates slide, your cash value is siphoned off to the insurance portion to maintain the level of coverage you want.

Variable Life Insurance: A Variety of Investments

Another major type of cash-plus-death-benefits insurance is called variable life, which has a heavy investment component. So much so that agents selling it must be registered representatives of a broker/dealer because the cash portion usually goes into mutual funds or securities.

With variable life, you decide where the cash portion is put—stocks, bonds, mutual funds, money-market instruments. As time goes by, you can switch funds and investments. If the investment does well, your cash value grows faster. Poor performance may mean you have to increase payments to maintain your coverage level.

> *"When the praying does no good, insurance does help."*
>
> —*Bertolt Brecht*

In arranging for variable life, you have two options for paying premiums. You can choose a fixed schedule of payments (monthly, quarterly, etc.) and a set amount; naturally, this kind of coverage is called *scheduled premium variable life*. Or, you can select a policy that allows you to vary when you pay and how much. And this is called—you guessed it—*flexible premium variable life*.

THE COST OF COVERAGE

There's no getting around it—insurance can take a noticeable bite from your monthly budget. This is especially true when you venture into the coverage-plus-savings policies because of the

IF YOU'RE TOTALLY CONFUSED

The insurance business has become so huge and labyrinthine that it has spawned an industry to help consumers find their way. These firms aren't selling insurance, they're selling information, usually for a fee. However, some also act as brokers and sell term insurance from an assortment of carriers.

- The Life Insurance Advisers Association (800/521-4578) is a group of insurance advisers who, for a flat fee, specialize in assessing coverage, premiums, and costs for individual policyholders.
- Insurance Information, Inc. (800/472-5800) provides price comparison information on term policies for $50.
- The National Insurance Consumer Organization (703/549-8050) is a membership organization ($30 per year) that provides information on all types of policies.
- SelectQuote Insurance Services (800/343-1985) evaluates existing policies and offers policy price comparisons. It also sells term insurance.
- The National Insurance Consumer Helpline (800/942-4242) is an industry-sponsored information service on life as well as other types of insurance.

added fees for managing the cash portion. That's the bad news. The good news is that insurance costs decline the longer you keep a policy. While the short-term policyholder will get clobbered by expenses, the long-hauler's burden gets lighter as years go by.

Price should not be the sole factor in your insurance decisions, but it will certainly play a key role. Insurance costs consist of sales charges and administrative expenses, including:

• Up-front sales commissions: On some policies, particularly whole life, commissions can range from 25 to 125 percent of the first year's premiums.

• Annual fees: Imposed to cover administrative, marketing, and sales costs. For example, on a universal life policy, fees may total 5 percent of annual premiums.

• Surrender fees (also known as a back-end load): Some policies charge a fee if you cancel before a certain number of years. The fee is taken from the cash value and can consume the entire amount if you cancel within the first year or two.

The total cost of your insurance can be confusing because some types of policies don't break the pieces out, or "unbundle" them as the trade puts it. By and large, fees are delineated in universal life policies but not whole life policies. Instead, payments are quoted as single sums, and how much of your premium goes toward commissions and expenses is a mystery.

One way to compare costs, even when they're not broken out, is through the interest-adjusted index number that represents the insurance company's calculation of the cost of a policy. Index num-

CELEBRITY LIFE INSURANCE

You've seen the ads on TV: Well-known celebrities selling "afford-able" life insurance to the over-55 crowd for only $6.95 a month and no health exam. Tempted by these endorsements? Think again.

The American Association of Retired Persons says about these ads: "If you buy a policy advertised on television for '$6.95' a month ($6.95 per thousand dollars of insurance a month), you'll pay almost $21,000 for a $25,000 policy over ten years time. But your cash value after ten years will be only $5,100. Compared to other ordinary life policies we reviewed, this insurance is not 'guaranteed affordable.' It's very expensive."

Life Insurance for Older Adults, American Association of Retired Persons

bers figure in commissions and expenses, as well as any reinvested dividends or earnings, and are standardized among all companies. The lower the index figure, the lower the costs.

But you can't put index numbers side-by-side for all companies and all policies. You must match up every policy variable—age and health of the policyholder; type of coverage and benefits, premiums, and riders. And while you're comparing policies, you might want to consider the issuing companies. Many experts prefer the large, solid national carriers with long histories of payouts.

Some carriers offer "no-load" or "low-load" policies with fees that are a fraction of full-commission policies. Insurance from these carriers is sold over the phone, not through agents. Expenses for low-load insurance run about 20 to 25 percent of total premiums, and for no-load expenses about 5 to 10 percent. The one drawback with these policies is that their carriers are generally small, somewhat new companies that have not been graded by the rating services. Consumers should be very cautious with new, unrated carriers.

ORNAMENTS ON YOUR POLICY: RIDERS

Riders are the extras on a life insurance policy that may either extend or limit the coverage and alter the cost. Different companies and policies offer an assortment of riders. Here are some of the possible riders you can attach to your policy:

• Accidental death benefit: Pays an added benefit if you die accidentally. This coverage is also called double indemnity.

• Automatic premium loan: Automatically makes a premium payment from the policy's cash value when the payment is overdue.

• Cost of living: Allows the policyholder to buy additional term insurance in line with cost-of-living increases.

• Guaranteed purchase: Promises you can buy additional insurance without a health exam. Usually this rider is offered to people under 40.

• Waiver of premium or insurance charges: Conditions for keeping a policy in force without paying premiums if a policyholder becomes totally and permanently disabled.

QUESTIONS YOU MAY HAVE ABOUT LIFE INSURANCE— WITH ANSWERS

Q. Does everybody need life insurance?

A. No. If you're single, have no kids or dependents, or will have an estate large enough to care for your survivors and pay its taxes, you don't need life insurance.

Q. How much life insurance do I need?

A. One rule of thumb pegs the amount at seven times your annual income. Insurance Information, Inc., an advisory service that monitors rates for term insurance, offers this formula for calculating the necessary coverage for a family's breadwinner:

1. Survivor's needed monthly income (pre-tax): $____
2. Survivor's available monthly income:
   Income from work $____
   Social security $____
   Pension benefits $____
   Other $____
3. Subtract total of number 2 from number 1. Result is survivor's monthly income goal. $____
4. Multiply number 3 by 12 for annual goal. $____
5. Divide by an assumed annual rate of return (e.g. 0.05). $____
6. Other financial obligations in today's dollars (these figures will vary, depending on when you will need the money):
   Children's education $____
   Estate $____
   Other $____
7. Add the total of number 6 and number 4 (goal in today's dollars). $____
8. Subtract assets that will contribute to goal:
   Other insurance coverage $____
   Pension fund $____
   Personal investments $____
   Other $____
9. Total is amount of life insurance needed for primary income earner. $____

Q. What are the ups and downs of switching a policy to another carrier?

A. There are more downs than ups. Moving your policy will bring another round of commissions and fees, and possibly a surrender penalty on your cash portion, especially if you jump ship within seven years of climbing on board. Switching is advised only in special situations: If the annual return on your money seriously lags behind like investments, such as corporate bonds or corporate bond mutual funds, or if your carrier is near the brink of insolvency.

Switching also takes time. It can be weeks before the paperwork has been transferred, so don't cash in your present policy until you've signed up a new carrier. If you do switch and the cash value of the original policy is more than what you've paid in premiums, avoid current taxes on the difference by executing an Internal Revenue Code Section 1035 exchange to transfer the money to the new carrier.

Q. How easy, and smart, is it to borrow from your life insurance policy?

A. Life insurance companies typically allow policyholders to borrow amounts equal to 90 to 92 percent of the cash value of their policy. (Since term insurance has no cash value, obviously you can't borrow from it.) Of course, you pay interest on this loan, and while you don't have to repay it, the amount will be subtracted from the policy's death benefits or cash value.

Q. What's an "Insurance Adviser?"

A. This is a new breed of insurance professional who provides policyholders with information and policy evaluations. Usually, the adviser is an independent consultant, although he or she can be the agent of a firm, who works for an hourly fee ($75 to $150) and assesses individual policies. Consumers confused by competing sales agents recommending various types of coverage may seek out an opinion from such an independent adviser. The adviser may also help you buy a policy, and choose the best options and riders. These insurance experts sell advice, not policies.

Q. What are the chances of my insurance company going belly-up?

A. Not likely, but not impossible. Since 1975, 170 life insurance companies have gone under, and

40 percent of these between 1989 and 1991. Most of these were small companies and represent a small fraction of the total insurance written by the approximately 1,600 life insurance companies in the United States.

Ratings companies (A.M. Best, Standard & Poor's, Moody's Investor Services, Duff & Phelps, and Weiss Research) scrutinize a carrier's holdings and its ability to sustain a drop in their value. A drop in a carrier's rating, even a seemingly small move from "A" to "B," may signal ill health.

Insurance experts advise consumers to stick with companies that have been in business at least 25 years, with a history of weathering hard times, have at least $3 billion in assets, and are licensed in New York State, which has the most stringent licensing requirements.

If an insurance company does become insolvent or state regulators believe failure is imminent and seize it in order to prevent runs, consumers have limited recourse. States have guarantee associations pledged to pay policyholders when a carrier that's either headquartered or licensed in the state becomes insolvent. State funds don't actually have the money on hand—when a carrier goes under, the healthy ones operating in the state pay into an assessment fund for the policyholders of the failed insurer.

State guarantee funds don't cover all losses. Payouts are usually limited to a percentage of a policyholder's claim (in California, it's 80 percent, for example) and are capped, typically at $100,000 or $300,000. Furthermore, some experts believe a state's fund would not cover the failure of a major insurer.

"I detest life-insurance agents: they always argue that I shall some day die, which is not so."

—Stephen Butler Leacock, Canadian economist and humorist

Q. What do I need to know about insurance agents?

A. Life insurance agents are licensed and regulated by individual states, not by the federal government. The closest to a national standard imposed on the industry are the educational requirements of the industry's trade school, The American College in Bryn Mawr,

WHAT ARE RATING SERVICES?

Rating services provide information to consumers over the phone or with a written report. Bear in mind that some ratings services charge an insurance company a substantial fee (in the $25,000 neighborhood) to obtain a rating and that some well-established, highly solvent insurance companies have not been rated. The raters examine a company's balance sheet—its assets, liabilities, income, and equity— for a sense of its solvency and ability to weather hard times. But the raters aren't foolproof; none of them flashed clear early warning signs when Mutual Benefit and Executive Life were drowning. The ratings companies:

- Standard & Poor's (212/208-1527). Provides free ratings for up to three insurers. Scale: AAA to CCC.
- A.M. Best. Ratings reports available at libraries. Will send written evaluations, "Best's Advance Company Report," for $15. Ratings by phone (900/420-0400) for $2.50 per minute. Scale: A+ to C−.
- Duff & Phelps. Ratings guides available at libraries or by phone (312/368-3157). Scale: AAA to D.
- Moody's. Ratings by phone (212/553-0377). Scale Aaa to C.
- Weiss Research. Ratings by phone for $15 per company (800/289-9222). Written ratings on individual annuity, life insurance, and brokerage companies. "Personal Safety Brief" available for $25 per company. Scale: A+ to F.

Pennsylvania. Salespeople who pass its courses and exams can use the designation CLU, "chartered life underwriter." Some agents also use the label ChFC, (char-tered financial consultant), which requires a slightly different course and set of exams also from The American College.

Though these tags guarantee

nothing, they are indications that an agent has experience and working knowledge of the field. Though writing life insurance policies is not brain surgery, it requires familiarity with complex financial calculations. So you want someone who can handle the technical aspects and who knows the pros and cons of all sorts of policies.

Probably the two most important qualities in a life insurance agent are candor and enough perspective to recognize when people don't need coverage. *Money* magazine reports that 75 percent of the people who buy insurance rely on just one agent's advice. If you talk to more than one, you'll most likely hear different recommendations about the kind of coverage you need. Consumers who know exactly the coverage they need can probably find a good agent through friends or coworkers. But if you're unsure, talk to at least a couple of agents. Be cautious and skeptical—agents are first and foremost salespeople, and may recommend coverage you don't need. Avoid agents you don't understand—don't be numbed by jargon.

An insurance agent either works for a single company, selling only its policies, or is indepen-

dent, offering policies from a number of carriers. While the agent for a single company may have fewer choices to offer, he or she often represents one of the large, established, safe carriers.

The issue of commissions will be part of your discussion with various agents, but it shouldn't obscure all other issues. It should be the litmus test for selecting an agent only when someone refuses to fully explain what portion of premium payments are siphoned off in commissions, expenses, and fees.

You may also encounter agents who offer discounts in the form of lower commissions or rebates on policies. Discounters may devise a "blended design" for a whole life policy, which charges a lower commission by either reducing premiums or putting more money into its savings component. Another discounting method, allowed only in Florida and California, is "commission rebating," with an agent actually returning to a policyholder 40 to 70 percent of the commission. Naturally, insurance companies don't like rebating, and may refuse to use agents who rebate. As a result, an agent who discounts may not offer coverage from the carrier you prefer.

LIFE INSURANCE TRUSTS

The very wealthy may not need life insurance because their estates contain more than enough to take care of dependents, funeral expenses, and unpaid debts. However, life insurance does have one feature that puts a glint in the wealthy individual's eye: its tax appeal. Death benefits are usually not subject to income tax. They do, of course, become part of a person's estate. If that estate is worth more than $600,000, then estate taxes kick in. However, by setting up a life insurance trust, a policyholder can deflect that hit.

The mechanics of a life insurance trust are relatively straightforward, while the results are somewhat serpentine. A life insurance policy is added to the assets of an irrevocable trust, which is untouchable and immovable. If the life insurance is purchased by the trust or existing policies are put into the irrevocable trust at least three years before the policyholder dies, the policy avoids estate taxes. In this way, a person can add to an estate without increasing the taxable portion. The downside is that the life insurance money is truly locked up; the cash value can't be withdrawn or borrowed against. So a life insurance trust is best left to someone wealthy enough to have no fears of a future cash shortage.

DISABILITY INCOME INSURANCE

Disability income insurance won't put any additional cash in your pocket like some kinds of life insurance, but it will stem the flow of money trickling out. In essence, disability income insurance is income protection. Though it may be costly, this insurance provides a safety net for all the other assets you have accumulated.

This net is essential for many. Insurance professionals say that one-third of all people between ages 30 and 65 will be disabled for at least three months sometime in their lives. Before arranging for disability income insurance, you need to assess other sources of income if you're not able to work. Does your employer provide any form of paid sick leave or disability coverage? (An estimated 70 percent of U.S. companies don't have this coverage.) Other possible sources include Social Security if you're out of work for

WHAT ARE THE CHANCES YOU'LL GET SICK?

In 1989 there were approximately 6.6 million job-related injuries and illnesses. The probability of a man between the ages of 20 and 60 becoming temporarily or permanently disabled is 19.1 percent; for women in the same age group, the probability is 15.3 percent.

Health Insurance Association of America

more than a year, or other types of coverage if you're a government employee. State worker's compensation may pay you if the disabling injury or illness is work-related. Personal savings and retirement plans can also fill the gap from lost income.

Find out how long this other money would last and what portion of your income it would cover; then aim for disability coverage that replaces 60 to 70 percent of your earnings. Remember, payments from disability insurance aren't taxed if you—not your employer—paid the premiums.

Disability policy payments can extend from one year to a lifetime. Policies come in three sizes: short-term for up to two years, long-term for at least five years and up to age 65, and lifelong. Most people need coverage only until age 65, when other kinds of income, such as Social Security, kick in.

In selecting a disability policy, pay special attention to the section that defines "disability." This definition is the heart of the policy, setting out the boundaries for coverage.

A policy with an "own occupation" definition will make payments if you can't perform your usual work, even though you may be able to do other types of work. So if a schoolteacher is disabled and can't stand in a classroom all day but can do desk work, "own occupation" coverage would pay. Another definition, the "any occupation" clause, would allow for payments only if the policyholder cannot do *any* work.

A "total and residual policy" pays for both partial and total disability, while a "total policy" covers only complete disability. Some policies cover only sickness or accidents; consider coverage for both.

Disability policies can also differ according to their terms for renewing, when benefits begin and how long they last, and premium levels. A policy that is "guaranteed renewable" can't drop policyholders regardless of what happens; however, the carrier *can* raise premiums for blocks of policyholders. On the other hand, "noncancelable" insurance means the carrier can't drop the coverage or raise the premiums.

The "elimination period" refers to how soon the insurer begins accruing liability for payments, which can be literally days following illness or injury, a year later, or longer. Most people opt for insurer liability to begin accruing in around 90 days. Clearly, the longer you wait to receive payments, the less you'll pay out in premiums.

Your premiums can be "level" or "rising" (known as a "step-rate") and a policy that is noncancelable will not raise premiums beyond the levels stated when issued. The amount of your premium will depend on the amount of income you're replacing and the particulars of your policy. To give you an idea of costs, a 45-year-old aiming for a $2,500 monthly benefit with a 90-day waiting period will pay annual premiums of around $1,200.

Disability policies can have pages of riders, which may include cost-of-living adjustments, renewability extensions, a waiver of premiums while the policyholder is disabled, an option to buy more coverage without a medical exam, as well as coverage for recurring disabilities.

THE ULTIMATE PIGGY BANK: ANNUITIES

Annuities are like a piggy bank that you feed regularly and can't get into unless you go to unusual lengths to shake money free, or break it. They're a kind of forced savings plan—you put money in periodically, or sometimes in a lump sum, the money grows, and years later (you decide when), the money flows back to you along with the interest it has earned. The earnings that it has accumulated over the years are not taxed until you take out the money, unlike other investments for which you owe taxes on gains even though you haven't withdrawn any money (remember zero coupon bonds?).

DID YOU KNOW?

"Annuity" comes from the Latin, "annus," meaning year, and originally meant a sum payable once a year. It now means a sum payable at regular intervals.

Although the annuity concept is simple enough, the term bewilders some people. In fact, the word "annuity" is considered so disconcerting that some investment professionals will go to great lengths to avoid using it. They'll describe a special kind of savings account or a unique long-term investment similar to a mutual fund or CD, when in fact they're talking about an annuity.

What distinguishes an annuity from other long-term savings is that your money is out of reach unless you want to sacrifice part of it. Once you decide where to save it, you may not be able to move it to another savings place, and if you insist on taking out your money and breaking the annuity, you may pay a heavy penalty to the IRS.

Annuities are popular because they force people to save, they provide a tax shelter for investment earnings, and they can give you a steady retirement income. With an annuity, you can arrange for payments that are dependable and predictable—a predetermined amount every year beginning at a certain age for the rest of your life.

They share some qualities with IRAs because the money grows tax-deferred and if you withdraw it before age 59½, you pay 10 percent penalty on the earnings. But annuities differ from an IRA in that there's no limit on how much you can put in every year and no tax deduction going in.

Given their attractions, it's not surprising that a host of companies sell annuities. They're sold not only by insurance companies, but also by mutual fund companies, brokerage firms, banks, thrifts, and financial service companies. (In truth, annuities are "manufactured" only by life insurance companies, but lots of other companies sell them.)

Not all annuities are alike, and their major differences center around these choices:

• How payments are invested: in fixed and guaranteed instruments or in variable investments.

• How payments are made: periodically (regular or irregular) or as one sum.

• When payments begin: immediately or deferred.

FIXED DEFERRED ANNUITIES

Fixed deferred annuities (also called guaranteed annuities) promise a certain rate of growth on your money, usually an amount competitive with current interest rates on bonds. But although your annuity is pledged to this investment scheme, the fixed rate is generally guaranteed for only one to three years. After that time, the annuity company renews the rate to reflect the current interest rate, which may be higher or lower than the original.

Obviously, annuity companies can't predict the future direction of interest rates. However, they usually have a track record of rates that gives investors a fairly good idea of how much the rate will move.

Besides a guaranteed rate, an annuity may have an interest rate floor, typically 1 percent below the rate you first received. If rates drop below that minimum, then you can take out the money without penalty or fees. This provision is known as a bailout clause.

However, there's a trade-off for this solid floor: policies with bailout provisions often pay less than those without. More to the point, a bailout clause may not protect you from sinking interest rates. If your annuity rate drops and you bail out, very possibly you won't find better rates anywhere else because they'll have dropped for all investments.

ANNUITY FACTS

• One in five Americans own annuities.

• The average age of an annuity buyer is 51.

• Americans bought about 3 million annuity contracts in 1990, and annuity sales for the year totaled $45 billion.

• The average initial deposit is $15,000 to $20,000.

• About 80 percent of annuities pay fixed returns.

• People typically begin withdrawing money from their annuities after eight years.

Q *I've been keeping some of my retirement money in CDs, but lately, every time they mature I have to buy one with a lower interest rate. Would I do better with an annuity?*

A *A fixed annuity is similar to a CD in that it pays a steady rate for a certain period, typically one to five years, then the issuer adjusts the rate. The advantage to an annuity is that your money grows tax-deferred; the downside is that it has expenses that CDs don't, and that are recouped only over the long term. If you're willing to lock it up, look at annuities.*

Guaranteed or fixed annuities are generally safer than other types of annuities. While their returns are usually less, your money is not likely to be eaten away by poor investments.

To make annuities more appealing, some companies tout returns much higher than prevailing rates. Investors should beware of a fixed annuity paying extraordinary rates. Often, dazzling rates indicate that annuity money is going into risky investments like junk bonds. Another possibility is that this so-called bonus yield is not as stunning as it looks. A fat yield today may translate into a below-market return later or a reduction in the return if you try to withdraw money before annuitization. Your best protection is to look at the insurance company's interest rate history on annuities sold five and ten years ago.

Yet a third variation on high rates that can evaporate is what's known as a "tiered rate." In this case, the annuity company dangles two levels of interest rates, one especially alluring. But if you grab the higher rate, you receive it only after your money has accumulated and you annuitize, receiving a rather ordinary return—the average of the two rates. That is, after years and years, and who knows what kind of interest rate gyrations.

Expenses and fees on a fixed deferred annuity are less than for variable types. There's no "asset management" fee for guaranteed annuities; expenses associated with managing the fund reduce the guaranteed interest rate return. However, some contracts may charge an annual administrative fee of $25 to $30, and you may be slapped with a surrender fee if you take out your money early.

THE RACY SIBLING: VARIABLE DEFERRED ANNUITIES

Fixed annuities offer safety and certainty—sometime years hence, your money will come back to you exactly as planned. The alternative to this type of annuity, one that makes no promises but raises the possibility of earnings far above guaranteed rates, is the variable annuity. In the world of annuities, admittedly relatively tame investments, deferred variables are as racy as they get.

As its name implies, a variable annuity allows you to invest in a variety of outlets—such as stock and bond funds—with no hard-and-fast rate of return. Your guaranteed pay-out is deferred until a future date (another type makes immediate payments—more about this later).

Variable deferred annuities behave more like an investment than insurance. Nonetheless, they are annuities: Dividends and capital gains build up tax-free until you withdraw them; early withdrawal brings down tax penalties and surrender charges; and in the end you can either take out a lump sum, receive a series of payments, or annuitize your investment to receive payments into the future.

If you're purchasing a variable annuity, say some investment professionals, put your money in a fund composed primarily of stocks rather than bonds or money market instruments. Using a variable to invest in sedate, steady growers like bonds may miss the point of a variable annuity: the prospect of robust growth.

Most variable annuities have a stock component. In fact, government regulators consider them a kind of security. Thus, they issue prospectuses and companies selling and managing them must be licensed broker/dealers. Variable annuities have another appealing quality: The managing investor or insurance company is not allowed to mingle the money with its general accounts, thus keeping it safe

HOW'S YOUR ANNUITY DOING?

Variable annuities, as their name promises, vary in their rates of growth. Many variable annuities hold an assortment of investment funds. So, comparing variable annuity performances is often an exercise in comparing apples and oranges. Nevertheless, this chart reflects the performances of types of variable annuity investment funds for one year and five years through October 1991.

Stock Funds	1 Year	5 Years
Capital appreciation	+43%	+64%
Stock	+37%	+69%
Small-company growth	+75%	+101%
Growth and income	+32%	+75%
Equity income	+31%	+53%
Global	+9%	N.A.*
International	+5%	N.A.*
Flexible	+24%	+57%
Income	+28%	+51%
Fixed-Income Funds		
Money-market	+5%	+35%
U.S. Government	+14%	+43%
Corporate bonds A	+15%	+47%
Corporate bonds BBB	+14%	+42%
General bond	+15%	+27%
High current yield	+34%	+41%
World income	+9%	N.A.*

*N.A.: Not available. Fund established less than five years. Lipper Analytical Services, Inc.

from troubled accounts.

When you purchase a variable annuity, you put your money in a particular fund, just as you would with a mutual fund. You can go into a fund dedicated to aggressive growth, long-term growth, growth and income, or even funds with more specialized focuses, such as a specific industry or area of the world. You may be able to move your investment between funds managed by the same company. However, if you want to roll it into a brand-new annuity and haven't held it beyond the surrender charge period, it may cost you. Regardless of where you stash your money, it will grow undeterred by taxes until you take it out.

The expenses and fees associated with a variable annuity are similar to those of a mutual fund. You are subject to an annual maintenance fee (usually around $30) and an annual asset-management fee (usually a percentage between 0.5 percent and 1.5 percent of your holdings). Alas, there's more: an annual assessment to the fund for "mortality and expense" risk, which covers company expenses, should you outlive your annuity payments. This assessment is normally around 1 to 1.5 percent of the fund.

Also, chances are good that the annuity charges a "surrender fee" in the event you have to take your money out early. Surrender fees (also called a "back-end load" or "deferred sales charge") generally run 5 to 10 percent and disappear after five to 10 years. However, some deferred sales charges run over 10 years, regardless of whether you stay in that long.

The bottom line? Fees for variable annuities typically run higher than those for mutual funds. For example, average annual fees for a general stock mutual fund are 0.82 percent, versus 1.13 percent for a variable annuity in a general stock fund. The comparison becomes somewhat complex, however, because mutual funds charge fees up front while annuity charges run toward the back end. Nevertheless, the best way to justify the annuity fees is to be prepared to hold your annuity for at least 10 to 15 years.

VARIATIONS ON A THEME

Annuities are arranged in a variety of configurations, with an assortment of offshoots from the basic two shapes, fixed and variable. Here's a tour down the annuity side roads.

Single Premium Deferred Annuity (SPDA)

You make one sizable payment instead of regular premium payments, and receive the payout years hence, but not before age 59½. The minimum required is usually around $5,000 and there's no limit on how much you can stash away. During the investment period, your money earns a fixed return, which piles up tax-free.

After you reach your magic age, you decide how you want to receive your annuity money. You have three choices: You can take it back in a lump sum and put it into another SPDA or a totally different investment. Or, you can take it in periodic payments. Or, you can "annuitize," that is, receive equal-sized payments until you die. The annuity company will calculate this for you based on your life expectancy (no, it doesn't have any divine knowledge, just a detailed set of actuarial tables).

Flexible Premium Deferred Annuities

This annuity flexes where many people want it most: in the premium payments. You have the freedom, with certain limitations, to skip a month's payment or to vary the amount you contribute every year. Often these annuities have a "stop and go" feature, allowing you to stop paying for a couple of years, after which time you reactivate the policy.

A Word About "Annuitization"

All deferred annuities allow you (no, encourage you) to tuck away your money for years and not think about it until the day comes when it's due to be paid back. At this time, you'll be offered a choice: take the money all at once or in periodic payments. This latter process is called "annuitization."

If you decide to annuitize, the insurance company pledges to pay you every year for a certain period. This might be a set number of years or for your, and your spouse's, lifetime. You work out with the annuity company, depending on the size of your policy and certain actuarial facts of life, how long your money will run. An important point to remember about annuitization is that you can stretch out paying taxes as you receive the earnings. With a lump sum, taxes are due pronto.

Instant Gratification:
Immediate Annuities

A whole other class of annuities pays off immediately; they're more like a regular paycheck than a long-term investment. Immediate annuities are often used by people who have received a lump sum—for instance, from a retirement plan like a 401(k) or a deferred annuity—and want to convert the sum into income for the rest of their life.

The basic features of an immediate annuity are standard: your lump sum is paid back to you in regular installments for a certain period. The size of your monthly check depends on your age, gender, how much you put in, and whether payments stop when you die, continue for a number of years, or go until a beneficiary dies. Monthly payments are usually not adjusted for inflation, an important consideration if you're looking 20 years ahead.

While the features are standard, immediate annuities differ among their issuers. Companies don't pay the same amount, even given identical circumstances, so this is where shopping can improve your payout. Companies vary in their calculations for individual life-times and return on investments, so their estimates for payments traverse a large map. A sampling of insurance companies offering a 55-year-old woman a $100,000 immediate annuity with monthly payments for life range from $611 to $766; for a 55-year-old man the same policy payments can run from $609 to $832. Stretch these payments over decades and they span many thousands. If you're built for longevity, you'll get your money back and much more; but if you die next year, your lump sum can disappear. The amount paid on an immediate annuity will vary greatly with the level of interest rates. You will get more when rates are high and less when rates are low (the amount is fixed for life).

You can purchase a lifetime plan for yourself and someone else (spouse, longtime friend). Called a "joint-and-survivor" plan, it pays until both you and the beneficiary die. When one of the policyholders dies, payments can be lowered to a percentage (e.g., 66.6 percent, a "joint-and-two-thirds survivor") of the original monthly checks.

Another variation is the "installment refund" policy. If you die early, this promises to pay your original investment to your beneficiary. A further refinement of this arrangement is the "cash refund" policy—if you die early, your beneficiary receives in a lump sum the balance of your payments.

Clearly, lifetime annuities are something of a crap shoot, with long-lived policyholders purchasing a goose that lays golden eggs. For this very reason, annuity companies have devised alternative plans.

The lifetime-only plan (also known as "straight life") pays until you die, whether that's tomorrow or in 20 years. The fickleness of the payment period (and life!) enables companies to offer the highest monthly payments for these types of annuities (not the joint-and-survivor variety). They're typically purchased by people who need immediate income and have no dependents or desire for an estate.

A variation on this plan is the "life-and-certain" policy, which promises to pay for life and a minimum number of years (e.g., 10, 15, or 20). If a policyholder dies before the certain period has lapsed, then payments are made to a beneficiary to the end of that time. The guaranteed "certain" period means that these policies tend to pay less than a lifetime plan.

SOURCES FOR LEARNING MORE ABOUT ANNUITIES

- *Annuity & Life Insurance Shopper* (United States Annuities, Englishtown, NJ; 800/872-6684). Quarterly newsletter with rates of different types of policies. $20 per issue or $45 per year.
- *Individual Investor's Guide to Low-Load Insurance Products* (Glen Daily, International Publishing, $22.95).
- *Comparative Annuity Reports* (Carmichael, CA; 916/487-7863). Monthly newsletter that ranks annuities according to interest rates and surrender penalties. $12 per report.
- *Variable Annuity Research and Data Service Report* (Miami, FL; 305/252-4600). Monthly newsletter. $49 per month or $698 per year.

ANOTHER HYBRID:
THE REAL ESTATE ANNUITY

A species of variable annuities is one that invests in real estate. These real estate investments may be in the form of REITs, real estate stock, or a portfolio of actual properties. As a real estate investment, this annuity shares the market's ups and downs, and its sticky liquidity. It may pay off better as an investment than as a retirement vehicle.

A WORD OF CAUTION

The life insurance debacle of the early 1990s has also tainted the annuity industry. Heart-wrenching accounts of retirees who scrimped and paid into deferred annuities only to find their life savings gone with the wind, and with junk bonds, are a reminder that caution counts. When you buy an annuity, you're signing up for a long-term relationship, and you need to know that your partner will be there to the end.

Annuities, unlike accounts at banks or savings and loans, are not federally insured. Money lost is not readily recouped. (States have guarantee funds, but they pay off only in bankruptcies and usually only up to $100,000. If a state seizes a troubled insurance company to prevent a run on its accounts, annuitants can be left empty-handed.) So care and caution in choosing which company to team up with are essential. At the very least, your would-be partner should have these qualities:

- A long record (at least five years) of payments.
- Top ratings (As) from at least three independent rating services.
- Rates of return competitive with the general market, not unusually high rates that declare, "desperately seeking customers."

Chapter 5

PLANNING FOR SOCIAL SECURITY AND MEDICARE

Whether you're among the 134 million people currently paying Social Security taxes or one of the 40 million now receiving benefits, the Social Security system may well touch your life more than any other government program.

How Social Security will affect your retirement life varies. For some, the average annual benefit of $7,548 for retired workers ($12,792 for retired couples with one earner) can be the difference between living in poverty and achieving a modest level of comfort. For those with personal savings, investments, insurance, and pension income, Social Security's monthly check may be icing on the cake. Maybe it will help pay for that freewheeling summer of travel or perhaps it will give you extra cash to help a grandchild with college bills.

However you plan to spend your government retirement funds, don't make the mistake of counting on Social Security to finance your way to a better life.

AUSPICIOUS BEGINNINGS

The very first American to ever receive Social Security pension payments was a law clerk in Vermont, Ida May Fuller, who retired in 1940. (The Social Security law was passed in 1935 and the first FICA taxes taken in 1937.) Her first check was for $22.54. Ida Mae, who had paid but $22 into the system before she stopped working, lived to be over 100. All in all, she tucked away about 420 monthly government pension checks, racking up $22,000 in benefits.

Many working Americans nearing retirement believe Social Security will be their *primary* income source once they no longer work. That's a mistake. Social Security is intended as a floor of retirement income, not the whole structure. The average retiree needs an income equal to 60 to 80 percent of annual working salary to maintain the same lifestyle, and Social Security doesn't come near to filling that bill. For the average American, the benefit equals 42 percent of income, and for those in upper income brackets, the portion covered by Uncle Sam's insurance is 27 percent or even less.

But whether it buys bread and butter or a week abroad, Social Security's annual contribution to your retirement well-being is a benefit you've earned. All your working life you paid into the system and once you retire you get to reap the rewards.

HOW DOES SOCIAL SECURITY WORK?

You pay taxes into the system during your working years, whether you want to or not, so that you and members of your family can receive monthly benefits once you retire or become disabled. And there is the added protection of survivors benefits: Should you die, your spouse and other dependents can collect benefits, too. Since its inception in 1940, Social Security's main goal has been to provide a "basic" level of financial support and health care for the elderly, workers with disabilities, the surviving dependents of deceased workers, and the elderly poor.

To do that, Social Security is broken into three main parts: Old Age and Survivors Insurance, Disability Insurance, and Medicare.

If you're working and are not self-employed, both you and your employer pay taxes to fund the three main sections of Social Security. You've seen that big tax bite on your W-2 form that says FICA? That stands for Federal Insurance Contributions Act and it goes to Social Security and Medicare. The current tax amounts to 7.65 percent taken out of your gross salary. Your employer pays the same amount, 7.65 percent, to cover his share of your retirement obligation. FICA taxes are "capped," meaning you and your employer do not have to pay on income that exceeds a certain

---

"Social Security was never envisioned as the only benefit a family would get upon retirement. Social Security needs to be viewed as one leg of a three-legged stool. People facing retirement should be looking not only to Social Security, but to a pension and to savings."

—*Gwendolyn S. King, former commissioner, Social Security Administration*

Q I plan to travel a lot when I retire, to places like Asia and South America. Will I still get my Social Security check when I'm away?

A Your travels won't affect your benefits, but there are some countries (Albania, Cuba, North Korea, for instance) where Social Security won't send checks. Notify SSA of any trips lasting more than 30 days, and it will tell you how to arrange to receive benefits while you're abroad.

WHO'S UNCOVERED . . .

Contrary to popular belief, not everyone gets Social Security. There are a few working citizens covered by other government plans who won't ever see that green monthly check from the Social Security Administration. Federal workers covered by the Civil Service Retirement System, about 20 percent of state and local government employees, and most railroad workers come under a different pension umbrella.

Social Security Administration

limit. In 1993, Social Security's limit is $57,600. Medicare takes an extra nibble in the form of a 1.45 percent tax on both you and your employer of anything you make over $57,600 (in 1993) and up to $135,000.

If you're self-employed, the burden of paying the entire 15.3 percent Social Security tax on the first $57,600 you earn is on your shoulders. That means you must send the money to the government on time, as well as handle the paperwork to make sure your FICA payments are credited in a proper fashion to your Social Security account. The self-employed also pay the entire 2.9 percent Medicare tax on all income between $57,600 and $135,000.

HOW MUCH CAN I EXPECT TO RECEIVE?

In the past, finding out what your future benefit might be was tricky and often inaccurate. But now the Social Security Administration can easily give you a personalized benefit estimate. All you have to do is call (toll-free) 800/772-1213 and request a Personal Earnings and Benefit Estimate Statement (PEBES), otherwise known as Form SSA 7004. The form will ask you to fill in last year's actual earnings, this year's estimated earnings, and when you expect to retire.

You also have to guess at your future earnings. Be conservative. You may be hoping your income will skyrocket in the next ten years, but don't be unrealistic or your estimated benefit may be way off the mark. Once you return the form, Social Security will mail back your work history and estimates of how much you will receive if you retire at 62, 65, or hold off until you are 70. (You can also get disability estimates or information about survivors benefits.) Gathering this information usually takes about six weeks.

REVIEWING YOUR SOCIAL SECURITY RECORD

Whether you're 35 or 55, it's a good idea to find out how much money you can expect to get from the U.S. Government once you retire. Many experts suggest you review your record every three years, although realistically most Americans do it only once or twice in a lifetime. For retirement planning purposes, it's essential to have some idea of just how much Social Security will contribute to your post-working-world lifestyle.

THE BENEFIT FORMULA

Your benefits are based on your earnings averaged over most of your working career. Social Security averages your income over your 35 highest-earning years (if you have more than 35 years, low

---

OLDER, WISER . . . AND RICHER

As a group, older people are at the top of America's wealth distribution chain, making up 20 percent of the population but owning 40 percent of the wealth. Most own their homes, many outright. In the last 30 years, the median income for families headed by someone 65 and older has risen faster than any other age group. Thanks in large part to Social Security, less than 11 percent of the elderly live below the official poverty line.

---

years are discarded; if fewer than 35 years, zero-earning years are averaged in). Then a complicated formula is applied that determines whether you will be closer to the low end of the benefits barrel ($529 per month in 1993) or the top ($1,128).

To qualify for Social Security, the rule of thumb is that you need to have been working for ten years. When you work and pay Social Security taxes, you earn Social Security credits; most people earn four a year. The vast majority of citizens (those born after 1929) need 40 credits to be eligible. You don't have to have worked ten consecutive years; working Moms who have taken a few years off to raise children can qualify as long as they have at least 40 credits.

WHAT A DEAL

"Many a worker imagines that he or she would be better off without compulsory Social Security taxes. But it takes a lot of money to guarantee yourself a monthly income for the rest of your life—especially one that rises with the inflation rate."

—Jane Bryant Quinn, as quoted in the Washington Post

The table on the next page gives some idea of the range in which your benefit will fall. The figures are based on the assumption that you have and will continue to work steadily and receive pay raises in line with the U.S. average throughout your working career.

Generally, if you're in the top 10 percent of American wage earners during most of your life, you can count on the higher monthly figure. Conversely, if you toiled most of your working life in low-wage jobs, the minimum figure is closer to what you will receive. Remember, these figures are in constant 1993 dollars. Of course the actual amounts you will receive may be much higher, due to cost-of-living increases.

MISTAKES CAN BE COSTLY

Keeping track of the entire work history of some 200 million Americans is no mean feat and the Social Security Administration does a fairly good job. But mistakes are made. The General Accounting Office, Congress's watchdog agency, says that nearly ten million workers have not had all of their earnings credited to their retirement accounts. The mistakes cost an average $204 a year in lost retirement benefits, says the GAO. But the impact on you may be much greater if SSA

MONTHLY BENEFITS BASED ON YOUR PRESENT ANNUAL EARNINGS

Your Age in 1993	Present Earnings				
	$12,000	$20,000	$30,000	$42,000	$57,600
65	$529	$728	$970	$1,066	$1,128
64	522	718	956	1,053	1,118
63	526	723	965	1,066	1,136
62	529	727	970	1,076	1,152
61	530	729	973	1,082	1,163
55*	528	728	977	1,102	1,215
50	502	692	930	1,062	1,195
45	505	698	939	1,074	1,233
40	509	703	943	1,080	1,255
35	488	675	902	1,034	1,205
30	478	663	883	1,013	1,182

*The figures start dropping for those who are 55 in 1993 because the day when retirement benefits are paid in full begins to rise for this age group, this making the payout at 65 slightly less.

Reprinted with permission of William M. Mercer, Inc.

inadvertently fails to record some of your top earning years.

Usually the mistake is a clerical one. Incorrect reporting by employers and errors by data clerks in the Social Security Administration account for the bulk of the foul-ups. But simple things, such as an unreported name change be-cause of marriage, can cause a snag. Even if you are diligent about reporting name changes or mistakes you catch along the way, glitches can occur.

For example, married women who kept their surname and are self-employed but file income taxes jointly with their husbands

TODAY'S RETIREES GET BACK EVERYTHING THEY PUT IN, AND MORE

Jack and Jill retired in January of 1981. Jack had been contributing to Social Security from the time of his first job in 1937 until he quit working 44 years later. His jobs paid average wages. Jill raised the kids and didn't work outside the home. She gets spousal benefits and Medicare, too.

How long does it take for Jack and Jill to be paid back every penny, including interest, that Jack contributed to the system?

Answer: *Three years and six months.*

National Taxpayers Union Foundation Chartbook

should be doubly sure to check their earnings record. In the late 1980s, FICA payments made by many women in this category slipped through a rather large crack in the Internal Revenue Service's computer program. They may not have gotten credit for FICA taxes they paid.

Once you receive a breakdown

DON'T TOSS THOSE FILES

Pack rats, you get the last laugh. If keeping every income tax return or W-2 form for the last two decades has made you the butt of family jokes, your time has come. Detailed financial records of your working life will make it easy to double-check your income history against the one maintained by Social Security. Since the size of your retirement check depends on how much you made during your working life, maintaining an accurate record is nothing to laugh about. Everyone else will have to rely on memory. Can't you just hear it now: "Gee, I'm sure I made more than that during that summer job in Alaska in 1958 . . ."

of your earnings from Social Security, check the record against anything you can: old W-2 forms, income tax returns, pay stubs. Self-employed people must have both tax returns and canceled checks to verify taxes they paid. If you think there's a problem, call the number on the form. If you still haven't resolved the matter, there's an appeals process, which can go all the way to court if you want to push it that far. (Fact Sheet No. 05-10041, available from SSA, explains your rights on appeal. If you don't want to deal

THE DREAM TICKET

The annual average benefit check for a retired man has risen from less than $30 in 1940 to more than $9,500 today. Given normal inflation for the next half century, and assuming you work in a high-paying job, your annual Social Security income could be as high as $60,843 if you retire in the year 2020.

Sounds like a bundle, but remember, it will buy what $19,608 will buy today. And who knows if benefit levels will remain as generous three decades hence. But don't let that stop you from dreaming . . .

	Average Annual Benefit	
Retirement Year	Current Dollars	1992 Dollars
2000	$ 19,324	$14,285
2010	35,963	17,268
2020	60,843	19,608
2030	104,026	21,920
2040	170,992	24,321
2050	281,218	27,044

1992 Annual Report of the Board of Trustees of the Federal Old-Age and Survivors Insurance Trust Fund

SOCIAL SECURITY FACTS

Beneficiaries, retired workers . . . . 24.1 million

Average monthly benefits, retired worker $567

Estimated average earnings $21,597

Elderly receiving benefits . . . . 92 percent

Fast Facts & Figures About Social Security, U.S. Department of Health and Human Services, Social Security Administration, 1990

Q When Ross Perot was running for President, he talked about getting wealthy individuals to refuse their Social Security benefits. Doesn't everybody have to take benefits by the time they're 70?

A To receive benefits at any age after 62, you have to apply. You can choose never to apply and, in effect, let the government keep the money.

over the phone or through the mail, you may visit a Social Security regional office—see the appendix—for assistance and information.)

GO EARLY OR STAY LATE?

The biggest decision you'll have to make regarding Social Security is whether to retire early, at age 62, and start drawing reduced benefits. Or should you wait to age 65, when you will receive the "full" retirement amount? Or what about putting off Social Security until age 70, when your credits rise to the maximum allotted? Every year you delay receiving benefits, the bigger they get.

If you retire at age 62, you'll have a smaller monthly benefit for the rest of your life. That's in part because you will probably have lower earnings than if you continued working but also because Social Security reduces the payout to reflect the fact that you will be drawing benefits for more years. The benefit is generally trimmed by about 20 percent. If you wait until age 63½, your monthly check will be cut about 10 percent.

Ironically, the lower payout doesn't discourage most people from taking advantage of the opportunity to get out while the getting is good. About 60 percent of retirees begin payments when they hit the magic 62-year mark.

Why begin early? For some people, health has a lot to do with it. Elderly Americans who are in ill health or simply tired of working may want to move on to the next phase of their life as quickly as possible rather than wait for a higher monthly income from Social Security. Then there are retirees who have planned for their post-work world. For them, Social Security is a supplement to their retirement income and the 20 percent loss in benefits won't hurt them over the long haul.

Social Security offers a hefty inducement to workers to delay retirement, though few actually do.

Q I'm a captain in the Navy and I'm wondering if all my compensation—pay, benefits, even my uniform —is counted for Social Security credits.

A Members of the military are covered by Social Security and receive additional credits ($100 for every $300 earned) for the value of housing, food, and clothing they receive. However, you get no extra credits if you have been in the service less than two years.

If you wait until after your so-called Normal Retirement Age (NRA) of 65 to claim your benefits, they will be increased by a percentage regardless of your earnings. If you turned 65 in 1993, for example, you will receive a 4 percent annual increase in your

DON'T WORRY ABOUT THE EARNINGS LIMITATION IF YOU WIN THE LOTTERY

Fortunately, not all your possible sources of cash will count toward the earnings limitation. You can win the lottery, be given an expensive china collection from Aunt Mary's estate, or even have rental income, and it won't affect your Social Security benefits. Also outside the earnings limitation are: gifts or inheritances, investment income, interest, annuities, capital gains, income from trust funds, moving or travel reimbursements, and some sick pay paid by your employer. Even jury duty pay is off-limits.

Social Security benefits every year you delay your claim. For citizens born after 1942, the increase is even bigger: 8 percent per year.

When you reach age 70, Social Security stops counting credits toward your benefits. You've reached the top. Even if you continue to work, pay FICA taxes, and opt not to apply for benefits, you'll receive no more at age 75, for example, than you would have five years earlier.

From a "total benefits received" point of view, unless you are still working and would lose a major portion of your Social Security benefits, you should start taking them as soon as you can. Only 15 or 20 years later will you

know for sure if you made the right decision. High inflation or a very long life expectancy are two of the main reasons for delay—but who can accurately predict either of these in advance? It takes a long time to make up for the benefits not received between 62 and 65.

WAITING FOR NORMAL RETIREMENT AGE

Americans are living so much longer after retirement than they once did that Social Security is boosting its age levels to cut down on the number of retirement years it has to finance. The metaphorical "average" 65-year-old woman, for example, will live to the ripe old age of 83. Men get a little less time, statistically speaking, but will still make it to 79 on average.

So, to catch up with today's longer life expectancies, Social Security will begin an incremental increase in its definition of normal retirement age, starting in the year 2000. The change will affect everyone born after 1938. Under the current plan, if you were born in the 1960s and beyond, you won't receive "full" benefits until you are 67 (see table, page 246). Of course, it's possible that by the time you're ready to move onto Easy Street, the age level may be even higher. There is another consideration for younger workers: You will still be able to start your government retirement pension at age 62, but the benefit will eventually be reduced to 70 percent, instead of the current 80 percent, as the full retirement age rises.

LIMITS ON WHAT YOU EARN

If you decide to keep working past 62 or 65, it may make sense to wait before you start to collect Social Security benefits. That's because if you earn more than a rather tight limit set by the government ($7,680 for those under 65 in 1992 or $10,560 for those between 65 and 69), the government will cut your benefits. If you are under age 65, your benefits will be reduced by $1 for every $2 you earn over the limit. For those over 65, the cut is $1 for every $3 over. Thus, if you're making a comfortable $75,000 at age 62, or 65 for that matter, the earnings limitation will reduce your benefits by one-third.

Of course a retiree earning an extra $15,000 a year selling homegrown herbs and vegetables from the family farm faces a challenge in figuring out whether the extra income is worth the reduction in benefits. Furthermore, if you go over the earnings cap, your spouse's benefits will be pared down, too. And keep in mind that most Social Security benefits are free from state and federal income tax (and more FICA taxes), whereas earned income is not.

WHAT COUNTS AS INCOME

What constitutes income under the earnings limitation test is narrowly defined. For the most part, it means money you make from either self-employment or

WHEN THE GOING GETS GOOD

Tom Jones, who will be 56 in 1993, wants to retire when he turns 62. But he's worried about the size of the monthly benefit and is wondering if he shouldn't hang on until 65, or even 70. The table below, which compares maximum benefits in constant dollars (that is, assuming no inflation and no increase in Tom's wage) provides a guide. The table also assumes Tom was employed continuously from the time he was 22 years old and that there was no increase in his average wage, or in the CPI. Tom can expect a payout of $948 per month in 1999. If he waits until 2002, he'll receive $1,218. If he doesn't draw benefits until age 70, it's $1,684.

AGE YOU RETIRE/AMOUNT YOU RECEIVE			
Retirement Year	62	65	70
1993	$ 893	$1,128	$1,289
1994	902	1,118	1,324
1995	912	1,135	1,395
1996	920	1,151	1,384
1997	929	1,163	1,439
1998	939	1,174	1,440
1999	948	1,185	1,448
2000	946	1,196	1,464
2001	945	1,207	1,509
2002	944	1,218	1,523
2003	942	1,215	1,567
2004	940	1,212	1,581

AGE YOU RETIRE/AMOUNT YOU RECEIVE			
Retirement Year	62	65	70
2005	938	1,209	1,626
2006	945	1,204	1,639
2007	953	1,200	1,684
2008	960	1,195	1,683
2009	967	1,204	1,711
2010	973	1,211	1,707
2011	979	1,218	1,730
2012	985	1,226	1,724
2013	990	1,233	1,743
2014	996	1,239	1,753
2015	1,000	1,244	1,760
2016	1,003	1,248	1,766
2017	995	1,252	1,771
2018	986	1,255	1,775
2019	976	1,257	1,778
2020	967	1,244	1,781

Reprinted with permission of William M. Mercer, Inc.

work for a company or another person. It doesn't include income from investments, pensions, or capital gains, for example.

For those who want to earn money after age 70, there is good news: The sky is the limit. Your benefits won't be cut regardless of how much outside income you make.

THE PAPERWORK

As with everything to do with the government, reporting your earnings requires piles of paperwork. If you earn more than the limit, every year you must complete an Annual Report of Earnings. In this report you describe your exact earnings for the previous year and provide an estimate for the current year. It must be filed by April 15 of the current year or a penalty may be assessed.

If your situation changes and, say, your home herb business takes off and it looks as if you're going to make twice what you estimated, call Social Security right away. It will send the proper forms for an update. (There is a fact sheet available, "How Work Affects Your Social Security Benefits," No. 05-10069, which lays out all the details.)

DON'T FORGET TAXES

If you thought figuring out your taxes was tough before you retired, welcome to the land of the truly complicated. Say you decide to keep working even after you start drawing Social Security benefits: You must still pay FICA taxes on any earnings. You may also have to pay income taxes on half of your Social Security benefits if your income tops the government threshold. The government considers anyone with an income over $32,000 (couple filing jointly) or $25,000 (single retiree) to be well-off. If your annual income passes one of these thresholds, you have to pay federal income taxes on either half of the combined income over the threshold or half of your Social Security benefits, whichever is less. Included in establishing a combined income are earnings, pensions, and even interest from tax-free bonds. Also, add to the combined income half of the Social Security benefits you received. (Who says life gets simpler when you retire?) Here's how it works:

Mr. and Mrs. Jones,
Both Aged 65

1. Taxable earnings from business:	$10,000
2. Taxable income from corporate pension:	30,000
3. Tax-free income from municipal bonds:	5,000
4. ½ of Social Security benefits:	6,000
Base total:	$51,000
Subtract threshold:	− 32,000
5. Excess income:	$19,000
6. ½ excess income:	$ 9,500
7. ½ of Social Security:	$ 6,000

Use the lesser amount of 6 or 7 to compute the adjusted gross income subject to federal income tax. In this case it is Social Security (line 7). Add taxable income: line 7 plus line 1 plus line 2 ($6,000 + $10,000 + $30,000).

Total adjusted gross income = $46,000.

FAMILY CONSIDERATIONS

Your spouse is eligible for his or her own Social Security benefits if he or she worked the minimum 10 years. Even if your spouse didn't make any income, however, he or she is entitled to benefits, based on your record, in addition to what you receive. If you retire at age 65, the monthly amount for both you and your spouse should total about 150 percent of the benefits you qualify for on your own. A 65-year-old spouse is eligible for 50 percent of the working partner's benefits. If you and your wife decide to retire early at age 62, the rate your spouse receives is reduced to 37.5 percent of your benefits.

One piece of good news: Social Security lets you take whichever amount is higher—the amount

BUSY, BUSY, BUSY

Social Security and Medicare run the largest consumer telephone networks in the world. As you can imagine, busy signals are not uncommon and it can take more than a few tries to get through. If you're calling between 9 and 5, don't get frustrated. Set your alarm the next morning and call again. The best times to get through are 7 to 9 A.M. and 5 to 7 P.M. Social Security's hotline, 800/772-1213, is open between 7 A.M. and 7 P.M., anywhere in the U.S., weekdays. If you can't get through or want forms or publications, visit a local office.

from your working years or the 50 percent benefit based on your spouse's working record.

There are other situations where family members can get

AGE TO RECEIVE SOCIAL SECURITY BENEFITS

If you were born in . . .	Your full retirement age is . . .
1937 or earlier	65
1938	65 and 2 months
1939	65 and 4 months
1940	65 and 6 months
1941	65 and 8 months
1942	65 and 10 months
1943–54	66
1955	66 and 2 months
1956	66 and 4 months
1957	66 and 6 months
1958	66 and 8 months
1959	66 and 10 months
1960 and beyond	67

Social Security Administration

monthly cash from Social Security once you retire:

• Your husband or wife qualifies at any age if he or she is caring for your child and that child is under 16 or disabled. (But you must have been married for at least one year if your spouse isn't the parent of your child or hasn't adopted the child).

• Your children can qualify for benefits, too, if they're unmarried and under age 18, or under 19 but still in high school, or older than 18 but disabled.

There is a maximum family benefit, however. If you retire, have six dependents and a spouse all drawing on your Social Security account, you will top the family limit allowed on each Social Security record. The cap is generally less than 200 percent of your retirement benefit. If your family goes over that limit, checks will be scaled back proportionately.

DEATH AND DIVORCE

Not everybody fits the neat Ozzie and Harriet family profile of a husband and wife nearing retirement after 30 years of marriage. Death, divorce, or both, can affect your benefits. For instance, say your second wife died before the two of you reached 60. You can draw on her Social Security account or on your own, depending on whose benefit is higher. You can even split it up, if you prefer. For example, you could receive your widower benefits at the 82.9 percent level when you turn 62 and then switch to your own higher full retirement amount at age 65.

Divorce doesn't mean you lose access to your ex's benefits. If you were married for ten years and are 62 or older and haven't remarried, you may be able to qualify for part of your former spouse's retirement benefits even if he or she has remarried or hasn't yet retired. Generally, you need to have been

divorced for two years to qualify, though the waiting period doesn't apply to every situation.

When death and/or divorce is involved, the best rule of thumb is, don't assume anything. Call Social Security's toll-free number and ask what your options are. They may be more varied than you think.

WHEN THE TIME COMES: HOW TO SIGN UP

Once you've figured out at what age you want to tap your government pension, what do you do? You can apply for benefits at any of the 1,300 Social Security offices nationwide or by calling SSA's toll-free number (800/772-1213). The Administration recommends that you sign up for retirement benefits about three months before you want the monthly checks to start. (If you plan to retire sometime in the coming year, talk to Social Security in January and a representative will help you decide the best time for benefits to begin.)

Before picking a date, make sure you review your Social Security account, carefully checking

Q I've heard Social Security described as the "third rail" of American politics. What does this mean?

A To touch it, politicians warn, means instant death (as with the electrified middle rail of a train).

that there are no discrepancies between what the agency thinks you have earned and your own recollections. That way if there are any disagreements, you can take care of them before benefits are scheduled to start.

Once your benefits begin, the checks will generally arrive on the third day of every month. Or, you can receive your payment through direct deposit into your bank account. Most people choose direct deposit—it's easier and more convenient. All you need to do is supply a voided check or papers that show your bank account number when you sign up for Social Security's retirement benefits.

The records you need when signing up vary depending on your circumstances, but here's a partial list:

• Social Security card
• Birth certificate
• Marriage certificate (if signing up for spouse's benefits)
• Divorce certificate
• Most recent W-2 form or tax return if you are self-employed

If you can't find your birth certificate, don't panic. Social Security can help you get the information you need, or at least tell you where to look.

WILL SOCIAL SECURITY BE AROUND WHEN MY TIME COMES?

The future of Social Security is as much a political question as an economic one. Predicting the stability of a social program decades hence is a bit like mapping the long-term change in weather patterns. Not surprisingly, polls show that most working Americans in their thirties and forties don't expect to receive the same level of benefits their parents and grandparents get today. That's a fair assumption, especially for younger Americans, but it's important to note that even the most pessimistic forecasters aren't predicting the outright demise of Social Security.

Economists' worries center on demographics. The work force is shrinking and the number of retirees is expanding. Right now Social Security takes in significantly more in taxes than it spends in order to save for those "crunch" years that will begin around 2010, when a big bulge of baby boomers marches full stride into retirement. But no one can really predict whether today's savings will be around in three decades. Some economists say FICA taxes might have to be as high as 40 percent in the year 2020 if tomorrow's recipients are to receive benefits as generous as today's.

For young working Americans, it's wise to be wary. Social Security will probably still be there when you retire but it may not provide the same steady stream of monthly income that today's retirees, rich and poor, enjoy. Solid financial planning for your retirement is even more important for you than it was for your father and grandfather.

For Americans nearing retirement now, there isn't much question that Social Security can be counted on to kick in sums similar to what today's over-65 crowd enjoys. Your benefits are safe for the foreseeable future because the system is on firm financial footing, at least for now. It also helps that politicians are scared to mess with Social Security because they don't want to tangle with the so-called gray lobby. And for good reason —a high percentage of elderly Americans vote.

That doesn't mean, however, that there won't be attempts to make minor changes aimed at trimming Social Security and Medicare costs. The money crunch in Washington has politicians scrambling for ways to trim budgets. As the federal government's most expensive social programs, Social Security and Medicare—which paid out $417 billion in 1992—make tempting targets. The most likely changes, however, would have only a minimal impact on your benefits:

• Higher taxes on benefits for wealthier retirees. Under current rules, roughly 50 percent of Social Security benefits are taxed if the recipient makes more than $25,000 (filing singly or $32,000 for a joint return). Some politicians have suggested taxing upwards of 85 percent of the benefits of the wealthy, including Medicare.

• A decrease in automatic cost-of-living-adjustments (COLAs). Social Security's payments are pegged to the consumer price index, so as costs go up in the general economy, so do your annual benefits. Offering a less generous rate of increase could save the government a bundle.

• A raise in the retirement age. The age at which most Americans can begin to receive full benefits is already going up. If you were born

UP, UP, AND AWAY

What goes up doesn't always come down. The amount of income subject to FICA taxes has risen steadily since 1937, when the government took a maximum $30 annually from every paycheck—that is, from all those who made a whopping $3,000 or more.

Year	FICA Tax Rate (%)	Maximum Earnings Taxed Annually	Maximum Annual Tax (Including Medicare)
1940	1.00	$ 3,000	$ 30.00
1950	2.00	3,600	72.00
1960	3.00	4,800	144.00
1970	4.80	7,800	374.40
1980	6.13	25,900	1,587.67
1990	7.65	51,300	3,924.45
1993	7.65	57,600	5,528.70

Reprinted with permission from William M. Mercer, Inc.

after 1960, for example, you won't be able to pull down the full amount until you're 67. The age could be raised still higher.

• A raise in the income threshold subject to Social Security tax. The maximum earnings subject to FICA taxes have increased every year since 1972 (when it was $9,000). In 1993 the ceiling for Social Security's portion is $57,600. It rises every year in relation to general earnings increases. However, Congress could raise the base in order to pay for changes in benefits.

OTHER BENEFITS: DISABILITY AND SURVIVORS

Social Security also serves as a giant insurance program, providing financial protection for millions of Americans who are disabled and for families whose primary breadwinners are either dead or unable to work because of illness. It pays monthly income to dependents if you die, and it replaces part of your income if you are seriously disabled.

That's the good news. The bad news is that the coverage can be pretty meager. For example, the

> **Q** *My roommate has AIDS. Can he get disability benefits?*
>
> **A** *Yes, if he's no longer able to work or is severely limited by the disease.*

most your family could get if you died at age 55 and were a top wage earner (making more than $57,600 per year) would be $1,927 per month, or $23,124 a year. Even though most, if not all, the benefits would be tax-free, that won't come close to making up the financial loss. What's more, if the living spouse has to return to work to support the kids, the mother's or father's benefits may be cut or even reduced to nothing (children's benefits continue). Disability benefits are generally less than those for survivors.

SURVIVORS BENEFITS

When a family breadwinner dies, at no matter what age, dependents and spouses are usually entitled to monthly Social Security benefits. Even a worker's parents are eligible if they were dependent on a deceased son or daughter for at least half of their support. Other family members who can collect income include:

- A widow or widower who is 60 or older.
- A widow or widower who is 50 or older and disabled.
- A widowed mother or father of any age who is caring for a child under 16 or a disabled child.
- Children if they are unmarried and under 18 or under 19 and still in high school or were severely disabled before age 22.

Social Security does have some limitations on whom it will cover, however. The insured worker needs to have earned enough credits to make his or her family eligible for benefits. For older workers the cutoff is generally the same as for retirement benefits: if you've worked for ten years, your dependents are covered.

But what if you're younger? Social Security makes allowances for early deaths. Workers under 29, for example, become eligible after paying Social Security taxes for a mere 18 months. The liberal time frame means that almost every family in America is covered should a breadwinner die. Of course, your income at the time of death affects how much your family will get.

Young widows and widowers don't receive Social Security's survivors benefits indefinitely. Once a deceased worker's children are 16, the insurance is cut off (except if the child is disabled). The widow or widower is then on his or her own until age 60 (50 if disabled within seven years of being widowed), when they can receive reduced retirement benefits. Or he or she can wait until age 65 for the full retirement pension.

SSA'S FINAL PAYMENT

If you die and your family is eligible for survivors benefits, it can receive an additional one-time payment of $255. That's not a lot, but it's worth a call to Social Security.

Working parents, or children for that matter, may lose some or all of their survivors insurance if they earn more than a limited wage during the years they're eligible to draw monthly income.

Large families, too, are at a disadvantage since Social Security will not ante up enough income to keep, say, seven kids between the ages of 1 and 15 in food and clothing. There is a limit, a rather low one, to the system's generosity. The "maximum family benefit" for survivors ranges from 150 percent to 188 percent of what the worker would have received, beginning on the date of the death.

DISABILITY BENEFITS

To qualify for Social Security's disability benefits you have to be incapacitated by illness. Medically certifiable illnesses can range from mental, such as schizophrenia, to physical, such as an incurable brain tumor. Whatever the illness, the criterion is that your doctors think it will last for a year or more, or will end in death. In addition, the insured must be unable to perform any "substantial, gainful" work.

Generally, any job that earns you $500 a month is considered substantial. But SSA's brochures warn that just because you have a doctor's note stating that you're disabled "does not mean you will be automatically eligible for disability payments." Believe it. You could qualify for benefits provided by your work and still not pass Social Security's litmus test. As long as you can flip burgers, even if you can't perform your old job as a crane operator, you probably won't qualify. You must be really sick, and likely to stay that way, to pass Social Security's test. There is an appeals process if you think you've been unfairly denied benefits and this is often worth pursuing. Almost two-thirds of SSA's initial denials of disability applications are reversed on appeal.

As with survivors benefits, you don't have to have worked very long to qualify for disability coverage. If you're under 25, for example, you're eligible if you worked for 18 of the previous 36 months. For people between 31 and 42 years old, you can qualify with just five years in the working world. There's a second test for disability benefits: before age 31, you must have worked half the years since age 21. After 30, you must have worked five out of the ten years before the disability began.

Disability coverage starts after

the fifth full month of disability, but if you think you are eligible, don't wait until then to apply. By filing as soon as you realize you won't be able to work again, all the paperwork and doctors' certifications will be done before your first check is due.

When you first contact Social Security you should be able to provide names, addresses, and phone numbers of your doctors and the hospitals and clinics where you received treatment, as well as a copy of any records that substantiate the nature of your illness. You'll also need a summary of your employers in the last 15 years and the kind of work you did. In this way, the office can assess whether or not you're fit to continue working.

Social Security checks up on you periodically to make sure your condition has not improved to the point where you could return to "substantial work." The agency can even order you to undergo an exam by doctors they have selected. (They will pay for any special exams, however.)

As with all other programs, members of your family are also eligible for benefits should you, the breadwinner, become disabled. The rules generally follow those for survivors benefits.

Another important benefit: People with a certifiable disability qualify for Medicare beginning in the twenty-fifth month that disability payments are paid. Even if you have private insurance, Medicare can help pay your medical bills.

MEDICARE

With all the concern about the cost and availability of health care in this country, it should be of some small comfort to know that once you reach age 65, the government's comprehensive Medicare program—the largest health care insurance system in the country—will take care of the majority of your health care needs. Unlike private insurance companies, Medicare can't refuse you coverage for a pre-existing condition, raise your rates because you are drawing heavily on the benefit, or cancel your right to coverage.

This isn't to say that Medicare is perfect. Some long-term illnesses could still leave you teetering on the verge of bankruptcy. And Medicare is bare-bones coverage. It won't pay for a top-of-the-line, fully automated wheelchair, for example, if you can get by with the old-fashioned hand-driven type. But, as a backstop for the majority of illnesses and health care problems elderly Americans face, most people feel that Medicare is worth every penny they paid into the system.

In recent years, Medicare has become even more important for the elderly as retirees have seen their health care benefits gutted in response to corporate cutbacks. Even when used solely as a backup in case your own insurance is scaled down or canceled, Medicare can provide some peace of mind.

A MULTITUDE OF MYTHS

Of all of the government's social programs, Medicare is the most easily misunderstood. Few people, even the elderly covered by its many benefits, really understand what Medicare pays, and what it doesn't. One myth is that Medicare won't begin until you retire. Actually, coverage begins at age 65 no matter what your work status is. Other misconceptions are that the program covers extended nursing-home care for seniors who can't take care of

Q I plan to retire when I'm 62, and I'll start Social Security benefits then too. Can I also get Medicare?

A No. Medicare starts when you're 65, even if you're already retired and on Social Security. (With two exceptions: if you're already getting disability benefits or have chronic kidney failure that requires dialysis or transplant.)

themselves, and that it provides unlimited amounts of physical rehabilitation, following a stroke, for example. The program does neither.

Even worse, recent reports indicate that there is so much confusion about Medicare's fee schedules that some patients are getting billed for services performed by doctors who, either knowingly or unwittingly, are charging more than the law allows. (Doctors are not supposed to deviate from prices established by the Health Care Financing Administration, Medicare's administrator.) The following should clear up some of the confusion and help you decide about how much of a role Medicare will play in your retirement health care plans.

PART A AND PART B

Medicare has two parts. Part A is hospital insurance. Anyone aged 65 (and eligible for Social Security or railroad retirement) is automatically eligible for Medicare Part A—it's the portion financed by the taxes you paid all of your working life. Your spouse, if he or she didn't work, will qualify for Part A coverage, too, when he or she turns 65, assuming you meet the standards to receive Social Security.

Part B is medical insurance, which covers such things as doctors' fees, most outpatient services, and other medical care. Part B is financed by both general revenue from the U.S. Treasury and a monthly premium paid by the beneficiary. Part B is available to everyone 65 and older regardless of work history, as long as they pay the monthly premium. The 1993 premium for most retirees is $36.60 a month. But if you're already getting Social Security, the agency will begin deducting premiums the month before you hit 65. People still working have to sign up for Part B at their local Social Security office.

Inside Part A

Hospital insurance: The good news is that Medicare's Part A insurance should shield you from the exorbitant cost of most hospital care and some but not all recovery care after major illnesses. This includes inpatient care in a skilled nursing facility, some home health care, and hospice care. However, the coverage is not consistent. When it comes to hospice care for the terminally ill, for example, Medicare's coverage is generous, and will even pay for counseling. But just the opposite is true for nursing-home care, where the standards for qualifying are extremely tight.

Overall, however, Medicare's Part A will help you handle the hospital costs of anything from a hip replacement to a stroke. As long as the care is deemed "medically necessary," Medicare's Part A coverage will kick in.

That doesn't mean all the services you might need in the event of a major illness will be covered by Medicare. There is a deductible, and there are limits to coverage. If you enter the hospital on an inpatient basis you must pay the deductible, which in 1993 is $676. This deductible is not a yearly figure. Say, for example, you were hospitalized twice in 1992, once in January for 15 days and once in September for 20. You would have paid the deductible twice, unless you had received skilled care throughout the period.

Once you pay the deductible, however, things look up. Medicare will pay all of your expenses (assuming the services are covered, which most are) for up to 60 days per stay. Very few health crises require longer stays than two months, but if you do need long-term acute care, Medicare starts to get a bit more stingy. From days 61 through 90, the patient must make a $163-a-day contribution for hospital care, with Medicare picking up the remainder. Beyond that, there is a once-in-a-lifetime benefit that allows you to draw on another 60 days of hospital coverage at an even higher cost to you of $326 a day.

As with most insurance, the list

DON'T EXPECT THE RITZ

Medicare is a bare-bones policy. It won't pay for some things that you might consider essential to your hospital stay, for example a telephone or television to keep your mind off the pain. In most cases, it won't pay for top-of-the-line medical equipment if a basic model will do. Private rooms are also not totally covered. But there is an upside to Medicare's cost controls: You won't have to worry about getting charged $14 for a box of Kleenex or $2.50 for an aspirin. Medicare won't allow outrageous prices.

of what is covered when you're confined to a hospital is generally rather inclusive:

- Semi-private room and meals
- Nursing services
- Operating and recovery room

DON'T PANIC, BUT HERE'S A TYPICAL HOSPITAL BILL

Matilda, aged 67, broke her hip while dancing and was taken to the hospital by ambulance. Not one to settle for anything less than first-class service, Matilda insisted on "luxury items"—private room, private nurse, and television—which Medicare won't cover.

Matilda's medical care included surgery to replace her broken hip with a prosthetic hip joint and seven days in the hospital. After that she moved to a skilled nursing home for physical therapy and continued treatment on her hip. She stayed in the nursing home a scant four days and was discharged to her own home, where she recovered. At home she needed a wheelchair, a special hospital bed, and follow-up visits from both a nurse and a therapist.

Expenses	Charge	Allowed	Paid	Matilda's bill
Ambulance	$ 75	$ 70	$ 56 (80%)	$ 19
Hospital	3,660	3,445	2,793*	867
Anesthesiologist	360	300	240 (80%)	120
Surgeon	1,380	1,150	920 (80%)	460
Private nurse	120	0	0	120
Amb. to nursing home	75	70	56 (80%)	19
Skilled nursing home	400	360	360	40
Amb. to residence	75	70	56 (80%)	19
Wheelchair	50	42	32 (80%)	18
Hospital bed	125	100	80 (80%)	45
Home visits, therapist	95	95	95	0
Home visits, nurse	95	95	95	0
Prescriptions	120	0	0	120
TOTALS	$6,630	$5,797	$4,783	$1,847

*Medicare's payment to the hospital was the allowable charge minus the $652 deductible paid by Matilda.
Reprinted with permission from William M. Mercer, Inc.

• Intensive care/special coronary care

• Drugs, lab tests, X-rays, CAT scans, and other high-tech diagnostic procedures

• Medical supplies

• Physical therapy and other rehabilitation services

Skilled nursing care: The guidelines say that Medicare will pay for 100 days in a skilled-nursing home. It will cover all services for the first 20 days, but there is a coinsurance payment of $81.50 per day on the next 80.

In reality, Medicare's coverage of nursing-home stays is scanty indeed. That's because to qualify for coverage you have to meet standards that are extremely strict. For instance, the patient must require physical therapy, skilled, or rehabilitative care every day. You wouldn't be covered, for example, if after a stroke you have trouble functioning on your own but only need speech therapy once a week. You must also have been in the hospital for at least three days before entering the nursing-home facility. Even if you meet all the criteria, however, Medicare may not cover the whole 100 days. If your condition stabilizes and/or the improvement from daily ther-

apy levels off, Medicare may cut your coverage whether or not you are able to care for yourself at home.

Another caveat: The nursing home must be Medicare-certified. There have been horror stories in past years about the sorry state of some nursing homes that cater primarily to Medicare patients. Recently, tougher and more thorough examinations by HCFA and state agencies have helped clean up the industry. But don't enter a nursing home, or place a relative in one, without thoroughly checking the institution. These days many decent nursing homes accept Medicare patients, so there is no reason to get substandard care. (However, just because a home doesn't have Medicare-certified beds doesn't mean it's shoddy. It may simply prefer not to deal with the bureaucracy.)

Home health and hospice care: The standards for Medicare's coverage for health care are tough but once you meet them, the agency will pay for visits from so-called home service agencies, basically "Nurses-on-Wheels." For instance, if you need chemotherapy and are confined to your home, Medicare might pay for the once-a-week intravenous infusion of cancer-killing drugs to be given at your bedside, rather than in a hospital or outpatient facility. Intermittent skilled nursing care, physical therapy, and speech therapy are among the home-based services that Medicare will pay for if you qualify for coverage. There is no coverage, however, for full-time nursing care, or for drugs or food delivered to your home.

Hospices are private programs that provide pain relief and support services for the terminally ill and their families. Many AIDS and cancer patients turn to a hospice in their final days of life. Medicare will help pay for hospice care if the program is certified, and many are. Medicare's hospice coverage is extensive and even pays for "respite care," which provides a nurse or other backup to give the patient's primary caretaker (usually a friend or family member) a temporary break. Other hospice coverage includes:

- Doctors and nursing services
- Medical appliances and supplies, including pain-relieving drugs, whether delivered on an inpatient or an outpatient basis. There are minimal charges for prescription drugs.
- Physical therapy

- Home health aid and other home services
- Medical social services
- Counseling

One important note with hospice care: it's last-ditch insurance. When you choose hospice benefits, you lose other Medicare benefits, except for physician services and treatment of conditions not related to the terminal illness. The hospice becomes, in effect, your medical manager.

Inside Part B

Medicare Part B pays for doctors' bills and other non-hospital medical services and supplies. You pay a premium for Part B coverage and if you receive Social Security, the premium is simply taken out of your monthly retirement check. Like all health insurance, Medicare's premiums are going up. They're scheduled to rise from $36.60 in 1993 to $46.10 in 1995. Still, that's less than a quarter of what the average senior citizen could expect to pay for individual coverage with a commercial policy.

Part B is more like regular insurance, which means its headache quotient is up there in the ozone.

As with most private insurance plans, there is an annual deductible ($100) and a co-payment for most services (generally the government pays 80 percent, you pay 20 percent).

But that's where the similarity to commercial insurance ends. Medicare tightly controls what it pays to doctors, and what they can charge you. Problems can arise, however, because Part B is so

ALPHABET SOUP—HMOs AND CMPs

Medicare is pushing to get you to sign up for health maintenance organizations (HMOs) and competitive medical plans (CMPs). These so-called coordinated care plans handle all your health care needs for a fixed monthly sum, which is generally paid by Medicare. The benefit for the patient is that there is less exposure to costs in the form of high deductibles or limits to hospital care. But the downside is a limited choice of doctors and other service professionals. HMOs generally have in-house doctors from which you choose, and you must go to their doctors (and the hospitals they designate) unless a visit to an outside specialist is authorized by your main HMO physician, who serves as your health care coordinator.

CMPs differ from HMOs in that the doctors are not all housed under one roof but are a collection of individual health care providers who may have private practices on the side.

In a coordinated health care plan, either CMP or HMO, a network of providers, including doctors, hospitals, skilled nurses, etc., are all contracted with Medicare to provide the full range of services you might need. Medicare makes a monthly payment to the plan for you and you don't have to worry about the high co-payments or deductibles. Sometimes there are nominal co-payments, such as $100, for a hospital stay. More of your potential exposure to cost from a catastrophic illness is covered. Sometimes even prescriptions are included.

complex, and the paperwork so voluminous, that patients don't always know if they're being fairly billed, the subject of an unwitting error, or getting ripped off by their doctor. If you are seeing more than one doctor, the problems compound.

A host of services: Whether in a doctor's office, ambulance, or outpatient clinic, Medicare Part B patients can generally breathe easier knowing their bill will be largely paid by Uncle Sam. The list is long and includes the usual services you might need:

• Medical and surgical services, including anesthesia
• Diagnostic tests
• Blood transfusions, medical supplies, and drugs that have to be administered by trained staff
• Ambulance transportation
• Most outpatient treatment
• Radiation treatments
• Home dialysis equipment
• Surgical dressings, splints, casts, braces, and other supplies ordered by a doctor
• Artificial body parts, such as hips or limbs

What's not included: Basic health care coverage provided by Medicare doesn't include some things that you might well need as

the years pass. That's why most people have supplemental insurance as well. There is also the question of quality in what it will provide. For instance, if you need an artificial leg, Medicare won't pay for a state-of-the-art prosthesis but for a standard model, which may not provide you with the flexibility and look you desire in your new appendage.

The list of what Medicare won't pay for is long:

• Custodial or long-term care of someone who isn't fit to manage daily activities but is not sick enough to require daily medical care. If you can't eat, take a bath, or walk on your own and need help, Medicare won't pay for it.
• Care you get while traveling outside the U.S.
• Dental care
• Routine physical
• Most prescription drugs
• Eyeglasses or hearing aids
• First three pints of blood used for transfusions

NONE OF THE ABOVE: SPECIAL MEDICAL SITUATIONS

Mental illness: As with most commercial insurance, covering the mental health of America is

SCAMS

In spite of Medicare's best efforts, there are those in the medical profession who have found ways to rip off both the system and the patient. One common scam: providing services that aren't needed— such as high-cost, high-tech diagnostic exams—to jack up the bill Medicare will actually pay.

Another problem: Although your doctor is supposed to follow cost-containment guidelines, there have been slips in the system that have resulted in doctors charging far more than they are allowed, to the detriment of patients who have to make up the difference.

If you think you've been charged too much, call Medicare and find out what the rate is for the service you received. (Medicare indicates the charge limit on the explanation of medical benefits when a doctor charges more.) Be sure the "diagnostic code" used by the doctor fits the description of your care.

If you can't make heads or tails of the medical terminology, call your state insurance office for help. Many states have offices designed precisely to help senior citizens sort out problems with medical claims. And AARP (American Association of Retired Persons), the largest organization of senior citizens, has volunteer programs in most states that will help you through the maze of forms and filings. Or your local hospital may help with translations of medical jargon. If you've been wronged in any way, contact Medicare and your state insurance office.

not a top priority with Medicare. The Part A insurance will cover no more than 190 days of inpatient psychiatric care *per lifetime* if it's in a psychiatric hospital. Mental health care in a general hospital is not limited by the 190-day-lifetime limit; it is instead subject to Medicare's regular hospital coverage limitations. But most general hospitals don't have the sort of services to supply care for long periods of time to the critically impaired.

As any person with a history of mental problems or the family of a person with mental illness knows, 190 days of hospitalization in a specialized institution is just a blip of time. Many severe mental illnesses, such as schizophrenia or manic depression, can require long, frequent hospital stays over a lifetime. Coverage is limited for outpatient treatment, too. Medicare usually pays just 50 percent of recognized charges and there are limits as to how long Medicare will pay the bill for your weekly or biweekly visits to a psychiatrist.

Even worse, some top-notch psychiatrists may not accept Medicare patients because the "recognized" charges are much lower than their normal rates. However, some states, such as Massachusetts, have made it illegal for doctors to refuse to treat Medicare patients.

Alternative medicine: Medicare's generosity when it comes to exploring alternative medical options is limited. Medicare's Part B will pay for one type and one type only of treatment by a licensed Medicare-certified chiropractor: manual manipulation of the spine for those who have a vertebra out of place. Medicare won't pay for the X-ray or any other diagnostic service provided by a chiropractor but it will hand over the cash to have your back treated, provided you can prove that a subluxation (dislocated joint or vertebra) is your problem.

As for acupuncture, forget it. Even in cases where acupuncture might be deemed helpful by your physician, as in treatment for repetitive motion syndrome in the hands for example, Medicare won't pay for it.

APPLYING FOR MEDICARE

Medicare is available the month you turn 65, even if you aren't receiving Social Security benefits, are working full-time, and have private health insurance. Your age makes it your right—if you want it, you get it, regardless of your situation. Medicare is also available to most people who have been receiving Social Security disability benefits for two years and to those with chronic kidney disease, no matter what age.

Your application to Medicare will be handled automatically by SSA if you're already receiving, or have applied for, Social Security benefits. But if you plan to work past age 65 and don't intend to draw on your Social Security benefits, be sure to sign up for Medicare three months before you turn 65. There is a rather tight seven-month period that you have in which to enroll—from three months before the month you turn 65 to three months after. If you happen to be covered by an employer plan (or spouse's employer), your enrollment window is also seven months, starting with the month your employment ends or your insurance ends, whichever comes first.

If you miss the first window of opportunity, you're given another chance, once a year, between January and March (but your benefits won't start until the next July.) Obviously, if you think there's any possibility you are going to use Medicare, sign up. If something unforeseen happens after you turn 65, a heart attack or stroke for example, you may not have the luxury of time to wait until the following July to get your benefits.

Even if you still work, have private insurance, and don't yet receive Social Security, you should apply for Part A. That way if something happens to your private insurance, say your company's group policy is canceled, you'll have a backup. And as for Part B, if you hesitate until you are older, the premium will be higher.

AVOID DOUBLE COVERAGE

If you already have health insurance when you become eligible for Medicare, is it worth it to sign up? Since Part A is free, the answer is yes, even if you use Medicare as a back-up to an employer plan. But Part B costs money, even though it's not a lot. The kind of coverage that will fit your likely medical bills is never easy to figure out. The first step is to talk to your insurance agent about your options.

If you're part of a group health plan through your work or your spouse's, you don't have to enroll in Medicare until you retire or the coverage ends, and you won't be penalized for waiting beyond the normal sign-up age of 65.

A key test of whether you should keep both is how well your private plan integrates with Medicare. If it covers the same services as Medicare and leaves off others, such as most nursing-home care, then you should reconsider. If your private policy is better than Medicare and doesn't cost you much, you might want to keep it. Some commercial insurance is much better than Medicare, some isn't. You'll have to compare the plans closely.

IF YOU HAVE MORE THAN ONE TYPE OF INSURANCE

If you're working and are part of an employer-provided health care plan, Medicare will be your secondary payer. That means your private commercial insurance company will be billed first and Medicare covers anything left over (to the extent the service is reimbursable).

In reality, Medicare as a secondary payer is not likely to fork over the funds to cover the 20 percent you are usually left paying. That's because Medicare will pay bills only to the extent the private carrier doesn't and only to the extent the bills don't exceed Medicare guidelines on how much the care was worth. For example, while one insurance company may pay 80 percent ($1,000) of your bill ($1,250) for doctor visits and test-

ing of an irregular heartbeat, Medicare may recognize only a portion of that cost, say $600. Since your private carrier has already paid more than that, Medicare pays nothing. In most other situations, such as with Medigap policies (see page 270), Medicare pays first, then your Medigap kicks in to cover the rest.

DOCTORS AND BILLS: HOW MEDICARE WORKS

One of Medicare's biggest problems is how to handle the health care claims and paperwork generated by 30 million patients, their doctors, nurses, and hospitals and still keep a lid on soaring health care costs.

One solution to cost containment in Medicare—and it's managed to keep administrative costs to a miraculous 2 percent of outlays—is to scrutinize every benefit payout to make sure not a single cent is being spent for an unnecessary service. If an "i" isn't dotted or a "t" crossed, your claim can get rejected. The whole billing process is a bureaucratic maze that can leave the most savvy consumer bewildered, and possibly holding the bag for expensive medical treatment that would have been covered but for want of the proper diagnostic code or some other clerical miscue. (If you get the right info, you can resubmit bills.)

FIGURING DOCTORS' FEES AND CHARGES

There are two types of doctors in the Medicare world—those who accept "assignment" (medical jargon for doctors who agree to limit their charges to Medicare's federal fee scales—the word has nothing to do with being "assigned" anywhere) and those who don't. The vast bulk of doctors in today's world accept Medicare's strict cost controls most of the time, even though they usually charge more for the same service for non-Medicare patients.

In any event, a doctor who takes you on as a Medicare patient, whether he or she accepts assignment or not, is subject to limits as to what he or she can charge. If your doctor doesn't accept "assignment," you'll be expected to pay the excess, but there are still cost controls. In 1993, the charge can't exceed 115 percent of the level set by Medicare. Your

Q My doctor doesn't accept assignment, so when he treated a small growth on my back in his office, I paid him. That was six months ago and I'm still waiting to be reimbursed by Medicare, which says it hasn't gotten the bill. What's going on?

A Your doctor has 12 months to file Medicare claims, so to get your money, you have to urge your doctor to file.

doctor is supposed to submit a form to Medicare to find out what is the top rate is for a particular service before charging you.

REIMBURSEMENT

Doctors who accept assignment get reimbursed directly by Medicare. Those who don't may expect you to pay for your service. If you go to a doctor who doesn't accept assignment, generally you pay up and are then reimbursed. The doctor's office is still responsible for sending the bill to Medicare, which will then send a check to you for 80 percent of the covered charge. (If you have supplemental insurance, Medicare will send along a copy of the bill to your Medigap carrier, though extra paperwork on your part may be needed, too.)

Here are two hypothetical examples (with thanks to William Mercer, Inc, compensation and benefits consultants) of how much your doctor can charge:

• Dr. Roberts accepts assignment. He is a "participating physician." When Mark Jones makes his bimonthly visit to have his diabetes monitored and checked, Dr. Roberts bills Medicare for $50, which is the amount HCFA deems appropriate for this care. (Dr. Roberts may charge his non-Medicare patients $60 for the visit, but that fact should not affect Mark Jones's bill, or treatment.) Medicare then sends Dr. Roberts a check for $40 (80 percent of the allowable charge). Dr. Roberts bills Mr. Jones for the remaining 20 percent, or $10, that Medicare didn't cover.

• Dr. Winthrop is not a participating physician. He sees Mark's wife, Maude, once every three months to check for a recurrence of cancer. Dr. Winthrop usually charges his patients $75 a visit. Even though he does not accept Medicare assignment, he has accepted Maude, a Medicare patient, which means he is constrained in what he can charge. For nonparticipating physicians Medicare crops 5 percent off its allowable costs, in this case $50, to establish a base. Dr. Winthrop can charge only 115 percent above that base. So deduct 5 percent ($2.50) to establish a base price of $47.50. Dr. Winthrop cannot charge Maude more than 115 percent of that figure, or $54.62. Maude pays the bill, and later Medicare reimburses her for 80 percent of the allowable charge of $50. Maude pays the rest.

The advantage to going to a doctor who accepts assignment is threefold: It's less complicated since the doctor handles most of the paperwork, it's cheaper, and you don't have to wait to be reimbursed. There's another bonus, too. If you have diagnostic testing, such as a CAT scan, done by a service provider (either an outpatient clinic or a doctor) who accepts assignment, Medicare will pay 100 percent of the bill.

RESOLVING PAYMENT DISPUTES

Every time Medicare is billed for a procedure, it will send you an Explanation of Medicare Benefits. If you receive a form with big fat zeroes, that means that Medicare refused to pay your bill for one stated reason or another. Usually the problem is simple, such as an inaccurate diagnostic code or some other filing foul-up. Medicare lists a toll-free number on the form so you can check what went wrong. Once you figure out where the problem lies, contact the provider, be it your doctor, hospital, or ambulance service, and have them resubmit the bill.

If Medicare refuses to pay your otherwise legitimate medical bill, don't panic. There are avenues for recourse—you can appeal a decision made by Medicare. If that doesn't result in a satisfactory conclusion and the amount's over $100 (for a Part A claim) or $500 (Part B claim), you can go to an administrative law judge; $1,000 disputes get you to federal court.

HOW TO FIND PARTICIPATING DOCTORS

To get a list of doctors in your area who accept assignment, call Social Security and ask for the toll-free number of the Medicare carrier in your state. Your state's Medicare carrier (usually a private company like Blue Cross/Blue Shield handles the paperwork for the federal government) can send you a free copy of its Participating Physician/Supplier Directory.

QUALITY CONCERNS

Don't think that you have to settle for substandard care or switch doctors simply to get one who accepts assignment. Most doctors today accept Medicare patients and many accept assignment on a case-by-case basis. Such are the growing numbers of elderly that most medical professionals find that they have to deal with Medicare or risk seeing their patient population shrink. Cosmetic surgeons for the rich and famous may not handle Medicare patients, but nearly everyone else does. Many top-notch doctors who are leaders in their fields have opened up a part of their practice to Medicare patients.

IS MEDIGAP NECESSARY?

Medigap insurance is designed to fill the cracks in Medicare. Unfortunately, in years past, many unscrupulous insurance agents sold policies to worried senior citizens that either duplicated coverage they already had or didn't adequately stop up the holes in Medicare's coverage.

The market was ripe for exploitation precisely because there is a need: Most benefit experts recommend that you buy Medigap insurance to protect your wallet in the event of a major medical catastrophe that might, even with Medicare, leave you exposed to financial ruin.

There are some exceptions to this blanket recommendation, such as low-income seniors eligible for state-sponsored Medicaid programs. Medicaid generally covers what Medicare won't. Also, Medicare beneficiaries enrolled in health maintenance organizations or so-called competitive medical plans probably don't need extra coverage. But nearly everyone else does; thankfully, the fed-

eral government has made the job a bit easier. And if you sign up for Medigap coverage within six months of enrolling in Medicare medical insurance (Part B), you can't be denied coverage because of any existing health problems. Wait more than six months and you have to meet the Medigap carrier's health requirements.

To stop fraud and abuse, new laws (as of July 1992) govern exactly what private carriers can and can't offer in the way of Medigap insurance. Under the new rules, there are ten standardized benefit packages that private insurance carriers offer to most Americans. This doesn't mean that those searching for Medigap insurance can do a one-stop shop for a policy. There will be different levels of coverage within the scope of the ten allowable policies. But it does mean there will be much less confusion. And each of the ten policies, by law, must include a "core" benefit package that plugs Medicare's biggest gaps.

The cost of these plans depends on the carrier and where you live. Generally, they range from around $400 a year for the basic Plan A upwards to $2,000 for the most comprehensive. There's a good chance that your premiums will go up every year—some experts say as much as 15 to 20 percent.

THE CORE PLAN

The core benefits pay the patient's 20 percent share of Medicare's approved amount for physician services (after the $100 deductible) as well as the cost of a long hospital stay. If you're in the hospital beyond 60 days, your Medigap coverage will absorb the whopping $163-a-day charge you're liable for up to day 90 and the $326-a-day charge you're expected to pay between days 91 and 150. Medigap isn't limitless, though. Coverage stops if you spend over a year in the hospital.

Medigap's core also pays for the first three pints of blood not covered by Medicare.

The ten standard benefit packages range from the simple core described above, Plan A, to the most expensive and comprehensive policy, Plan J. (Plan J, for example, includes coverage for preventive medical care and for 50 percent of the cost of prescription drugs up to $3,000 per year, after a $250 deductible.)

When shopping for Medigap, keep the guide on page 274 handy because insurers have to follow

MEDIGAP GAPS

It may be called Medigap, but don't be fooled. These policies do not constitute fail-safe protection for your pocketbook in the event of a major medical emergency or long-term illness. The biggest gap in Medigap? Long-term care. It can be expensive and in most cases neither Medicare nor Medigap will cover nursing-home care for people who don't need "medical attention" but can't manage day-to-day living, such as bathing, eating, and walking, without help.

the prescriptions to the letter. They can't change the name or rearrange the benefits.

Some states have not approved all ten plans and a few others already have their own standardized programs, so your choices will depend on where you live. Check

SHOPPING TIPS FOR HEALTH INSURANCE

Hidden Restrictions. Policies differ as to coverage, cost, and service. Ask about the "loss ratio," which is the portion the insurance company actually pays out of every premium dollar it receives. By law, insurers must pay at least 65 to 75 cents in benefits for each premium dollar they receive for Medigap policies. For any insurance, the 65 to 75 percent rule is a good one to follow. If the company won't tell you what its loss ratio is, find another company. It may be taking in $1 in premiums for every 6 cents it pays out. That could mean the policy is filled with hidden restrictions that make it tough to collect benefits.

Consider Alternatives. Depending on your needs, and finances, you may find you don't need Medigap but are more concerned about the long-term cash drain of a debilitating medical illness (say, for example, Alzheimer's runs in your family) and would be better off with long-term-care coverage. Or you may want to continue the group coverage you have at work, or to join a health maintenance organization or competitive medical plan.

Report High Pressure Tactics. If anyone tries to pressure you into buying Medigap or other insurance, call your state insurance office right away. Don't be frightened by tales of financial ruin. If any salesperson says he or she represents Medicare or any other government agency, get their name, and address if possible. Then call the federal toll-free hotline, 800/638-6833, with the information. It's illegal for any salesperson to say they are associated with the U.S. government.

1992 Guide to Health Insurance for People with Medicare, U.S. Department of Health and Human Services

Check for Pre-Existing Conditions. Most states require Medigap policies to cover pre-existing conditions after the policy has been in effect for 6 months, but not all do. (And Part B Medicare enrollees after November 1991 can't have more than a 6-month waiting period). Many other commercial insurance policies don't cover health problems that you have at the time of purchase. Don't be fooled if the policy says "no medical exam is required." If you make a claim 3 months into the policy, the company will find out from your medical provider whether the illness existed before the contract started.

Maximum Benefits: The Bottom Line. Check the limit on benefits. Some policies restrict the dollar amount that will be paid for treatment of a condition. Others restrict the number of days for which care will be paid. Compare policies to be sure you are getting the best coverage for your premium dollar.

Renewal Rights. Make sure your policy is renewable. Companies should be allowed to refuse renewal only if you didn't pay your premiums, lied about your health, or committed fraud. Never buy a policy that allows a company to refuse to renew on an individual basis. That gives the insurance company a license to dump you should your bills start running up.

Ask for a Simple Outline. Companies will provide a clear, understandable outline of coverage if you ask. Do so. This will let you know for sure what your rights, and coverage, are.

THE MEDIGAP GUIDE:
THE TEN STANDARD MEDICARE SUPPLEMENT BENEFIT PLANS

Core Benefits	Plan									
	A	B	C	D	E	F	G	H	I	J
Part A: Hospital (days 61–90)	X	X	X	X	X	X	X	X	X	X
Lifetime reserve days (91–150)	X	X	X	X	X	X	X	X	X	X
365 hospital days/100%	X	X	X	X	X	X	X	X	X	X
Blood	X	X	X	X	X	X	X	X	X	X
Part B: 20% co-insurance	X	X	X	X	X	X	X	X	X	X

Optional	Plan									
	A	B	C	D	E	F	G	H	I	J
Skilled nursing home co-insurance			X	X	X	X	X	X	X	X
Part A deductible		X	X	X	X	X	X	X	X	X
Part B deductible			X			X				X
Part B excess charges						X	80%		X	X
Foreign travel emergency			X	X	X	X	X	X	X	
At-home recovery				X			X		X	X
Prescription drugs								1	1	2
Preventive medical care					X				X	

1. Coverage for 50 percent of the cost of prescription drugs up to a maximum annual benefit of $1,250. There is a $250 annual deductible.
2. Coverage for 50 percent of the cost of prescription drugs up to maximum annual benefit of $3,000. There is an annual $250 deductible.

1992 Guide to Health Insurance for People with Medicare, Department of Health and Human Services

with your state insurance department. (See Appendix C to find out what's available in your state.)

The new regulations, of course, don't apply to any policy you may have already purchased. You may want to switch, but check carefully to make sure the new policy provides better benefits, better service, or a more affordable price. If you decide to swap Medigap policies, the new insurer must, under most circumstances, waive any preexisting-condition clause.

BASES MEDIGAP DOESN'T COVER

Medigap insurance, in spite of its name, does *not* cover all the holes in Medicare. For instance, Medigap policies do not address the problem of "custodial" or long-term care, the type of daily care needed by many Alzheimer patients or paralyzed stroke victims. It's not a bad idea to look into long-term-care insurance, but be careful—many policies promise more than they deliver.

Some seniors think they need so-called specified disease insurance, that is, a policy that covers only one disease, usually cancer. The value of such a policy is questionable—the benefits may not fill holes in Medicare's coverage. If you're considering dread-disease coverage, ask yourself:

• What is the likelihood of my getting the covered disease? (Some policies cover truly rare diseases, like polio.)
• Am I covered if I've already had the illness and was "cured" or am in remission? (If you had cancer 30 years ago, you may not be able to get coverage for it today.)
• Is the promised daily benefit adequate to cover a day's hospitalization? (Frequently, benefits fall way short of what you may need.)

Hospital indemnity insurance is another type of policy frequently sold to older Americans. It probably isn't necessary unless you're willing to pay dearly to cover almost every imaginable medical disaster that might befall you.

Chapter 6

Estates, Wills, and Trusts

"I leave my entire estate to my wife, Grace, and request that she be appointed executrix without bond." That's all it took for U.S. President Calvin Coolidge to make known his final wishes when he died in 1933.

Too bad life, and death, aren't so simple now. Back in "Silent Cal's" day it was a lot easier to get by with one-liners. Today, writing even a simple will can stress out the most serene person. Planning for your own demise goes far be-

yond the question of inheritance. You have to ponder critical medical decisions as well, such as whether you would want to be sustained on life-support equipment. None of these issues is fun to think about. It's no wonder 60 to 70 percent of Americans die without ever writing a will.

And that's too bad.

President Coolidge could rest in peace knowing that his last wishes, however brief, would be carried out. But if you die without having taken certain basic steps, your life's savings can end up with someone you haven't chosen. Even worse, if you have children under 18 and you and your spouse die without a will that names a guardian for them, the state may decide who gets to raise your kids.

Should your sister or your par-

PRESIDENTIAL PARDONS?

President Coolidge had the foresight to make a will, but other Presidents were too busy with affairs of state to worry about their own fate. At least that's probably how Abe Lincoln, a lawyer no less, rationalized the neglect of his personal affairs. Presidents Andrew Johnson, Ulysses Grant, and James Garfield died without wills, too. But they were in good company. Thomas Jarmon, considered one of the world's greatest experts on wills, died without one.

Town & Country

ents raise your kids in your absence? If you're incapacitated because of illness or accident, do you want your life sustained indefinitely by feeding tubes or repeated resuscitations? Do you want your loved ones to have the power to make such decisions of life and death for you? Only you can answer these questions. But if you don't, some bureaucracy may do it for you.

It doesn't all have to be so bleak. Once you learn the legalities, the whole process becomes a matter of choices that you can control. Take a positive approach and you can plan to your advantage, and your beneficiaries', while you're still around to enjoy the rewards of a well-thought-out financial, medical, and personal road map.

WHERE THERE'S A WILL . . .

There's no more important document than a will. It creates an everlasting bridge between the people you love and the property you own. A will can be prepared one of three ways—formally, handwritten (or holographic), or orally—but your best bet is to go for the formal variety. Some states

Q *Where should I keep my will, and is it necessary for me to hide it?*

A *You don't have to hide it, but it shouldn't be kept in your safe-deposit box since the box might not be opened until months after you die. Keep two copies in separate places (in case of fire), and tell two people where the copies are.*

allow handwritten wills, a few allow oral, but most want the "i's" dotted and the "t's" crossed in the most rigorous legal tradition.

To create a formal will you don't have to hire a lawyer—some good books and software programs are available that will help you craft a legally binding document. But you do have to make sure it is signed, dated, and witnessed according to your state's requirements, which can be very strict. Most states require two witnesses; some require three. And some require a notary to put a seal on the whole thing. The cost of hiring a lawyer, however, may be less than you think and may well provide much peace of mind.

Most assets can be passed on through a will. The main exceptions are property owned in joint tenancy with right of survivorship; life insurance, retirement plans, and IRAs that name a beneficiary; and assets that have been placed in trust. Joint tenancy is when you and your spouse (or someone else) own something jointly, say a savings account or real estate.

If you don't have a will, the state has one for you. Your estate will be considered "intestate" and an administrator will be appointed by the courts. Your loved ones won't have a say in how your assets are distributed—a state formula will decide.

In fact, there really is no good excuse for not writing a will. Once you do shoulder up to the task, and before you consult a lawyer about writing a will (or attempt to do it yourself), there are three basic decisions to make.

Decision one: *The Guardian.* If you have minor children (under 18 or 21, depending on your state), this can be the hardest decision

ANCIENT RITE

Planning for death is an ancient rite of passage that some people actually enjoy, or at least face up to with a measure of responsibility. Jacob, the father of Joseph, is said to have made the first will. In 1540, England was the first country to establish wills as a legal vehicle for inheritance, much to the delight of the landed class, which wanted the court— and the King's muscle—to protect their heirs' right to property.

Town & Country

you must make. The guardian decides where the children live, go to school, even go to church, until they're old enough to decide for themselves. The children don't automatically live with the guardian.

Many people avoid making wills simply because they can't decide whom they would want to care for their kids. Tough as it is, it's better to make a choice, even an imperfect one, than to let the state do it for you. If you have trouble deciding between your sister and your best friend, consider that the state might not pick either one. It's also a good idea to name a substitute guardian in case something happens to your first choice, either death or a change in circumstances, making it impossible for them to care for your child.

It's absolutely essential to talk to your chosen guardian *before* the will is drawn. Don't assume your parents will be happy to take over your children's care. It's a big responsibility, financially and personally.

Decision two: *The Executor* (called a personal representative or administrator in some states). An executor will carry out the terms of your will. Your designated executor will offer the will for probate in court, collect and inventory your assets, have them appraised, pay any due taxes and, finally, distribute the assets to your heirs. The executor is also charged with investing the proceeds from the estate before the inheritance is doled out. It can be a big job, and if things get complicated, it can stretch 3 years.

Most people name their spouse or another principal beneficiary to take on this weighty task. Sometimes, a bank or trust company will be appointed, particularly if the estate is large or complicated. If you want an executor with a personal touch, stick to friends or family. Say, for example, your son requests early distribution of some of your assets because he has fallen on hard times; an executor who was close to you might be better able to make that sort of personal decision. On the other hand, an estate with complicated wrinkles, such as a family business, is probably better handled by a bank or other professional familiar with such cases. Professional executors generally charge from 0.75 to 2 percent of an estate.

Remember to name an alternative executor in case the first person dies or can't serve for some reason. Again, it's very important to ask the person you're thinking of choosing.

THY WILL WON'T BE DONE IF YOU . . .

It takes only a little mistake to throw your will out of court and your heirs into chaos. Whatever you do, don't make these common mistakes:

- Don't get out the camcorder. Videotaping may be more fun than writing, but courts won't recognize your "final wishes video" as a valid will.

- Don't have a loved one, such as your wife or your daughter's husband, serve as a witness. Anyone who stands to benefit financially from your will cannot affix their John or Joan Hancock to it, for obvious reasons. Agatha Christie isn't the only one who suspects family fealty can be in short supply when money is involved. The state does too.

- Don't sign the thing and then go over to a neighbor's house to get a witness. You have to sign your will *in the presence* of the witnesses or a court may declare the whole thing invalid.

WHAT WILL IT COST ME?

Here's the price range for drafting a will in three cities, according to a survey by the American Association of Retired Persons. It should provide you with some sort of guide.

	San Diego	Milwaukee	Wilmington
Low	$ 50	$ 75	$ 70
Average	173	149	143
High	500	300	400

Decision three: *The Beneficiaries.* Some people don't bother with the details but stick to relatively simple arrangements, such as splitting their entire estate into equal parts among their children. That leaves it up to the beneficiaries to decide who gets the china and hall clock. Others prefer to parcel out their belongings down to the last pair of earrings and gardening tool. You might think it's crazy to inventory everything you own, but if you don't divide up your personal property, your executor will have final say. That can be a big burden if your heirs start squabbling about who gets what. Even the tightest of families can fall apart when it comes to dividing up a lifetime of memories.

In addition to your friends and family, now is the time to consider charitable gifts. These usually are specified dollar amounts or pieces of real estate. Depending on how much you own, trusts might make sense (more later on gifts). Be sure to cover what happens if the intended beneficiary dies *before* you.

CHANGING WISHES, CHANGING WILLS

Although a will is set in stone when you die, don't think of it as an immutable object to be forgotten once written. Changing a will is normally done through what's known as a codicil: an amendment to the original document. It must be drawn up, signed, witnessed, and dated to meet the same standards required of the will itself. Don't be tempted to cut corners and pull out your old will, scratch out changes, and write your new wishes in the margins. Courts won't accept such informal handiwork. You can revoke the entire will simply by drawing up a new one (as long as it states that it replaces the old version).

Some people wield their wills as family power tools, changing beneficiaries as this person falls out of favor or that person moves to the front of the line. Whatever you do, don't keep the old wills stashed around the house. Who knows which one might be entered into the court as your latest? It's a good idea to destroy an old will when you write a new one.

WHAT TYPE OF WILL?

Once you've decided on a guardian, executor, and beneficiaries, you have to turn to what type of will you need. There are four basic types of wills and two of these create testamentary trusts, which are activated when the person dies. A trust is nothing more than a legal vehicle in which you can park assets for a specified time and distribute the income and principal as you desire. (Living trusts, which are established before the death of the person who is setting them up, called the trustor or settlor, are discussed later.)

SINGLE OR DIVORCED PARENTS—THE PRESSURE IS ON

If you are a single parent, it's absolutely essential to write a will appointing a guardian for your child. The cold, hard facts are that a child of a single-parent household has a much greater chance of being left alone than the child in a two-parent family. Those odds are bad enough. Don't take any other chances with your child's future.

If you're divorced, you may want your former spouse to raise your child. Saying so could prevent a fight between your relatives and the spouse. If you don't want your spouse to take over, make that clear, too. State your reasons why, so the judge has something to go on.

DO-IT-YOURSELF SOFTWARE

Pop a disk into your computer, fill in a few blanks, answer a couple of questions, and print out the results. *Presto!* You have a legitimate, credible, readable will. Sound good to you? It does to some millions of Americans who have purchased do-it-yourself will and living trust computer software kits.

But are they legal, and more to the point, will they stand up in court? Experts say that generally the more popular programs are safe bets, at least if your estate is straightforward, uncomplicated, and under $600,000. If your estate is larger, you need a professional to do tax avoidance planning. Most computer programs fall short of that.

One bestseller, Willmaker (Nolo Press) has a good track record. It costs about $36.99, has sold more than 250,000 copies since 1985, and so far, so good. The publisher says none of its wills has been struck down in court. WillPower (Jacoby & Meyers) has gotten good reviews as has Will Builder (Sybar Software) and Expert Will (Expert Software).

Other bestsellers that create wills and other legal documents include Home Lawyer (MECA Software), It's Legal (Parsons Technology), and Personal Law Firm (BLOC Publishing).

Simple Will

Under a simple will, everything passes to your spouse (or children or other beneficiaries). The advantage of this type of will is obvious: it's simple. There are no lists of personal belongings to inventory, no complicated decisions about who gets what, or when.

For tax purposes, leaving everything to your spouse has a great advantage: Uncle Sam allows an unlimited marital deduction. Your spouse won't pay a penny of federal estate tax on anything you leave behind. But if your spouse doesn't remarry, there could be substantial estate taxes due when he or she dies if the value of the combined estate—both spouses—equals more than $600,000. (If your spouse remarries and provides for the new spouse, rather than the children, taxes are dodged once again.) If the combined total of your estates could be worth more than the federal tax threshold when the second spouse dies, you may well be better off with another option.

Stated Dollar Amount

This will allows you to pass a specific amount to your spouse or main beneficiary. For example, you could decide that you want to leave a portion of your estate that you figure your spouse will need and no more. Or you may wish to pass on an amount that will roughly equalize the size of your estate and that of your spouse so that each is taxed as its lowest possible rate. Some states dictate how much of your estate you must leave your spouse.

It's generally possible to disinherit your kids, but many states won't allow you to completely cut out your wife or husband. A stated-dollar-amount will allows you to control the nickels and dimes. Some families whose main

asset is a business run by the children use this sort of will to pass a fixed amount to the surviving spouse while the business goes directly to the kids.

Credit Shelter Trust

This type of will contains what's known as a "bypass trust," which passes on half of an estate valued

Q My 78-year-old widowed father is marrying a much younger woman. Will she inherit everything when he dies?

A It depends on his will and the state where he lives, but chances are she'll inherit the bulk. Some older couples use prenuptial agreements to ensure that inheritances go to children and grandchildren rather than to new spouses.

NOTHING SIMPLE ABOUT BRIGHAM YOUNG'S WILL

Brigham Young, a founder of the Mormon Church, died in 1877 leaving behind an estate of about $2.5 million, a tidy sum in those days. He also left behind 18 wives and 48 children.

Town & Country

from $600,000 up to $1.2 million, to a spouse. The survivor doesn't pay estate taxes on the $600,000 since spouses can inherit any amount without a federal tax bite. The remainder of the estate goes into a trust for other beneficiaries, usually children, grandchildren, or a charity. These recipients won't actually receive any inheritance until the remaining spouse dies. The surviving spouse can't touch the trust capital—it is being held in "trust" for other heirs—but can receive the income from the trust.

The advantage of this is that it effectively doubles up to $1.2 million the amount of inheritance free of federal taxes. That's because the $600,000 you left your beneficiaries in trust neatly falls under the estate tax threshold of $600,000.Then when your spouse dies, the other half, the $600,000, is passed on tax-free, too. Let's say you had simply willed your entire estate to your mate. When that person died, the children would pay taxes on everything over the federal threshold.

If your estate is less than $600,000, this arrangement has no tax advantages. But if your estate is over $1.2 million, this is still a smart setup. In this case, the beneficiaries trust still gets $600,000

SEVEN REASONS TO CHANGE YOUR WILL

As if it wasn't bad enough writing the thing in the first place, here's a partial list of reasons to have another go at it. You get married • You have a baby • You get divorced • You retire • You move to another state • Your spouse dies • You inherit money.

and the spouse gets the rest.

Credit shelter trusts, or marital share plans, are a good idea if your estate is over $600,000 and you want to leave a "safety net" for your spouse in the form of income from your assets. Remember, too, that even if the trust has grown to more than $600,000 when the second spouse dies and it's distributed to your heirs, it's completely free of estate tax.

Another Kind of Trust: The QTIP

A will establishing a Qualified Terminable Interest Property Trust, or QTIP, is tailor-made for modern America, where half of all marriages end in divorce.

A dissolved marriage can give rise to all sorts of inheritance complications. Say you married, had children, then divorced and remarried. You most likely want to make sure that those children get their portion of your inheritance after your second spouse dies. If you leave everything to your second spouse, he or she is essentially free to do anything with your estate regardless of your children's needs. Or, you may be worried that after you die, your spouse will remarry and leave

your life's savings to this second love.

If these sorts of questions apply to your circumstances, a will creating a QTIP is for you. A QTIP arranges for your spouse to receive income and have access to some of your assets (at the discretion of the trustee), but your spouse has no voice in what happens to your assets once he or she dies. What happens to your estate then depends on what the QTIP specifies. For instance, it may provide for your kids by making sure they—not your husband's second wife—get your inheritance.

PROBATE

Let's face it, probate has a bad reputation. Charles Dickens blasted the court process required of all wills in his book *Bleak House,* a multigenerational legal saga. The stories told today aren't any less torturous. Most of us get our ideas about probate from television and tabloids, in which generally nasty heirs gather in court to battle over kindly Grandpa Herb's multimillion-dollar estate. By the time the lawyers are done, there's nothing left to fight over anyway.

It happens in the real world, too. Remember the Johnson & Johnson probate spat? When J. Seward Johnson of the Band-Aid company died in 1983, his six children challenged his will because they didn't like the fact that Dad left most of his pharmaceutical fortune, in trust, to his third wife. Enough dirty laundry was aired to taint the entire clan and keep tabloid editors happy for months. Eventually the warring Johnson tribe settled the case. Needless to say, the final dispensation of Mr. Johnson's assets—including $10 million to the lawyers—bore no resemblance to the wishes he had stated in his will.

Sure, probate can be costly—up to 5 percent of an estate in some states—and it can take as long as three or four years if there is a complication or a dispute among beneficiaries. One infamous Minnesota case took more than 40 years to wind its way through the courts. But those cases represent the exception, not the rule. Most wills pass through probate in about a year with only modest costs, 1 to 2 percent of the estate. And in response to demand, many states now have a fast-track procedure for smaller estates. In Minnesota, for example, there are two types of probate, formal and informal. Informal probate for cut-and-dried cases can be wrapped up in four months.

In many states, lawyers may charge an hourly or a fixed fee for handling probate, rather than a percentage, and that may reduce costs. In some jurisdictions, a layperson may be able to handle many aspects of the proceeding without an attorney. That can cut probate fees substantially, too.

The purpose of probate is to make sure that the estate taxes and debts of someone who has died are paid, and that the remaining assets are distributed according to law and the wishes of the deceased. When a person dies, the executor of the will (or whoever is handling matters if the deceased didn't have a will) must file a notification of the death with the probate court in the county or city where the person died. In most cases there is a specified time within which the court must be notified, usually nine months.

Any person who expects to receive an inheritance from the dead person's estate can start the probate proceeding by filing the appropriate form with the court. Then a judge will authorize someone to administer the estate. If there is a will, the executor will be officially charged with the duty. If not, the court will decide who should handle affairs.

Everything in a person's estate falls under the court's authority, with a few important exceptions: (1) life insurance and retirement plans that name a person as a beneficiary (the proceeds are simply paid to the person for whom they were intended); (2) assets placed in trust; (3) property owned jointly with right of survivorship.

JOINT TENANCY

Joint tenancy is the biggest loophole in the probate process. Anything with more than one name on the ownership papers—a home, a car, or a bank account, for example—avoids probate upon death of one of the owners. (Technically, joint tenancy avoids probate only when the ownership paper reads "joint tenancy *with rights of survivorship*." But this isn't a legal document, so just visualize those four words whenever you read "joint tenancy.")

For example, if Mr. and Mrs. Jones have a joint savings account and Mrs. Jones dies, all Mr. Jones

CHARLES DICKENS, DISGUSTED

Everyone knows what Charles Dickens thought about Britain's treatment of orphans in the nineteenth century. Well, he didn't much like probate, either. In 1853 he wrote that the British probate system "so exhausts the finances, patience, courage, and hope; so overthrows the brain and breaks the heart, that there is not an honorable man among its practitioners who would not give the warning, 'Suffer any wrong that can be done you rather than come here.' "

has to do is file a notice with the bank to transfer the assets into his name alone.

Often, older persons will place some or all of their assets in joint tenancy with a son or daughter. This way if the other person be-

Q My mother's will is now being probated and the lawyers say some of her things are "probate property." What does this mean?

A It means that it has no "right of survivorship," or put another way, that the court must decide who gets the property.

comes disabled, the child can take over management of the assets. (Real estate or securities require both joint owners to sign the deed or ownership papers.) But it's important to note that a joint owner in a bank account has full rights to the cash that's in that account. That means he can withdraw every penny while you're not looking and there won't be a thing you can do about it. Only the most trusting families use joint tenancy as a way to give children control in the event parents can't manage

their own affairs.

There's liability to consider, too. If your daughter's name is on your securities and she is sued for damages, your savings could be held hostage. Likewise, her creditors, which could include the IRS, might be able to tap your funds.

Don't think that property or assets held in joint tenancy will avoid the tax man. Uncle Sam will figure out your portion of that jointly held beachfront condominium and include it in your estate.

SIDESTEPPING PROBATE: LIVING TRUSTS

In the world of loopholes for avoiding probate, joint tenancy is a relatively narrow one compared with living trusts. A living trust can render probate into little more than a short footnote to your beneficiaries' plans.

Living trusts, or "loving" trusts, as they are sometimes called, have become so popular they're hyped on late-night TV like vegetable shredders. They're especially hot in states such as California, New York, and Connecticut where probate costs can eat up a big chunk of an estate.

Despite the word "trust," which suggests a rich estate, many middle-income Americans are turning to living trusts as an alternative to a will, and no wonder. These trusts let your heirs seize control of their inheritance from the moment you die, leapfrogging the potentially costly and time-intensive probate required of an ordinary will.

Setting up a living trust is relatively easy. Although you can write it yourself—you've probably seen advertisements for mail-order do-it-yourself kits for less than $200—play it safe and get a lawyer to draft a legally binding document. Loving-hands-at-home legal work is asking for trouble-

FACE-OFF: LIVING TRUSTS VS. WILLS

Attorneys charge more to write living trusts than they do to write wills. In the short run a will is cheaper, but when probate costs are added in, a living trust will save you more. The following comparison, however, doesn't include the cost of transferring assets.

Living Trust: 77-Year-Old With $80,000			
	San Diego	Milwaukee	Wilmington
Low	$300	$ 300	$150
Average	598	540	350
High	850	1,000	600

Will and Probate: 77-Year-Old With $80,000			
	San Diego	Milwaukee	Wilmington
Low	$1,848	$1,580	$1,428
Average	1,971	1,654	1,501
High	2,298	1,850	1,758

Product Report: Living Trusts & Wills, American Association for Retired Persons

some complications. A lawyer will charge anywhere from $1,500 to $10,000 for the work.

Think of a living trust as a safe-deposit box into which you put any or all assets of your estate. Once your lawyer has established the trust, you should place your property titles into it. That means your real estate (including your home, if it's not jointly owned or you're not planning to refinance), stock portfolio, and antique furniture, for instance, are owned by the Your Name Trust instead of yourself. However, you haven't relinquished that much control. You can serve as trustee, thereby controlling all of the assets as long as you live. When you die, a successor picked by you takes over. A living trust is "revocable," meaning you can modify or nullify the arrangement anytime you wish, and you can change beneficiaries, or buy and sell assets.

Another feature of a living trust is that you can name the trustee who will manage your finances should you become disabled. This means if you get Alzheimers or some other debilitating illness, your family won't have to go through the emotionally wrenching process of going to court to arrange for a guardian or conserv-ator to handle your affairs.

Upon your death the living trust becomes irrevocable and the terms can't be changed. At this time, your designated successor trustee, usually a family member, will hand out the assets according to your instructions. And here's the part that really appeals to people: There's no waiting. Unlike a will, which has to go through the laborious probate process before heirs will see a penny of their inheritance, a living trust trustee can disperse your assets ASAP.

Living trusts are particularly practical for families who own real estate in more than one state because although wills might not travel across state lines, living trusts usually do. With a living trust your heirs avoid having to file a will and go through probate in all the states in which you owned property.

THE MYTHS

Now that you've heard all the good news about living trusts, a few words of warning. If not properly crafted, a badly drawn living trust can leave your estate in a mess. Be sure the lawyer you hire to do it has experience in your state. Another good sign is if the lawyer is a member of the American College of Trust and Estate Counsel. All sorts of salespeople are hawking living trusts; beware of anything that sounds too good to be true. Unscrupulous financial planners, accountants, and attorneys sell living trusts by making claims about their cost and tax features that just aren't true. Here are the most common misperceptions.

Myth 1. "Living trusts are cheaper than a will." In fact, overall prices are not much different. And there are some hidden costs with living trusts that can push the price well above the original cost of drawing up the document. Often there are additional charges for transferring your assets, redrawing deeds, and changing titles into the trust.

Myth 2. "Once the document is drawn up, signed, and dated, I don't have to think about it anymore." No. Your work has just begun—now you have to transfer your assets, and if you don't, the trust is worthless. Sadly, many people go through the trouble of writing a living trust but then never transfer their property, stocks, and bonds to the trust. It works only if you follow through and place your assets in it.

Myth 3. "There is no legal difference between property held in my name and in the living trust." Generally, that's true. But sometimes problems can arise if you've placed your home in the living trust and later want to refinance it. Some banks insist the title be held by an individual, not a trust. It can also be difficult to get some types of car insurance if the car title is held by a trust.

Myth 4. "Administering trusts is easy." Living trusts require

Q Are living trusts and living wills the same thing?

A Not at all, although they sound similar. A living trust is an estate planning device for keeping your assets out of probate court. A living will has to do with your health and tells people what you want in terms of medical intervention should you become incapacitated or unable to communicate.

some additional paperwork, which sellers of these estate planning devices tend to gloss over.

Myth 5. "A living trust has tax advantages." Wrong. A living trust is not a tax saving device. The assets in your trust will be included in your estate for tax purposes. It has no special tax benefits at all. A living trust won't save your heirs a penny in taxes.

CLAIMS BY CREDITORS

Another twist that living trust advocates sometimes forget to mention is that in some states there's no deadline for filing claims by creditors against trust assets. With a living trust, suits against your estate can be brought for years after you are deceased. On the other hand, with a will there is a deadline, usually four to six months after the will has been admitted to probate. If the creditors miss that narrow window of opportunity, tough luck—your checkbook is off-limits.

THE POUR-OVER WILL

What happens if you inadvertently leave some assets out of your living trust? For instance,

you forgot about those 45 shares in a small growth company that you bought on a whim one day. If those assets aren't included in the living trust, then that portion of your estate will have to go through probate after all.

But there is a way to catch any assets that fall through the cracks, and that is a pour-over will, which allows those assets to "pour over" into the trust. A knowledgeable lawyer or financial planner will always recommend this supplement. A pour-over will catch any assets not tucked into the living trust safe-deposit box. Of course, creating a pour-over will adds to your legal costs.

LIVING WILLS AND BEYOND— PREPARING FOR HEALTH CARE CRISES

Sparing your family the agonizing choice of deciding whether to prolong your life or hasten your death if you can't make the choice yourself is even more important today, thanks to the Supreme Court. Take the case of Nancy Cruzan: She lay in a vegetative state in a hospital for years while her family appealed unsuccessfully to state courts to allow doctors to pull the artificial life-support plug. Eventually the Supreme Court held the state was right to continue treatment, even though there was no hope of recovery, because Nancy hadn't made her wishes clearly known before the car accident that put her in a coma. (Later the family unearthed new evidence of Nancy's wishes, and the state allowed her feeding tube to be withdrawn.)

Nobody likes to contemplate such morbid possibilities, but in today's high-tech medical world, you must. A living will outlines your feelings on the subject should you be unable to voice an opinion if tragedy strikes. These documents are usually relatively brief and general, instructing your doctors to let you die naturally if you have an "incurable injury, disease, or illness certified to be a terminal condition." They also let you choose to continue medical care under specified conditions.

Because the subject is so touchy, states can be demanding about how you set up a living will. Many states have a standard approved form of living will. Most require that a living will be signed, dated, and witnessed by two people who are *not* relatives and who do not stand to inherit upon your death. Officials don't want the son who's getting all your worldly goods to have anything to do with your decision to end your life.

The question of unlimited medical intervention is not a theoretical one. As many as 10,000 patients are being kept alive today in situations very much like the one that kept Nancy Cruzan's family in the courts, and in turmoil, for years.

The emotional cost to your family is just one aspect of the horrifying prospect of spending your final years hooked to a machine. There is a financial toll, too. The cost of complicated life-support systems could wipe out your family's assets in no time at al!. Of course, you may wish to be kept alive and this, too, may be the wish of your family; but if that's not your desire, you must make it known.

Today, there is a double reason for making a living will—if you don't, some courts may view your lack of action as evidence you *want* unlimited access to life-support technology.

But for all they do accomplish,

living wills are not a panacea for all medical crises. There are some shortcomings:

• Living wills are not always followed by medical personnel. A 1990 study of nursing-home residents in the *New England Journal of Medicine* found that doctors and nurses frequently make treatment decisions that directly contradict a patient's living will. Many health-care experts say that doctors are often reluctant to withhold medical treatment on the basis of a piece of paper, even a legal one.

• Most living wills are general— they simply state that the writer doesn't wish to have prolonged life-support measures if their condition is "terminal." But many medical decisions fall in a decidedly gray zone—for instance, what to do when a patient has had a stroke, is in a coma, and doctors are uncertain about whether or not she will awaken. In such a case, the wishes of a 87-year-old widow may be very different from those of a 42-year-old mother of three, yet both may have a living will that uses similar language.

• Some states won't recognize a living will if it's executed before a terminal condition is diagnosed.

Only if you know you have a terminal illness will those states honor your wishes. If you have an illness such as cancer that could cost you your life, you should update your wishes regarding medical intervention.

• In some states, such as California, a living will automatically expires after five years. You have to update it to keep it active.

• Most states honor only living wills made within their borders, with many states imposing specific standards for a living will.

DURABLE HEALTH-CARE POWER OF ATTORNEY

Health-care experts say that giving someone else durable power of attorney is the best way to ensure that a patient's wishes will be respected when they can no longer voice their own opinion. Giving someone power of attorney means you authorize him or her to act for you should you be unable to make decisions on your own. Durable health-care power of attorney means you limit that power to medical decisions, and you can specify what you want the "attorney" or "agent" to handle by granting broad powers to decide your health care or by limiting the power to specific medical situations.

This option is really for the person who lives by the Boy Scout's credo—be prepared. Giving someone durable health-care power of attorney is more flexible than a living will because it can be invoked for a variety of reasons—say, if you're incapacitated and in a vegetative state but not "terminal." But you have to be sure you trust the person implicitly to make decisions on your behalf. The person has to know you well—and be able to judge whether you're just acting slightly eccentric, or whether you're seriously, permanently impaired. It's a huge responsibility to place on the shoulders of a loved one.

The power of "health-care proxies" as they're also called, varies from state to state. All states have laws governing durable power of attorneys, but only recently has the concept of medical care been applied. Check your state's laws before you make any move or contact Choice and Dying (212/366-5540), which can provide information on proxies and living wills.

TALKING TO YOUR FAMILY ABOUT DYING (GULP)

Some people can talk about their financial affairs with the same ease with which they discuss summer vacations. But for most families, sharing ideas about death and money ranks up there with sex on the privacy scale.

Sometimes children have a hard time raising the "what-happens-after-you-die" topic for fear of looking like gold diggers. Or they don't want to contemplate their parents' death. Parents may avoid the topic for the same reason—who wants to face their own mortality?

Forging through the awkwardness is tough but necessary. Many kids want—indeed, need—to know what their parents have planned. With life expectancies getting longer and longer, it isn't unreasonable for your children to wonder if your planning is adequate to cover life's unexpected hazards, a major illness, for example. If children may someday be picking up the tab should Mom and Dad live beyond their means, the kids have to know. On the other hand, if you have socked away a couple hundred thousand in savings, which you intend to pass on, the kids should know that, too. It might affect a decision about a new home or job, or what college their daughter can attend.

If parents have left potential mines in their wake, such as leaving most of their property to one child, it's only fair to make the decision public. That way the chosen beneficiary won't have to suffer the slings and arrows of slighted siblings who can't understand why Mom and Dad did this. Likewise if you're giving all of your money to charity, don't keep it a secret. Your kids deserve to know.

There's another reason for bringing up the unmentionable. When parents become ill or die, children usually want to carry out their final wishes. It can help to know what they are beforehand. A time of mourning over a father's recent death in Colorado is not the time to discover he wanted to be buried in Wisconsin on the old family farm.

The first key to tackling this touchy subject is timing. Don't bring it up at Thanksgiving dinner just before the pumpkin pie. Choose a time that experts call a "moment of opportunity" a major life change, such as retirement, a milestone birthday, a move to a new home, or the death of a rela-

tive. Major life-shaking events can more easily give way to a powwow over other big things, such as Mom and Dad's late-life planning. Also, be sensitive to where you bring up the subject. Around a table in the middle of a busy restaurant is no place to raise delicate, "What ifs?" Your home is probably the best place, but make sure guests aren't expected within the hour and no one is about to run off for a dental appointment.

One way to ease into the topic is to ask, or answer, the easy questions first, then move into the emotion-heavy questions later. Unless you know already, you should cover these topics:

• Where important documents —the will, life insurance policy, social security cards, and bank account numbers—are stored.

• Who will be the executor? If a decision hasn't been made, talk about the decisions an executor will need to make and how they should be made. For instance, should the executor be the only authority or should decisions be made by consensus? What if family members disagree with the executor? Does the executor receive a fee, and how much?

• How should personal effects

DISINHERITANCE: THE ULTIMATE JAB

" To my son I leave the pleasure of earning a living. For 28 years he thought the pleasure was mine, but he was mistaken." So read the will of an exasperated father who certainly got in the last word on the subject.

Disinheritance is not a laughing matter, however. Nor is it easy. Some states won't even allow a spouse to be completely disinherited no matter what his or her crime. If you write a will specifically leaving out an obvious heir, say one son out of three, it is wise to state your exact reasons for doing so. That way the court will have some idea of your state of mind, reducing the chances the disgruntled child will be able to contest the will. On the other hand, the specified reasons may give the son grounds for challenging the will. The best route? Talk to a lawyer.

Some experts recommend living trusts if you intend to disinherit a family member. They are harder to challenge and courts are more reluctant to fiddle with them.

be handled? Will the Steuben crystal collection go to Cousin Jake, and who gets the Biedermeier dresser? Attached to the will should be a letter explaining how jewelry, clothing, and personal items should be divided (although in many states, this letter isn't legally enforceable). Another possibility is to give heirs the choice of deciding what they want. A third way is to discuss now what each child would like, and assuming there's no big conflict, put their preferences in the will.

• How do you feel about organ donations, transplants, and autopsies? Air your thoughts now, and put them in writing.

• What about burial and funeral preferences? Talk about cremation, ashes, memorial services, burial plots, or any other thoughts you have about "procedural" matters. Some people like the idea of a wake or party in their memory, and like to organize and fund such an event in advance.

FINDING A WILL, TRUST, OR ESTATE ATTORNEY

Along with everyone else who has to sell a service to make a living, lawyers are waking up to the graying of America. Many attorneys now claim to cater to retirees' needs—drawing up wills, setting up trusts, negotiating probate. But how can you be sure? By the time someone discovers the lawyer messed up the wording in your will or failed to add assets to your trust, it's usually too late to do anything about it. Most people don't find the little mistakes—their heirs do.

There are no guarantees of competence, but a little background checking can help you avoid sloppy work and costly mistakes. One way to minimize surprises is to locate an attorney who specializes in problems of the elderly. You may not be in that group yet, but aging issues—wills, trusts, durable powers of attorney, etc.—are often not addressed until later years; thus the area has come to be called "elder law."

One place to start is to ask the trust officer at your local bank if he or she knows a qualified lawyer. If you're near a law school,

call a professor who teaches probate or estate planning and ask for names of experienced practitioners. A sure bet for finding a good referral is to attend free seminars on the subject you're interested in. But be careful. Usually attorneys or professionals who present free seminars at a community college or association are on the level, but not always. Occasionally, a speaker uses these occasions more for selling than for educating.

Checking with local agencies that follow aging issues is another good way to get referred to someone with experience. These associations may have listings of lawyers who have the experience you want:

- The American Association of Retired Persons
- Area Agency on Aging
- Children of Aging Parents
- Health Insurance Association of America
- National Citizen's Coalition for Nursing Home Reform
- Older Women's League
- Support groups for specific diseases
- State offices on aging
- State or local bar association (use this as a last resort since usually all it takes to be listed is to be

a member or pay a small fee; there is no screening)

Also, check whether the attorney you have picked is a member of a professional organization like the American College of Trust and Estate Counsel. A professional association has standards for membership that at least provide you with a modicum of certainty your lawyer is familiar with the topic areas.

ATTORNEYS

Many people want more than someone to write their will; they want someone to handle all their financial affairs. A widow more interested in Caribbean arts and crafts than in worrying about the Dow Jones average is a good candidate to hire an attorney to help manage her finances and legal matters. An attorney can provide an array of services, from managing investments to filing tax returns, establishing trusts, maintaining legal documents, and paying certain bills.

The advantage of having someone else manage your financial affairs is obvious: It frees you to do other things. On the other hand, it's a big commitment, so take your time choosing a good attorney. Ask for references and interview them, as you would anyone you're thinking of hiring. You can begin slowly, letting the attorney handle only certain matters until you're comfortable with his or her decisions. And follow the same guidelines above for finding a good lawyer or trustee.

The question of whether to grant this person power of attorney, which would give him or her total control over your finances, is not to be taken lightly. Be suspicious of an attorney, financial planner, or bank trust department that urges you to completely turn

Q Don't I want an estate attorney to help me with estate planning?

A An "estate attorney" probates estates after death. Before that day, you want an attorney who specializes in estate planning or elder law.

over the reins to your estate by giving total power of attorney. Unless you're obviously ill, be wary if they raise the subject first. If you're going to need someone to make decisions for you, you initiate the discussion. (For more on lawyers as financial planners, see page 41.)

FUNERAL PLANNING

There are 22,000 funeral homes in the United States and some 2.1 million deaths per year. One would think dealing with a funeral home, which people do every day, would be easy. But often it's not. Few things are approached with more dread than the obligatory visit to the funeral parlor after a loved one dies.

That's one reason why many elderly people pre-plan their funerals. Morbid as it may seem, it does save wear and tear on relatives, who are probably already distraught enough without the added trauma of looking at the price tags on caskets.

Advance planning of funerals is becoming so common that mortuaries today offer an array of funding mechanisms that can be as varied as the investment options at

the neighborhood bank. The simplest contracts are those that are "guaranteed." You make an up-front payment and the funeral home promises to provide the services and merchandise you selected when you die, regardless of how much costs have increased by then.

But some people—and many funeral directors—prefer to fund future funerals with more creative financing. There are special bank trust funds, annuities, savings accounts, even life insurance contracts, that can be set up to pay for your funeral when the time comes. All of these financing mechanisms are complex, so don't be bullied into making a quick decision. Talk to your lawyer or financial planner about which contract, if any, makes sense to you.

One reason funeral homes promote financing schemes is that they're often crafted to the benefit of the mortuary. For instance, be alert to what happens to the "excess" cash buildup in any account you establish. Say you set up a savings account and assume that it will make 7 percent interest, compounded, over the next 15 years. Suppose the interest is actually higher and instead of building to $4,500—which is what your fu-

On the Lookout for Obits

An obituary notice in your local newspaper may do more than alert your spouse's friends and co-workers that he or she has died. It also signals that a widow or widower is about to come into money, at a time when defenses are down. That's a combination that has enriched the pockets of many an unscrupulous scam artist. Be wary of the following:

- Any merchandise or other item that arrives COD, supposedly ordered by the deceased.
- Unusual bills that come too quickly after your loved one's death. Most state probate courts have a grace period for notifying and paying off creditors. Don't pay any bills before the specified waiting period is ended. That way you won't be tricked into paying a phony outstanding debt. You should, however, continue to pay ordinary monthly bills, such as a mortgage or auto loan.
- Phone solicitations or home visits by "agents" who have an investment "deal" for you. Ask any salesman where he got your name and number. A cold call from someone selling you the investment opportunity of a lifetime should be ignored. He probably picked your name out of the newspaper obituary section.
- You'd be surprised how friends and relatives suddenly need a small loan for this emergency or that crisis. It's probably best to stall until you are better able to make a decision. You could say you don't have access to the inheritance yet. That's probably not a big lie since even a living trust takes a while to distribute.

neral will cost—the fund grows to $5,000. If it isn't in writing that any extra money goes to your estate, it'll end up lining the funeral directors' pockets.

Another note: You're generally responsible for income tax on any interest earned on an annuity, savings account, or trust fund regardless of the fact that the funeral home, and not you, gets the proceeds in the end.

The average cost of a funeral today is $3,533, according to the National Funeral Directors Association. That price, however, doesn't include cemetery costs or a gravestone.

If you think picking out a casket is the biggest funeral-related decision someone has to make, think again. You'll have to ponder whether you want the casket to be left open or not. Whether you want to be cremated or buried. Where your ashes are to be placed or spread. The list goes on. Funeral services usually include:

- Professional services of a funeral director or staff
- The hearse and other transportation services
- Embalming and preparation, if an open casket
- Facilities for your loved ones to pay their last respects
- The funeral ceremony
- Other services, such as music or religious services

FUNERAL DOUBLE-SPEAK

This is a true story: A father and his son made the dreaded trip to a funeral home in California to make arrangements for their newly departed wife and mother. Although they agreed they wouldn't be talked into any superfluous add-ons, the funeral director convinced them to pay an extra $100 for a more "dignified" wood cremation box than the normal cardboard variety.

Later, when the family went to transfer the ashes into a special urn, the father noticed the "box" was simple cardboard, not the oak veneer he had paid for. He called the funeral home to ask what happened.

"Oh, sir," purred the receptionist. "I think you are confusing the cremains with the remains."

The extra "dignified" box, it turns out, was for the remains, which no one ever saw because they soon become the "cremains." Moral: Watch out for fast sales talk even from funeral people.

And there's the merchandise:

• Casket for your body or urn for your ashes

• Any other burial container, such as a cemetery vault

• Flowers, notices, and or thank-you cards. Funeral homes these days are veritable Hallmark stores and they are happy to arrange flowers too, if that's appropriate.

WATCH OUT

There are some questions you should definitely ask before you commit to a funeral plan. The biggest is, what happens if you move and want to change funeral homes? Some morticians will let you out of a contract if you move, others won't. Get it in writing. Likewise, has the funeral home guaranteed the price no matter how many years have passed and how much costs have increased by the time you make the final trip in the front door? What are the tax consequences of any funding arrangement you might enter? Is there a grace period during which you can cancel the contract? Changing your mind, at least for a fixed period of time, should be allowed.

Obviously, planning for your death can be as simple, or as complicated, as you want it. But go into the process clear eyed and you'll save yourself and your family a lot of hassle and grief.

ESTATE PLANNING

You don't have to be a Carnegie or a Rockefeller to have an estate. *Everyone* has an estate. Boiled down, an estate is what you leave behind when you die. It's the sum of all of your assets minus debts, and includes your house, pension, life insurance, stocks and bonds, bank accounts, everything, even your old Barbie doll collection or that Hank Aaron signature baseball. Don't make the common mistake of overlooking retirement benefits and insurance policies. A big portion of your net worth may come from your company's retirement, profit-sharing, or employee stock option plan, other company-sponsored retirement benefits, or your own IRA.

ADD UP YOUR ESTATE

Add it all up and you'll probably find your estate is bigger than you think. This is particularly true if you live in a part of the country where housing prices have appreciated rapidly these past several decades. To figure out the worth of your assets, start with what you think you could sell your home for today. What you paid for it back in 1968 doesn't count. It's the market price when you die that the IRS uses to calculate the value of your estate. Taking today's price is the closest you can get to an educated estimate. Next, add in stocks, bonds, pension payout, savings, life insurance, and anything else of value that will be passed on to your heirs. Use the item's current market value, not what you paid.

THE NUT OF ESTATE PLANNING: WHAT HAPPENS TO YOUR PROPERTY

The main reason you go to the trouble to do estate planning is to disinherit the IRS. You want to make sure your heirs get as much of the reward as possible, and that Uncle Sam gets as little as possible. That's the theory and goal, but in practice the state and feds, through various estate and inheritance taxes, may get a good piece of your worldly goods.

A tightfisted Uncle Sam has wiped out most of the tax shelters and generational transfer schemes that once made it so easy for the wealthy to place much of their life's loot out of the federal government's reach. Today, estate planning is no less an art form, but there are a lot fewer tools to work with. It's a sign of the times that one of the most popular estate planning vehicles, which uses an irrevocable trust funded with life insurance, is designed not to avoid taxes but to ensure your heirs have enough cash to *pay* them. And another tax-saver, the charitable remainder trust, works only if you *give away* some of your assets to a charity.

When the subject is estate planning, people are lumped into one of two categories that are pretty clear-cut: those with estates valued under $600,000 and those with estates over $600,000.

For people passing on with less than $600,000, estate planning is relatively simple, with the federal government taking nothing. But slip over the $600,000 line and the scenery changes entirely. Federal estate taxes are so high on anything over the $600,000 that to avoid planning is simply foolish. For example, if your estate is worth $2 million, the net federal

OW! THAT TAX BITE

"There is only one difference between the tax collector and the taxidermist—the taxidermist leaves the hide." And that came from a former commissioner of the IRS, no less.

Federal estate taxes are no laughing matter. As if they aren't bad enough now, there is no guarantee Washington won't raise the tax rates, or lower the threshold amount, in the future. As of 1993 these are the tax rates (over the $600,000 exemption):

Amount	Tax Percentage
$ 600,001– 750,000	37%
750,001–1,000,000	39
1,000,001–1,250,000	41
1,250,001–1,500,000	43
1,500,001–2,000,000	45
2,000,001–2,500,000	49
2,500,001 and up	50

estate tax is $488,400 (the figure takes into account the federal and state credits). Clearly, some planning and legal maneuvering can save your heirs a bundle.

THE $600,000 LIMIT

All estates enjoy an exemption of $600,00 from federal taxes. Basically, when you die the govern-ment gives you a tax credit of $192,800, which would be equal to the tax on $600,000. So you're al-lowed to bequeath $600,000 with-out the amount being taxed.

That tax floor, by the way, is a *net* figure; it's figured after all of your debts, including funeral ex-penses, medical expenses, and do-nations to charity, are paid off. The figure does not mean every-

Q My husband is a Mexican citizen. Does this make a difference to my estate planning?

A It sure does, because noncitizens don't qualify for the marital deduction. Talk to a lawyer about establishing a special trust for him.

one in your family gets to inherit $600,000 but rather that your estate can give away $600,000 in one check or in dozens of checks, with no federal tax bite.

As noted earlier, the most common estate planning strategy is to divide a married couple's estate into two parts, so that the wife and husband each have an estate and can bequeath $600,000. This, in effect, doubles the tax-free exemption to $1.2 million.

UNLIMITED MARITAL DEDUCTION

Remember, there is a special break for married couples— you can leave as much as you want to your surviving spouse, whether that is $6 or $60 million— and he or she won't pay a cent in federal estate taxes. (However, when the second spouse dies, the estate will pay taxes on anything over $600,000. So if you leave everything to your spouse, your children could pay more taxes on the death of the second parent.)

The vast majority of Americans —more than 95 percent—have nothing to fear from Uncle Sam's final attempt to drain their pockets because their estates fall below the threshold. (There may be a state pinch, though.) If you're under the $600,000 ceiling, you don't need to worry about complicated estate planning. But that doesn't mean you can rest easy. At the very least you still need a will or its substitute, a living trust.

But, should you be among the fortunate 5 percent and your assets total more than $600,000 or close to it, you need some extensive estate planning. Otherwise your money may end up filling the vaults at the U.S. Treasury Department instead of your daughter's bank account. And the tax bite isn't small change, either. Federal estate taxes in 1993 range from 37 percent to 50 percent.) Thankfully, there are many ways to trim the federal bite down to size. With a little forethought, you could disinherit the IRS.

HOW ABOUT GIVING IT AWAY?

After all the talk about death and disability, here is some good news. In the otherwise tight-as-a-drum tax code there's a tidy loophole when it comes to gifts. Every year you can make tax-free gifts of as much as $10,000 to anyone and any number of people. If you have fourteen grandchildren and a pile of cash to distribute, go right ahead, as long as each handout doesn't exceed $10,000. Your spouse has the same right—so be-tween you, you can give away $20,000 per recipient every year.

Go over the $10,000 top, however, and the IRS will exact a heavy price. Any excess over the threshold will be subtracted from your $600,000 freebie when your estate tax is figured at your death. That means your heirs will eventually pay 37 to 50 percent tax rates on their inheritances because of the gifts you made years before.

If your estate is nowhere near the lofty level where estate taxes kick in, your gifts, no matter how large, will be free and clear of taxes for the recipient. That is, if you have the cash to be handing out megadollar presents.

GREAT EXPECTATIONS

The wealthiest generation of retirees in American history is, to put it bluntly, reaching the end of their days. Sad as that may be, it's good news, financially speaking, for the 64 million baby boomers who'll directly benefit from the coming wave of inheritances. Some economists predict that as much as $7 *trillion* in inheritance money will be passed on between now and the year 2011 as the parents of the baby boom generation die. Of course, not everyone will benefit equally in the redistribution of wealth. A scant 1 percent will get one-third of the inheritance kitty. Nine percent will inherit the next third. The remaining 90 percent get what's left.

There's another tax twist to keep in mind. If your gifts include assets such as stocks, bonds, or artwork, there could be unintended income tax consequences. For example, if you give your daughter stock you bought for $10,000 in 1978 that is worth $28,000 when she decides to sell it, your daughter will have to pay capital gains taxes on all $18,000 of the appreciation. The reason is that there is no so-called "step-up" in the income tax basis for assets that are given away during your life. (Assets bequeathed to an heir are, however, "stepped up" —increased in valued from their original cost to their current value —when their owner dies, not before.) So estate planners sometimes recommend giving cash before death, or assets that haven't appreciated very much.

There are other gift traps, too:

• Sometimes a parent will give her home to the kids before she dies and continue to live there rent-free. It may sound like a good deal, but beware. The IRS will pull the house back into the estate if the parent has been living there rent-free. As far as the IRS is concerned, this situation is a no-go. In order for it to work, the parent must pay rent on the house and have a written lease, and the child should not only hold title but also pay taxes, insurance, and upkeep for the property.

• Likewise, sometimes parents will give away stocks and bonds to their children but keep the dividends or interest for themselves. The IRS won't fall for this trick and will consider the gift a part of the estate upon death.

If you have a large estate and want to use the gift tax to whittle down your financial empire, you should consult a financial planner or tax attorney. There are lots of creative ways to give while you are still here on Earth rather than waiting until you are gone. But don't be foolish. Give what you can afford, and no more. Don't be in a rush to parcel out your assets if there is even the smallest chance you might need them later on.

"PUT YOUR MONEY IN TRUST"

"Put not your trust in money, but your money in trust." So said Oliver Wendell Holmes in 1858. His words hold true today, especially in estate planning,

INVENTORY

Don't make your spouse or children search through a lifetime's worth of bits of paper to find the certificate for that IBM stock you bought in 1967. One way to help add up your estate is to write out the following inventory list. With each item, be sure to include its approximate value and where it is stored. It will force you to get organized, and will provide whomever you leave in charge with an easy-to-follow reference guide for your important papers.

- Birth certificate (yours and children's)
- Marriage certificate
- Life insurance policies
- Accident, sickness, or disability insurance policies
- Business agreements/contracts
- Checkbooks and bankbooks
- Savings accounts, CDs, and other bank accounts
- IRA accounts
- Pension and/or work retirement funds
- Stocks, bonds, or other securities
- Real estate deeds
- Automobile registration and title
- Loan payment books (for home and auto)
- Notes receivable
- Notes payable
- Wills and trust documents
- Recent income tax form
- W-2 forms
- Other assets
- Social Security number
- Military discharge papers/ Veterans Administration number

where trusts are as important to the job as a saddle is to a professional jockey. Without trusts, you don't get very far. Two of the most common types of trusts, the credit shelter and the QTIP trust, were discussed in the section on wills. Other frequently used trusts are Life Insurance Trusts, Charitable Remainder Trusts, and Grantor Retained Income Trusts (GRITs).

LIFE INSURANCE TRUSTS

One way to leave cash to your heirs tax-free is to put life insurance into an irrevocable trust.

(Your lawyer may call this a "wealth replacement trust"—it's the same thing.) Irrevocable means that it can't be changed, amended, or revoked. The permanency of this option is absolute: Once you establish the trust you've given up all rights to the life insurance held by the trust and you can't get it back. You can't get a loan against the policy, either, since technically it isn't yours anymore.

To use an example, Steve Savvy sets up an irrevocable trust that buys a $200,000 life insurance policy and names a trustee other than himself. Steve contributes $2,500 each year to pay the premium and that contribution is tax-free because it's considered a "gift" to the trust (and it's under the $10,000 gift limit). When Steve dies, the $200,000 insurance booty in the trust goes to his kids according to his directions. The entire payoff is tax-free.

There are a couple of catches (aren't there always?) that can trigger trouble with the IRS. If Steve's wife is named a beneficiary, the life insurance may be pulled back into the estate because the IRS judges a husband and wife as one unit. Or if Steve places an existing policy in a trust, rather than buying a new one, he'd better not die for a least three years (as if he has any say!). If three years haven't passed since the life insurance was transferred to the trust, the IRS will include the amount in the estate and not let it pass tax-free.

Financial planners recommend these life insurance trusts as one way to ensure your kids have the cash they'll need to pay estate taxes. Sometimes heirs have to sell property they might not want to get rid of, solely for the purposes of raising money to satisfy the IRS. These trusts provide a pile of cash that can be raided for precisely that purpose. Small-business owners whose children inherit a healthy concern but tight cash flow are good candidates for these types of trusts.

Charitable Remainder Trusts

Charitable remainder trusts have become very popular as an estate planning tool. Some estate planners are promoting them more as tax shelters than philanthropic gestures. If you want to leave something to charity, and get a tax break in the here and now, this is one way.

In this scenario, Steve has an estate worth $1 million, which includes a $300,000 piece of beachfront property in Delaware that he bought 30 years ago for a mere $25,000. Now he wants to sell his slice of the Delaware seashore and he also wants to leave some money to a children's hospital. With those two goals in mind, Steve puts the property in a charitable remainder trust.

Steve reaps a double tax bounty with a huge deduction on his income taxes because the charitable trust can sell property without incurring capital gains taxes. If Steve had sold the assets himself, he would have been slapped with a 28 percent capital gains tax bill on the $275,000 gain. Instead, the trust sells the Delaware real estate and invests the proceeds in stocks and bonds, and (this is the attractive part) Steve receives the income from the portfolio. When Steve dies, the trust is dissolved and the hospital gets the principal.

When most people set up a charitable remainder trust they let the charity handle the investments. Most colleges, community foundations, hospitals, and other big charities have experts who run charitable remainder trusts and other investments. The appeal is clear: Financial pros manage your money and it's in their interest to do a good job since they get whatever is left when you die. The downside is there are no guarantees as to how the experts will perform. If you're counting on the income from the trust to maintain your standard of living, be careful. The charity's investment managers may try to do a good job, but if they botch it, your income stream could slow to a trickle.

And there's another small matter you might consider: the kids. If you put all of your assets into a charitable remainder trust, your children may not be pleased. That's why many wealthy retirees use some of the income from the charitable trusts to set up irrevocable life insurance trusts for their kids. In Steve's case, some of the income from his trust buys two policies, one each for his daughter and son. That way everybody is happy and the government has been aced out of a chunk of cash it would have received had Steve sold his property himself, or left it in his still sizable estate.

Final note: Don't forget that a charitable remainder trust is irrevocable. Once you give away the principal, you cannot, under any circumstances, get it back. Nor can you later decide you want son Billy to have the money after all. These things are set in stone.

GRANTOR RETAINED INCOME TRUSTS—GRITS

For people living in a pricey hunk of real estate, Grantor Retained Income Trusts can help save a tidy bundle. The strategy works best for people whose home constitutes a big part of their estate and whose mortgage is paid off, or close to it.

With a GRIT, you essentially transfer ownership of your home while continuing to live in it. You give your house to a trust for a fixed number of years and name a trustee. The beneficiaries of the trust, usually your children, receive the house when the trust expires.

WOODY ALLEN, PHILOSOPHER

"The key, I think, is not to think of death as an end, but to think of it as a very effective way to cut down on your expenses."

But the finish line for a GRIT is not simply to give away your house, but to outlive the term of the trust. Then, you get the tax benefits of the deal. Let's say Steve Savvy is 70 and creates a ten-year GRIT for his home. When he "gives" the house to the trust, he computes the gift tax on a portion of the value, based on actuarial tables. Say the home is worth $300,000; in this case, the tax is applied to about 38 percent of the value, or $115,663. (Why 38 percent? It goes back to the age of the trust. Let your estate lawyer do the figuring.) Since the first $10,000 is free under the gift-tax exclusion, Steve computes the tax on $105,663. No gift tax is actually paid, though. The $300,000 gift to the trust is considered to be part of Steve's exemption.

This GRIT gets very tasty when Steve outlives the 10-year term because that signals the end of estate tax liability. There won't be any more taxes on the family home even though it's transferred to his heirs. So 62 percent of the house, or $186,000, is shielded from the IRS, saving the kids at least $68,820 or 37 percent (that's the lowest tax rate on estates over $600,000).

One small footnote: Steve

needs a roof over his head, and once the trust expires, he has to either move out or make a deal with the new owners, his kids, to let him live there. And he has to pay fair market rent for the privilege of staying in the house or the IRS won't allow the tax break. A more serious problem can crop up because Steve has lost control over his largest asset. What happens if he gets sick while the trust is active and needs to sell the house to cover medical bills? The trustee may not be able to sell the property, depending on how the trust is worded.

But let's back up for a minute. What if Steve dies before the trust expires? This unpleasant turn of events ends the trust and the value of the house is drawn back into his estate. In this case, Steve is out the cost of setting up the trust.

ONE POTATO, TWO POTATO . . . CHOOSING A TRUSTEE

Who will carry out the terms of your trusts? Manage any investments? Round up all those titles, contracts, and bank accounts? Have property appraised, and sold if necessary? Deal with your creditors? And what about filing those estate and inheritance tax forms with state and federal governments? The answer to all these questions is contained in a single word: a trustee. But given all there is to do, the lucky designee must be chosen with care and thought.

You might automatically assume that one of your children should serve as trustee. People generally name their children out of love, and because it saves the money required to hire a professional trustee. Annual fees charged by banks, lawyers, or other experienced trustees range from 0.75 percent to 1.5 percent of the estate. But, serving as a trustee for a relative really is a labor of love—accent on the labor —and it can backfire. Often a trustee who is family or friend doesn't have the financial dexterity to do the job well, particularly if it involves investing. A Rhode Island father named his daughter trustee of his living trust worth $2 million. The daughter made a series of bad investments and six months after her father died the trust was worth $1.5 million. The result: a suit against the daughter by her two angry brothers. The moral: be sure whoever you ask to be trustee is up to the task.

Hiring a professional has pitfalls, too. If the bank or law firm is doing a bad job it can be very hard for heirs to unseat them, unless the trustee is in flagrant violation of the law. If a bank's investment performance isn't up to par it may cost your heirs money, but there is little they can do about it. However, you can carefully structure trust documents so that beneficiaries have some power over a trustee whose exploits fall short.

When choosing someone to manage your trust, consider this:

• Do you have complete faith in the person? Removing a trustee requires a lot of legal muscle. If the trustee doesn't follow your instructions to the letter, your heirs would have to take the trustee to court. The state won't look out for your, or your heirs', interests as it would with a will. Furthermore, if the trustee has misspent your estate or not followed your instructions, it may be hard to recover anything, unless he or she has deep pockets.

• Does the person want the job? Just because you name someone, doesn't mean he or she will accept. So, don't assume your golfing buddy wants to handle your affairs.

• Where does the person live? It isn't impossible to handle an estate across state lines, but it's much smoother if the person you appoint is a resident in your home state. Some states insist on it.

• If you appoint a professional manager—a bank trust department, for example—what is its reputation? Ask for references at the bank and talk to others in your community. Ask for copies of investment reports on the bank's investment accounts for the previous four years. Find out the trust department's investment philosophy; for instance, does it aim to preserve your estate or make it grow? Where will it invest your money if you don't specify the kind of portfolio you want? Check with the local Better Business Bureau and Chamber of Commerce to see if there have been any complaints lodged against the bank.

STATE TAXES

If you thought the federal government was the only hand in your coffer, don't look now but there's another. Where the feds leave off, the state steps in.

States can collect three kinds of

death taxes: "pickup" taxes (which all states impose), estate taxes, and inheritance taxes.

Inheritance taxes (as of November 1992) are imposed in 17 states and range from 1 percent in a couple of states to 32 percent in Montana. (Bear in mind, these are marginal rates not flat taxes, and they apply to different categories of beneficiaries. For an explanation of marginal rates, see Chapter 7.) Exactly what pieces of your estate the state nibbles on varies from state to state.

Five states that don't impose inheritance taxes (taxes applied to individual bequests) do levy estate taxes (taxes applied to entire estates), collecting a percentage of entire estates. Most of these states offer unlimited marital deductions and some exempt property—for instance, Mississippi exempts property up to $600,000. The five states are Massachusetts, Mississippi, New York, Ohio, and Oklahoma.

The third species of state tax is the "pickup" tax, a clever catch-all that's used by all 50 states. Its name highlights its main characteristic: It's a tax that allows states to claim a portion of your federal estate tax. The amount it picks up is the credit for state death taxes allowed by the federal government. It doesn't actually cost the taxpayer anything extra since it is a bite out of the federal pie. Essentially, the state grabs for itself a slice of Uncle Sam's dessert. The pickup tax is the only death tax in most Western states and in some east of the Rockies, including Maine and West Virginia.

It pays to check out what your state is doing since many have a much lower threshold (read "exemption" or "credit") for what can pass through untaxed than the federal government has. For instance, in Massachusetts, estates of over $200,000 are subject to some tax. Be warned that state legislatures have a habit of frequently fiddling with death taxes, particularly in times of budget crunch. What's true today may not be so tomorrow.

Here are the states that have either an estate or an inheritance tax, in addition to the universal pickup tax: Connecticut, Delaware, Indiana, Iowa, Kansas, Kentucky, Louisiana, Maryland, Massachusetts, Michigan, Mississippi, Montana, Nebraska, New Hampshire, New Jersey, New York, North Carolina, Ohio, Oklahoma, Pennsylvania, South Dakota, and Tennessee.

Chapter 7

DODGING TAXES AT RETIREMENT

No matter what you've earned or saved, taxes are a drain. There isn't a working person who hasn't stared at his or her pay stub and thought of a hundred better uses for all the money snatched by federal and state taxes. Typical Americans pay 40 percent of their earnings into state and federal tax coffers. Taxpayers toil from January to the first week of May to earn the money they owe in taxes, says the Tax Foundation, which keeps track.

These facts are probably nothing new to you—you've lived with them since your first day of work. But if you're eager for the day you

The IRS has a special publication for retirees called "Tax Information for Older Americans," Publication 554. It is available from the IRS and is worth sending for.

retire and can say good-bye to tax aggravations, there's some bad news—taxes never go away. You may retire from work but *never* from paying taxes. So along with retirement planning, you must plan your tax strategy.

DON'T TURN YOUR BACK ON THE IRS

Retiring can be as much a tax event as a personal milestone. When you retire (for now, assume that's at 59½), much of the money you've socked away tax-deferred into organized retirement plans can emerge without penalty. You can start spending your investment income (also called "unearned income") and owe taxes only on what you take out of a retirement plan. Of course you'll owe taxes on this income, as you will on other income, but if you're not on someone's payroll, odds are your tax bill will have noticeably shrunk.

However, before you thumb your nose at the IRS and throw away your tax guides, remember the taxpayer's credo: What the Tax Man Giveth, He Also Taketh Away. Just when you thought

Q When I retire I plan to move to a state with lower income taxes. Although I'll be retired from my job, I'm going to be doing part-time consulting from my new home. Any way I can deduct my moving expenses?

A Deducting moving expenses because they're related to your work is allowed only if you are working full-time in your new job for most of the year you move and you move at least 35 miles from your old home.

your tax burden was lightening, other obligations may pile on. Despite what you may have been led to think, senior citizens and retirees are given little special tax treatment. It's your income, regardless of whether you're 32 or 82, that determines the taxes you'll pay. It doesn't take a big annual paycheck to make you a taxpayer: in 1993 its $10,900 if filing jointly and under 65; $12,300 if filing jointly and both over 65; $6,050 if single and under 65; $6,950 if single and over 65.

It seems unfair, after years of spending and paying taxes, that your retirement can be threatened by tax liabilities. But it's true, and anyone on the brink of retirement has to be especially vigilant. Taxes can hurt even more at retirement because people may have exhausted or relinquished deductions that have helped to pare their tax bills. If you're not working, you can't claim business deductions; if you've paid off your house, you have no more mortgage deductions.

True, if you're over 65, you qualify for a slightly higher standard deduction—for married joint filers in 1993 an additional $1,400, and for single filers an additional $900. But this is about the limit of the government's largess for retirees.

Retirees who leave a company but take up other kinds of work also face taxing situations. Not only is your working income taxable but so, too, may be up to half your Social Security benefits. If your income (adjusted gross income plus tax-exempt interest income and half of Social Security income) is over $25,000 (for a single filer) or $32,000 (joint filer), those green checks from Social Security are taxed.

Being tax smart doesn't require an accounting degree. It's a readily learned skill not unlike that of dieters who have memorized the calorie counts of various foods and, when eating, tote up the damage. So, too, can reducing taxes be an automatic reflex that's part of any money decision.

This chapter offers some facts and strategies to boost your tax IQ and reduce what you hand over to the tax collectors.

KNOW THE LANGUAGE, KNOW THE LAND

Many people find the subject of taxes not only boring but also unfathomable. The IRS Tax Code fills out entire bookshelves and tax regulations are often as easy to decipher as Sanskrit. However, tax laws and practices are not quantum physics; given a little patience and study, the average person can crack the code.

Typically, people are deterred by the language of taxes. The multisyllable tongue twisters and terms composed of adjective heaped upon adjective confuse even the most lucid minds. Toss in a dash of math phobia and a distrust of anything emanating from Washington, and the average citizen capitulates and hands over all tax matters to a professional. While it's always helpful to consult a pro to act as translator, you should know what key tax terms mean. What follows is a brief tour through the language and laws of tax accounting, a pocket guide to Tax Land, as it were.

"Due to the imposition of special taxes on the elderly [for instance taxes on Social Security], many of today's workers will face higher marginal tax rates when they retire than during their working years."

—*Aldona and Gary Robbins,*
National Center for Policy Analysis,
as quoted in Consumer's Research

TAX RATES

Your tax rate is the percentage of your taxable income owed for federal income taxes, and it's set at three levels, depending on your income and your filing status.

Single taxpayer income	Tax rate
$1–22,100	15%
$22,100–53,500	28%
$53,500 and up	31%

Head of household income	Tax rate
$1–29,600	15%
$29,600–76,400	28%
$76,400 and up	31%

Married filing jointly income	Tax rate
$1–36,900	15%
$36,900–89,150	28%
$89,150 and up	31%

Married filing separately income	Tax rate
$1–18,450	15%
$18,450–44,575	28%
$44,575 and up	31%

EFFECTIVE TAX RATE

Your taxable income puts you squarely in a tax bracket, but this is not necessarily what you pay in taxes. You pay an "effective tax rate," which is the actual percentage of your gross income after you have taken deductions, exemptions, and any tax credits.

MARGINAL TAX RATE

As you just read, the IRS has created three major tax brackets that lump together various levels of wage earners. Your income is taxed incrementally (remember, the U.S. has a progressive tax system, meaning higher earners are taxed more). The tax rate on the dollars you earn early in the year starts low and rises through the brackets as your income increases. So the percentage of taxes you pay on early dollars is less than what you pay on later dollars. The last, highest rate you pay is your marginal tax rate. For instance, a couple filing a joint return with an adjusted gross income of $40,000 pays a 0 percent tax on the first $10,900 and 15 percent on

YOUR TAX RATE

Americans face two tax rates: the effective or average tax rate, which is the percentage that the bulk of their income is taxed at, and the marginal tax rate, which is the percentage that their highest earnings are taxed at. This table shows the two rates paid by various categories of taxpayers in 1992:

Taxpayer and Income	Average Rate	Marginal Rate
Single, $25,000	11.5%	28%
Single, $35,000	15.3%	28%
Single, $50,000	18.3%	28%
Married, two dependents, $25,000	5.9%	15%
Married, two dependents, $35,000	8.5%	15%
Married, two dependents, $50,000	10.4%	28%

Advisory Commission on Intergovernmental Relations

the next $29,100 earned.

Taxpayers have to be wary of marginal rates, anticipate when certain income may push them into another bracket, and if possible, defer or divert income to the next tax year.

ALTERNATIVE MINIMUM TAX

This tax guarantees the government will extract some taxes from most people, regardless of how many deductions and tax credits you claim. When figuring your taxes, if certain deductions (e.g., those from investments, such as accelerated depreciation, or tax shelter losses) reduce your tax bill to nothing or less than what you would pay on normal income, you must pay the alternative minimum tax. In 1993, the alternative minimum tax rate (ATM) was 24 percent. Consult your tax preparer to figure whether you must pay the AMT.

AGI: WHAT YOU EARN

The IRS rarely uses simple language to describe what you earn. The closest it comes is the term "adjusted gross income." This is the amount on which your taxable income is computed, but it's not everything you earn in a tax year. It's generally less than what you pocket and decidedly less if you're contributing to a retirement plan. Here's a rough idea of how to figure your AGI.

Begin by adding up your gross income, which consists of salary, wages, tips, interest, dividends, income on rental properties, annuities, pension, and royalties. Don't include money that's not subject to taxes, for example, interest from municipal bonds, gifts and inheritance, and Social Security benefits (up to a certain income level).

Next, subtract allowed expenses, for instance, certain business expenses, including operating losses; contributions to a Keogh, SEP, or deductible IRA; expenses related to rental income or royalties; alimony payments; penalties for early withdrawal of savings; and half of any self-employment tax you pay. And, voilà, the number you're left with is your AGI.

UNEARNED INCOME: AN UNFAIR LABEL

The term "unearned income" (also called "portfolio income") is money that comes from investments. The label implies a lack of thought and effort, but there's nothing easy about making smart investments.

CAPITAL GAINS: THE REWARDS OF SUCCESS

If you think of "capital" as another word for investment or asset, then this term becomes crystal clear. It's the amount your investment has grown over what you paid for it. Put another way, it's the difference between the original price and the price when you sell it. (What you paid is also referred to as your "cost" or "basis.") This gain could be appreciation on a house, the increase in the price of stock you own, or the added value of a business you own. Of course, not all investments move upward; some tumble, and the result is a capital loss.

Capital gains are often distinguished by whether they are long-term or short-term, referring to how long an investor owned or held on to the investment. If a year or less, the IRS says it's a short-term investment; a day over 12 months and it becomes long-term.

This distinction is more than calendar watching because short-term gains are taxed as regular income (up to 31 percent), while long-term gains are taxed at a maximum of 28 percent. There was a time when long-term capital gains were taxed at a much lower rate than regular income, which is why investors are rooting for Capitol Hill to return to that golden era. But the issue of taxing long-term cap gains has become a political football, and the game's not likely to end for many seasons.

TAX CREDITS: RARE GEMS ·

A tax credit is indeed a rare and valuable gem. Unlike a tax deduction, which reduces your gross income and so lowers your taxes according to your tax rate, a tax credit reduces your actual tax bill, dollar for dollar.

A special tax credit exists for seniors and for the disabled. You qualify for this credit if you're under 65, retired, and permanently and totally disabled, or if you are over 65. The credit is 15 percent of a base amount ($5,000 for single filers or $7,500 for joint filers) or a maximum of $750 or $1,125. This base amount is lowered, however, by nontaxable Social Security income and by pension income. It's also lowered by half the amount that your adjusted gross income exceeds $7,500 if you're single, or $10,000 on a joint return. If these add up to more than the base amount, you can't claim the credit.

TAX SHELTERS: FADING FAST

These are investments in which your money is allowed to grow with low or no tax liabilities or where the amount you invest creates a tax deduction or credit. Popular and prolific in the 1970s and 1980s, the sheltering qualities of many of these deals have been largely razed by tax reform laws requiring investors to be actively involved in a project to qualify for a deduction.

PLOT YOUR PROGRESS

To whittle down your tax bill you need all the backup you can muster. You can find support from a tax professional who knows the laws and regulations, and is experienced in preparing returns for people with financial backgrounds similar to your own. This pro may be a CPA, a public accountant, an enrolled agent (a tax preparer recognized by the IRS for presenting cases), or a seasoned tax preparer.

Q Every now and then I get a phone call from someone promoting some kind of tax shelter. The amount of taxes I pay makes me angry, so I'm tempted to get into one of these, but I'm afraid of a scam. How can I tell if a shelter's any good?

A For starters, don't buy any investment over the phone unless you know the person. An abusive tax shelter typically offers write-offs many times greater than the investment, may not own any real assets, and isn't intended to produce profits but just losses.

The pro knows the laws and regulations. You're in charge of the backup—all the documents and records to substantiate your figures. Most people keep some type of tax records, but too often they're incomplete or fragmented. A shoe box or shopping bag stuffed with receipts sounds like a joke, but for many taxpayers, it's their primary filing system!

A simple way to keep track of tax-related expenses is to create separate folders for major categories of income or expense so that tucking a receipt into its proper file becomes as routine as opening the mail. Starting in January each year, here's what you need to file and/or document.

• Pay slips or check stubs from employers. If you're paid for a freelance or consulting job with a simple check, keep the deposit slip and note the source.

• Record of cash income such as tips. The IRS is sensitive about people not reporting cash income. A written record of what you received and when will help reassure the agency that your reporting is accurate.

• Confirmation slips from brokers when you buy or sell any stock.

• Receipts for maintenance work, improvements, and insurance on rental property.

• Receipts for nonreimbursed medical expenses, including insurance, prescription drugs, and transportation to medical care.

• Records of real estate taxes paid.

• Records of home mortgage interest paid.

• Records of cash and other contributions to qualified charities or educational institutions.

• Record of safe-deposit box rental if you use it to store income-producing securities.

• Receipts for fees paid for tax preparation.

• Record of moving expenses if you changed jobs.

• Pocket diary of incidental expenses related to your work.

• Mileage for business use of your car.

• Investment expenses.

• Self-employment expenses (more later on this).

RULES OF THE ROAD

Armed with basic tax language skills and a solid set of records, you're well equipped to navigate through thickets of tax forms and returns. As you venture through tax land, remember these fundamental rules:

Rule 1: Defer, defer, defer. To put off paying taxes as long as possible, the simplest way is to defer receiving income. You owe taxes on income you actually received during the calendar year, not income promised you. So if you're owed money in December and don't need it immediately, ask the payer to send it in January, thus putting off taxes until another year. The payer may not want to put off paying you because that defers when he can deduct the expense. However, a check made out on December 31, 1992, and received by you on January 2, 1993, is a 1992 payer expense and 1993 income to you.

The logic behind this rule—that next year Congress may lower tax rates—may seem questionable. The constant chatter from Capitol Hill about lowering the deficit usually circles back to raising taxes as the most obvious solution. However, over the long run, while the trend has been to push up taxes on property and luxury items, federal income taxes have been holding their ground and slipping south. While President Clinton has talked about raising taxes on high incomes, making high earners consider not deferring, there are no certainties whatsoever when it comes to taxes and politics. In deciding whether to defer, ask yourself, "How lucky do I feel?" then opt for the safest strategy, which is always Defer, Defer, Defer.

Corollary to Rule 1: While postponing receiving income, immediately grab any deductions. Don't wait to match income and corresponding deductions. Pay January business expenses, mortgage loans, and state taxes in December so you can deduct them a year earlier. When it comes to deductions and paying taxes, your philosophy should be to hold on to your money as long as possible and cut your taxes as soon as possible.

Rule 2: Keep the money you save in taxes in a growing investment. Try not to spend it or, as many people do, use it as a vacation fund. Whether age 59½ sounds far away or just around the corner, you're going to need more money for retirement than you think. Hoarding your tax savings is a relatively painless way to beef up your retirement account.

Rule 3: Never travel alone. No matter how small your income or how simple your tax returns, let a professional help you organize and file your taxes. This person's experience and knowledge of the tax code will save you more than you'll ever spend in fees. (And don't consider this chapter a substitute for expert advice. The information here is general and summary; you need an expert looking at your special situation.)

Rule 4: Your records can never be too complete. Even though you may have duplicate records (canceled checks and receipts), or records for expenditures that may not be deductible (limited medical expenses), keep every piece of documentation. The value of thorough records when preparing your returns or in case of an audit far outweighs the nuisance of regularly stashing receipts into a tax file.

PINPOINT WHERE TAXES CAN HURT YOU

Although there's little escape from taxes, not everyone's situation is the same. Where you're vulnerable to heavier taxes depends on a host of conditions, including your income, expenses, financial habits, where you live, and how you spend your retirement days. What follows is a sur-

vey of various categories of income and expenses, their tax features, and how you might reduce taxes.

TAXABLE OR NONTAXABLE INCOME?

Not every dollar you earn is taxed, as you already know. The dividing line between taxable and nontaxable income becomes blurred as you begin to receive retirement income from a variety of sources. Wages are taxable, of course, but what about payoff from an insurance policy for a personal injury? (It's not taxable.)

The IRS reports that much of the income older Americans receive is nontaxable, particularly the following:

• Public assistance or welfare. (This includes money from a state fund for crime victims, mortgage assistance, energy or utility bill assistance, and food benefits; it does not include unemployment compensation payments.)

• Sickness or injury benefits (this includes worker's compensation, compensation damages for injuries or illness, insurance payments from an accident, payments through the Federal Employees'

> Q *I'm retired and receiving disability payments. Do I owe taxes on this money?*

> A *It depends on how the disability coverage was financed. If you receive the money through an employer-paid plan, it's taxable. However, if part of the money is from worker's compensation, some of that isn't taxed.*

(mustering-out pay, combat zone or MIA pay, allowances for housing, uniforms, rations, most VA benefits).

• Payments for reimbursement for out-of-pocket expenses from support services or such volunteer groups as: Retired Senior Volunteer Program, Foster Grandparent Program, Senior Companion Program, Service Corps of Retired Executives, and Active Corps of Executives.

Alas, the list of income that is taxable is much longer and may include money from sources that you didn't realize were taxable. Income from these sources is either partially or completely taxable:

Compensation Act, but not money that's a continuation of your pay while the claim's being decided).

• Gifts, inheritances, bequests. (But if you inherit an investment that produces income, you owe taxes on that.)

• Interest on frozen deposits (if your financial institution is bankrupt or its deposits frozen and you can't get at them, you won't owe on the accumulating interest until you get it).

• Certain veterans' benefits

• Compensation (wages, salaries, fees, commissions, bonuses, tips, some fringe benefits)

• Interest (except from municipal bonds)

• Dividends

• Rental income

• Royalties

• Sale of assets

• Retirement plans, pensions, annuities (but not the return of your after-tax money contributions)

• Disability insurance income

(if premiums paid by employer)
- Military retirement pay
- Lump sum distributions
- Interest on insurance proceeds
- Social Security or Railroad Retirement benefits (if income from other sources reaches certain levels)

WORKING INCOME

As you know, salaries, wages, tips, bonuses, and commissions are all taxable. You may not know that nonfinancial compensation is also taxable. If during retirement you undertake a job, and make some type of barter arrangement in which you receive goods or services in return for your work, you'll owe taxes on the fair market value of what you receive. Most nonfinancial compensation, for example a free trip or discounts on merchandise, is taxable.

If you retire from a full-time company job and do freelance work or consulting, the responsibility of making regular tax payments falls in your lap, not the individual or company signing the check. Self-employment requires making quarterly tax payments based on an estimate of your annual income (if the check you have to write on April 15 is at least $500). In fact, any income may generate more estimated tax liabilities. Your quarterly tax payments for the year have to add up to at least 90 percent of what you'll owe or 100 percent of taxes paid the previous year. However, if your current tax bill is going to vastly exceed last year's, you won't be able to get away with estimated payments based on last year's taxes. Failure to pay your quarterly taxes will reap you penalties.

"The greatest disruptive factor for retirees in recent years has been the decline in interest rates and changes in the tax laws."

—William Goldberg, National Director, Personal Financial Services, KPMG Peat Marwick, as quoted in the Wall Street Journal

Working for yourself, along with the allure of being your own boss, can also bring a heavier tax burden. The self-employed don't have an employer to withhold federal taxes from each paycheck, so they estimate their earnings and pay the appropriate taxes quarterly. Since there's no employer, the do-it-yourselfer is also responsible for paying the entire Social Security tax, which is normally split between employer and employee. The 1993 FICA tax is 15.3 percent of your first $57,600, with your employer picking up 7.65 percent. The Medicare tax is an additional 1.45 percent on income up to $135,000. But if you're toiling for yourself, you pick up the entire Social Security tab. (But since the self-employed pay with net earnings dollars, the effective rate is really 14.2 percent if you're in the 15 percent bracket).

The best way for you to save taxes on self-employment income is to be a meticulous record-keeper, and to take advantage of every single deductible expense coming to you. Read on to find out what that can include.

PENSION INCOME: LUMP SUM OR REGULAR PAYMENTS?

If you've toiled for years for an employer that provides you with a pension, one of the weightiest decisions you must make at retirement is what to do with that golden egg. Taxes will wield a powerful influence on your decision, and these are your choices:

1. Accept your pension in regular payments and pay taxes on the taxable portion you receive. To receive this money without owing early withdrawal penalties, you have to be at least 59½, quit your job after 55, or "annuitize" your payments.

Annuitizing entails setting up a schedule for taking out money in portions equal to the actuarial estimate of your lifetime (or joint life with a spouse beneficiary). With such a schedule, regardless of your age, the IRS will not penalize you for early withdrawal although you'll owe regular taxes on the income.

Annuitizing sounds complicated, but it isn't. The IRS publishes tables with estimated lifetimes. For instance, the tables show that if you're 50, you should expect to live another 33 years. With this number—33—in hand, the 50-year-old can annuitize by withdrawing approximately ⅓₃ of the total value of his or her pension. If you start annuitizing before you're 59½, you have to keep it up for five years or until you hit 59½. Otherwise, you'll owe penalty taxes.

2. Accept your pension in a

lump sum, deposit it in an account that you gives you immediate access but where it's not sheltered from taxes, and pay taxes on the entire taxable portion. Married people wanting to take this road generally need their spouse's written consent. This route contains a sizable tax bite, but it can be dulled somewhat by a maneuver called "five-year forward averaging," or for people born before 1936, ten-year averaging. This averaging enables you calculate your lump sum taxes based on a hypothetical five (or ten) years.

Starting in 1993, the employer handing out your lump sum has to withhold 20 percent of the amount to help pay your income taxes on it. Instead of a $100,000 payment, you would take away $80,000 and have $20,000 of withholding that you can't get until you file your tax return, even though you would owe taxes on it also! The only way to avoid the withheld $20,000 is to have your employer directly transfer the entire lump sum into an IRA or new employer's plan. (Needless to say, this new law discourages taking lump sums out of retirement plans.)

3. Accept your pension in a lump sum and have your employer transfer the entire amount into an IRA or another employer's retirement plan (thereby avoiding the 20

HUGE TAX BITES

Here's what Uncle Sam can take out of your lump sum pension distribution, if you choose that route.

Lump Sum	Tax Bite
$100,000	$ 31,000
$200,000	$ 62,000
$300,000	$ 93,000
$400,000	$124,000
$500,000	$155,000

percent withholding), and pay taxes only when you withdraw money and only on that amount, not the lump sum. (Again, you may need your mate's approval.) With this option, you can avoid withdrawing any money and hold off the IRS until you reach 70½. At that time, you *must* begin taking out money and paying taxes.

Of course, the question of what to do with your pension also hinges on your financial picture. If you need the money immediately, whether for living expenses or to invest in a new enterprise, and can't afford to stash it away, then taxes are inevitable. But keep in mind that the decision of whether to take the money or roll it into another retirement plan comes once in a lifetime. You can't decide to put the money into a liquid investment and a year later deposit it into an IRA and expect to not pay taxes on the entire amount. (But you can opt to cash out a portion of your lump sum, and pay taxes on it.) Once you've decided whether to annuitize, accept a lump sum, or roll over, you can't change your mind or break your money into portions and treat them differently. You make the decision once, and that's it.

IRA, KEOGH INCOME

An IRA or Keogh plan can also dump a large sum of money in your lap and raise the question of whether to take the lump sum, annuitize, or roll over.

Furthermore, if your pension has done exceedingly well and is especially flush, you may face another taxing situation: a 15 percent excise tax on what the IRS considers "excess distributions." In the eyes of the Internal Revenue Service, depending on the type of distribution, "excess" is defined in 1993 as a lump sum of more than $750,000 if you qualify for income averaging or more than $150,000 from an IRA and other types of pensions or qualified annuities. So, if you retire at 65 and receive $200,000 in one year from your IRA and, for example, a tax-sheltered annuity, you owe $7,500 (.15 × 50,000).

The most obvious way to avoid this tax is to take the money out over time so that your annual take is less than $150,000. And remember that money considered not part of the "excess distributions" includes after-tax contributions to a plan and nondeductible amounts that you roll over to an IRA, as well as amounts transferred to an ex-spouse under a divorce decree.

SOCIAL SECURITY INCOME

As many seniors have discovered, their monthly Social Security check is sometimes less than expected. Regardless of what you paid, benefits are scaled back if a person works and earns over

---

Q My mother, who's 70, has an IRA she won't tap into until she needs it, which will be a while. For now she has a good pension income. What'll happen to her money if she doesn't start taking it out at 70½?

A Awful things, namely a 50 percent penalty tax on the minimum amount not taken, plus regular income tax on what she does take out.

---

certain amounts. In 1993, if you're 62 to 64 and earning more than $7,680, you lose $1 of benefits for every $2 you earn; if you're 65 to 69 and earning more than $10,560, you lose $1 for every $3 earned. These amounts are adjusted for inflation and so inch upward yearly. But, hallelujah, after age 70, you can earn all you like and not lose any benefits!

Every year, you report what you earned to both the IRS and Social Security. If you earned over the limit and you received full benefits, you'll have to pay Social Security back. It works the other way, too: If you overestimated income and received lower benefits, Social Security owes you.

Every year, the IRS performs an "earnings test," meaning it scrutinizes how much you earn from both wages and self-employment to see if your earned income exceeds the levels mentioned above ($7,680 or $10,560). If you pass the test level (it feels like *failing* a test!), then Social Security lowers your benefits according to your earnings.

Taxes can also eat into your Social Security benefits. When figuring your annual tax bill and adding up your adjusted gross income, you must include in your taxable income the lesser of 50 percent of your Social Security benefits or 50 percent of the excess of adjusted gross income, plus tax-exempt income, plus half your Social Security benefits over a base amount. The base amount is $25,000 for single filers or $32,000 for joint filers.

INVESTMENT INCOME

Investments can be divided into two families: taxable and tax-free. Generally, people opt for tax-free investments when they're paying fat tax bills and don't want any more tax liabilities. Usually, peak earning years are the forties and fifties, not retirement time. But if you're cruising into retirement making bundles of unearned income and not much to hold the tax man at bay, you want to think about tax-free investments. The tax-free rides can be municipal bonds exempt from federal taxes (often exempt from state taxes, if you're a resident of the issuing locale) and bonds, notes, and bills from the U.S. Treasury (exempt from state taxes only). Chapter 2 gives lots of details on these.

Yet, even if your investments are whipping up taxable gains, you can take steps to pare the taxes you'll owe. Generally, your tax bill will be smaller if you invest in long-term-growth mutual funds as opposed to funds that produce a steady stream of income.

To understand why, remember that not all investment returns are taxed the same way. Investments in securities spawn three types of money: interest, dividends, and capital gains. Furthermore, how long you hold an investment affects its taxes. Interest and dividends are taxed the year they're earned at the same rates as ordinary income, even if the money stays in a mutual fund and you don't actually receive it. Such income may be taxed at 31 percent.

Long-term capital gains are also taxed at the same rates as ordinary income, *but* only in the year the investment is sold and the gain is realized, and only up to the 28 percent tax bracket. If you're in a 31 percent tax bracket, your long-term capital gains are taxed at a lower rate. And, capital losses can offset capital gains, but only losses up to $3,000.

What this means for the investor is that bond funds and high-yield funds that generate great chunks of interest and dividends could create a bigger tax bill than a mutual fund spinning off a steady stream of capital gains.

But consider avoiding a situation in which a mutual fund's assets consist of large amounts of realized but undistributed capital gains. These cap gains have been known to make up as much as 40 percent of an individual share price. When this happens, you pay an inflated price for the stock because it includes gains taken before you invested and you'll owe taxes on these gains. Look at the mutual fund's prospectus for a history of its price. Price spurts coupled with above-normal capital gains holdings point to times (usually around year end) when you should think twice about buying.

INCOME FROM ANNUITIES

The tax benefits from annuities fade a little when the time comes to, at last, collect. Over the years, the earnings on your annuity have been quietly piling up and multiplying, out of sight and mind of the tax man. But when you start to tap into these funds, you tap into taxes, too. If you opt to receive a lump sum, then all the deferred earnings that have accumulated are taxable in that one year. The other option—annuitizing and getting your money in regular payments—creates different tax ripples.

Annuity income, for tax purposes, is split into capital and earnings. The portion you receive that represents capital—that is, the principal you originally invested—is not taxed; the portion that represents earnings is taxed. Annuity companies send policyholders IRS Form 1099-R, "Distributions from Pensions, Annuities, Retirement or Profit-Sharing Plans, IRAs, Insurance Contracts," showing the taxable and tax-free figures for what they paid.

But if you're trying to contain your taxes, it's useful to know well before Form 1099-R appears in the mailbox how much of your annuity must go to Uncle Sam. So, here goes . . .

Whether you've purchased a single-premium annuity or a flexible-premium annuity (either fixed or variable), you begin by adding what you have paid in premiums minus what you've received back in dividends, refunds, or rebates. Call this "Total Investment."

Next, figure out how much you're going to get from your annuity. With a fixed annuity, it's the total of the annuity payments you'll receive for a full year multiplied by the number of years the policy runs. Call this "Total Return." Now, divide Total Investment by Total Return and that percentage is the tax-free portion of your annuity payments. (If you think about it for a minute, this makes sense. You're not going to pay taxes on what you invested because you originally put in dollars you'd already paid taxes on.)

If you have a variable annuity, you don't have a guaranteed return—it depends where your money is invested and how it performs. So add up how much money you expect to get and call this Total Expected Return. To arrive at your tax-free portion, divide your Total Investment by Total Expected Return. This percentage is the amount of each check that will be tax-free.

The unknown in figuring either how much you're going to receive or for how long pops up immediately with lifetime annuity payment options. People who decided on a lifetime annuity payment signed on for an uncertain period. To clear up the mystery, at least in tax land, the IRS has published an actuarial table with estimates of how long you and your spouse (for joint-and-survivor policies) will live. The table appears in IRS Publication 939 and is available from the IRS or your tax preparer.

Once you've determined the tax-free percentage, simply multiply this by the total annuity payments you'll receive each year. The result will determine the non-taxable and taxable portions.

All this adding and dividing becomes clearer with an example:

Years ago you invested $20,000 in a fixed annuity (Total Investment) that will begin paying you $4,000 yearly at age 65 and will continue for your lifetime. The IRS life expectancy table says you'll live another 20 years. Here's the equation:

Total Investment: $20,000

Total Expected Return:
$4,000 \times 20 \div $80,000

Percentage:
$20,000 \div $80,000 = 25\%$

Tax-free portion each year:
$4,000 \times 25\% = $1,000

Taxable portion each year:
$4,000 - $1,000 = $3,000

When preparing your income tax return, you report $3,000 as taxable annuity income; the taxes you pay will depend on your tax rate. This example gives you a general idea of how to estimate the taxable portion of your annuity—the annuity company will give you a Form 1099-R with the actual taxable amount to use for your return.

INCOME FROM THE
FAMILY HOMESTEAD

One of the few genuine breaks given senior citizens is a one-time exemption from taxes on the sale of a home. This is an extraordinary tax savings that any senior selling a home should consider cashing in on.

Congress has decreed that homeowners aged 55 and over can sell their principal residence (and he or she must have occupied it for at least three of the five years preceding the sale) and not owe *any* taxes on the realized gain in the value of the home up to $125,000. Say you're 56, have owned your home for ten years, and paid $100,000 for it; if you sell it for $225,000, you owe no taxes. However, if you sell it for more, you can shelter only $125,000. This is such a deal that the government allows you to do it only once.

There is one potential glitch in this exemption: married couples are allowed only one exemption between them, not one each. If you sell your home, claim the exemption, then divorce, you can't apply the $125,000 break to your next home sale.

Tax experts paint one situation in which you may not want to claim this exemption. If you sell your home at a profit much less than $125,000, and plan to put the proceeds into another, more expensive home, save this once-in-a-lifetime break for a later sale that may produce larger profits. It makes little sense to use the exemption to avoid taxes on a home sale that turns up, say, a $20,000 profit, if a subsequent home sale may spit out a $100,000 gain. Of course, there's no way to know for sure what real estate values will be tomorrow, but this exemption may well be worth hoarding.

THE DEDUCTION GAME

The bulk of taxpayers don't itemize their deductions, and instead claim only the standard deduction. This is a fixed amount that any taxpayer can subtract from his or her adjusted gross income; in 1993, the standard deductions were $6,200 (joint filer), $3,700 (single filer), $5,450 (head of household), and $3,100 (married filing separately).

While your accountant should know all the deductions you have coming, you can't keep the right records unless you know where deductible expenses may crop up. Here are some deductions you might have overlooked or assumed would be coming to you when they're not.

HOME EQUITY LOANS

These loans are the only remaining consumer loans with tax-deductible interest. So if you're in need of money, you may want to seek out a home equity loan and deduct the interest on your annual tax return. (See Chapter 4 for details on home equity loans.)

HOME MORTGAGE EXPENSES

Interest paid on home mortgages on both a first and second home continues to be deductible, but homeowners should not assume that all mortgage costs are deductible. Points (transaction fees charged up-front and equal to 1 percent of the total purchase price, also called loan origination fees or premium charges) paid to buy your principal residence are deductible. However, points paid to refinance a home mortgage are deductible only over the period of the loan, not in the year paid.

REVERSE MORTGAGE EXPENSES

If you arrange for a reverse mortgage (also called a home equity conversion loan), you receive a loan based on the value of your house and you will owe interest on that loan. As loan payments are made to you, the interest you owe also accumulates. However, you cannot deduct this interest until you actually pay it, which usually happens when the house is sold and the loan is closed out.

MEDICAL AND DENTAL EXPENSES

Alas, as you get older, medical expenses tend to snowball. While they may not have been sufficient to deduct when you were younger (expenses have to exceed 7.5 percent of your AGI), they may now hit a point where you can begin to write them off (because your expenses may be higher and your AGI lower). Medical expenses that can be itemized and deducted are fees for medical services, hospital fees, insurance premiums for medical and dental care, meals and lodging associated with medical care up to $50 a night, special equipment such as a motorized wheelchair, and insulin and prescription medicine. You also can deduct an array of special items, such as false teeth, glasses, hearing aids, cost of a guide dog, cost of special phone or television equipment for the hearing-impaired, oxygen equipment, and legal fees associated with mental health commitment.

Another category of deductible expenses is those that make your home more accommodating if you're disabled. These improvements include ramps, wider doorways, railings, altered kitchen appliances, and modified stairs.

Medical expenses you can't write off are health club dues, programs for stopping smoking or losing weight, Medicare insurance, nonprescription drugs, cosmetics or toiletries, unnecessary cosmetic surgery, trips to improve your general health, and illegal treatments or operations.

Nursing-home expenses, if you're there primarily because of a physical condition or for medical care, are deductible. But if you're in the home for personal or family reasons, you can't write it off.

SELF-EMPLOYMENT EXPENSES

If you retire from a salaried job but continue to earn through consulting, freelancing, or running a small business, you have a vast number of possible deductions in your future. Basically, anything you spend, buy, or invest that is used or applied to your income-producing efforts is tax-deductible. There's a fair amount of gray here, especially when activities include a bit of work and a bit of personal interest, and your accountant will help you navigate by asking, "Is this expense ordinary, necessary, and related to generating income?" or "What percentage of this expense can you allocate to your work?"

What the IRS wants to weed out are hobby expenses, which are not deductible. It considers anything a hobby that isn't dedicated to making a profit. If you can show a profit in three out of five consecutive tax years, whether it's knitting toaster covers or trading baseball cards, you've got a business, not a hobby.

The kinds of self-employment expenses that you can deduct include supplies, office space (home office if the space is your main place of business and dedicated *solely* to your work), office equipment and furnishings, travel, meals, car expenses, publications, entertainment, education, research, dues, and professional

STATE TAXES (1992)

	Top Income Tax Rate (%)*	Sales Tax (%)
Alabama	5.0	4.0
Alaska	0.0	0.0
Arizona	7.0	5.0
Arkansas	7.0	4.5
California	11.0	6.0
Colorado	5.0	3.0
Connecticut	4.5	6.0
Delaware	7.7	0.0
District of Columbia	9.5	6.0
Florida	0.0	6.0
Georgia	6.0	4.0
Hawaii	10.0	4.0
Idaho	8.2	5.0
Illinois	3.0	6.25
Indiana	3.4	5.0
Iowa	9.98	5.0
Kansas	7.75	4.9
Kentucky	6.0	6.0
Louisiana	6.0	4.0
Maine	9.89	6.0
Maryland	6.0	5.0
Massachusetts	12.0 (on cap. gains) 5.95 (on after-inc.)	5.0
Michigan	4.6	4.0
Minnesota	8.5	6.0
Mississippi	5.0	7.0
Missouri	6.0	4.22

National Conference of State Legislatures and Advisory Commission on Intergovernmental Relations

	Top Income Tax Rate (%)*	Sales Tax (%)
Montana	11.0	0.0
Nebraska	9.92	5.0
Nevada	0.0	6.5
New Hampshire	5.0 (int. and div. only)	0.0
New Jersey	7.0	6.0
New Mexico	8.5	5.0
New York	7.87	4.0
North Carolina	7.75	4.0
North Dakota	14.0	5.0
Ohio	6.9	5.0
Oklahoma	7.0	4.5
Oregon	9.0	0.0
Pennsylvania	2.95	6.0
Rhode Island	27.5 (of fed. inc. tax)	7.0
South Carolina	7.0	5.0
South Dakota	0.0	4.0
Tennessee	6.0 (int. and div. only)	6.0
Texas	0.0	6.25
Utah	7.2	5.0
Vermont	34.0 (of fed. inc. tax)	5.0
Virginia	5.75	3.5
Washington	0.0	6.5
West Virginia	6.5	6.0
Wisconsin	6.93	5.0
Wyoming	0.0	3.0

*Personal income tax on earned and/or unearned income. Rates as of October 1992.

fees. However, you can't use the deduction for home-office space to the point where you create a loss from your business.

Frequently, a self-employed person will take a trip, pick up a meal tab, or buy a small piece of equipment that is partially connected to work. When this happens—which is often because for many self-employed, activities and lifestyle blend almost seamlessly—you must apportion expenses, assigning one-third, one-half, or whatever is reasonable to the personal, nondeductible category. This business of apportioning deductible expenses is acceptable to the IRS, however, only if you keep thorough records. Recasting events and estimating expenditures after the fact or at tax time won't cut it. Get your tax adviser's help on setting up records before you start spending.

A CHANCE TO MAKE CHANGES: FILING AN AMENDED RETURN

Your deductions are good for more than a year—if you forgot to take one, you can amend returns filed in the past three years or for taxes paid in the past two years. An amended return, which is a restatement of a tax return

filed erroneously a previous year, enables you to claim missed deductions or credits, report income, and request a refund. Of course, the converse also holds true: If your reported deductions were really less, then you have to tell the IRS with an amended return and pay the taxes, interest, and possibly penalties.

AN ASSAULT ON ALL FRONTS: STATE AND LOCAL TAXES

Of course, federal taxes aren't the taxpayer's only burden. People are clipped by taxes from virtually every corner of their lives —as homeowners, consumers, employees, vacationers, students, drivers, drinkers, shoppers, ad nauseam. There's no one reading this who doesn't pay a variety of taxes just to get through a day. Often these taxes are small—a few cents, a few dollars—but the expression, "being nickeled and dimed to death" surely originated with taxpayers.

After Uncle Sam, your state government probably takes the biggest bite from your wallet. But only "probably," not "certainly," because states are literally all over

> *"Thirty states have enacted tax increases that will raise a total of $17 billion in new revenue in fiscal year 1992, making fiscal year 1991 the biggest revenue-raising year in history at the state level."*
>
> —*Gregory Leong, Director of Special Studies, the Tax Foundation*

the map in their taxing habits. Some leave residents alone and rely on specific industries, such as oil and gas, or sales taxes, to fund them while other states are notorious for their omnivorous appetites for income tax revenues.

In recent years, states have been reaching out for an ever-growing amount of tax revenues, upping the rates they already charge and devising new tax angles. The prize in 1992 for creative taxation went to California, which imposed a tax on snack foods, but not other foods, thus forcing merchants to tax as a snack food, for instance, bite-size pieces of matzo but not full-size matzo sheets.

A few of these taxes appear aimed squarely at older citizens and those readying for retirement.

Taxes on investment income, estate taxes, and gift taxes all bite into the sixtysomething crowd a little harder. Although these taxes are largely inescapable, there are ways to whittle them down.

SOURCE TAXES

As states struggle with tight revenues and billowing expenses, a number have devised a method for boosting revenues called a "source tax." This tax allows states to impose income taxes on the pensions of former residents who have retired elsewhere. Retirees who left California, for instance, and settled in Nevada because of its low state income tax

---

THEY WILL FOLLOW YOU

"They scared the socks off me. I had no idea I owed them money."
—*Reaction of a 75-year-old retiree living in Nevada when she received an $8,000 tax bill from California.*

Wall Street Journal

Q *I live in Massachusetts and have a condo in Florida, where I spend most of the winter and weeks here and there throughout the year. How do I establish Florida as my state for paying taxes since it doesn't impose any individual income taxes?*

A *You're allowed one "principal residence" for tax-paying purposes. To establish that residence, it helps to be registered to vote, have a driver's license, and register your car in the state. The state where you earn your income makes a difference, too. Talk to your accountant to find out individual state guidelines on residency.*

are receiving tax bills on pension benefits from former employers in the Golden State.

At present about 40 states have such laws, although tax experts say only a handful of states are actively trying to collect from out-of-state pensioners. Some are going after IRA checks sent to one time residents, and other states are pursuing IRA payouts only if a resident moves the same year he begins taking out IRA money. Others tax only certain types of pension incomes, such as railroad retirement money, military retirement payments, or "nonqualified" pensions (that is, pensions that are more for deferring compensation and not recognized by the IRS for tax advantages).

The situation becomes even messier for people who have lived, and accumulated pensions or set up IRAs, in a number of states. Presumably, they must file nonresident tax forms for every state with a source tax in which they've worked. The result of this patchwork of tax collecting, notes money expert Jane Bryant Quinn, is "The Tax Return From Hell." And, say tax experts, the trend toward states collecting taxes on their former residents' pensions is spreading.

STATES THAT HAVE THEIR HAND OUT

The 16 states that tax Social Security income, according to 1992 data collected by the U.S. Advisory Commission on Intergovernmental Relations, are Colorado, Connecticut, Iowa, Kansas, Minnesota, Missouri, Montana, Nebraska, New Mexico, North Dakota, Rhode Island, South Carolina, Utah, Vermont, West Virginia, and Wisconsin.

Not surprisingly, many people believe source taxes to be unfair and are vigorously protesting, claiming they're being taxed without representation since they have no vote where they no longer live. A group called Retirees to Eliminate State Income Source Tax (RESIST) is tracking state taxing practices and pushing for federal legislation to outlaw this variety of source taxes.

Until that happens (and it may not), pensioners should consult with a local tax expert before moving or making decisions about receiving pension payments. Some states, for instance New York, don't tax pension annuities but do chase after lump sum payouts. Individual state tax laws are in flux and some states have no firm policy on how much an IRA recipient, who made contributions while living in numerous states, owes that state. And some states have no way of tracking pension money that's leaving their boundaries if the pension manager doesn't notify them. The best way to deal with this tax is to talk with a tax professional before retiring and moving out of state.

CHIPPING AWAY AT SOCIAL SECURITY INCOME

The federal government taxes Social Security Income—50 percent—if your total income reaches a certain level. This is a well-known source of irritation to many retirees, but less publicized is the fact that 16 states also tax Social Security income. These states tell residents to add in 50 percent of their Social Security benefits when totaling up taxable income and if the final figure goes over $25,000 (single filer; $32,000 for joint filer), taxes are due. Some, however, do exclude pension income, which may include Social Security, up to a certain amount. For example, in 1991, Colorado had a $21,000 exemption. The rest of the nation allows taxpayers to exclude Social Security benefits from their state income tax calculations. In those 16 states, Social Security checks are being taxed twice—first by the IRS, then by your state capitol. How big a piece they will demand depends on their individual income tax rates.

Pension Income

Another taxing area where states differ and apply quirky exemptions or heavy-handed taxes is in the area of pension income. Some insist that you include all of it in your formulas for figuring taxable income; others allow you to count only part; and a few say you don't have to add it in at all.

But exactly what they do and don't count is as individual as the state flowers, so here's a summary of who counts what (states not listed have complex ways for figuring income or don't have state income taxes; an accountant in the

state will know how it figures pension income). In some cases, a state considers "pension income" to include all kinds of payments—Social Security, private benefits, civil service benefits, railroad benefits—and others have a narrower definition. And, these figures are for 1992 and states can change their mind. Again, consult a knowledgeable tax preparer.

• Exempts pension income: Hawaii, Illinois, Pennsylvania, Tennessee.

• Exempts a portion of pension income: Arizona, Arkansas, Colorado, Connecticut, Delaware, Georgia, Maryland, Mississippi, Montana, New Jersey, New Mexico, North Carolina, Utah.

• Exempts pension income (all or part) paid to certain employees (e.g., teachers, police, state or federal government workers, military): Alabama, District of Columbia, Idaho, Indiana, Kansas, Kentucky, Louisiana, Michigan, New York, North Dakota, Oklahoma, South Carolina, West Virginia, Wisconsin.

• Includes pension income (with some exceptions): California, Iowa, Maine, Massachusetts, Minnesota, Missouri, Nebraska, Ohio, Oregon, Virginia.

PRICE TAGS AND TRUE PRICES

The true price of an item, once you factor in sales taxes and taxes on the income used to buy it, is much higher than the price tag. According to a study by the CATO Institute, a couple with an annual income between $34,000 and $53,400 living in an average-tax state (e.g. Michigan, which has a 4.6 percent income tax) has to earn much more than sticker prices in order to afford to buy certain items. And a self-employed person, as many retirees are, pay even more because of self-employment taxes.

	$ Price	$ for Couple	$ for Self-Employed
Car	10,000	17,038	18,776
Computer	1,500	2,568	2,748

SALES TAXES

Local sales taxes were first collected during the Depression (New York City in 1934) as an alternative source of revenue beyond property taxes. Land values were falling faster than property tax rates, and these taxes plus widespread foreclosures created great public hostility toward property taxes.

Depending on where you live, sales taxes can eat into your budget like a swarm of hungry termites. And like termites, they sometimes appear smaller and more inconsequential than they really are. In fact, a Washington think tank, the CATO Institute, has studied state taxes and points out that the adage, "My take-home pay won't take me home" is truer now than ever. While some states impose no sales taxes, others reach deep into taxpayers' pockets. The effect of sales taxes, combined with state income taxes and federal taxes, can readily double the cost of an item you buy.

Taxpayers may dodge sales taxes by buying costly consumer items where possible in nearby states that have lower sales taxes. But if you happen to be surrounded by states with equally

PROPERTY TAXES: A SAMPLING

These were the 1990 property tax rates in U.S. cities compiled with a mind toward geographic diversity. They're stated as the rate per $1,000 of assessed value (assessment levels are often a percentage of actual, or market, value).

City	Rate	City	Rate
Tucson, AZ	$148.84	Carson City, NV	$ 20.46
Hot Springs, AR	37.60	Nashua, NH	35.30
Fresno, CA	10.84	Santa Fe, NM	15.40
San Diego, CA	10.36	Saratoga Springs, NY	251.14
Colorado Springs, CO	58.02	Asheville, NC	6.85
Greenwich, CT	29.97	Corvallis, OR	33.78
Coral Gables, FL	20.34	Philadelphia, PA	78.65
Winter Park, FL	17.16	Greenville, SC	133.70
Savannah, GA	28.60	Bristol, TN	72.00
Hawaii	8.50	Corpus Christi, TX	21.53
Garden City, KS	137.30	Provo, UT	15.40
Lexington, KY	5.30	Manassas, VA	11.80
New Orleans, LA	143.68	Spokane, WA	14.89
Prince Georges County, MD	24.80	Charleston, WV	8.63
Biloxi, MS	103.49	Kenosha, WI	23.83
Helena, MT	411.64		

Advisory Commission on Intergovernmental Relations

greedy sales taxes, you may have little recourse or way of saving. And although state income, real property, and personal property taxes are deductible on your federal return, sales taxes are not.

PROPERTY TAXES

Taxes on personal property and real property can form a sizable chunk of annual taxes. States and local taxing authorities (cities and counties) calculate these taxes according to the value of the real or personal property. "Real" property is real estate—your home, vacation place, or an undeveloped lot. "Personal" property can mean a virtual yard sale of items —automobiles, telecommunications equipment, household items, clothes, investments, and tools used in a business. Each state has its own definition; some, like Delaware, don't tax personal property while others, like Arizona, have numerous categories of personal property.

It's important to remember that local authorities impose many more property taxes than states do —more than 90 percent of property taxes are local, according to the Tax Foundation.

Taxpayers have little control over property taxes, short of not owning a home or curtailing improvements. Taxes are often calculated as a certain number of dollars per $1,000 of assessed value. Probably the only recourse, but one that seems to be used with more and more success, is challenging local authorities on the assessment they use as a basis for property taxes. Often cities and counties use dated, sometimes inflated, market prices for determining the value of a home or piece of property. Taxpayers can ask local authorities to check whether an assessment accurately reflects current market prices. Such a request may well produce a lower assessment.

TAXES AND LIVING ABROAD

Living in a foreign country won't protect you from the IRS. Much of what you earn—salary, bonus, commissions, fees—is taxable. And this applies whether you're on someone's payroll or self-employed. But the income limits and filing schedules for U.S. citizens living in foreign countries are different than those here.

One break you get by living

A BIG AIRMAIL BILL

Social Security mails about 340,000 checks every year to retirees living in foreign countries.

abroad is a more lenient filing schedule—if you're out of the United States on April 15, you have an automatic extension to June 15 to file, although you must pay estimated taxes or you'll owe interest on any taxes due.

The truly generous allowance is the income ceiling for taxes. Income earned abroad up to $70,000 is not subject to U.S. income taxes and you can exclude any amounts you receive from an employer for housing. Or you may be able to deduct housing costs not paid by your employer. (And if you're not working for someone but producing freelance income, you can deduct housing expenses that go over your foreign-earned income exclusion of $70,000). As a foreign resident, you can choose to claim the $70,000 exemption or deductions related to that income or foreign tax credits. When you opt for the $70,000 exclusion, you can't

write off business deductions, IRA contributions, or foreign taxes related to the excluded income. And, you're committed to taking this route in all coming years unless you formally revoke your decision, in which case you can go back to taking deductions. But you need the permission of the IRS.

With living on distant shores making tax-paying almost painless (but not quite), the IRS has established, of course, strict guidelines for claiming a foreign country as your "tax home." Under one test, you have to physically be in the country 330 full days during any period of 12 consecutive months.

Unearned income is a different

NOT FOREIGN ENOUGH

The Internal Revenue Service doesn't consider these places to be foreign countries that qualify for the foreign earned income exclusion: Puerto Rico, Virgin Islands, Guam, American Samoa, and Northern Mariana Islands.

matter—it doesn't qualify for the wonderful exclusion. Income from annuities, pensions, investments, and Social Security may be subject to the same U.S. taxes regardless of where you're living.

Furthermore, the foreign country in which you're living may tax your income, including Social Security payments from the States. To avoid U.S. citizens' money being taxed twice, the United States has signed tax treaties with a number of countries. These treaties typically allow tax credits on a foreign return for U.S. taxes or vice versa. IRS Publication 901 lists the countries the U.S. has tax treaties with and what's taxed, what's exempt, and when credits are given.

Chapter 8

Taking Care of Your Health

The best retirement plans are worth little without your health. Piles of money and years of foresight won't bring you much pleasure in your senior years without a well-functioning body and freedom from debilitating illness. This may be clear as spring water to you, but reports suggest that large numbers of older Americans neglect their health.

The truly good news is that many of the unpleasant changes in health associated with aging can be diminished. According to Dr. James F. Fries, a nationally recognized expert on aging, the following health conditions can be modified by your behavior, including diet, weight control, exercise, and smoking:

- Physical fitness
- Heart reserve
- Mobility
- Blood pressure
- Intelligence
- Memory
- Reaction time
- Heart Disease
- Cancer
- Arthritis
- Agility

SHEDDING MYTHS ABOUT AGING

Many seniors ignore their health because of myths surrounding aging and personal health.

Our very ideas about what is "old" are being challenged. People in their sixties today are thought of as middle-aged, hardly "elderly" (if you have any doubt, check out Paul Newman and Jackie Kennedy Onassis). This makes sense if you look at how life spans have lengthened—people born in 1900 had a life expectancy of 47 years; now the average lifetime is 75 years—78.5 for women and 71.8 for men.

"There are three periods in life: youth, middle age, and 'How well you look.'"

—*Nelson Rockefeller*

The question of exactly how far our lives can be extended is hotly debated in the medical community. One side argues that the human body usually starts to wear out in the eighties simply because it's biologically programmed to do so. Other researchers contend that because of life-saving therapies and healthy lifestyles, the threshold for when the body runs out of steam may be closer to 115 years.

When it comes to myths, it will surprise no one that sex is another source of illusions. For instance, nothing stands in the way of having a normal sex life into your nineties, medical experts say. Impotence, once shrugged off as a consequence of aging, is now often treatable. Menopause, of course, is an inevitable event but it doesn't necessarily have to hamper your sex life.

Brain cells remain vibrant in the elderly, contrary to the image of older people as fuzzy and forgetful. These are symptoms of a medical disorder, not a reflection of the calendar. While short-term memory might fade a tad in the elderly, reasoning and judgment can get sharper.

Another common fable is the idea of "wearing out" your body, as if it were an automobile good for only so many miles. This quaint notion sprung from a late 19th-century medical analogy comparing the human body to a machine. It was given further credence in the 1920s with researchers expounding on the "rate of living theory" and "stress theory," which held that the more energy you spent, the shorter your life span.

The human body doesn't automatically begin to disintegrate in middle age and fall apart in old age. Sure, aging brings a decline in muscle mass and quickness, along with very gradual hearing loss and increased farsightedness. Biologically, our bodies decline about 1 percent a year beginning in middle age. And, certain diseases and chronic conditions plague older people more. But this decline can be lessened through better habits, especially regular exercise.

Unless you've been living in a cave the last few years, you've heard about the wondrous effects of exercise. Exercise has become the darling of researchers, who say it's the closest we've come to an anti-aging elixir. Recent studies show it remarkably rejuvenates the muscles, lungs, and hearts of older people. In one study, a group of people between ages 87 and 96 joined an eight-week exercise program and at the end of their training, they could lift loads three times as heavy as they could at the start of the program.

This raises a chicken-and-egg dilemma: Are the elderly who are physically active less likely to suffer from diseases because they exercise? Or, are they able to exercise and stay active because they've never suffered from serious disease? Scientists aren't sure of the answer yet, but one thing is clear—there's a steel-link chain connecting exercise and the ability to fend off aging, at least for a while.

HOW WE AGE

As if you didn't know! Of course, many signs of aging are unmistakable: gray hair, sagging skin, farsightedness, high-tone hearing loss.

"To me, old age is always 15 years older than I am."

—Bernard Baruch, on his eighty-fifth birthday

Making the process even more vexing is the fact that various parts of the body age at different rates. At 55, you might be one of the lucky ones who look into the mirror and see a 30-year-old's complexion. But, alas, you may see it through bifocals that other people may not wear until their sixties or seventies. In the final

"The myths about aging are in error, at least for a great many old and very old persons," says Dr. T. Franklin Williams, director of the National Institute on Aging. "Absent disease and with a good lifestyle, most organ systems of older people can and do continue functioning at essentially the same levels as in younger adults."

Washingtonian

analysis, how you age has a lot to do with heredity, and also with how you take care of yourself.

What follows is a tour through our various body parts as they age, with some pointers for slowing down the steady march.

THE SAGA OF SAGGING SKIN

Changes in the skin come naturally with age: as it becomes drier it begins to sag, crinkles form at the corner of the eyes, and spots and growths appear. Also, cells regenerate more slowly, so blemishes take longer to heal.

However, people hasten the deterioration of skin by overexposure to the sun and by smoking. The sun's rays can also precipitate skin cancer. But diagnosed early, most skin cancer can be cured, so stay alert for these warning signs: the appearance of a new skin spot, or changes in the color, size, shape, or surface of moles.

While the signs of age can't be held off forever, certain palliatives exist. A couple of wrinkle-fighting topical lotions have been shown to reduce fine wrinkling by causing the skin to peel—Retin-A and alpha hydroxyacids.

Other more costly methods of battling wrinkles and sagging skin are collagen injection; dermabrasion, a kind of surgical sanding of the skin; chemical peel, which chemically burns off the top layer of skin; rhytidectomy, or facelift, a surgical procedure to tighten or remove fatty tissue; and blepharoplasty, surgery performed to remove bags from the eyes.

The American Society of Plastic and Reconstructive Surgeons reports collagen injections and blepharoplasty are the most popular treatments. But chemical peels are gaining fast, probably because of a new chemical agent, trichloracetic acid, a milder chemical than phenol, which monopolized the field before.

Collagen treatments have run into trouble because they've been associated in the public's mind with silicone breast implants, a treatment that's been sharply curtailed because of medical problems. Collagen, taken from cowhide, is injected into wrinkles and scars, and treatments must continue three or four times a year. The procedure has been linked to serious health problems, including lupus, scleroderma, and localized skin death. Think twice —no, think very hard—about doing it.

RETOOLING MUSCLES

Starting around age 20, Americans typically lose 6.6 pounds of muscle fiber for each decade that ticks by. Fat volume, meanwhile, creeps up, even if your weight is the same at 60 as at 30. Scientists estimate that the average, sedentary 65-year-old woman is about 43 percent fat, up from 25 percent when she was 25 years old. Men are typically a bit leaner, with body fat of 18 percent at age 25 and 28 percent at 65.

This change in the proportions of fat and muscle contributes to many health problems associated with age, but it can be held off for a time by a nutritious diet coupled with exercise.

Fewer calories are needed to maintain fat tissue, which is inactive, than are required for muscle, which is active tissue. Because fewer calories are needed for fat tissue, the body shifts to a lower metabolism rate. However, many

Q I know lifetimes are getting longer for men and women, but still, what are the odds that I'll outlive my husband? (He's 48, I'm 39.)

A Statistically, you'll live at least seven years longer than your husband, which means you'll be around for 16 years after he's gone. Today, women over 65 outnumber men by three to two, and this disparity is getting larger, not shrinking.

people rarely change their eating habits as they age and continue to chow down as in their youth. The inevitable result: more pounds.

By the time people realize the weight should come off, it's hard to do because the body is burning calories at a slower rate. On top of it all is probably a more sedentary lifestyle. You can break the cycle with exercise and consuming fewer calories. This will help in re-tooling your muscles, which in turn will burn up more calories and speed up your metabolism.

Some muscles are more suscep-tible to aging than others. Of the two kinds of muscle fibers, the fast-twitch and the slow-twitch, the former are the ones that atro-phy with age. The slow-twitch fi-bers take care of posture and low-intensity movement, while the fast-twitch fibers rise to the de-mands of high-intensity move-ment, such as lifting heavy loads and sports.

Researchers once thought the decline in muscle strength that comes with old age was irreversi-ble, but studies of older people and their response to exercise has changed their minds. In one study, men aged 60 to 72 who lifted weights for 12 weeks, three days each week, proved that older peo-ple can exhibit as much muscle growth as young people doing the same amount of exercise. So don't give up your gym club member-ship just because you're getting older.

SAVING THE EYES

Normal changes in your vision usually start in the forties. A common scene is suddenly discov-ering you cannot read the menu in a dimly lit restaurant. You find yourself holding telephone books and newspapers farther and far-ther away to bring the print into focus. Time to see the eye doctor. When you do, you'll likely be told about presbyopia, or creeping far-sightedness.

But such a diagnosis is no rea-son to fret. These flaws are easily corrected with glasses or contact lenses. Of greater concern—and a

"If you're the average middle-aged person, your problem is not excess weight so much as it is excess body fat coupled with too little muscle."

Prevention Magazine

EYE CARE RESOURCES

• For free information on eye diseases and a home eye test, contact the National Society to Prevent Blindness, 500 East Remington Road, Schaumburg, IL 60173; 800/221-3004.

• For a list of products and services for the visually impaired, contact the Vision Foundation, 818 Mt. Auburn Street, Watertown, MA 02172.

• For information on a public service program that brings medical eye care to disadvantaged older people, contact the National Eye Care Project, American Academy of Ophthalmology, P.O. Box 6988, San Francisco, CA 94120-6988; 800/222-EYES.

reason for regular checkups for your eyes, even if you're still seeing clearly—are various diseases of the eye to which older people become more susceptible. Some of these have no palpable symptoms and can be detected only by an eye specialist. The most common eye diseases among the elderly are cataracts, glaucoma, macular degeneration, and diabetic retinopathy.

Normally the lens of the eye is clear, allowing light to penetrate and fall on the retina inside the eye. Cataracts form cloudy or opaque areas on all or part of the lens and your vision becomes hazy, almost as if you were peering through a waterfall, which is the meaning of the Latin word "cataracta." The disease usually develops gradually and without pain or other signs of trouble, and surgery is the only effective treatment. The operation removes the lens itself, a frightening idea but the procedure is safe, with a long history of success. Sight is restored through special eyeglasses, contact lenses, or lens implants.

Glaucoma is the term for several diseases characterized by a buildup of fluid pressure, which can injure the optic nerve and destroy vision. Its cause is not known, but early diagnosis and treatment can control the disease and prevent blindness. Since the pressure causes no pain, to catch glaucoma early you need routine eye exams. Treatments include prescription eye drops, oral drugs, laser therapy, and surgery.

Age-related macular degeneration, caused by damage to a small portion of the retina called the macula, develops most often in people over 65. Millions of older Americans have at least a touch of the disease, but most maintain a degree of useful vision. Depending on the damage, laser surgery may stop the degeneration.

Diabetic retinopathy, the most serious eye condition related to diabetes, also attacks the retina, the layer of nerves at the back of the eye that sends visual messages to the brain through the optic nerve. The disease weakens the blood vessels in the retina, which can cause them to leak. Some victims experience blurry vision, but typically there are no symptoms in the early stages. In some cases, laser surgery is recommended to seal the leaking vessels and preclude the loss of vision.

SAY WHAT? YOUR HEARING

How many times in the past week have you asked someone to speak up or heard complaints that you didn't answer the doorbell? If this happens a lot, have your ears checked.

SHHH . . .

Self Help for Hard of Hearing People is a national group that can help in coping with a hearing loss and provide information about new hearing aids and technology. Write SHHH, 7800 Wisconsin Avenue, Bethesda, MD 20892.

Among the more than 16 million Americans who are hearing-impaired, 60 percent are 55 or older. But deafness is not that common —only 2 percent of this group is classified as legally deaf.

Looking at the odds another way, about 30 percent of adults aged 65 to 74 experience some degree of hearing loss. This increases to 50 percent in people between 75 and 79.

The medical term for hearing loss that worsens with age is presbycusis, an ailment that's more common and more severe in men. The impairment is permanent because nerve cells degenerate. It strikes both ears equally, and high-pitched sounds are usually the ones that can't be heard.

Aging is not the only factor in the disorder. Heredity, infections, prolonged exposure to very loud noise, vascular problems, head injuries, tumors, and certain medications can all play a role.

Sounds can be amplified by a hearing aid to compensate for hearing loss, but before buying a hearing aid, talk with a doctor about whether you can benefit from one.

HOLDING ON TO A FULL SET: TEETH AND GUMS

Teeth are meant to last a lifetime —but it takes vigilance. Faithful daily brushing with fluoride toothpaste, flossing, rinsing with fluoride mouthwash, and regular dental checkups are all part of the routine.

This discipline must be maintained even if you wear dentures; otherwise gum irritation sets in, not to mention teeth staining and bad breath.

For those who still have their teeth, gum disease, or periodontitis, can cause tooth loss. Periodontitis develops if plaque is not removed every day. Plaque, or bacteria, irritates the gums, and if the irritation goes untreated, pockets of infection form, causing the gums to recede. If the infection spreads to the roots of the teeth, they can loosen and fall out.

Regular checkups can also detect mouth cancer, which can go unnoticed in the early painless stages when it's curable. If you notice red or white spots, or sores in your mouth that bleed or don't go away within two weeks, see your dentist.

FOR MEN ONLY

Women outlive men by about seven years on average. Why? And can men do anything about it?

DENTISTRY PLUS GERIATRICS

General dentists can handle the dental problems of most older patients, but some specialize in the elderly. Names and addresses of such specialists are available from the American Society of Geriatric Dentistry, 1121 West Michigan Street, Indianapolis, IN 46202.

ALZHEIMER'S SYMPTOMS

Symptoms of Alzheimer's disease generally fall into three stages. However, symptoms are not uniform in every patient, and stages can overlap. Here are some noteworthy symptoms:

FIRST STAGE: TWO TO FOUR YEARS

- Progressive forgetfulness
- Confusion about directions, money management
- Loss of spontaneity and initiative
- Repetitive statements and actions
- Disorientation of time and place
- Changes in mood, personality, and judgment

SECOND STAGE: TWO TO TEN YEARS (THE LONGEST STAGE)

- Difficulty recognizing friends and relatives
- Wandering
- Hallucinations
- Occasional muscle twitching
- Difficulty in logical thinking, inability to do simple arithmetic, write name, or read signs
- Loss of impulse control, sloppiness
- Irritability, teariness

THIRD STAGE: ONE TO THREE YEARS

- Inability to recognize self in mirror
- Emaciation
- Mutism
- Compulsion for touching and putting things into mouth
- Bowel and bladder incontinence
- Inability to swallow
- Increased need for sleep, then coma, and eventual death

The question has many answers. Researchers say one-third of the gap in longevity is attributable to the way men behave—they smoke more, drink more, and take more life-threatening chances. This makes them more vulnerable to disease-induced death as well as death by a variety of other means. Men are victims of the top ten causes of death at twice the rate of women: They're victims of murder three times more frequently than women; commit suicide at two to three times the rate of women; and are killed in car accidents at twice the rate of women.

Besides behavior, genes and hormones probably play a role in the longevity gap. The female hormone estrogen guards women against heart disease through their forties, a time when heart disease topples men at three times the rate that it kills women. After menopause, when estrogen levels drop, women become more susceptible to heart problems.

Another factor tipping the scale against men might be their own male hormone testosterone. Studies suggest this hormone lowers the level of "good" cholesterol, which sweeps away harmful deposits on artery walls left by "bad" cholesterol.

On the other hand, men are generally more fit than women, a major factor in overall good health. They have about 10 percent less body fat than women, and their metabolism is about 6 percent faster, enabling them to burn up calories more efficiently than women and to stay lean.

WATCH OUT!

One of the biggest health hazards of growing old is accidents. As you age, you become more prone to accidents, largely because of diminished eyesight and hearing, and because of diseases of the musculoskeletal and nervous systems. While people 65 and older make up 12 percent of the population, they incur 27 percent of fatal accidents. The high accident rate is compounded by the fact that the elderly's injuries tend to be more severe and slower to heal.

It was once widely believed that men were dying faster than women because of the stresses of work. But holes have been punched in this hypothesis because women who have entered the work force in droves since 1950 are as healthy as women who stay at home, researchers say.

Men seem to be wising up. They now live on average for 71.8 years compared with 78.5 years for women, having closed the longevity gap by almost one year, from 70.8 years, since 1970. This trend may be attributable to a change in their lifestyle: less smoking and drinking, and better eating.

COMBATING THE ILLNESSES OF AGING

Some of the health hazards of growing older, are avoidable (at least until you're *very* old). For many people the reasonably

---

AVOIDING ACCIDENTS

Some 27,000 people aged 65 and older die from accidental injuries each year, and hundreds of thousands of others suffer months of pain and confinement. To avoid accidents, follow these tips:

- Provide plenty of lighting throughout your home.
- Install handrails on both sides of stairways, and mark the first and last steps with bright, contrasting tape.
- Cover slippery surfaces with carpets or rugs firmly anchored to the floor.
- Use nonskid floor wax on linoleum floors.
- Arrange furniture so it doesn't create obstacles in pathways.
- Use nonskid adhesive strips or plastic mats in bathtubs, and install grab bars on bathroom walls.

healthy with no strong family history of a particular illness—confronting the illnesses of aging is like dodging bullets. Whether you get hit depends somewhat on how quick you are in anticipating danger, and also on luck. Knowing exactly what the bullets look like—and this section offers a glimpse—may help you duck a little faster.

There are serious diseases that can be deflected by certain precautions and healthy living. Others are more difficult to combat, but can be managed if they're spotted early.

ODDS AGAINST ALZHEIMER'S

Are you misplacing your keys more often or writing more lists to prompt your memory? Don't worry, it probably isn't Alzheimer's, just a normal part of aging. However, if your memory keeps fading, you feel your personality changing, and confusion moves in, it's time to see a doctor.

Extreme forgetfulness, mood changes, and disorientation may spring from dementia, and the most pervasive form of dementia in old age is Alzheimer's disease. About four million adults are afflicted with Alzheimer's, the fourth leading cause of adult

BRIDGING THE LONGEVITY GAP

"The gap isn't shrinking because women are acting like men," says Deborah Wingard, an epidemiologist at the University of California at San Diego. "It's shrinking because men are behaving more like women."

deaths. Among 65-to 84-year-olds, about 10 percent have Alzheimer's, and the rate jumps to more than 47 percent in people over 85.

The cause of the dread disease is unknown, and there is no prevention, cure, or treatment. Moreover, diagnosis is complicated because there's no single diagnostic test, and doctors must rule out other causes of the dementia before landing on a probable diagnosis of Alzheimer's. Even then, it's an assumption—an absolute diagnosis would take analysis of the patient's brain cells.

In Alzheimer's victims, symptoms begin slowly and become

steadily worse, advancing through three stages. It starts with problems remembering recent events and ends in total helplessness. Death comes three to 20 years after the onset of symptoms.

The symptoms are a result of the death of a large number of cells in the person's brain, where tangles and plaques form. Researchers have determined the structure of the protein that forms the core of the plaques, but they don't know whether the protein is a cause or an effect of the disease. Since they don't know exactly why the nerve cells die, it's incurable for now. But that doesn't mean you can't do anything to fight it. Counseling for people in the early stages of the illness, or for the people taking care of them, helps combat the confusion and anger. Counseling may also be the first step to finding a support network.

ACHY BREAKY ARTHRITIS

Arthritis, or inflammation of the joints, is not a disease in itself but the result of more than 100 diseases, the most common being osteoarthritis, which touches nearly everyone who reaches old age.

In fact, evidence of osteoarthri-

"Osteoarthritis is far from a hopeless condition," says Dr. John L. Decker, chief of the Arthritis and Rheumatism Branch at the National Institutes of Health. "Crippling is very uncommon. In fact, the swelling and pain have a tendency to disappear after a year or so, although X-rays may show that the arthritis has progressed."

tis—the wear and tear of the cartilage at the tip of the bones where the joints are formed—shows up on X-rays of virtually everyone over 60. Osteoarthritis mostly affects the hands and the joints that bear a person's weight—hips, knees, and ankles. However, evidence of degenerating cartilage doesn't mean you'll necessarily feel the stiffness and pain associated with arthritis; most people don't.

Other types of arthritis often found in older people are rheumatoid arthritis, which afflicts women three times more than men, and gout, which hits men more often. Altogether, half of people 65 and older suffer from some form of arthritis.

The cause of rheumatoid arthritis, one of the most disabling forms of arthritis, is a mystery but doctors believe it may stem from an inherited trait that leads to a breakdown in the immune system. The disease typically attacks 15 or 20 joints at once, inflaming the membrane surrounding them. It's characterized by alternating periods of remission and exacerbation; cycles that can last as long as months or years. In some cases, the arthritis abates permanently.

Gout flares up when levels of uric acid are too high. It starts with the liver, which manufactures the acid. When too much acid is produced and the kidneys can't excrete it all, crystals of sodium urate settle in the joints, causing painful inflammation, often in the big toe. This mechanism gave rise to the misconception that you could get gout from stuffing yourself with rich foods containing uric acid. Doctors insist that overindulgence is an unlikely cause of gout.

Most forms of arthritis can't be prevented or cured, but gout can be combatted with medicines that block the body's production of uric acid and facilitate its excretion. Treatments for other forms of arthritis include painkillers, such as aspirin, anti-inflammatory drugs like ibuprofen, heat or cold treatments, weight control, and individualized exercise regimens.

ARTHRITIS HELP

Free booklets describing various forms of arthritis and their treatments are available from the Arthritis Foundation. Look up local chapters, listed in the telephone directory, or contact national headquarters, P.O. Box 19000, Atlanta, GA 30326; 800/285-7800.

In extreme cases, surgery is the answer, such as removal of the diseased membrane for chronic rheumatoid arthritis or joint replacement surgery, primarily in the hips and knees, for crippling osteoarthritis. In fact, among seniors, joint replacement surgery has become very common and is highly successful. "People unable to walk due to extreme pain often walk out of the hospital free of pain," says John L. Decker, of the National Institutes of Health.

THE CURSE OF CANCER

Three out of ten Americans develop cancer, and the chances of getting it increase with age, with more than half of all cancer victims over 65.

"Cancer" generally refers to more than 100 diseases in which normal cells mutate into renegade cells that run amok and multiply out of control. No one knows why normal cells turn into cancerous cells, but both genetic and environmental factors play starring roles in the onset of the disease.

The environmental factors include diet, tobacco, and alcohol as well as cancer-causing agents in the air, water, and workplace. Cancer-causing agents, called carcinogens, are X-rays, sun rays, certain viruses, and some substances in familiar products, like arsenic in pesticides and asbestos in insulation.

Cancers grow slowly, usually appearing five to 40 years after exposure to a carcinogen. Malignant cells appear, and then metastasize, or travel to other parts of the body and start new tumors.

Early detection is crucial—before the cancer spreads—to enhance chances for recovery. Pain is rarely an early sign, but other symptoms can tip you off.

Even without symptoms,

Q I'm 45 and just had hip surgery, and the doctors didn't seem to give me any time to recover. The anesthesia had barely worn off before the therapist was getting me to move and exercise. What gives?

A Though moving may be hard and painful, they're doing you a favor. Doctors have found that a mere two weeks of complete bed rest can cause your bones to lose as much calcium as would a year of aging. So the sooner you're using your muscles, the better.

CANCER SIGNS

The following symptoms can be linked to certain kinds of cancers, although they may be signs of other ailments:

- Lung: cough that lasts more than two weeks; coughing up blood
- Colon and rectum: change in bowel habits; blood in stool
- Skin: sore that doesn't heal; change in shape, size, color of wart or mole; sudden appearance of mole
- Breast: lump or thickening in breast; discharge from nipple
- Uterus, ovary, cervix: bleeding after menopause; unusual discharge from vagina; swelling of abdomen, pain during intercourse
- Prostate: difficulty or pain while urinating; impulse to urinate often, especially at night

though, you should be on the lookout for cancer in your senior years. Beginning at age 40, women should have a mammogram, an X-ray of the breast, every two years (annually beginning at age 50) and should self-examine their breasts monthly. They also should have regular Pap smears (beginning around age 18 or after they've become sexually active) to detect cancer of the cervix and pelvic exams to find cancers of the uterus or ovaries. Men over 40 need annual exams for prostate cancer. And every older person should have periodic rectal exams and fecal occult blood tests, which can find cancer in the colon or rectum.

Although no one knows how to prevent cancer, you can greatly improve your odds with certain lifestyle adjustments. You've probably heard this before, but that's because evidence continues to mount that some personal habits increase your risk many times over. By now you know you help your chances considerably by not smoking and by avoiding unnecessary X-rays, following a low-fat, high-fiber diet, and drinking in moderation. You can also discourage cancer by avoiding excess exposure to the sun, whose ultra-violet rays play a role in 90 percent of cases of skin cancer, which afflicts more people than any other form of the disease. If you're a woman taking estrogen to alleviate menopausal symptoms, take the smallest possible dose; studies show that high doses increase risk of cancer of the uterine lining.

Despite the gloomy odds of getting cancer, prospects for victims are looking up. Nearly half of all cancer patients can be cured,

CANCER TREATMENTS

Surgery: removal of the tumor and any nearby tissue that may contain cancer cells.

Radiation therapy: also known by several other names—X-ray therapy, radiotherapy, cobalt treatment, and irradiation. It's primarily a local treatment, but for some cancers, like leukemia and lymphoma, the whole body may be radiated. High-energy rays damage cancer cells so they are unable to grow and multiply.

Chemotherapy: a treatment by which anticancer drugs are used to disrupt cancer cells' ability to grow and multiply. The drugs, taken orally or by injection, travel through the bloodstream so they can affect cells throughout the body.

Hormone therapy: a treatment applied because some types of cancer depend on hormones for their growth. This therapy may be recommended to block the body's production of hormones, or surgery may be performed to remove hormone-producing organs. Hormone therapy is most often used to treat cancers of the breast, prostate, kidney, and uterus.

Biological therapy: the newest area of cancer treatment, using both natural and man-made substances. Two examples are interferon, a substance that stimulates the body's immune system to fight cancer cells, and interleukin-2, a protein that regulates cell growth.

which doctors define as surviving without recurrence for five years, and the outlook continues to improve with scientific advancements. And, there is no telling how many people *didn't* get cancer because they paid attention to their health.

A DEADLY CATCHALL: CARDIOVASCULAR DISEASE

Cardiovascular disease, which attacks the heart and blood vessels, causes as many deaths in the United States as cancer and all other diseases lumped together. Heart attack, by itself, is the nation's number-one killer, claiming more than half a million lives yearly, and stroke is number three after cancer.

Other diseases that come under the cardiovascular disease umbrella are high blood pressure, atherosclerosis, angina pectoris, and congestive heart failure.

High blood pressure hits one in three American adults. Also called hypertension, it's been dubbed "the silent killer" because it can damage the heart, blood vessels, kidneys, and eyes, all without symptoms. High blood pressure increases your chances of having a stroke eightfold, and of congestive heart failure threefold.

Blood pressure, the force generated by the heart as it pumps, is measured in the arteries by two numbers: the first is systolic pressure, when the heart contracts, and the second is diastolic pressure, when the heart relaxes. A healthy blood pressure is 120/80; more than 140/90 is too high. By having your blood pressure checked at least once a year, you can get a jump on controlling hypertension.

Although there's no cure for high blood pressure, medication, weight control, and a low-sodium diet can rein it in. People who consume too much sodium, a primary component of salt, can increase their risk for high blood pressure, and excess sodium can exacerbate high blood pressure in those who already have it. To maintain normal blood pressure and volume, and to keep muscles and nerves functioning properly, you need only about a teaspoon a day of sodium, but most Americans ingest at least twice that much.

Exercise can be especially effective in lowering blood pressure. In one study, workouts of 45 minutes, three days a week, dropped blood pressure 14 points. "There is a significant drop in death rates of hypertensives with higher fitness," says Larry Gibbons, medical director of the Cooper Clinic at the Institute for Aerobic Research in Dallas.

A danger with high blood pressure and atherosclerosis—thickening of artery walls from fatty deposits—is strokes, which kill brain cells by depriving them of blood. Dead blood vessels in the brain create blood clots or hemorrhaging, which causes a stroke. The aftereffects of strokes may be temporary or permanent, depending on how long the blood flow is blocked. If the low flow of blood to brain cells persists, there's permanent damage, such as weakness or paralysis, abnormalities of thought or motion, and difficulty speaking and seeing.

Warnings of strokes are numbness in the face, arm, or leg, difficulty speaking, dimness of vision, and unexplained dizziness. The symptoms usually last up to five minutes, but may go on for up to 24 hours and still be temporary. If you see your doctor or get to a hospital emergency room immediately, these warnings can save your life.

A heart attack strikes when a blood clot forms in a defective coronary artery, usually one narrowed by the buildup of fatty substances. If the blood supply to the heart is cut off, heart cells die, and depending on the extent of the damage, the attack can end in death or disability.

Angina pectoris can indicate a susceptibility toward heart attacks. An attack of angina feels like a dull ache, tightness, or a burning sensation in the middle of the chest and discomfort in the neck, jaw, or both arms. These symptoms are the result of the narrowing of the coronary arteries by atherosclerosis, thus restricting the flow of blood to the heart. If angina hits when you're resting, that's a strong warning. Angina can be treated with medication— nitroglycerin, beta-blockers, calcium antagonists, and aspirin.

You can stave off heart attacks with drugs that dissolve clots or by coronary bypass surgery or balloon dilation of narrowed coronary arteries. And, major lifestyle changes may be in order.

Another bullet in the cardiovascular disease arsenal is congestive heart failure. Caused by a weakened or stiffened heart muscle that fails to pump blood efficiently, it is relatively common among seniors. The good news is there are numerous treatment possibilities.

Congestive heart failure can be triggered by disease of the coronary arteries or heart valves, high blood pressure, or alcoholism, and symptoms include shortness of breath and swelling in the legs. Treatment depends on the cause: surgery if heart valves are diseased; otherwise, drugs to remove excess salt and water from the body (called diuretics), widen the blood vessels (vasodilators), and inhibit the body's production of substances that constrict blood vessels (ACE inhibitors). The most widely known treatment, used for more than 200 years, is digitalis, a cardiac stimulant and diuretic derived from the dried leaf of the common foxglove plant.

The likelihood of developing any of these cardiovascular illnesses increases with age, but your heredity, race, and gender also figure in. Overall, blacks experience a higher overall death rate than whites from cardiovascular disease, and men are generally more prone to develop these medical problems than women.

Still, women, especially those over 65, aren't in the clear at all. During the later years, they're more likely than men to have high blood pressure and a much higher rate of strokes. Their chances for

THESE HEART ATTACK WARNING SIGNS CAN SAVE YOUR LIFE

Not all these warning signs must be present to indicate a heart attack. If any of them occur, call your local emergency medical service immediately. When a heart attack occurs, prompt medical attention may save your life.

• Uncomfortable pressure, fullness, squeezing, or pain in the center of the chest lasting two minutes or longer.
• Pain spreading to the shoulders, neck, or arms.
• Severe pain, dizziness, fainting, sweating, nausea, or shortness of breath.

cardiovascular illnesses increase from one in nine for women aged 45 to 64, to one in three for women 65 and older.

Obviously you have no control over these factors. But you do have a say over lifestyle risks, and this say can be significant. You can stop smoking, get the proper exercise, watch your weight, and eat a diet low in salt and fats and high in fiber, thereby taking yourself partially out of harm's way.

DEALING WITH DEPRESSION

If you think of all the struggles you might face in your retirement years—chronic illness, death of a spouse and close friends, money worries—it's enough to depress anyone. But in too many older people, temporary blues deteriorate into full-fledged clinical depression.

Around 15 percent of people over 65 are clinically depressed, a percentage that rises to 25 percent in nursing homes. Depressive disorders appear more often in older women than in older men, in part because women live longer and so suffer more losses associated with aging.

Depression rears many ugly heads: feelings of emptiness or worthlessness, persistent sadness, anxiety, lack of interest in life, irritability, trouble concentrating, remembering, and making decisions, change in sleep patterns, persistent fatigue, nagging aches and pains, and digestive problems. At its worst, depression leads to suicide.

Although these symptoms sound cut-and-dried, diagnosing depression in older people is a slippery undertaking. Often symptoms are mistakenly dismissed as simply part of aging, confused with Alzheimer's disease, or may stem from medications taken for arthritis, hypertension, or heart problems. As a rule of thumb, when any of these symptoms lasts two weeks or more, it's time to get medical help.

The truly sad news is that some 60 percent of the elderly who suffer from depression live with their pain rather than get medical help. It doesn't have to be this way. Depression can be effectively treated with a combination of drugs and psychotherapy, support groups, or electroshock therapy.

Treating depression can be a matter of survival in elderly people fighting disease. According to a yearlong study of 454 nursing-home residents, depression weakened the immune system and markedly increased the likelihood of death by 59 percent.

SERIOUS DAMAGE FROM DIABETES

Diabetes upsets the body's ability to turn food into energy, a job that requires sufficient amounts of the hormone insulin. The disease appears in two main forms. Type I, or insulin-dependent diabetes, accounts for only 10 percent of the 6 million cases in the United States and most often afflicts younger people. (You might know it as juvenile diabetes, but it strikes adults, too.) This type is treated with insulin injections because the pancreas fails to produce the hormone.

Type II, or non-insulin-dependent diabetes, appears when the body produces enough insulin, but resists absorbing the hormone (insulin unlocks the cells so that the fuel foods can get from the bloodstream into the cells). As a result, body fuel, such as glucose and blood fats, builds up and damages the walls of the blood vessels and retards circulation.

Type II diabetes can often be controlled by regular exercise and proper diet, although insulin injec-

Q I have a good friend, a woman in her fifties, who I think is severely depressed. She's unhappy and angry much of the time, and isn't sleeping well. She says her problem's related to work and a messy divorce, but I think she needs help. How do I get her some?

A One of the biggest problems with mental illness is denial—people denying that they have a medical problem, not just a temporary tough time. Suggest she get a checkup —a sharp internist or general practitioner will recommend antidepressant medication or steer her toward a psychologist or psychiatrist.

tions and drugs may have to be given from time to time. And smoking is definitely out of the question. This type is more likely to afflict older people. Women are more likely to develop the disease than men, and blacks and Hispanic women are even more susceptible. Also, this type has a stronger hereditary factor than Type I.

Watch for these warning signs of diabetes: thirst, fatigue, frequent urination, slow healing of cuts and bruises, steady weight gain or recent weight loss, dental disease, and difficulties seeing.

Although very treatable and manageable, diabetes shouldn't be underestimated. It can be a serious threat to your health, leading to heart disease, stroke, kidney failure, sexual problems, and amputation of legs and feet (all caused by inadequate circulation of the blood). It's the leading cause of adult blindness in the United States.

INCONTINENCE: A SIGNAL OF SOMETHING ELSE

Urinary incontinence—the involuntary loss of urine—is at last out of the closet. Until recently this signal that something is wrong was dismissed as an embarrassment that comes naturally with aging. Although not a disease, it is a condition that's treatable, if not curable. Among women over 60, almost 40 percent suffer from it.

It shows up in different forms, ranging from slight involuntary voidance to frequent wetting. The two most common types are called stress incontinence and urge incontinence. Stress incontinence is leaking urine during physical exertion, anything from a sneeze to

LEARN MORE ABOUT DIABETES

For free or low-cost publications about diabetes, contact the American Diabetes Association, 1600 Duke Street, Alexandria, VA 22314; 800/232-3475, and the National Diabetes Information Clearinghouse, National Institute of Diabetes and Digestive and Kidney Diseases, Bethesda, MD 20892.

demanding exercise, that puts pressure on the bladder. Urge incontinence is a sudden need to urinate that can be so powerful it's difficult to reach a toilet in time. This type, although it can exist in healthy older people, occurs most frequently in victims of stroke, dementia, and other serious diseases.

Usually incontinence is caused by:

- Infections
- Weak pelvic floor and abdominal muscles
- Hormonal changes during menopause
- Certain diseases, including diabetes, Alzheimer's, bladder cancer, and strokes
- Medications, such as diuretics
- Abnormal positioning of the bladder, which can result from surgery, such as a hysterectomy

Treating incontinence depends on the cause, but generally doctors recommend the most conservative therapies first, like exercising to strengthen pelvic and abdominal muscles, and training the bladder to follow a schedule for emptying. Medications are available, but they may have unpleasant side effects such as dry mouth and eye problems. Surgery is an option for problems related to blockage or the bladder's position.

Many people afflicted with incontinence make themselves prisoners in their own homes for fear they'll have an embarrassing accident. Such isolation is truly unnecessary. If you suffer from incontinence get medical advice so you can get your life back on track.

MANAGING MENOPAUSE

A natural event in every woman's life, menopause marks the end of menstruation and the ability to have children. Typically, it happens around age 50 as the body produces less estrogen and so the ovaries stop releasing eggs.

Although many women sail through menopause without a big fuss, the symptoms make some women miserable for years. One of the earliest signs is irregular periods, along with a lighter and shorter blood flow. Other signs are vaginal burning and itching as the vaginal lining becomes thinner and less flexible, which can contribute to discomfort during intercourse. (An easy way to counter the discomfort is to apply lubrication—water-soluble surgical jelly, not petroleum jelly).

GET HIP (HELP FOR INCONTINENT PEOPLE)

HIP is an organization providing support and education for people suffering from incontinence. The group recommends that you get a complete medical examination if you have an incontinence problem. Before seeing your doctor, keep a diary to record your daily trips to the bathroom and include notes on when and how incontinence began, frequency, and times of day of the involuntary loss of urine, the activities you were involved in at those times, and any medications you're taking.

Call HIP for further advice: 800/BLADDER, or write to P.O. Box 544, Union, SC 29379.

Estrogen reduction also leads to loss of calcium in bones, which can contribute to the bone-thinning disease called osteoporosis, and to fractures. Hot flashes often accompany a woman's transition out of the childbearing years, as do some mood swings, with more nervousness, irritability, and mild depression.

If symptoms are severe, the doctor may recommend drug therapy, the most common being estrogen replacement. But this hormone therapy is prescribed with caution because studies have linked it to higher risk for breast and endometrial cancer, and concerns about heart disease.

If menopausal and premenopausal conditions become intolerable, your doctor may recommend surgery to remove the uterus, a procedure called a hysterectomy. While many women who have had hysterectomies feel it was worth the surgery, there are those who say this operation is performed too cavalierly. Sometimes it is not the best remedy and patients are not properly advised about possible consequences. Women have reported loss of sexual feeling and desire, fatigue, depression, protruding abdomen, bloating, urine leakage, and premature graying and hair loss. So before proceeding, research all options and, if possible, get more than one doctor's opinion.

FRIGHTENING FRACTURES: OSTEOPOROSIS

Some bone loss is natural in aging but when it's exaggerated, it becomes osteoporosis. Scientists don't fully grasp why the disease develops, but they say decreasing hormone levels, too little calcium in the diet during early years, and inactivity play a role.

Osteoporosis is a bone-thinning disease that is a major cause of fractures—it's blamed for 1.3 million bone breaks a year in people 45 and older. When it leads to a broken hip, it can even magnify the risk of death. Between 12 and 20 percent of patients with broken hips die during the first six months after the fracture, and 20 percent of the survivors end up in nursing homes, often for the rest of their lives.

More than 24 million Americans have osteoporosis, striking eight times as many women as men. One in four women over 60 develops osteoporosis, and white and Asian women with petite frames and a family history of the disease are the most susceptible. Although men are less likely victims, their risk increases in their advanced years.

Osteoporosis happens gradually and without pain as not enough

RECOMMENDED CALCIUM INTAKE	
Age	Mg calcium per day
Infants	
Birth–6 months	400
6 months–1 year	600
Children and young adults	
1–10 years	800
11–24 years	1,200
Adults	1,000
Pregnant and lactating women	1,200
Postmenopausal women not on hormone therapy	1,500
National Academy of Sciences, National Institutes of Health	

new bone is formed to replace old bits that are routinely worn away. An early sign of it is a loss of height and curvature of the spine. Often you break a bone before osteoporosis is diagnosed.

You can help fend off osteoporosis in a number of ways. For instance, by taking in calcium and getting sufficient vitamin D, which helps the body absorb calcium. Good calcium sources are dairy products and sardines with bones. Vitamin D can be found in fortified milk products. You can also pick up some D by basking for a few minutes in the sun whenever possible. You can increase bone mass with weight-bearing exercises like walking, running, and riding a bicycle. In addition, estrogen therapy is sometimes recommended because it reduces the amount of calcium extracted from bones. But hormone therapy has a cancer risk attached to it and it can't restore lost bone mass. Men are protected from bone loss by the male hormone testosterone.

PROSTATE PROBLEMS

Problems with the prostate, a male reproductive gland that adds secretions to sperm during ejaculation, are widespread among

SPOTTING QUACK CURES

Regard the following characteristics in ads for so-called cures with a large dose of skepticism:

- A quick and painless cure.
- A "special," "secret," "ancient," or "foreign" formula, available only through the mail and only from one supplier.
- Testimonials from satisfied users as the sole proof that the product works.
- A single product that works for a variety of ailments.
- A scientific "breakthrough" or "miracle cure" that has been held back or overlooked by the medical community.

men 50 and older. More than half the men in their sixties develop an enlargement of the prostate, and up to 90 percent do so by the time they are in their seventies and eighties.

Prostate cancer, one of the most common forms of cancer, strikes mostly older men—about 80 percent of prostate cancers afflict men over 65. But if the cancer is found early, treatment increases the prospects for a good recovery.

Symptoms of prostate disease include difficulty urinating, dribbling after urination, the need to urinate frequently, especially at night, and occasionally the inability to urinate.

If the enlargement is mild and benign, the symptoms may disappear on their own. If they don't, balloon dilation of the urethra may be called for in some cases. So far, drug treatments have proved ineffective. If symptoms persist, surgery to remove the portion of the prostate that is putting pressure on the urethra and causing urinary problems may be necessary.

With early-stage cancer, surgery entails removing the entire prostate and surrounding tissues. New techniques for this surgery, called a radical prostatectomy, keep the nerves that go to the penis intact, allowing the patient to have erections after the operation. More extreme treatment—radiation, hormone drugs, and chemotherapy—may sometimes be necessary.

A man's best protections against serious prostate problems are regular checkups and acting swiftly when symptoms arise.

QUACK CURES: NO PANACEAS

None of these diseases or conditions is easy to live with, and people frustrated by the limits of conventional treatments are often tempted to find miracles where none exist. People overwhelmed by illness want to believe there's a cure-all, and this makes them susceptible to quack cures.

The sick and desperate are easy prey to quacks selling pills, potions, and devices said to cure everything from arthritic pain to male pattern baldness. Americans spend billions of dollars each year on fraudulent products that don't work and can be harmful, especially if they prevent someone from seeking genuine medical care.

The biggest areas mined by quacks are arthritis, cancer, fitness, and weight loss. Arthritis is rich territory because symptoms may come and go, so those who have the disease may be suckered into thinking they've been cured by a fraudulent product. Over 30 million Americans suffer from the disease, and $2 billion (true!) is spent every year on quack cures, from snake venom to lemon juice to dangerous use of steroids. It's easy to avoid being taken in by this quackery by just remembering that no cure for arthritis has been found.

Perhaps the cruelest, and certainly the most costly, fraud against the sick is cancer quackery. Seemingly legitimate clinics, often outside U.S. boundaries and outside the reach of U.S. authorities, provide untested diets or drugs that are no cure and often produce more health woes.

Quack cures are often aimed at older people, who need to be especially wary of pitches and advertisements that sound too good to be true. Beware of advertisements claiming effectiveness for health-care products not screened by any government agency. Authorities can take action only after ads appear, but by the time a duped customer pursues a "money-back guarantee," the fly-by-night operator has skipped town.

Q I've seen ads in very respected magazines for guaranteed treatments for arthritis. Doesn't the fact the ads appear in these publications mean they're legitimate and approved by the government?

A No government agency screens magazine ads before they appear. Truth-in-advertising standards are promoted by consumer organizations and the magazine industry.

HAZARDS TO HEALTHY LIVING

STRESS CAN MAKE YOU SICK

Stress is a normal response to the physical, mental, and emotional challenges of life. A steady diet of stress can hurt you—leading to nervousness, high blood pressure, stomach ulcers, and mental problems. If you're already sick, stress can exacerbate your pain and slow your recovery.

When you're under stress, your body revs up to meet the difficulty or challenge. Hormones speed up their output and nerve impulses accelerate, making the heart beat faster. Blood vessels in the stomach and intestines contract to divert blood to the muscles for swift reaction. You breathe faster to take in more oxygen. These reactions bring about muscle tightening, shallow breathing, clenching, headaches, digestive disturbances, and irritability. If the signs of stress go unheeded and ignored, depression may follow.

You can defend yourself from prolonged stress by identifying what's causing it, then taking steps to relieve or remove it. For instance, anger and hostility are extremely stressful, and studies have linked them to increased risk of heart disease. People inclined to lose their tempers easily and to harbor grudges need to recognize what sets them off and find ways to control and channel their anger.

Some of the most stressful events of life fall during the later years, such as the death of a spouse, retirement, changes in financial status, or the death of a close friend. Keep in mind that should these eventually crash in on you, you should get help from a counselor or therapist.

KNOWING YOUR LIMITS: ALCOHOL AND TOBACCO

After 50, your body becomes more sensitive to alcohol because of a slowdown in the digestive processes. It takes less alcohol to affect you, and its effects last longer.

Alcohol is a powerful depressant, slowing the brain's activity and impairing your mental quickness and reflexes. This immediately heightens the risk of falls and other accidents, and over the long haul increases the risk of serious illnesses such as cancer and cardiovascular disease. Years of heavy drinking can permanently damage the brain, central nervous system, liver, heart, kidneys, and stomach.

Mixing alcohol and drugs is dangerous at any age, but the changes in your body's ability to absorb and dispose of drugs and alcohol mean you should be particularly careful as you age. Alco-

SIGNS OF TOO MUCH: RISKS OF HEAVY DRINKING

- Cancer of the mouth and esophagus
- Cancer of the liver and bladder
- Ulcers
- Heart disease
- Diabetes
- Cirrhosis of the liver
- Influenza and pneumonia
- Malnutrition
- Impaired mental functioning
- Memory loss
- Accidental injury and death
- Decreased life expectancy

hol, combined with certain drugs, interferes with desired therapeutic effects; worse yet, the mixture can be life-threatening. Always check with your doctor before drinking when you are taking medicine, whether prescription or over-the-counter drugs.

If you're over 50 and healthy, moderate drinking probably won't hurt. However, people with a chronic health problem or a proclivity toward dependency should avoid any alcohol.

Smoking has no redeeming features when it comes to your health. It prematurely kills 390,000 Americans each year and seriously disables millions more; it causes several types of cancer; and it promotes the high blood pressure and high blood cholesterol that lay the groundwork for cardiovascular disease. It irritates and inflames the lungs and air passages, and incites the production of excess mucus. Chronic bronchitis is a likely result, and long-term damage can end in emphysema, which prevents normal breathing. Furthermore, smokers are at a higher risk for pneumonia and influenza, to which older patients are especially vulnerable anyway.

As if this isn't enough, studies have shown that smoking may increase the risk of osteoporosis. That's because smoking may lower blood concentrations of estrogen, a hormone that influences bone formation.

The precise risks you face from smoking depend on how much you smoke, how long you've been smoking, and how deeply you inhale. Cigars and pipes are less risky for lung cancer, but they can cause mouth, tongue, and throat cancer.

Quitting smoking can improve

your health immediately, no matter what your age. It's never too late to quit, medical experts say.

LEARNING TO EAT BETTER

Some 85 percent of older Americans suffer from chronic diseases that can be fought with better eating habits. Unfortunately, a study of people over age 60 showed that half don't eat enough of at least one nutrient on a list of essential vitamins, minerals, and proteins. In another study, just 13 percent of people 55 to 74 years old said they ate the daily minimum of five servings of fruit and vegetables.

As you grow older, your eating habits may deteriorate because your appetite is diminished. Your sense of taste or smell may also have been dulled by age. Loneli-

WHY QUIT?

Even if you've smoked for years, you can save your life by quitting now. Here are some big reasons to stop:

- Your risk of shortened life expectancy will be lowered.
- Your chances for getting smoking-related cancers will begin to shrink as soon as smoking stops, and within ten years the risk will be reduced to that of nonsmokers.
- Your risk for cardiovascular disease will decline to that for nonsmokers within one to five years.
- Risks for respiratory disease will be lessened.
- Your physical stamina will improve.
- Your taste and olfactory senses will get sharper.
- Your teeth and dentures will stay whiter.
- Your breath, body, and clothes will smell better.
- You'll save money on tobacco products and medical bills.

Q *I've seen a lot of ads lately for a nicotine patch to help a smoker quit. Does it work?*

A *The patch, which is worn on the upper arm or torso, slowly releases nicotine into the blood. It does reduce nicotine cravings. But for it to work, doctors warn, patch wearers have to quit completely (no occasional puffs) and confront their behavioral and psychological addiction.*

ness and depression can take away your appetite, too. Finally, you may not eat nutritiously because you're not sure what's healthy and what's not.

Information on diets and the special needs of the elderly is readily available from consumer advocacy groups, medical associations, local social service agencies, and the federal government. Or, from your doctor. You owe it to yourself to be informed—it's literally a life-or-death issue.

A NEW LOOK AT VITAMINS

Recent research has raised the stock of vitamins, which are being studied for their effect on illness and aging. Preliminary research has shown that vitamins, sometimes in higher doses than usual, may boost the immune system, lower cholesterol levels, reduce risk of cataracts, cancer, stroke, and heart attack, and even decelerate aging.

"Along with exercise, a proper diet that supplies a full complement of vitamins can go a long way to help us stay vigorous and prevent disease—and prevention is the key to a long, healthy life," says Dr. Jeffrey Blumberg, assistant director of the U.S. Department of Agriculture's Human Nutrition Research Center on Aging.

The earlier you start increasing the intake of certain nutrients, Blumberg suggests, the sooner the aging process would be stymied. "If we can retard or reverse a phenomenon like the decline in immunity with nutritional intervention in older adults," he says, "then it's reasonable to speculate that we can slow age-related changes by having a relatively high intake of these nutrients in the middle years."

The new information from the studies is causing a stir in the medical community, where experts are reconsidering whether the RDAs (Recommended Dietary Allowances) for nutrients fit the aging population. As it stands, all people aged 51 and older are lumped into one big average group. The RDA chart breaks down other ages into more restricted groups, so why should it be assumed that all older people fit one category? Someone 91 years old surely requires a different diet from that of someone who is 51, the experts reason.

Three vitamins of the antioxidant family play starring roles in the research: vitamins E, C, and beta carotene, a form of vitamin A. Antioxidants stop loose electrons, called free radicals, from damaging cells. The radicals are set free in your body when fat and proteins mix with oxygen. In their search for a place to settle, the radicals invade your cells, causing them to break down. According to one theory, aging is the outcome of free-radical barrages over the years. But antioxidants can squelch the attacks by latching onto the free agents before they crash into the cells and damage them.

In one recent study, beta carotene cut the risk of heart attack and stroke in half in a group of men who showed signs of heart disease. The men ate 25 mg of beta carotene daily, equivalent to a cup of cooked carrots.

The vitamin C studies show that the nutrient may be responsible for slowing the accrual of cellular sorbitol, a sugar that gets some of the blame for cataracts. The vitamin may also prevent some complications of diabetes, such as neurological damage and clogged arteries. Good sources of the vitamin are citrus fruits, strawberries, cantaloupe, broccoli, and peppers.

Vitamin E supplements helped the immune systems of people over 60 years old in one study, and other studies using higher amounts showed a potential for reducing the risk of cancer and other chronic diseases. Foods that contain vitamin E are wheat germ, peanut butter, almonds, and leafy green vegetables.

Researchers have a distance to go before recommending amounts of vitamin E that would be helpful and safe at the same time. At the daily level of 8 to 10 mg recommended by the National Academy of Sciences, vitamin E helps build red blood cells and guards disease-fighting white blood cells. Experimental levels of the vitamin reached at least 80 times the recommended daily amount.

In yet another study, doses of more than 500 mg a day of vitamin

WEIGHTS FOR MEN AND WOMEN BY AGE

Height	35	45	55	65
5'0"	98–127	106–135	114–143	123–152
5'1"	101–131	110–140	118–148	127–157
5'2"	105–136	113–144	122–153	131–163
5'3"	108–140	117–149	126–158	135–168
5'4"	112–145	121–154	130–163	140–173
5'5"	115–149	125–159	134–168	144–179
5'6"	119–154	129–164	138–174	148–184
5'7"	122–159	133–169	143–179	153–190
5'8"	126–163	137–174	147–184	158–196
5'9"	130–168	141–179	151–190	162–201
5'10"	134–173	145–184	156–195	167–207
5'11"	137–178	149–190	160–201	172–213
6'0"	141–183	153–195	165–207	177–219
6'1"	145–188	157–200	169–213	182–225
6'2"	149–194	162–206	174–219	187–232
6'3"	153–199	166–212	179–225	192–238
6'4"	157–205	171–218	184–231	197–244

Rubin Andres, M.D., Gerontology Research Center

B_3, or niacin, lowered levels of blood cholesterol, which forms plaque on arteries. In normal amounts, about 16 mg a day, niacin contributes to the conversion of carbohydrates, fats, and proteins into energy. Medical experts caution against increasing niacin in the diet without consulting a doctor, because it can lead to serious side effects, including liver damage. Niacin is found in whole grains, leafy greens, poultry, tuna, and peanuts.

Vitamin B_6 also raised hopes in recent anti-aging research. When B_6 was taken out of healthy elderly subjects, their immune response functioned less efficiently. The amount needed to restore the immune response was higher than the 2 mg currently accepted as the proper daily intake. With higher doses, the immune system truly rallied. While absorbing this good news, it's important to remember that 50 mg a day of B_6 can be toxic.

In other vitamin B developments, preliminary tests have shown that supplements of B_6 and B_{12} may improve memory and learning ability, and lack of B_6 can cause mental confusion, nervousness, irritability, and insomnia. Good sources for B_6 are poultry, fish, beans, corn, whole wheat, and low-fat dairy products.

THE BATTLE OF THE BULGE: FAT CONTROVERSY

For many people, gaining weight as they get older seems as unavoidable as liver spots. Metabolisms slow down, and life in general becomes more sedentary. Gaining a pound a year as they course through their forties and fifties feels inevitable. Yet for years, nutritionists have been saying that you should *not* add pounds as you age, that what you weigh at age 50 should be what you weighed at age 30. Recommended weight charts issued by the life insurance industry reinforce this position by offering desired weight ranges according to gender, height, and frame size but not age. The Metropolitan Life Insurance Company chart shows the same weight range for people aged 25 to 59.

But now scientists at the Gerontology Research Center are turning years of long-held wisdom on its head. They have reviewed longevity and mortality studies, and claim that recommended weights should differ only according to age and height, not gender or frame size, as has traditionally been held.

BEWARE OF ADS FOR NUTRITIONAL SUPPLEMENTS

While preliminary research on vitamins is exciting, be wary of ads that imply high-dose supplements of vitamins and minerals will improve appearance, enhance sex life, prevent or cure diseases, and even lengthen life. Too much of a good thing can be a waste at the least, and toxic at the worst.

For instance, vitamin A, while essential for healthy skin, hair, and bone growth, can cause headaches, nausea, diarrhea, and eventually liver and bone damage if overdosed. Too much vitamin D can end in kidney damage and even death. Vitamin B_{15}, also called pangamic acid or calcium pangamate, hasn't the least bit of medical usefulness, scientists say. Still, it's held out as a treatment of heart disease, diabetes, glaucoma, allergies, and "aging" in general.

Consult your physician before taking supplements. If you have been taking supplements without medical consultation, talk with an expert about stopping. It may be advisable to reduce the amount slowly rather than doing it cold turkey.

Talk about stirring up a hornet's nest! By devising recommended weight ranges according to age and height only, the Gerontology Research Center is challenging common wisdom about how men and women age, and whether gaining weight over the years is healthy. It does stress that its weights are recommended only according to their impact on mortality. Nevertheless, people interpret them as standards for general health, not just longevity.

Whatever recommended weight range you choose to consult, experts all agree that being overweight or obese, particularly as you get older, markedly raises your risk of deadly diseases like heart attacks, strokes, and cancer.

An older person needs the same nutrients as a younger adult—proteins, carbohydrates, vitamins, minerals, and a bit of fat. But, given a slow rate of burning food for energy, seniors need to consume fewer calories. On average, women 51 and older should limit daily calories to 1,600, and men to 2,400. To do this, say nutritionists, you should adopt a nutrient-dense diet.

FAT AND FIBER

B y now we are all repeating the health mantra of the 1990s: "Fat is bad. Fat is bad." After de-cades of educating people about calories, salt, and sugar, health experts now say that an overload of fat in the diet is probably more hazardous to your health than any other item on the menu.

Fats have lots of calories, so they're a concentrated form of energy and help your body absorb vitamins A, D, E, and K. Fats also build and repair cells, and make certain hormones. The problem is that people eat too much of them; about 40 percent of their caloric intake is made up of fats on aver-

---

GUIDE TO A WELL-BALANCED DIET

To eat a wide range of nutritious foods, your daily diet should include:

- 2 to 3 servings* of low-fat milk or dairy products such as cheese, cottage cheese, or yogurt
- 2 to 3 servings of protein-rich foods, such as poultry, fish, eggs, beans, nuts, or lean meat
- 5 to 9 servings of fruit and vegetables, including a citrus fruit or juice and a dark green leafy vegetable
- 6 to 11 servings of breads, rice, pasta, or cereal products made from whole grain or enriched flours

* Serving means a single helping, e.g. 1 cup of milk or yogurt; 2 ounces cheese; 3 ounces beans, meat, poultry, or fish; ½ cup pasta or cereal; 1 slice bread.

---

age—10 percentage points higher than the level recommended by the American Heart Association, American Cancer Society, and the surgeon general.

Curtailing the fat in your diet prevents weight gain and high blood cholesterol, as well as disease such as diabetes, heart disease, high blood pressure, and some cancers.

Fats come in various shapes, some worse than others. Particularly hazardous are fats in a group of foods called lipids, which include saturated fats, unsaturated fats, and cholesterol. Saturated fats, usually solid at room temperature (like lard), are found in animal foods, and in coconut and palm oils. Unsaturated fats, usually liquid at room temperature (like olive oil), are in vegetable and fish oils. Cholesterol is a fat-like substance found in meat, dairy products, and seafood, and it's manufactured in your body. Some foods, like red meats and cheese, are loaded with both cholesterol and saturated fat.

Fiber in your diet, though not fully understood, may protect you against some cancers and, combined with low fat, can help prevent non-insulin-dependent diabetes. Dietary fiber (matter from plant cells that humans digest partially or not at all) also aids digestion and works against digestive disorders like constipation and hemorrhoids. Good sources are whole-grain breads, cereals with oats, vegetables, and fruit.

The typical American eats 11 grams of fiber each day, barely half of the minimum intake of 20 to 30 grams recommended by the National Cancer Institute.

FITNESS: A MODERN MAGIC WAND

If you could do something simple and painless to lower your risk for heart attack, stroke, cancer, and other chronic diseases, would you? And, if you could at the same time strengthen your muscles, trim your waistline, and elevate your mood, would you? If your answer is yes to both, then take a brisk walk—the easiest of exercises—and start the trip to rejuvenation.

Researchers studying exercise in the elderly say it can actually turn the clock back in some ways as much as 25 years, so a 60-year-old can potentially function like a 35-year-old if a rigorous exercise regimen is followed. Even a modest level of exercise brings re-

TOO MUCH SPRINKLING?

Use the following key to estimate the amount of salt in your diet:

Less than once a week = 1
1–2 times a week = 2
3–5 times a week = 3
Almost daily = 4

How often do you:
1. Add salt to cooking water? _____
2. Eat cheese? _____
3. Use prepared dinners? _____
4. Salt food before tasting? _____
5. Eat salted snacks? _____
6. Use condiments or seasoning mixes to cook? _____
7. Eat canned vegetables or frozen vegetables with sauces? _____
8. Eat cured or processed meats like bacon, hot dogs, or sandwich meats? _____
9. Eat commercial soups? _____
10. Eat fast-food meals? _____

Scoring:
10–20: You're doing pretty well.
21–30: Fair, but be careful.
31–40: Poor. Do yourself a favor and cut back on salt.

The National Council on the Aging

wards. At one time, doctors considered deterioration of the muscles, bones, heart, and lungs to be a natural part of aging. Now they believe it is, in great part, a result of inactivity.

Q *I recently started a low-fat diet but now I'm hearing about people not getting enough fat. Is it possible to eat too little fat?*

A *It sure is. If you're taking in less than 10 percent of your calories from fat, it may well be too little. An ultra-low-fat diet can leave you deficient in HDL, the good cholesterol, which helps fight heart disease.*

The benefits of exercise for older people become clearer with every scientific study. A Canadian study of women aged 50 to 62 compared the bone densities of two groups: those who regularly did aerobic and stretching exercises and those who were sedentary. While the exercisers showed an increase in bone mass, the inactive women actually had a loss in bone mass. Even fears that frailty in older people would put them in danger of injury during exercise have been stifled by successes in studies of the "oldest old," those 85 years old and up. By exercising, one group of oldsters increased muscle mass by 10 to 15 percent and in a walking test increased speed and balance by 48 percent.

Studies of the flip side of exercise—inactivity—simply reinforce the importance of physical activity. For instance, people forced into prolonged bed rest show a dramatic decline in the capacity of the heart and lungs, and in muscle function.

In the fight against chronic diseases, exercise lowers the risk for high blood pressure, strokes, heart disease, cancer, osteoporosis, and non-insulin-dependent diabetes, and it helps to ease the symptoms of arthritis.

Exercise works various forms of magic on different body parts. Here's a stem-to-stern look at how it performs:

• Lowers blood pressure (and guards against cardiovascular disorders) by keeping the circulatory system humming smoothly so blood can be pushed through with less force from the heart.

• Cleans artery walls (and pro-

HOW EXERCISE PAYS OFF

Recent research on how exercise affects older people has provided some promising statistics:

- Men who exercise regularly suffer 50 percent fewer heart attacks than their sedentary counterparts.
- Women who exercise vigorously once a week lower their risk for non-insulin-dependent diabetes by 33 percent.
- People who maintain their fitness have a 34 percent lower risk of developing high blood pressure.
- Men who burn 1,000 calories a week during exercise cut their risk of colon cancer by about 50 percent.

tects against heart disease) by raising levels of high-density lipoprotein, the good cholesterol that scours away fatty deposits.

- Enlarges the diameter of arteries, working against blockages that could lead to a heart attack.
- Pushes food through the digestive system more quickly, and so discourages colon cancer.
- Strengthens bones, through weight-bearing exercise, and so lowers the risk for osteoporosis.
- Lowers body fat, and so fights non-insulin-dependent diabetes.

It seems a clear victory for exercise. There's simply no other single thing you can do that will improve your health as much and slow down the aging process too.

STARTING TO EXERCISE

If you're rising from the legions of couch potatoes, don't rush full speed ahead into an exercise program. Check in with your doctor first, especially if you have a history of heart disease or dizzy spells, become breathless when exerting yourself, or have some other physical problem.

You want an exercise that gets your heart and lungs working, but you also want something that's convenient and fun. It's hard to maintain an exercise program that's inconvenient and unenjoyable. Assuming you've found something you enjoy, also look for a combination of three types of exercises:

1. Stretching: to strengthen and tone muscles, and improve flexibility, coordination, balance, and joint mobility. Do slow, gentle stretching exercises during five- to ten-minute warm-up and cool-down sessions.

2. Aerobics: exercises that are brisk enough to elevate your heart beat rate to your target zone rate. Your maximum heart rate is figured by subtracting your age from 220. Your target zone, a rate you want to maintain for 20 minutes of exercise, is a percentage of your maximum rate. (Figure your target zone by multiplying your maximum rate first by 60 percent, then by 75 percent. If you're 60, for example, your maximum rate is 160, so multiply 160 by .60 to get 96, then multiply 160 by .75 to get 120, the numbers that tell you your target zone: 96 to 120.) To check if you've hit your zone, take your pulse for 10 seconds immediately after a vigorous workout and multiply by six. (If you have difficulty taking your pulse, ask your fitness instructor or doctor for help.) Aerobic exercises are brisk walking, swimming, dancing, and bicycling.

3. Weight-bearing exercises: strengthen muscles and help maintain strong bones. Walking is a good form of this type of exercise, as is training with weights.

To stay fit, exercise at least three times a week for 30 to 40 minutes per session, including warm-up and cool-down routines.

PROTECTING YOURSELF: TRENDS IN HEALTH INSURANCE

You can't take care of your health without looking ahead to your health insurance to make sure you're covered for a crisis as well as the chronic ailments that plague older people. Most people over age 65 are covered by Medicare, but that doesn't mean they should ignore other sources of health coverage.

WHAT'S HAPPENING AT THE OFFICE

If you work for someone else, you may have some type of health insurance. And if you're really lucky, your company's health coverage will last through your retirement. About one-third of American employers offer company-paid retiree health insurance, but their ranks are dwindling steadily.

Major upheavals in health-care insurance are rocking company health plans. Under enormous stress from changes in accounting rules and rising health-care costs, company plans for employees as well as retirees are being reconfigured and redesigned into various shapes. Today, about four out of ten employees can count on receiving health-care benefits when they retire. But this number is slipping fast, and companies are reorganizing and reducing benefit plans right and left. The result? Regardless of how company programs are refashioned, employees will have to pay more and may well receive less coverage.

Here are the various ways employers are altering their health plans.

• Introducing "managed care," meaning your employer has negotiated with certain doctors and hospitals for services at an established rate. Employees may be limited as to who can treat them and what care is covered. Individual claims will be carefully scrutinized before they're paid.

• Offering employees and retirees "cafeteria" plans with a selection of health-care services and different levels for deductibles, percentage of care paid by the employer, and routine medical expenses.

• Arranging for coverage from a preferred provider organization (PPO), by negotiating with a network of health-care professionals to deliver service at established rates. Employees can choose to see any doctor in the network. And while a company won't force an employee to use a preferred provider, it can provide incentives by establishing lower deductibles and paying a larger percentage of hospital bills and surgical fees. Employees who opt to go "out of network" pay more.

• Hooking up with a health maintenance organization (HMO) that will provide all medical (and sometimes dental) care from select doctors and institutions for set fees. Employees have complete coverage and usually have to pay only a very small fee per visit, but no deductible. However, they have little say over who treats them and may contend with administrative red tape, including long waits for appointments.

• Eliminating health coverage for future retirees and putting the money into a special fund, like an employee stock ownership plan or 401(k), which retirees can tap into for health coverage. The extent of the health coverage thus depends on how the fund performs, and there are no guarantees as to level of coverage.

• More sharply defining health benefits for retirees and limiting coverage to employees with a set number of years of employment (e.g., 10) and only at a certain age (e.g. 60). Thus employees who retire after only a few years with a company or who retire early won't be covered.

• Requiring larger employee contributions, especially for those wanting retiree coverage. Monthly premiums for employees may be especially high if they're older.

When it comes to health insurance, the bottom line for retirement planning is that it's probably going to cost you more than you think. Regardless of whether you have lifetime retiree benefits from your former boss or arrange for Medigap coverage to fill in what Medicare doesn't, the price tag will most likely be bigger than you anticipate. Given the frightening escalation in medical costs over recent years—a steady annual march upward of 10 to 15 percent —you must plan on everything costing more.

Financial planning experts recommend people take four steps to prepare for health coverage when they retire:

1. Learn everything about your current coverage and what happens to it at retirement.

2. Find out what Medicare will cover (see Chapter 5).

3. Explore alternative coverage, such as an HMO.

4. Save as much as possible earmarked for health care.

MEDICAID: INSURER OF LAST RESORT

Medicaid is health coverage provided by the government that is "means-tested." This means you're covered only if you're poor enough, whereas you get Medicare if you're old enough, poor or not. Some people do use Medicaid for long-term care without going into poverty, but the maneuver is ethically if not legally questionable.

Q *I've a friend who works for a large insurance company and whenever we talk about insurance, she raves about an "EAP." What is this?*

A *It's an employee assistance plan, which offers a host of benefits beyond basic health insurance. It usually encompasses preventive medical and mental-health benefits, for instance substance abuse counseling, fitness and nutritional information, stress-reduction workshops, and family counseling.*

Nursing homes, the most expensive of the ordinary long-term-care facilities, typically drain the family finances by $25,000 to $50,000 a year, sometimes more. To protect its assets and save a legacy for its children, a middle-class family may resort to some financial shuffling in order to qualify for Medicaid.

It's done this way: You put your savings into an irrevocable trust, specifying that the money and interest from it can't be applied to nursing-home costs. Soon you will be legally poor enough to qualify for Medicaid underwriting of your long-term care. There are lawyers and financial planners who specialize in this sort of loophole, and if the idea interests you, talk to one of them. You'll need expert advice immediately because you can't wait until you're forced into a nursing home to place your assets in the hands of your heirs. The government requires that the transfer take place at least two and a half years before benefits begin.

ONE SOLUTION TO LONG-TERM CARE

It's also possible to purchase long-term-care insurance—a policy that pays a certain amount every day, whether you're receiving care in a nursing home or at home. Most long-term-care policies are "indemnity" policies, meaning they pay a fixed amount every day; no policy covers all expenses completely. Typically, they cover nursing-home expenses or in-home care, including payment for nurses, physical therapists, nursing aides, medical supplies and equipment, and medication.

You decide how much coverage to take; it generally ranges between $40 and $150 a day. Given the cost of nursing-home care, it's not surprising that this insurance is expensive to begin with and becomes more so as you age. Many policies are adjusted for inflation, adding to the cost of premiums. Some examples of what this coverage costs (in 1991 figures):

• A 65-year-old, with a policy offering an $80 a day nursing-home benefit for four years, with a 20-day deductible, pays about $1,103 a year.

• A 79-year-old with the same policy features, pays about $3,989.

• A 50-year-old, with the same policy plus an inflation feature, pays $852 a year.

• A 65-year-old, with the same policy plus an inflation feature, pays $1,781 a year.

Long-term-care insurance is normally recommended for people with large assets to protect. For most recipients of long-term care, the fact remains that they'll rely on Medicaid—after their own money has been depleted. "You should have over $40,000 in savings ($100,000 for a couple) before considering buying a long-term-care insurance policy," says the Senior Health Cooperative.

AN OUNCE OF PREVENTION

All of these rather gloomy prospects are best thought about before you're blindsided by a health catastrophe. Making all the smart financial moves—consulting with experts, ensuring medical coverage far into your senior years —is easy enough, but don't forget the critical point made at the beginning of this chapter. Take care of yourself—eat right, exercise, avoid habits that jeopardize your health—to give your planning the best chance to produce a rich, full retirement.

Chapter 9

RETIREMENT LIFE: TIME TO LIVE THE DREAM

The basics are in place—financial plan, investments, tax strategies, estate preparation—and when the time comes, you'll be more than ready to give up the daily grind and savor your senior years.

But have you thought about where you'll live? What you're going to do? How you want to live?

Will it be the house overlooking the first tee with enough bedrooms for the grandchildren at holiday time? Or the cabin on the trout stream for just the two of you? Are you thinking about the friendly seniors' high-rise overlooking the Florida marina or the little business, the bed-and-breakfast on the west coast of Ireland?

Focus for a moment on what that B&B dream represents—namely retirement on your own terms, the chance to make new friends, the possibility of earning break-even income, and living exactly where you've always wanted to live.

What these elements add up to

—location, companionship, extra income, and a commitment to a particular activity in a special place—is a good definition of the Retirement Good Life.

CHEZ NOUS?

Like running a successful store, retirement success can hinge on three variables: location, location, and location. This is a vital decision, or rather two, because retirement runs in two stages—early, active years, and later when health and security concerns are foremost. In each stage, you have to decide where to live.

People happily retired strongly recommend that their younger friends not move immediately. "What I learned is that you must not move after you retire," cautions a 63-year-old former college professor in California. "You should give yourself a year to sort things out."

If remaining in your home is your preference, think for a minute about the physical setup: How suitable will it be in years to come? Look around to see how accommodating it is for someone with, perhaps, an arthritic hip,

weakening eyesight, or the need to use a walker.

Your early retirement years are the time to make modifications that will make your home comfortable in your older years. Inventory your home for fixtures or features that may be hard to negotiate as you age. Imagine you've aged 20 years and walk through your house, giving special attention to the kitchen and bathroom, looking for obstacles or potential trouble spots. How easy are they to negotiate if you can't see well, have difficulty reading, hear poorly, don't move well, can't stand for any length of time, or have limited hand or arm strength or flexibility?

One-third of all people over age 65 live alone (9 million in 1989). Family and friends provide a great deal of assistance with daily activities, but this is the most vulnerable and impoverished group of elderly.

Aging America

Modifying your home may require a few simple changes you can do yourself, like increasing the wattage in light bulbs or turning up the volume on phones and the doorbell. When major alterations are needed—installing handbars in showers or lowering kitchen cabinets—consult with a handyman or contractor familiar with the kind of work you need. You want to do this upgrading only once, so be thorough. A useful booklet is "The Do-Able, Renewable Home" by the American Association of Retired Persons (for a free copy call the AARP Publications Line, 202/434-2277).

For physical or financial reasons, you might be ready for a home that's easier to maintain, a better size for your needs, nearer to children, or in a warmer climate. In short, you may want to move.

A MOVABLE FEAST

Picking up and moving can be as natural a part of retirement as shedding your work clothes. When you start to think about moving and begin to focus on a particular spot, ask yourself (and your spouse) these questions:

• Will I like the climate year-round?

• Do I want to be this far from (or close to) my family?

• Am I willing to leave my support community—friends, religious group, social club, neighbors?

• Are public services equal to or better than where I am?

• Can I handle a new environment (i.e., country instead of city; suburb instead of small town; dense housing instead of spacious lots)?

PICKING AND CHOOSING

If you're seriously considering moving, you've no doubt visited your potential future homesite a number of times. But have you seen it as a non-tourist, in the off-season as well as peak season, from a resident's point of view instead of a hotel guest's point of view? If not, plan to do so before calling the moving van.

And you'll need to do more than sightsee to pick a spot for your retirement years. America's map (we'll look at foreign sites later) is dotted with wonderful places to grow old in. In fact, selecting retirement locales has become a specialty for some travel writers. One of the leading experts is David Savageau, who has written extensively about selecting a retirement paradise. He rates areas according to seven qualities, with each region or city receiving a score, number one being the best. His quality categories are:

1. Money matters
2. Housing
3. Climate
4. Personal safety
5. Services (e.g., doctors, hospitals)
6. Working
7. Leisure living

Weighing and evaluating each category, Savageau rates the following places as his top ten retirement spots:

1. Fort Myers, Florida
2. San Antonio, Texas
3. St. George, Utah
4. Pensacola, Florida
5. Brownsville, Texas
6. Phoenix, Arizona
7. Orlando, Florida
8. Clearwater, Florida
9. St. Tammany Parish, Louisiana
10. Hialeah, Florida

Another guru in sizing up retirement places is Peter Dickinson, who concentrates on regions. His

criteria are climate, living costs, housing costs, cultural and recreational outlets, and special services for seniors, such as transportation, community senior discounts, in-home services, good senior centers.

PICKING UP STAKES

Among people aged 55 to 64, about 7.1 percent moved in 1987–1988. For 65- to 74-year-olds, about 4.9 percent moved, and for those over 75, about 4.7 percent moved.

Statistical Abstract of the United States, 1991, *U.S. Department of Commerce*

Every part of the country has its pros and cons, its gentle breezes and harsh winds. Savageau's or Dickinson's ratings may be exactly what you need or a jumping-off point for devising your own list of important qualities. You may also consider access to a university, mountains for skiing and hiking, or distance to children's homes as more essential criteria.

For many retirees, the cost of living and housing are the first features they notice. They may zero

COST OF LIVING AROUND THE COUNTRY

These are the cost-of-living indexes, which indicate prices for consumer goods and services in various parts of the country. The national average is 100, so an area with an index of 105 is 5 percent higher than the national average. (GI = Grocery items index; HI = Housing index; HCI = Health-care index; the composite index also includes prices of utilities and transportation.)

Area	Composite Index	GI	HI	HCI
Albuquerque, NM	99.1	96.3	105.2	102.1
Augusta, GA	99.3	96.2	88.8	94.0
Austin, TX	95.4	98.0	83.9	94.9
Charleston, SC	99.5	95.9	97.1	98.8
Denver, CO	101.3	91.5	108.31	114.3
Greensboro, NC, area	96.8	92.5	97.6	93.6
Jacksonville, FL	96.7	96.1	90.4	96.1
Knoxville, TN	90.9	93.2	88.0	82.3
LA–Long Beach, CA	127.4	103.3	211.3	128.5
Miami–Hialeah, FL	112.2	100.3	123.0	137.8
Norfolk, VA	103.2	100.7	99.8	93.9
Phoenix, AZ	101.1	95.7	98.7	115.2
San Diego, CA	132.8	104.7	216.1	132.3
West Palm Beach, FL	106.7	102.8	102.1	110.7

Statistical Abstract of the United States, 1991

in on low state income tax and property tax rates. Although you shouldn't count on living expenses dropping dramatically when you retire, they will dip depending on how much you've been spending on work-related items such as clothes and commuting.

Retirees scouting for a new place not only want to live on less but also get more mileage for their money. Pinpointing a place with a lower cost of living means looking at consumer prices for goods and services, as well as tax rates. You can learn a place's cost of living by visiting and spending time there, and by consulting various reference books that track them, such as the *Statistical Abstract of the United States: The National Data Book,* available at government bookstores, or by writing the Superintendent of Documents, U.S. Government Printing Office, Washington, DC 20402, or by calling 202/783-3238. The cost is $28; the stock number 003-024-07260-2.

For people who've toiled most of their lives in cold, snowy climates, retirement may bring a long-awaited move to warmth and daily sunshine. To the warm-weather seeker, a place's average daily temperatures and days of rain make it heaven or hell.

REGIONAL WONDERS

Another way to approach your search is to examine the regions of the country for their unique attractions.

You want temperatures that don't fluctuate much? Think the coastal plains of the lower U.S. Atlantic and Pacific coasts and the entire Gulf region. Even as far as 200 miles inland, you can still benefit from the seas' year-round warming process. Think the Carolinas or Texas, and look into Alabama or the less populated areas of California. These areas are rich with culture and available resources. Away from the big coastal cities, you can enjoy the perks of the balmy weather imbued with a small-town atmosphere.

Looking for a quiet, slower life? The Midwest also has many opportunities for those seeking the small-town scene. If you don't mind seasonal weather, check out the "Golden Pond" lakes and pastoral scenery in areas such as Madison, Wisconsin, and Belleville, Illinois.

Like the crystal-clear skies and dry air of the desert? Hate the sticky humidity and sweaty sheen of the East Coast? New Mexico, and compass points in all directions from there are worth exploring. Prescott, Arizona, for instance, averages 45 percent humidity; the temperature range there is only about 12 degrees, 70 in the summer and high 50s in winter. On the desert floor, it's even dryer and less temperate—but lots hotter. If that's what you like, the

	FOLLOW THE SUN	
City	Daily Temperature (Sept.)*	Average Days Rain (Sept.)**
Phoenix, AZ	84.6	3
Sacramento, CA	71.7	1
San Diego, CA	71.0	1
Denver, CO	62.9	6
Miami, FL	81.8	17
Atlanta, GA	73.0	8
Des Moines, IA	65.1	9
Boston, MA	64.6	9
Reno, NV	60.2	2
Albuquerque, NM	69.0	6
Charlotte, NC	72.0	7
Memphis, TN	74.2	7
Dallas, TX	78.6	7
Houston, TX	78.4	9
San Juan, PR	81.9	17

* Normal daily mean temperature in Fahrenheit.
** Average number of days with precipitation over .01 inch.

Statistical Abstract of the United States, 1991

Southwest can be a compatible spot with magnificent scenery.

Always hankered for the cabin in the mountains? Check out sites around Boulder, Colorado, and Provo, Utah. There is outdoor recreation galore if you're comfortable with the altitude. With nearby colleges, there are plenty of educational opportunities and cultural events to attend. Mountain climates range from summer 80s to winter 20s, with low humidity and much sunshine.

RETIRING OVERSEAS

Maybe your dream spot lies beyond the Interstate. Maybe you've always wanted to live in Italy's Dolomite mountains or in Cabo San Lucas in Baja California. Now's the time to spread your wings, but slowly.

Unless you're an exceptionally seasoned traveler, you'll undergo a dose of culture shock when setting up house in another country. What made a place special to the temporary traveler—exotic food, different culture, and varying customs encompassing everything from when you eat dinner to how women dress in public—may be much more difficult for you to adjust to as a resident. Consequently, many Americans choose to live in areas with a high concentration of other U.S. citizens, giving them a support group while they adjust.

If you're thinking about moving to foreign shores, think ahead about possible ruts in the road:

• Homesickness for friends and family.

• Reduced standard of living in terms of services such as telephone, utilities, television, postal service, and medical care. Medicare won't cover you abroad, so talk to your insurance company about coverage in your foreign home. Also, the lack of convenient American products can make life more trying—at a time in your life when you don't want it to be trying more.

"In Guadalajara, Mexico, the largest American retirement community abroad, a couple can live well—including a full-time maid and two cars—on about $900 a month."

Changing Times

FAVORITE FOREIGN COUNTRIES

These are the countries with largest concentrations of residents who are U.S. citizens:

Mexico	425,000
Canada	259,000
United Kingdom	170,000
Germany	152,000
Philippines	120,000

Statistical Abstract of the United States, 1991

• Non-citizen legal status. As a foreigner, you probably won't have the same rights as a citizen. For instance, you may not be able to own property in certain areas.

• Language and communication difficulties.

• You get few tax breaks; at best, you escape state taxes, but you'll still owe the IRS on your U.S. income. One bright spot, however, is Social Security, which will mail your check virtually anywhere, unless you're living in one of the few countries (e.g., Albania, Cuba, North Korea) it won't send to. In these cases, it'll hold your check until you go elsewhere.

• Your retirement income can be eroded by foreign currency fluctuations. If the value of the dollar dips while you're living abroad, your pension buck is worth less. To protect yourself, talk to an investment professional about buying shares of funds that invest in the currencies of your new home.

On the sunny side, living abroad may well be cheaper than State-side and may offer a gracious, slower pace of living more to your liking. Countries considered retirement meccas because of their low cost of living are Uruguay, Spain, Costa Rica, and Portugal.

Before packing your dishes and giving up your season tickets to the symphony, make sure you've thoroughly investigated where you're moving and know what you will encounter. Have you:

• Visited the place at least twice, once in summer, once in winter, so you know the atmosphere the year-round? Better yet, have you rented a place there for a couple of months—a trial move, so to speak?

• Researched local real estate laws? How easy or difficult is it for a foreigner to buy, arrange financing, rent to someone else, and sell?

• Sketched out a budget for what it costs to live? Include everything, and then some; don't forget the cost of services that may cost you nothing in the United States, and airfare back to the States every now and then.

• Looked into available medical care (qualified doctors? hospitals? clinics?) and whether your present insurer will extend your coverage to a foreign home?

• Found out about any restrictions or limitations on your working in your foreign country?

STAYING AT THE PARTY

To dream the dream is not just about where, it's also about what you'll be doing. Forget the images of retirement as being "put

---

"One does not leave a convivial party before closing time."

Winston Churchill's response to questions about his retirement

---

out to pasture" or drifting into the sunset. Odds are your retirement is going to be a time of doing and discovering.

Active retirement is becoming the norm. Midlife and older workers are forming an ever larger part of the work force, a trend that will expand markedly after the year 2000, as your retirement era starts to open. An increasing component of that labor force will be women. In 2000, estimates the U.S. Department of Labor, almost 15 percent of the work force will be men over 65 and just over 7 percent will be women 65 and older.

Retirement no longer means keeping busy just for the sake of it, but rather taking advantage of the new time—2,000 hours a year, 40,000 hours in the average retirement life. Take this pop quiz:

THE 2,000 HOUR QUESTION: WHAT WILL I DO IN RETIREMENT?

1. I'm a worker type. I'll continue to work at something:
   a. full-time
   b. part-time
   c. occasionally or seasonally

2. I'm a people person. I'll volunteer:

a. full-time
b. part-time
c. occasionally for special projects or events

3. I have strong opinions and always want to say what I think. I'll be an activist for:
a. social causes
b. political issues
c. aging issues
d. special groups, such as women or the disabled

4. What I really want to do in retirement is "retire." I'll:
a. travel
b. develop a particular hobby or interest
c. go back to school
d. fish, play tennis, lounge on the beach and dream

5. Where I live in retirement matters more to me than what I'll be doing. The ideal location to me is:
a. seaside
b. mountains
c. desert
d. small town
e. near family
f. foreign country

If you weren't able to answer all these questions, this chapter will

---

TIPS FOR TRAVELING ABROAD

The State Department offers "Tips for Americans Residing Abroad" and "Background Notes," fact sheets on 170 countries with information on their culture, geography, government, economy, and political conditions. Available for $1 each from the Superintendent of Documents, U.S. Government Printing Office, Washington, DC 20402; 202/783-3238.

---

help you come up with ideas, showing what's possible, what's available, and where you can fit in.

ELDER ACHIEVERS

Retirement has its hazards, the two big ones being lethargy and boredom. These booby traps can bring on depression and ill health that in turn make real the stereotype of retirement as a period of

Computer company executive Ed Gistaro retired at 53, and decided he wanted his own company. At his high school reunion, he discovered an old friend had a similar dream. The two created Frescala Foods, producing fresh pasta for grocery chains and restaurants. "You have to be able to say, 'I can be out here on my own,' " Gistaro reflected. "It's 90 percent attitude."

New Choices

---

steady decline. The cultural myth that as people age they naturally slow down is perpetuated by behavior, not biology.

Positive behavior may take work, like any other goal you aim for. But the potential payoff is enormous. Read about how ordinary people have turned themselves into elder achievers, and made their lives rich and full.

• Beverly Gemigniani was 58 when she became fed up with her grandmotherly appearance and the aches and pains of advancing age. She enrolled in an aerobics class and hasn't been the same since. Encouraged, she wanted others to share the experience, so she founded "The Dancin' Grannies," an aerobic dance troupe.

The 25 Dancin' Grannies, ages 58 to 70 and all genuine grandmothers, have the figures and, more important, the energy of many women half their age. Almost all of these grannies had weight and health problems—from heart and cholesterol troubles to a brain tumor—before they joined. The program has not banished all their problems, but it has alleviated their ailments and given them the energy to cope. The exercise and companionship alone have helped several of the women overcome depression due to the death of loved ones.

• Elderly and achieving? Winfield Chace was 91 when he decided to take up bowling. At age 100, the Connecticut man was America's oldest active bowler, with a 98 scoring average.

• Philadelphian Lyman Frain bicycled from New York to San Francisco. The 3,244-mile journey took him 86 days—at age 80.

• George McManaman, a Harvard MBA, was already living in a

modest retirement community when he was jolted into becoming an elder achiever. He organized an enormous corps of fellow volunteers to help feed the homeless.

These are not movie stars or wealthy people who can tap into unlimited resources to preserve their youthful vigor and drive. They're ordinary people who are determined not to let the myths of aging set their pace.

LIFESTYLE: THE WORKING LIFE

Many people of retirement age are ignoring the assumptions of their parents' generation and in fact, are not retiring at all.

If you want to continue working with your present employer, you have a host of choices. You can rearrange your existing job: stay on with your employer with reduced hours, on-call, part-time, or sharing a job.

Some companies now permit management and professional employees to gradually reduce working hours to about 40 percent of full time during the last few years on the job as a way of easing into retirement. Salaries are adjusted accordingly. (The critical factor here may not be your job but what happens to your benefits, especially health coverage.) A gradual phase-out not only perks up your income and energy, but also helps you stay motivated while you decide what to do on full retirement.

Working at your career after retirement is a great idea, though still fairly uncommon. One poll shows that 84 percent of people over 65 have left the work force.

"If you keep working you'll last longer and I just want to keep vertical. I'd hate to spend the rest of my life trying to outwit an 18-inch fish."

— Harold Geneen, former chairman of ITT, who started a new business after retiring

As the normal retirement years approach, seniors who want to keep working find it's easier to get a job while they still have a job. It's difficult for unemployed older workers to get back into the job market, so the smart ones start looking for that first post-retirement job before the farewell dinner. Working elsewhere after retirement often means changing to a new occupation at a markedly reduced salary and without much job security. But these may not be as important in a post-retirement job. Congenial surroundings, a different pace, and new colleagues may well be the essentials.

Seeking that first post-retirement job while still drawing a paycheck can bolster your self-confidence while you struggle with some new realities. One of the uglier of these realities is a fact of life most seniors encounter: age discrimination.

AGE DISCRIMINATION: FACING THE FACTS

Age discrimination is illegal. And although the Age Discrimination Act of 1967 protects the working rights of everyone over 40, it doesn't stop discrimination from happening.

One reason age discrimination persists is that it's hard to prove. Of the estimated 17,000 cases reported yearly to the Equal Employment Opportunity Commission (EEOC), fewer than 200 are taken to court. Many are impossible to pursue, and even when the company is proven guilty, compensation has usually been small and slow to arrive.

But hidden in these statistics is an encouraging trend. As more age discrimination cases are brought to lawmakers' attention, new safeguards are being established to protect against such bias. For instance, a new law in Massachusetts allows plaintiffs to seek jury trials and double or triple damages in cases of age discrimination. Previously, straight damages—usually small—were awarded in such cases, which were presented only to a judge. This meant legal representation, already an expensive venue for the unemployed, was hard to come by. With jury trials now allowed, more lawyers will be involved, raising the expense of questionable layoffs for companies.

Cases are surfacing where laid-off people are called back to work because of pending legal action. High court costs are making companies take the cheaper way out and give the employee back his or her job. Said one lawyer: "Employers may find that in the short term it's more costly to discriminate."

Changes in the federal law also give more power to the plaintiff, and may make employers think

Studies by the U.S. Department of Health and Human Services show that while the unemployment rate for older workers (65-plus) is about half that of younger workers, once they lose that job, the older group stays unemployed longer. Older workers suffer greater income losses when, and if, they're rehired.

Aging America

twice. The 1987 federal law prohibits mandatory retirement, with limited exceptions such as professors, firefighters, and judges. And even these exceptions will be reviewed in 1994.

While people are becoming more aware, and intolerant, of age discrimination, demographic trends may well be the most powerful force for eliminating it. With smaller, younger generations now entering the work force, studies predict a growing labor shortage by 2010. Confronted with the aging population, the nation's employers are being forced to retool their attitudes toward the middle-

aged and older worker. Otherwise, they'll find themselves with empty offices and factories.

Fighting Back

The best weapon against age discrimination, say organizations that are fighting it, is individual testing. Age is not an accurate measure of an individual's capabilities, they maintain. If an employee is incapable of properly completing a job, it will become apparent regardless of how old he or she is.

Not until someone reaches his or her eighties is there a measurable decrease in intelligence or ability to do a full day's work. Although people's ability to memorize and learn new skills slips through middle age, much of the deterioration is because adults are out of practice at taking tests that measure these abilities.

Employers ridding their ranks of older workers argue that most age discrimination cases are the result of an unfortunate coincidence: industries jettisoning high-salary middle management to ease budget crunches or stay competitive, and a middle management that just happens to be comprised of older workers.

Gender has also become a sore point in age discrimination. A 1991 report of the Older Women's League (OWL) exposed some startling facts: Women over 45 have an average salary 60 percent below men the same age. Women's salaries peak at age 44, men's at 55. Men in their late forties earn 8 percent more, on average, than younger men; women in the same age bracket (45 to 54) earn 2 percent less than their younger, female counterparts.

According to the OWL report, older women are employed mainly in "traditional" female jobs: clerical, food service, nursing, teaching, and sales. Perhaps most alarming of all, college-educated women aged 45 to 64 earn nearly 10 percent less than men the same age who have only high school educations. The Older Women's League partially blames television: Roles for older women are hard to find on television and when they are cast, they're frequently as stereotypical characters. According to OWL, such mass media coverage only helps perpetuate the picture of the stubborn, slow, and unhealthy middle-aged woman. This in turn, states OWL, damages older women's job opportunities.

You can fight back, as older workers are learning. However, it's usually not an easy or inexpensive struggle.

Two department store vice presidents, both ousted at age 56, took their employer to court. One of the ejected employees won a $1.2 million verdict, but the company is trying to have the verdict overturned. As is typical, the company has the money to drag out the case for years while the two ex-$100,000-a-year executives live off savings.

A 60-year-old paper company vice president was subjected to verbal and written "age harassment" and eventually reduced to sweeping the warehouse floor. He was awarded $3.5 million and the decision was upheld by a federal appeals court.

An IBM employee, forced into early retirement after 30 years, was awarded several hundred thousand dollars' worth of damages after six years. (IBM has appealed.)

When discrimination is difficult to prove, the victory in such cases often comes more from the feeling of vindication than from financial awards. But with the growing number of precedents and anti-age discrimination laws being enacted, it's becoming easier to pocket a meaningful financial reward as well as the personal satisfaction that justice has been done.

GREAT JOBS FOR SENIORS

Some employers actively seek older workers: They're even considered drawing cards in some businesses. Banks and hardware stores find that customers have more confidence in older employees. Bank customers feel more confident with their money in the hands of older people and bank managers feel that older employees give their institutions a dignified appearance.

Hardware stores often like to make use of an older employee's lifetime of fix-it jobs as a source of good advice. So do travel agencies, whose clientele, more than a quarter of whom are over 55, relate more easily to someone of their generation. Hotels and fast-food outlets also value experienced seniors.

Resources for your job hunt are all around you: library, Yellow Pages, community center. Begin with the local and national nonprofit organizations that specialize in helping older workers. For instance:

• New York's Senior Career Planning & Placement Service matches retired executives with part-time employment across the country (257 Park Avenue South, New York, NY 10010; 212/529-6660).

NOW WHERE DID I PUT MY GLASSES?

You may fear that creeping forgetfulness is Alzheimer's, but it's unlikely. The incidence of Alzheimer's is really quite low in the under-late-eighties group, according to the Journal of the American Medical Association. *It reports the percentage of people over 65 with probable Alzheimer's (not counting those in institutions):*

65 to 74 years old: 3 percent	
75 to 84 years old: 19 percent	
Over 85 years old: 47 percent	

Aging America

• Operation ABLE, a nation-wide senior employment agency, deals exclusively in job-seekers over 50 (180 North Wabash Avenue, Suite 802, Chicago, IL 60601; 312/782-3335).

• The National Council on the Aging may list older workers' job-search organizations in your area (national office: 409 3rd Street, SW, Washington, DC 20024; 202/479-1200).

• The American Association of Retired Persons workshop "Think of Your Future" and free booklet *Working Options* help job hunters (AARP, 600 E Street, NW, Washington, DC 20049).

• The Senior Community Service Employment Program is a federal program that helps low-income seniors find work (U.S. Department of Labor, Older Work Program, Office of Special Targeted Programs, Employment and Training Administration, Room N-4641, 200 Constitution Avenue, NW, Washington, DC 20210).

• Forty Plus provides job-hunting support to unemployed managers and professionals (offices in California, Colorado, District of Columbia, Hawaii, Illinois, New York, Ohio, Pennsylvania, Texas, Utah, and Washington; check your phone book for a listing).

Part-time work is an increasingly important form of employment for 65-plus workers: 48 percent of all men still work part-time after 65, and 59 percent of all women work part-time.

Aging America

If you're quitting a full-time job at retirement, you might consider registering with a temporary employment agency. Temp agencies often provide the freedom of flexible hours and eliminate some of the stress of finding a permanent position yourself. And more than one person has used temp agencies as a way to scout the local market and find out what's available full-time. Temp work also means you can choose to take vacations and time off when your income approaches the cutoff point for taxable Social Security benefits. Most of the major national temp agencies (Manpower Temporary Services, Kelly Temporary Services, BSI Temporaries, Accountemps) gladly use older employees.

Consulting is another possibility if your career lends itself to it. Do you have the kind of expertise people would pay to hear about? Successful consulting requires one of two credentials: a highly skilled specialty, such as editing, accounting, or engineering, or a highly visible, successful position, like chief financial officer for a Fortune 500 company, that can be parlayed into managerial consulting.

Calling yourself a consultant and being hired as one are worlds apart. Anyone can hang out the "Consultant Is In" shingle. You'll need to market your services to local companies, a task that's no less daunting and demanding than job hunting.

GOING IT ALONE: ELDER ENTREPRENEUR

A New Jersey woman, on reading *O Come Ye Back to Ireland,* an entertaining tale about living on Ireland's west coast, took her retirement future in her hands. She quit her job as a general manager of a newspaper, sold her home, and bought a bed-and-breakfast at Slea Head on Ireland's Dingle Bay. She'd always wanted to do something like that, and the coincidence of indirect encouragement from the book brought the dream to the surface.

It might happen that way to you. Starting your own business can be an exciting adventure, and occasionally quite lucrative. But it's also an expensive and time-consuming risk. Be warned before sinking your retirement funds into a new business: A huge percentage of them fail within a couple of years—often taking all the owner's capital with them. Also—and this is particularly true in any kind of retail business—a start-up can require 12-hour days, seven days a week. The fantasy of handing over the start-up to a hired manager is often just a fantasy.

You may have an inkling that you've got the stuff of an elder entrepreneur. Perhaps you have an idea—it may not be a dream yet— a consuming interest, an achievement or goal you've always wanted to reach, or a talent that commands attention. These are the nuggets that can be mined into a fledgling business. But if you have to dig for an idea, driven simply by the desire to be your own boss, your venture could be unrewarding drudgery.

With a firm idea of what you want to accomplish, your first step is a plan. Sounds obvious, but most fledgling ventures fail because the principals didn't research the market and competition, anticipate trouble spots, or line up enough financing. They short-circuited the planning process.

Your plan needn't be a formal business plan. It can be an item-by-item consideration of every facet, such as management (Are you going to run everything? Where can you get advice?), marketing, sales, competitors, operations (activities or service—what you do or offer), and money (how much, where from, how to use it).

In 1991, about 18 percent of businesses three years old and under failed. The highest failure rate was businesses five years old and under.

The Dun & Bradstreet Corp.

A good test of your plan is to share it with other entrepreneurs or businesspeople. A useful source of expertise is the Service Corps of Retired Executives (SCORE, 409 3rd Street, SW, Suite 5900, Washington, DC 20024), an organization of more than 13,000 former executives and company managers who volunteer their time advising small businesses.

SCORE's main function is to help people think out their enterprise before launching it, and in fact, it counsels many clients against pursuing their dream business. They raise these questions:

• Is the location right?
• Why isn't the business you want to start already operating in the area you have chosen?
• Is there an existing clientele?
• Is this really something you'll stick with when times get rough?
• Have you talked to other people who are in the business?
• Do you know the downside for both your personal health and your financial well-being?
• Do you know your competitors? Why are they successful? Why will your business succeed over theirs?
• Do you have enough money? Starting a new business always takes more money than anticipated. Project your sales and profits as best you can through the first one or two years, figuring in all expenses (including your salary, taxes, and benefits) before calculating the gravy, your profits.

LIFESTYLE: THE VOLUNTEER

At least one in six people aged 55 to 70 are part-time or full-time volunteers. And no wonder; it can be personally fulfilling, a source of new friends, a means of being exposed to new ideas, and a way of involving yourself in community, social, or national issues.

While many modern volunteers work full-time elsewhere and can offer only a few hours a week, other "core volunteers" dedicate more than 20 hours a week to the cause, and more than half of this group are retirees.

DIVE IN

If there is a cause you feel deeply about, pick up a magazine that focuses on it, and turn to the back listings of possible opportunities. If there's no magazine, try your library for the cause's local chapters or get the national headquarter's address and write a letter asking for guidance.

A host of national and local organizations specialize in placing retirees in volunteer positions. The American Association of Retired People has a Volunteer Talent Bank at its Office of Volunteer

WHO VOLUNTEERS?

According to Modern Maturity *magazine, the 65- to 74-year-olds donate the most time each week (6 hours) while the 47- to 64-year-olds are those most likely to be volunteering (more than 47 percent in this bracket volunteer). Gender? Forty-six percent of all women are volunteers, and 44 percent of all men.*

Coordination in Washington, DC. The Retired Senior Volunteer Program (RSVP) is a government-funded national volunteer bank (929 L Street, NW, Washington, DC 20001; 202/289-1510). To connect with a volunteer bank in your area, try Volunteer—The National Center (111 N. 19th Street, Suite 500, Arlington, VA 22209).

Two national job banks for retired persons place executives in consulting positions. The already-mentioned Service Corps of Retired Executives is constantly recruiting new volunteers. The

National Executive Service Corps (257 Park Avenue South, New York, NY 10010-7304; 212/529-6660) has a similar program with a wider range of jobs in education, arts, social services, religious groups, and health care. Its affiliates, called Executive Service Corps, are active in 350 American cities. The NESC funds two other programs: Senior Career Planning and Placement Service, which connects executives with paid positions in nonprofit organizations and businesses, and the

---

DO "SOMETHING"

Bob Bertelson, president of the Service Corps of Retired Executives (SCORE), encourages retirees to pursue volunteer work. "After you've painted the house, fixed up the yard and taken a few trips, you find out retirement is better if you're doing something— especially something worthwhile."

Modern Maturity

Math/Science Education Program, which brings technical professionals into schools to expand the instruction of pre-college students in those fields.

Look around—volunteer opportunities are everywhere. Here's a start:

• Churches and temples always need volunteers, as do schools for tutoring or after-school education programs, from Head Start to adult GED (General Educational Development—the test for a high school equivalency diploma).

• The American Red Cross is 95 percent volunteer staffed, half of those folks over age 50. Find your local chapter in the phone book.

• The Salvation Army uses volunteers for ringing Christmas bells, staffing thrift shops, feeding the homeless, and much in between. Inquire locally or contact national headquarters (1318 9th Street NW, Washington, DC 20001; 202/234-7291).

• A local museum or library may need lecturers or tour guides.

• The "Y" and groups working with the physically and emotionally handicapped thrive on volunteers.

Are none of these challenge

enough? Well, how tough are you? Adventurous enough for the Peace Corps? President Jimmy Carter's mother, Lillian, didn't volunteer for India until she was well into her sixties. Some volunteers are in their eighties. Older Corps people are especially valued because of their experience and skill, patience and flexibility. Older workers can also accomplish much in cultures where elders are revered for their wisdom.

Of course, the Peace Corps is no packaged tour. The training is rigorous, particularly in language skills, and conditions are spartan compared with the U.S. Founded in 1961, the Peace Corps has placed 130,000 volunteers in 100 countries. Volunteers train for two to four months, often in the country where they serve. The Corps pays traveling and living expenses, with a slim $200 monthly stipend, but working under such conditions can be surprisingly rewarding. The learning experience is as great, if not greater, for the volunteers as it is for the people they help. For many, the experience has served as a catalyst for a new lifestyle or career. For information and applications, contact the U.S. Peace Corps, 1990 K Street, NW, Washington, DC 20526; 202/606-3010. Applications are due about nine months before you expect to leave for your post.

Lifestyle: Back to School

As older citizens crowd onto campuses and into classrooms, the demand for part-time higher education has exploded. Colleges and universities around the country now offer low-cost short-term education through post-retirement learning centers. What's more, free, state-funded, or low-tuition programs are becoming as commonplace as recycling centers.

Elder-student programs, dubbed learning-in-retirement institutes (LIRs), offer daytime no-credit classes on college campuses. Most are "peer oriented" (academic jargon meaning you'll be surrounded by men and women of an age similar to yours) and funded through volunteer memberships. Members also serve as instructors, free of charge. Generally, there are no exams or grades, and the programs are self-supported and semi-independent of the college proper.

The first such LIR was the New School for Social Research's Insti-

THE OLDER ADULTS COLLEGE

Marymount Manhattan College, in New York City, has some 3,000 seniors annually attending its more than 100 classes. The college's Center for Older Adults grew out of the realization that the neighborhood where the college is situated, in Yorkville, has one of the highest per capita elderly populations in the country.

Brookdale Foundation Group

tute for Retired Professionals, founded in New York City in 1974 to promote continuing education for seniors. Since the late 1980s, the number of institutes has skyrocketed. Notable ones are UCLA's Plato Society, which uses discussion seminars as its preferred learning method; the Athenaeum at Rochester Institute of Technology; University of Delaware's Academy of Lifelong Learning; and the Senior Ventures

program at several universities in the Northwest, which combines class time with travel and on-campus residence. For all, the emphasis is on "lifelong learning" and the idea that retirees want to remain intellectually stimulated.

Research shows that continuing-education facilities play a large role in where retirees choose to live, so businesses and colleges have joined forces to create retirement communities with easy access to educational opportunities. And post-retirement institute membership fees, which run between $100 and $300, usually include access to college recreational and educational facilities like the pool and library.

Perhaps the most successful educational program for seniors is Elderhostel, an international organization active in over 40 countries and drawing more than 200,000 students a year. Its only educational prerequisite is a desire to learn and participate.

Elderhostel's North American programs are mostly one-week (Sunday to Saturday) courses composed of three 90-minute class sessions a day covering three varied topics. Residence is usually in a college dorm, and meals are provided in the cafeteria. The living arrangements are generally comfortable and the classes of varying quality; cost is about $275 a head.

International Elderhostel courses, which run from $1,500 to $3,800 depending on location, last for three weeks. Some international programs have health restrictions because they involve hiking or unusual climates, but the variety is impressive. A course catalog is available from Elderhostel (75 Federal Street, Boston, MA 02110).

Interhostel, a combination study-tour program, is a two-week course in one of 24 countries for people over 50. Affiliated with the University of New Hampshire, it coordinates activities with foreign universities, colleges, and cultural institutions. (For information, write Interhostel, University of New Hampshire, 6 Garrison Avenue, Durham, NH 03824.)

ONE TUITION COVERS MUCH

For less than $300 per couple ($175 single), the College for Seniors, an affiliate of the University of North Carolina at Asheville, allows individuals 55 and over—no previous educational experience required—to attend any or all of its courses.

North Carolina Center for Creative Retirement, Asheville, NC

LIFESTYLE: TRAVEL AND LEISURE

Time to stop promising to see the Grand Canyon, Brazilian rain forest, Aztec ruins, or Greek islands. Or, if your imagination wanders a little wilder, whale-watching off the Sea of Cortez, hiking in Mexico, camping in Alaska, or visiting Kenyan game parks. In short, this is it—time to take all those adventures you've been putting off while earning a living, raising kids, and tending to family.

EASY AND WONDROUS: U.S. TRAVEL

You already know the United States is full of enjoyable vacation spots, natural wonders, and cultural locations. You may have flown over or passed through them

How About Home Study?

You can earn credit or just audit a variety of classes through correspondence schools. Instructors guide you via mailings for all levels of education, from junior high through graduate studies, and televised home learning is sometimes available. The National University Continuing Education Association has a "Guide to Independent Study Through Correspondence Instruction" which lists accredited institutions around the country. The cost is $8.95 plus $1.75 shipping and handling from the NUCEA, Peterson's Book Order Dept., P.O. Box 2123, Princeton, NJ 08543. A listing of technical/vocational private home study schools is available from the National Home Study Council, 1 Dupont Circle, NW, Suite 615, Washington, DC 20036.

on your way to a business meeting. If you're like many people, your travel experiences have generally consisted of bursts of energy and a spraying of money, as you crammed hundreds of miles of scenery or thousands of years of history into a one-week ''get away.''

Now, at last, you have time to soak up the sights, to smell and taste the exotic flavors. And, better yet, it's going to cost you less than in your younger years.

This is not a travel book with descriptions of dozens of regions or roadside amusements. Lots of other books already do a very good job of that. Instead, the information here will show you how traveling can be easy and affordable, regardless of where you head for.

Tourism, as you probably know, is big business in America. Americans in 1989 took more than 450 million vacation trips at least 100 miles from their homes. And where did they spend the most money? California, of course. Other states in the top five for vacation dollars are Florida, New York, Texas, and New Jersey. (New Jersey? Yup, it's got some great beaches.)

A host of companies, local governments, and private businesspeople are eager for your travel dollars, so naturally they offer enticements and discounts. One of the biggest promoters of U.S. travel is the federal government, and it has lots to offer.

Federal Park Perks

There are more than 300 national parks, campsites, and monuments in America—enough to satisfy the most extreme case of retiree wanderlust! There's the Iditarod Historic Trail in Alaska, Canyon de Chelly in Arizona, Point Reyes National Seashore in California, Everglades National Park in Florida, Antietam National Battlefield in Maryland, the Great Smoky Mountains National Park in North Carolina . . . You get the picture.

The national parks have special rates for older visitors. The "Golden Age Passport," for 62 and older, offers a free lifetime entrance as well as half price on federal use fees for camping, boating, and parking. To get this pass, apply in person with proof of age at any National Park or Forest Service station.

Regardless of where you visit, remember that this is the 90s, the decade of "crowds everywhere,"

so be sure to make reservations well (that's months) in advance. To reserve a spot in places like Yellowstone, Yosemite, and Cape Hatteras, call 800/365-CAMP.

Or, you can skip the crowds and visit some of the more secluded, less known parks and historical sites. For a description of these places, write for "The National Parks: Lesser-Known Areas" (Superintendent of Documents, U.S. Government Printing Office, Washington, DC 20402, stock number 024-005-00911-6; $1.50).

THE GOLDEN MARKET

"The over-50 population has a combined income of $800 billion, and it controls half the discretionary income in the United States and three-quarters of the financial assets, which is why it is becoming known to advertisers as the new 'Golden Market.'"

James Thompson, Manager, Consumer Affairs, American Association of Retired Persons, Los Angeles Times

DISCOUNTS GALORE

Getting around the country is cheaper as a senior citizen. Many major airlines offer seniors (at least 62 years old) discounts between 10 and 25 percent on domestic flights with the purchase of airline coupon books. (Discounts may not apply to special fare tickets, such as excursion rates.) United Airlines' Silver Pack coupons for seniors 62 and over cost $568 for four coupons for two round-trip tickets to the 48 states (Alaska and Hawaii excluded). Both Delta and American coupons cost $568 for four, $984 for eight.

Airline travel clubs offer worthwhile discounts. For instance, United Airlines' Silver Wings Plus Travel Club gives members (over 60) 50 percent off standby fares. Membership costs $75 for three years.

Amtrak gives seniors (62 and older) discounts of 15 percent on any fare. Bus companies also offer breaks: Greyhound and Trailways chop off 10 percent from any regular fare Monday through Thursday for the over-65 traveler.

Hotel chains also hanker for your business and will cut their rates for seniors, some even for folks only 55 years old. Although their discounts may not be advertised—you have to ask when making reservations or checking in—they can be significant. And some hotel chains have "clubs," such as the Days Inns' "September Days Club," that offer a slew of discounts.

Many hotel chains offer 25 percent and more off room rates, especially to members of senior clubs like AARP.

The *Mature Traveler,* a nifty newsletter that reports on travel opportunities for seniors, reports these discounts:

• Holiday Inn: Up to 20 percent discount worldwide to senior club members.

• Choice Hotels: 30 percent off for senior club members who reserve rooms; to those who don't, 10 percent off their "Senior Saver Rates." This discount includes such motels as Econo Lodge, Quality Inn, Comfort Inn, Friendship Inn, and others.

• Days Inns: 15 to 50 percent discounts, including discounts on local sights and car rentals for members of its September Days club.

• Howard Johnson's: 15 percent discount for senior club members. Some locations offer 30 percent off on advance reservations.

- Sheraton: 25 percent discount when rooms are available. Grandchildren stay free.

A number of senior organizations include travel discounts in their membership benefits. The National Alliance of Senior Citizens (202/986-0117) gives members

TEN TIPS FOR TRAVELING ABROAD

- Always keep your passport with you. Don't pack it in your luggage, and risk losing it.
- Pack old clothes that you wouldn't mind leaving behind on your travels, if wear and tear warrants it. This also frees up suitcase space.
- Take a phrase book: Even fractured sentences communicate better than grunts and hand signs.
- Be wary of duty-free shops: Their prices are frequently not a bargain.
- Ask your tour director or hotel concierge how to work the local phones.
- Tipping isn't automatic everywhere, so before dipping into your change purse, consult a travel book or your guide about local tipping customs.
- When paying a restaurant tab, always ask if a tip is included in the total figure.
- Don't assume museums' and shops' open hours are similar to those in the United States. Check first.
- Don't skip meals, even in a rush. Traveling takes energy, so slow down and savor the food and sights.
- Pack an empty collapsible bag in your suitcase to carry home souvenirs and presents.

Going Abroad: 101 Tips for Mature Travelers, Grand Circle Travel

a 10 percent discount at various hotel chains (Clarion, Quality, Rodeway, Comfort Inns, Econo Lodge, Friendship, Sleeper Motels) at all times and 30 percent with reservations. The National Council of Senior Citizens (800/ 322-6677) has a complete travel program, Vantage Travel, with many discount rates.

The AARP Travel Experience, a huge offering of tours coordinated by American Express, has hundreds of discount packages to every corner of America and the rest of the globe (800/927-0111). Grand Circle Travel, an agency in Boston, has been specializing in discount tours for seniors (particularly members of AARP) for years. If you're shopping for low-priced journeys, contact them (800/221-2610).

TRAVELING ABROAD

The world is shrinking. Political boundaries have melted, and telecommunications systems are bringing everyone closer. Venturing to the four corners of the globe is almost easier than commuting across a congested city.

If you've got feet fidgety for international sights, whether it's the crumbled Berlin Wall or Machu Picchu, be a stickler for detail in your preparation. With the right planning, your travels won't be ruined by running out of local currency, a head cold and no aspirin, an expired visa, or a lost wallet.

The State Department has several good pamphlets on international travel: "Travel Tips for Older Americans" and "Your Trip Abroad." For copies, write the Superintendent of Documents, U.S. Government Printing Office, Washington, DC 20402. Another useful brochure is "Going Abroad: 101 Tips for Mature Travelers," free from Grand Circle Travel (800/221-2610.) For copies, check first with your travel agent.

Passports and Visas Up-To-Date?

If you don't have a passport, apply for one at least three months before you travel. For your first passport, apply in person to a local passport agency; bring an official birth certificate or other proof of U.S. citizenship and identification, two identical 2×2-inch front-view photos, and a completed DSP-11 passport application (available from the passport office). A passport is valid for 10 years and costs $42. To renew, you can apply by mail with the

DSP-82 form; renewal costs $35. Sign your passport as soon as you get it, and fill out the emergency information on page four with pencil (so you can change it in later years). Also, make a photocopy of the passport's information page and keep it separate from your passport so that if it's stolen, arranging for a replacement is easier.

You need a passport before you can apply for visas, which are required in most non-European countries. A visa is a stamp in your passport that states that you are authorized to enter the country for a specific time period and for an expressed purpose (e.g., pleasure, business, study). Visas are obtained from local consular offices of the country, and take several weeks to clear.

Entry requirements for what you can bring into a foreign country differ for each nation, and a "Foreign Entry Requirements" listing is available for 50 cents from the Consumer Information Center, Dept. 438T, Pueblo, CO 81009.

Immunizations

That old-fashioned feverish-looking "yellow card" is still around to record the shots you'll need if you're a serious globe-trotter. Countries require some immunizations to prevent the spread of contagious diseases, others to protect the visitor's health. The international health certificate shows the dates of your immunizations and what exactly you're protected against.

Check your health records and the country's requirements before traveling. If you arrive without the correct vaccinations, the health office at the airport may insist on vaccinating you, or may provide a medical follow-up card that you must later present to show proof of vaccination. In rare instances, health officers may isolate you for the period in which the disease incubates—that would certainly put a crimp in your travel plans.

The most common requirements are shots against yellow fever and cholera; you may also want immunizations for polio, rubella, diphtheria, tetanus, measles, mumps, and whooping cough. International health regulations don't always require shots, but if you are traveling in regions where you risk exposure for malaria, typhoid, or another serious disease, you should take precautionary shots or medication.

Usually your physician or local

health department can advise you on your immunization needs. The U.S. Public Health Service publishes the handbook, "Health Information for International Travel," which contains immunization information and other advisories about health conditions abroad. It's available for $5 from the U.S. Government Printing Office, Washington, DC 20402.

The essential form you want is available in the PHS-731 booklet, "International Certificates of Vaccination as Approved by the World Health Organization," which you can get from your doctor or for $2 from the U.S. Government Printing Office.

Watch for Advisories

The U.S. Government publishes travel advisories for Americans going abroad to warn them of health or political dangers. The State Department issues three kinds of advisories: warnings recommending you not visit a country; cautions about unstable political or health conditions; and notices about inconveniences such as crime or currency changes. For instance, in June 1992, advisories were being issued for Bolivia, Pakistan, Bangladesh, Ethiopia,

Yemen, Tanzania, and Thailand. It's a good idea to check this listing (202/647-5225) before leaving the country.

What Kind of Insurance?

Think of travel insurance as you would an umbrella on a sunny day: You probably won't need it, but if you don't take it, chances are you'll wish you had! Travel insurance, available from tour operators, travel agents, and some insurance companies, can protect your deposit, trip payments, or added expenses from a host of disasters: cancellation, lost luggage, theft, accidents and illness, hotel screw-ups, airline difficulties, bad weather, even operator bankruptcy. Of course, not all policies

---

ON THE MOVE

Older Americans account for 30 percent of all travel; 32 percent of all hotel/ motel nights; 34 percent of all packaged overseas tours; and 44 percent of adult passports.

American Express/AARP Travel Experience

---

cover all contingencies—read the contract carefully. And check your homeowner's policy—it might cover some travel hazards.

If your travel agent is a member of the United States Tour Operators Association, you're automatically covered should the operator be insolvent or go bankrupt.

Trips that require sizable deposits or complete payment in advance make cancellation insurance essential. At the least, you should have coverage for the cost of a full-fare plane ticket home, not just the price of the tour, which may be less.

Think through all the "What ifs?" when buying travel insurance. For instance, a policy may pay if a traveler becomes sick but not if a close friend at home becomes ill. Also, coverage against tour operator insolvency usually doesn't include airplane tickets, car rentals, or train tickets purchased separately from the tour package. Check the insurance's cancellation policy and what emergencies are acceptable.

After travel insurance, remember health insurance. Health care abroad can be expensive, so review your health insurance policy before you leave. Your Medigap policy may cover international travel, but Medicare will not provide any hospital or medical care outside the United States (although hospital costs in Canada and Mexico are covered in special situations). Although some countries have nationalized medical service, meaning anyone, including foreigners, are treated for a small fee or free of charge, doctors may be hard to see and the country may have residency requirements.

Medicaid doesn't provide services outside the United States, but special short-term coverage called Medical Assistance Programs are available for people traveling outside the U.S. These usually cover the cost of hospitalization, medical care, and emergency evaluation. If you already have health insurance, your carrier can add on Medical Assistance Program coverage for the time you're traveling. Usually the cost is less than $50 for a couple of weeks' travel.

U.S. auto insurance usually isn't valid outside the United States and Canada, so if you're planning to drive in any other country, look into buying insurance there. If you rent a car in a foreign country, make sure insurance is part of the rental contract.

Take Your Medications

If you take prescription medication, carry a large supply in the original packaging and pack copies of prescriptions to prevent a misunderstanding. Because of strict narcotics laws, you need to know the generic names of your prescription drugs to avoid trouble. Any unusual drug should be accompanied by a physician's letter of explanation. Pack these items in your purse or carry-on luggage so they don't get lost.

In addition to medications, don't forget an extra pair of glasses or contact lenses, and hearing aid replacements.

If you have a serious health problem—high blood pressure or diabetes—consider wearing a medical alert bracelet. Also take along over-the-counter medications like antacids and aspirin; they can make a big difference in how you feel and may not be available where you're going.

Getting There in Comfort: Dos and Don'ts

• Avoid carrying a lot of cash—use traveler's checks and cash them only as needed. Take one internationally recognized credit card, just in case. Before leaving, obtain enough currency of the country you're visiting to get from the airport to your lodging; then convert dollars as needed while you travel.

• Pack a carry-on "survival kit" with passport, traveler's checks, medication, glasses, and a change of clothes and essential toiletries in case your luggage gets lost.

• Don't take anything valuable, including sentimental items. If you couldn't bear to lose something or it's irreplaceable, leave it home.

• Don't overplan. Leave a lot of blank space on your itinerary. Be open to spontaneous side trips or spending the day reading in a café. Take time just to enjoy being there.

• Leave a detailed itinerary with someone at home, including names, addresses, and numbers of contacts and hotels. If you change your plans, let someone know.

• Dress conservatively and comfortably. Be alert to avoid theft. One of the biggest deterrents to pickpocketing is the "fanny pack," a purse-like pouch worn around your waist.

• Don't be an ugly American—it's rude, and more to the point, it could land you in trouble. Some countries' customs and laws may be foreign to you—for instance, prohibitions about drinking and where women are allowed—and if you violate them, you could face fines, imprisonment, and deportation. And, of course, everyone knows how foolish it is to even *think* about using, buying, or carrying illegal drugs. Age makes no difference on this one, so don't think because you're over 30, you can get away with a little recreational fare.

• Check in with the U.S. consulate when you arrive. If you have any health or legal emergencies, such as injury, serious illness, or arrest, the consulate can help you.

• Reconfirm your flights at each stopover. Foreign airlines generally don't recognize your reservation unless you've reconfirmed.

• Most important, hang on to your passport—it's your most valuable asset abroad. Keep the passport number in a separate place so you can get a new one quickly if necessary. Hotels often ask to keep your passport for a short time to check you out with the local authorities. This is standard, but make sure you get it back as soon as possible.

What If, What If . . . ?

What if you don't register your arrival and location with the U.S. embassy in a foreign country?

In most western countries, it won't matter. But even in places like England and Israel, if you plan to stick around for more than a month, stop in at the embassy's consular office and tell them who and where you are. Trouble can erupt anytime, anywhere, even in the safest surroundings. No place is completely immune from natural disasters, political unrest, or terrorism.

If you plan to visit a country that has no U.S. embassy (there aren't many, but Cuba and North Korea are two, and parts of the former Soviet Union may be off the consular map), register your presence beforehand with the consulate of a neighboring country and find out who represents the United States where you will be traveling.

If you get into trouble overseas, the U.S. consul may be your only English-speaking contact and your sole source of aid.

What if you lose your passport?

If your passport is lost or stolen in the United States, contact the

Passport Services office at the State Department immediately. Outside the United States, contact local police and the U.S. consulate as quickly as possible.

What if you're robbed?

Contact local authorities and the U.S. consulate. The consul can contact banks, relatives, or employers at home to help you. Money can sometimes be wired to you through the State Department.

What if you get sick or injured?

The U.S. consulate can provide a list of reliable local medical practitioners. In serious circumstances, the consulate may even assist you in locating medical help, contact your family, or arrange transfer of funds to you from home. If you're unable to communicate, the consul will notify the contacts listed in your passport of your condition. Arrange medical evacuation as part of your traveler's health insurance before you travel, just in case.

What if my traveling companion dies?

About 2,000 Americans die traveling overseas each year, so this isn't an unduly morbid concern. Make local burial arrangements or transportation of remains home part of your travel insurance package. In the sad circumstance that your traveling companion dies, contact the next of kin and make the necessary arrangements to move the body. The U.S. embassy can explain the local requirements in such cases.

What if I get arrested?

Obviously you're going to try to avoid this under all circumstances! You're subject to local laws while traveling, so respect them. United States laws can't protect you abroad, and treatment of prisoners is less than humane in many countries. International agreements give you the right to contact an American consul, so do this as soon as possible. But consuls can't act as attorneys or post bail for you; they can explain your rights under local law, help get you legal aid, contact your relatives, ensure your fair treatment under local laws, and transfer food, clothing, and money to you from relatives.

Stay away from illegal drugs! Laws are fierce concerning drugs, resulting in long prison sentences, hard labor, large fines, inhumane treatment, even the death penalty.

What if I get caught in an uprising or natural disaster?

For starters, avoid traveling in unstable countries. Get to safety as soon as possible and try to stay out of harm's way. Don't imagine, with your camcorder or camera in hand, that you're going to scoop the world as a freelance journalist —if there's trouble, avoid it. You're a private citizen on vacation. Contact the embassy to let them know your whereabouts and condition. Contact your relatives to let them know you're safe.

Welcome Home

Have your papers ready to get through customs more quickly. You can verbally declare $400 worth of imports duty-free. After that, there are taxes and forms involved. If you've acquired many things, consider mailing them to yourself in the States. Although a heavy package may take a month or so to arrive, you avoid the hassle of customs (you must file a declaration when you mail it, stating the contents and value, and may owe duty) and the wrestling match with your bags when you arrive. You can bring foreign currency into the country, but not fruits, vegetables, seeds, or items made from endangered species.

THE JOYS OF GROUP TRAVEL

Many older people enjoy the company of others their age and the relative inexpensiveness of traveling in a group. Group travel is also safer or, if you will, tamer. Chances of missed connections, reservation foul-ups, and unpleasant surprises over accommodations are much less likely than if you're journeying solo. And numerous tour operators cater especially to seniors, offering a smorgasbord of packages and low fares.

Tours are sold mainly through travel agencies, and they vary from highly organized, structured tours to more independent, self-guided ventures. Group travel or a packaged tour usually means that airfares, accommodations, meals, ground transportation, and sightseeing are sold as a single trip. The trickiest part of tours is finding one that suits your traveling style and pocketbook.

As you read through brochures about various tours, note what's included and what's not. The United States Tour Operators Association recommends travelers

THE LANGUAGE OF PACKAGE TOURS

Knowing these terms can help you sift through the mountains of tour brochures you'll be reading in your search for a great trip.

Single room: room with one bed for one person.

Twin room: room with two beds for two people.

Double room: room for two people with a double bed.

Pension: a guesthouse or small inn.

Single-room supplement: difference in price between half of a twin room and price of a single room.

Double-occupancy rate: price per person based on two people sharing a room.

Double-room rate: full price of a room shared by two people.

Value added tax (VAT): tax on products or services imposed by local government. If you take a purchase outside the country, you can get a refund on the VAT. But be prepared to show the purchase to officials when applying for the refund.

Vouchers: documents issued by tour operators to be exchanged for accommodations, sightseeing, and other services.

Continental breakfast: usually bread, rolls, butter, jam, and tea or coffee.

American plan: meal arrangement that includes breakfast, lunch, and dinner.

Modified American plan: meal arrangement that includes breakfast and dinner.

Full board (full pension): includes all meals.

Half board (demi-pension): includes breakfast and either lunch or dinner.

Table d'hôte: published restaurant or dining room menu.

A la carte: unrestricted selection from the menu.

Tour escort/tour director/tour manager: oversees details of the tour and accompanies the group from one place to another.

Local host: representative of the tour operator who provides help, information, and sometimes sightseeing in a particular city or area.

Local guide: provides tours to specific sights.

United States Tour Operators Association

have a checklist for the kind of tour they want. Read carefully for this information:

• Tour price: Is it "all-inclusive" or for land arrangements only? If airfare is included, is it from your home city? If airfare isn't included, can you use the airline of your choice? What "extras" may be charged: Side trips? Taxes? High-season surcharges?

• Itinerary: Will you be "visiting" or "driving through" areas? How much time will you be spending on a bus, train, or en route? How much walking is involved? Is there enough free time (or too much) for shopping, exploring, or simply resting?

• Hotels: Every country has its own rating system, so "deluxe" in Portugal may not be the same as in Hungary. Where is your hotel located? Do you want to be in a throbbing city or a quiet countryside?

• Meals: How much "regional flavor" in your meals? How many and what kinds of meals a day are included in your package? Will you have menu selections or fixed fare?

• Schedule: How early does your day start and how long does it last? Will you be visiting lots of cities, with much packing and un-

packing? Do you prefer fewer stops and longer stays?

• Conditions: This is the fine print in many brochures. Pay attention, and notice details about reservations, cancellations, and refunds for the land and air legs of your journey. Also look for any conditions about meals, sightseeing, baggage allowance, and what's not included in the price.

CRUISING ALONG

A tour doesn't have to be by plane or bus. Cruise ships are ever more popular, and they navigate virtually every body of water in the world.

On these modern floating hotels, the food is often superb and the entertainment ample: from deck games to movies and gambling, golfing to aerobics, dances and music to educational lectures and on-board libraries. For details on cruises, from the sport-oriented ship to the formal cruise, your travel agent can give you all the particulars, including what clothes to take and tipping practices.

Your "Love Boat" might be an elegant cruise filled mostly with retired couples or a casual assemblage of families and children. The size of the ship will affect the atmosphere. Small ships carry as few as 200 passengers; the big ocean liners, as many as 2,500. Large ships (tonnage over 30,000) usually offer more services, more socializing, more lines; they also can't usually dock in ports and so must ferry passengers back and forth.

Cruise variations include pre- or post-cruise excursions; sightseeing trips around various ports; expedition cruises that emphasize exotic locations and education; theme cruises (you can sail with the Baltimore Orioles or play bridge for a week nonstop!); and yacht cruises that drench you in luxury.

When planning a cruise, allow for roughly $300 per person per day, which covers food, room, and entertainment. Some cruise price quotes include the airfare to the embarkation port from major U.S. cities. A few tips to keep costs down:

• The earlier you book your cruise, the greater the discount. Reserving six months to a year before the trip can mean large price reductions.

• You can reserve a less expensive cabin on a luxury liner, or a mid-range one on an older ship, without ruining your fun. As long as the room isn't near the engine room, galley, or dance hall (where the rooms are hot and noisy), you should have a pleasant voyage.

• Taking inland side trips at ports of call can rapidly escalate the expense. Get the full list of the cruise's additional expenses from your travel agent.

TRAVEL WITH A PURPOSE: HIGH ADVENTURE TO GOURMET INDULGENCES

You can travel to sightsee or you can travel to capture a special experience. Climb Kilimanjaro, raft down the Colorado River, retreat to a Tibetan monastery, bicycle through the French wine country, golf in Scotland, learn to cook in the restaurants of Florence. The possibilities are limitless and there for the taking. The most limiting part of adventure travel won't be your age or health, but the expense.

Of course, it's costly to travel across continents or wherever, but adventure travel adds another layer of expenses—the cost of renting the gear and paying a guide. Even when you're spending nights in a sleeping bag and eating canned stew over an open fire, when you're doing it in the Grand Canyon, expenses easily exceed $100 a day.

Adventure tours are booked through general travel agents and agencies that specialize in exotic experiences. Adventure agencies like Mountain Travel in Albany, California, or Seattle's Society Expeditions can deliver you to virtually any corner of the world. Mountain Travel offers adventure trips through the world's mountainous regions for the young at heart. About a third of its clients are of retirement age, going so far as tackling Tibet and hiking to the Everest base camp.

Society Expeditions has a different bent: educationally exotic locations from Antarctica to the Galapagos, from the Amazon to India. Tours feature informative presentations followed by first-hand experience with flora and fauna categorization, marine life research, or studying tropical ecology. The field work is very active; nevertheless, more than half the participants are over 55, many in their seventies and eighties.

Grand Circle Travel offers "Soft Adventures," educational and exploration programs in which travelers live in tent base camps

and explore and learn about an area, for instance an 11-day trip through Costa Rica with five nights in tent base camps.

Alaska Wildland Adventures offers a "Senior Safari"; Ten-Speed Tours offers bicycle tours of Europe; Eye of the Whale tours offers marine adventures around Hawaii; Cameras, Horses, and Trails offers four-legged trips around the United States; and Sub Sea Explorer offers glass-bottom-boat tours in the Caribbean. There are lots more, but you get the picture: any place and any activity you can imagine.

You can also book adventure tours through educational membership organizations such as the World Wildlife Fund (endangered species trips), the Smithsonian Institution (study tours), and the Sierra Club (bicycle or backpack outings).

THE LATER YEARS

As you age, circumstances may change enough to warrant your rethinking your living situation. A spouse may die or become disabled, your money may not be holding up as well as you had hoped, you may wish to have more people your own age living close by, you may want to be nearer your family. What, then, are the options?

Let's be honest: It's the rare healthy retiree who wants to live with the children. It's you who raised them, fed them, schooled them, loved them—and still do. But sharing a kitchen with a grown-up daughter or son is probably not what you have in mind for the golden years.

ARE YOU A MEMBER OF THE SANDWICH GENERATION?

By now you've heard of the Sandwich Generation. In fact, it's not unlikely you're part of it! Longer lifetimes—people living into their eighties and nineties—have converged with a shortage of inexpensive housing and of inexpensive elder care. Adult children tending to the needs of both their aging parents and their own young children feel trapped—sandwiched—often with all three generations living under the same roof.

Family sandwiching is not an arrangement many people would choose voluntarily; it's usually created by health and financial strains. If you're in this situation or see it coming in a few years, you want to know how it can be made convenient and comfortable. What works for you depends on your family, but here are some suggestions for how to make sandwiching work.

• Explore adult day-care: These programs are designed for older people living at home who either need medical supervision during the day while their children are at work, or who desire contact and activity during the day which they would not get staying at home. The cost per week ranges from $25 to $100. A local Agency on Aging can guide you to reliable services, as can the National Counsel of the Aging, 409 Third Street, SW, Washington, DC 20024.

Some older retirees may feel pressured by offspring to combine households. Their kids voice concerns—they think an older parent will become forgetful about such things as turning off the stove. While the concern is appreciated, it doesn't necessarily make the right decision any easier.

Nonetheless, the question of who, if anyone, you're going to live with in retirement is bound to come up. And you need to think about it, because for some elderly

- Explore support groups and respite care-givers for adults giving full-time care to elderly parents.
- Find out about "intergenerational day-care." With the demand for infant day-care increasing in the country, employers have lit on the bright idea of solving two problems with one program: employing the older parents of employees to help care for employees' children. You may not have toddlers who need day-care, but your live-in (or living nearby) parents may need something to do, a place to go to be useful and feel valued. Connecting them with an intergenerational day-care center, where they look after employees' youngsters, helps everybody.
- Explore geriatric-care managers. These are professionals who provide services for adult children who don't live near their parents and need someone to ensure their parents' well-being. Services vary widely, and their costs depend upon the services rendered, usually between $50 and $150 an hour. The service continually assesses the elder's ability to remain independent, and bases its services around those needs. To find a reliable manager, try the Children of Aging Parents organization (1609 Woodburne Road, Suite 302-A, Woodburne Office Campus, Levittown, PA 19056) and your area Agency on Aging (see Appendix).

people, loneliness and isolation are the demons that destroy their retirement.

The following information won't tell you whom you can or should live with. However, it will help you understand the choices, plus their emotional and financial ramifications, and help you begin to plan an arrangement best suited for you. Of course, the later years of retirement may still be decades away, but surveying the housing options now—when there is time to financially prepare for them—is important.

STAYING IN YOUR OWN HOME

Probably the biggest complication to staying in your home is if you need health care. But health problems shouldn't kick you out.

About six million Americans currently use home-care programs, which enable them to stay in their home as long as possible while receiving health care. There are several kinds, based on the health and ability of the senior. Be forewarned, though, that home care is the least regulated form of elder health care, so be a wary shopper. A referral service for reliable help is available, along with a list of accredited programs, from the National League for Nursing (350 Hudson Street, New York, NY 10014).

Chore services are available to help with cleaning and food preparation. The program workers are often volunteers, although sometimes a small fee may be included, usually monthly and based on services provided at the rate of $15 to $25 an hour.

Medical home care is available on two levels. A visiting nurse or doctor provides checkups, medication, and assistance with living needs. The frequency of the visits depends on the care you need—whether it's weekly, monthly, or just for a short time while you recuperate from a serious illness or surgery. Cost varies widely with the services.

Twenty-four-hour care is also available, with several specialists working in shifts. While this

"For the first time in history, the average American has more parents than children."

Age Wave

method is sometimes necessary, it can cost up to $50 an hour. A better solution may be live-in care, at a price of $10 to $20 an hour. This service provides a single caregiver to live in the house and be on constant call. The service helps with any physical assistance, whether it's bathing, dressing, or taking medication. Live-in care is also available for short periods after serious hospital treatment.

If you're healthy but have trouble getting around, many organizations have transportation services available for less than the price of a cab and with more convenience than a bus. You can locate these services in the phone book, or by getting in touch with your local Agency on Aging (see Appendix E).

Depending on how well you can get around, you may want to drop in on a senior center that offers social and activity programs for healthy and active older people. Beyond exercise equipment and recreational programs, the center may give tax form help and other useful instruction. Often transportation to the facility is available. Many of the centers are run by religious and fraternal organizations, so center fees are minimal, sometimes free.

Senior centers are also handy if you're still living by yourself at home. They provide outside social contacts and stimulating activities. There are nearly 10,000 such centers in the United States, including programs with the YMCA and YWCA. Again, the Agency on Aging near you will have local listings, or check the Yellow Pages under "Recreational Centers."

SPLENDID ISOLATION

Judging from the letters to Dear Abby from aging parents who feel neglected by their children, you may think most seniors feel this way. Not true. Three out of four people over age 50, says a *Los Angeles Times* poll, feel they have just the right amount of contact with their children. Even older widows and widowers may prefer living on their own to hooking up with children or a sibling or another spouse. So if you're looking forward to living alone, don't feel you need to apologize or explain.

However, if you're relatively new at solo living, keep in mind these points:

• Living alone costs more. No getting around it. Cooking for one and maintaining a household for yourself always cost more than if you're divvying up expenses.

• Living alone means you often must initiate social contact and events. You don't have live-in entertainment or someone to share your day with. So you must make the calls and the arrangements.

• Living alone requires few compromises and opens up all sorts of self-indulgences. You can listen to opera at three in the morning, eat breakfast in the middle of the afternoon, and stay out all night with no one to answer to.

• Living alone is not the same as loneliness. Lots of individuals living with someone feel lonely. Loneliness has less to do with your housing arrangement than with your ability to relate to other people.

PAIRING UP: SHARING HOUSEHOLDS, TYING THE KNOT

On the other hand, many find they don't want to live alone. You, too, may like the idea of having that special someone sharing your home. One of the nicer things about growing older is that people feel less constrained by convention and the opinions of friends and strangers. While you may

In California, an estimated 200,000 people live alone in houses that have three or more bedrooms.

Age Wave

never have subscribed to the idea of living with a friend in your younger years, regardless of the bedroom arrangement, now may be the time to consider it.

Sharing households, with a lover or friend, has much to recommend it. There are the obvious benefits of companionship and reduced cost, as well as the small perks that matter, like someone to share chores and the extra feeling of safety and security that comes with having someone else around.

You can share a home with one other person (an obvious option for empty-nesters with large homes and empty bedrooms) or live in a boarding-house arrangement with up to a dozen other people. Some community groups, such as churches and aging agencies, and organizations, like Alternative Living for the Aging in Los Angeles and the Shared Living Project in Boston, arrange group homes, bringing together as many as 15 seniors. The organizations may arrange the housing and locate a suitable building and, more important, help match people—finding a good housemate at any age isn't easy!

When the reality of aging, rather than love or family ties, is the driving force behind living together, you need to be especially careful in your decision. If you're considering living in an organized group home, sharing your home, or moving into someone else's, mull over these questions and be comfortable with the answers:

• Am I a reasonably flexible person? How set am I in my personal habits and ways around the house? For instance, how would I react to someone whose sleeping and waking hours are markedly different from mine? Am I a neatnik who can't stand to live around clutter? How do I feel about a housemate who smokes?

• Does this arrangement make financial sense? Is this the best way to spend my housing dollar? Can I comfortably share expenses without becoming obsessive over nickels and dimes, or constantly worrying that someone's not paying his or her fair share?

• How do I feel about having someone around most of the time? Do I need a lot of time and space to myself?

What if you decide to get married? Getting married late in life can be exciting, and frightening. Melding your life with someone new is never easy. Layer on decades of habits that may well have to be adjusted and compromised, and the prospect can be unnerving. But love and a desire to share a home with someone is a joyous feeling.

You need to plan carefully before you tie the knot. This entails several moves: deciding where you're going to live; confronting lingering emotions about earlier relationships, such as a previous marriage; talking about financial matters like household budgets and a prenuptial agreement; and telling the children.

Like all successful ventures, this relationship needs attention and thought. If you're going to set up housekeeping with a new spouse, talk about practical matters. Do you split all expenses? Who pays what? Who writes the checks? Are you going to keep separate checking and investment accounts? What are you going to share ownership in—the house?

beach cottage? You'll need a clear picture of what's yours alone, what's his (or hers), and what belongs to both of you. (If you both own a house and plan to sell one, do it before you tie the knot. Single people get a bigger tax break on home equity than couples. See Chapter 7 for details.)

You and your new mate have lots of ground to cover before mingling your dish collections. As you plow through the mundane business of "Your sheets or mine?" and "Do we really need two lawn sprinklers?" remember that the potential spoilers to your new relationship are money and false expectations. And both of these can be confronted beforehand with frank discussion and an honest airing of feelings.

RETIREMENT COMMUNITIES

Retirement communities have a slightly sour reputation. You hear the words and envision "white-haired ghettos"—clusters of senior citizens living bland lives and watching sunsets. Well erase that picture. The actual footage is much brighter and livelier.

For starters, a retirement community may be a neighborhood for anyone over 55 that boasts more tennis courts, swimming pools, and golf holes than walkers, wheelchairs, and pinochle games. By and large, these enclaves are dedicated to giving residents freedom and independence in safe, landscaped surroundings with dawn-to-dusk amenities.

Anyone toying with the idea of living in a retirement community first needs to understand that the term encircles three kinds of living situations.

Over-55 senior communities are for active and independent people living in apartments and homes in exclusive neighborhoods that contain an assortment of social and recreational outlets.

Continuing-care retirement communities (also called "life-care" centers) are residential areas that provide apartments, common living areas and dining rooms, and complete medical and nursing facilities. These communities are geared to taking care of you as you age and as (presumably) your health declines or you are less able to live independently.

Nursing homes are for the infirm who need regular nursing and medical care, and help with daily tasks such as dressing and fixing meals.

WHO'S A HOMEOWNER?

According to a survey of 1,000 people over age 65 by the Marriott Corporation, the majority of seniors (81 percent) own their own home, and over 90 percent of seniors who are married own their home. Seventy-one percent of widowed or divorced individuals own homes. About 18 percent of seniors rent a home or apartment.

Los Angeles Times

SENIOR COMMUNITIES

You've probably heard of some of the bigger senior communities, places like Sun City and Leisure World, where the fifty-something crowd bounces from an array of sports to stimulating lectures to rockin' parties. Like their names, these retreats are designed for active, vibrant adults who are hardly ready for rocking chairs.

The appeal of senior communities is their ability to combine services for an aging population with a host of recreational, intellectual, and social activities. In between the pools and social halls are fully equipped medical facilities, community dining rooms, cars and vans for transportation, and constant security and safety patrols.

Typically, moving into a senior community requires applying for residency (requirements usually insist on a minimum age and good health so you're able to live independently), then purchasing a home, apartment, or condominium on the grounds. Prices depend on what kind of home you choose; many communities have various types of housing, from rental units to $50,000 single-bedroom apartments to luxurious $500,000 homes. Residents also usually pay monthly fees for amenities plus security, grounds maintenance, and some utilities.

In choosing a senior community, experts suggest you scout the place thoroughly. Visit at least twice at different times of the year for a year-round sense of the activity. Look closely at the elements you're most interested in, for instance, the condition of the golf course or the quality of the housing or the convenience of transportation services. If making new friends and social events are important, meet the residents to see if you find them congenial.

Investigate beyond the services and amenities and learn about the community's financial health. It's important to know what percentage of the living accommodations are sold or occupied. A community having a hard time attracting residents is going to be squeezed for enough cash to run the place. Request a copy of the managing company's financial statements, and share them with your accountant or lawyer for a reading on its solvency and cash flow. Be wary of a place that can't keep to its budget and has to regularly raise dues or impose special assessments to cover routine maintenance. As long as you're requesting formal documents, ask to see the association's rules, regulations, and by-laws. Read these carefully—if you move in, you'll have to live by them. Put a call in to local regulatory or monitoring agencies—the Better Business Bureau, a consumer affairs office, or a state department of real estate —to see if complaints have been registered.

Lastly, walk around and talk to residents. Ask them what they like and dislike about the place. Some gentle probing will elicit a pretty good picture of what it's like to live there.

CONTINUING-CARE RETIREMENT COMMUNITIES (CCRCs)

These communities are for residents a little older, a little less healthy, than those in the senior communities. While they also may offer a full spread of amenities and recreational facilities, their main attraction is full-service medical care and attention. The typical resident is around 70, has a good 15 years left, and although reasonably healthy, has a chronic medical problem, such as a heart condition, that needs watching. She or he doesn't need a full-time nurse, but help with daily tasks such as laundry and meal service is essential.

The services in these communities depend largely on the needs of the residents. Usually, nursing professionals are on staff and most have an arrangement with a nearby hospital in case of serious medical needs beyond the home's range.

The financial exchange is generally different, too. Residents pay a nonrefundable entrance fee, usually a sizable sum, and a much smaller monthly fee. The entrance fee is basically health-care insurance; it guarantees unlimited nursing and medical care for the rest of your life. They operate on the concept of "risk pooling"—the fees of all residents, some of whom will not require medical care, pay for the costs of those who need nursing services.

The cost of buying into some of these homes reaches into the hundreds of thousands. One luxurious establishment in Florida demands an entrance fee over $600,000, while there are places in Arizona asking $60,000. However, residents don't simply hand over huge sums never to be seen again. The standard arrangement with a CCRC is that a portion of the entrance fee is returned to a resident's heirs, after the resident's death, depending on how long he or she lived in the residence. The CCRC promises a certain rate of return on the entrance fee money (which may or may not be a good deal, depending on inflation).

Some CCRCs don't require an entrance fee and charge only monthly, but usually this setup doesn't allow for regular, unlimited nursing care. A community that has limited care may not be advisable if your health is not 100 percent.

The monthly fees, which range from a couple of hundred dollars to thousands, cover the cost of housing, meals, and amenities. Monthly fees at a residence with an entrance fee of from $200,000 to $600,000 range from $1,500 to $2,200.

These CCRCs are usually your last home, and you'll probably liquidate most of your assets to afford one. For this reason, you want to make sure you're making the right decision. Continuing-Care retirement communities differ mostly in the amount of nursing care they offer, so you should choose one according to your health.

An *extensive-care* CCRC is an all-inclusive facility that offers unlimited nursing care without additional payment. Laundry service, transportation, swimming pools, meal service, utilities (excluding telephones), and housekeeping and cleaning are part of the package. Assisted living care, such as help with bathing and dressing, is also available. These places have a communal dining hall and often a resident purchases a specific number of meals a month.

Entrance costs for these communities begin around $50,000 to $60,000 for one-bedroom apartments, but the prices vary depending on location and luxury, and you can pay as much as $250,000 for a swank two-bedroom apartment. The average monthly fee is around $1,000.

A rung down in level of medical care are *modified-care* CCRCs, communities that provide nursing care for a specified number of days each year, usually 15 or less. Anything over this carries a daily charge, although residents often get discounts on health care over what outpatients would pay. With such a payment plan, residents may still have to "spend down," that is, deplete their personal assets, so that they qualify for Medicaid to cover nursing costs. Entrance fees for modified-care residences average $45,000 to $69,000; monthly fees range from $600 to $800.

A third kind of continuing care, *fee-for-service* facilities, guarantees access to nursing care, but you pay for each day of care you receive. The amenities are similar to those in the all-inclusive residences but personal care and meals are not typically included in the monthly fee. Many services, including communal dining, are available for an additional fee.

With services more limited, fees are smaller: On average, a $40,000 entrance cost with a $700 monthly maintenance will get you a one-bedroom apartment; a $60,000 entrance cost with a $750 monthly maintenance will get you two bedrooms.

Picky, Picky

The good CCRCs are as picky as you are about who lives in their communities. Many of them have long waiting lists; couples in their sixties may sign up for places ten years before they'll be ready to move. (It's kind of like putting your newborn on a list for a selective prep school!)

A CCRC wants people who can live independently, meaning able to dress and feed themselves, and can get around for a normal day's activity. Before admitting you, they'll insist on a complete checkup, perhaps even a psychological exam, and accept only applicants with a reasonably clean bill of health. Would-be residents debilitated by stroke, Alzheimer's disease, or cancer (even if it's in remission) are often not accepted. Furthermore, the home will protect itself by levying extra nursing charges for complications of a pre-existing condition.

The CCRC will probe the health of your assets as much as your arteries. It wants to be sure you can make the monthly payments for the remainder of your life. As a rule of thumb, a CCRC wants your total monthly income to be about double its current monthly fee.

Look Hard at the Dollars and Sense

Moving into a CCRC is a major financial commitment. Before pulling out your checkbook, know exactly what it's going to cost, and how fees and services are charged. Pose these questions to your prospective new home:

If I move in when I'm older, will my monthly fees be less than for younger residents? What are the chances that monthly fees will rise?

Most places don't scale fees according to the age of residents, although couples pay more than singles (of course). Monthly fees may well rise as services become more costly, and while entrance fees may be increased, the residences can't collect the higher amounts retroactively.

What if I change my mind? Can I get my entrance fee back?

Entrance fees have generally not been refundable, but competition has forced some communities to offer a refundable option. It usually works this way: You pay as much as a third less if you agree to a nonrefundable entrance fee. Nonrefundables make more sense for people without heirs or with limited funds. If you insist on a refundable fee, you can get it back only within a certain amount of time; refundable fees frequently decline by 1 to 2 percent a month, so that eventually the refundable portion is down to zero. Bear in mind that refundable fees may affect your taxes. The IRS may regard the entrance fee as a loan to the CCRC and tax it accordingly; talk to your accountant.

Some communities allow refunds if you move out soon after arriving and your apartment is reoccupied. And, naturally, if you die soon after moving in, your heirs will receive your fee.

What assurances are there that the place is financially healthy and will be operating for the rest of my life?

Financial security is, and should be, a big concern. You're

signing on for years, and you don't want a sloppily managed residence. If a place goes bankrupt, you're on the street. One answer to this question lies in occupancy rates: Low rates are what destroy continuing-care communities. Low occupancy—90 percent or less, particularly for several years running—can force these communities into bankruptcy. Too few residents equals too little operating money.

Ask for a copy of recent audited financial statements, and go over them with your accountant. As someone handing over life savings, you're entitled to know how your money will be handled. A CCRC can be a for-profit corporation or a nonprofit corporation; in either case, it should have audited financial statements. Walk away from a community that won't show you its financial records. As you study these statements, be sure the company has accounted for the future cost of nursing care. Also look at its level of debt: If the company's debt dwarfs its assets, keep looking.

Another financial safeguard is a CCRC director with experience running a residence and managing budgets. Ask about the director's background.

Before Signing on the Dotted Line

You've pored through financial statements, talked to staff and residents, handed over your financial and health records, but you're not there yet. There's one more round: reviewing the contract.

Get a copy on your first visit to the community; it may not be in the information packet, so ask for it. What you're looking for are these specifics (and it is important that you show it to a lawyer before even picking up a pen):

• The record on fee increases: how often, how much, and why.

• Added medical fees: What additional fees are involved if you have to stay in the medical wing?

• Resident rights of a bed in the medical wing: Are you guaranteed a bed? Who has the authority to put you there?

• Details of entrance fee refunds, to you or your estate.

• Rights concerning remarriage and the related fees.

• Rights concerning contract termination.

• Schedule of services and amenities, including how many meals and what services you're entitled to and how often.

And when you know more than you ever wanted to about a CCRC, and are mulling over your decision, step back from the facts and figures and ask this: Will you be happy there?

The Danger of Cheap Imitations

A number of CCRC look-alikes have sprung up—places that offer similar living but don't have the guaranteed medical care and financial resources. These places give off numerous tell-tale signs, each pointing to a precarious arrangement, and are nothing you want to sign with for life. Often they don't charge entry fees and services, meals, and health care are pay-as-you-go. Their medical care is a "continuum of care" (not steady and continuing but liable to interruption), meaning you're guaranteed a priority spot on the medical facility's waiting list, but not an immediate bona fide bed, as in a CCRC.

Services may also be skimpy and expensive, and large increases in monthly fees are a constant hazard. You may not be asked to sign a lease at a look-alike, but that's not necessarily a good thing. You could be evicted if you can't afford

SENIOR CLUSTERS

Only 7 percent of seniors live in retirement communities, according to the National Center for Health Statistics.

Los Angeles Times

the rising monthly fees.

The bottom line on these places is that they may cost less, and you get what you pay for, which may not be very much.

THE TRUTH ABOUT NURSING HOMES

You've read the stories, seen the pictures on TV, heard the tales: Nursing homes are awful places where only the most desperate go to live. That's the image, and while it does add a certain punch to the evening news, it's only a slice of the screen. In general, they're not as bad as you think, but finding a good one—a home that's clean, with ample medical care, competent and compassionate staff, and pleasant to live in—requires both sensitive antennae and full attention to detail.

If you're planning for retirement, you'd probably sooner test-drive a wheelchair than think about nursing homes. And, statistically speaking, odds are about even that you'll never need a nursing home. Government researchers report that about 43 percent of people over 65 will check into a nursing home at some point.

Nursing homes include a broad range of facilities and different levels of medical care. They can be 25-bed "homes" situated in rural countrysides; multistory, 100-bed facilities in the heart of a city; or clusters of buildings blended into a suburban neighborhood.

They usually offer custodial care, intermediate care, or skilled nursing care, with each level involving more intensive medical attention. Whereas custodial care may be little more than daily supervision, skilled nursing care may involve around-the-clock nursing treatment.

The cost of living in a nursing home obviously depends on the home, where it's situated, the quality and intensity of the medical care, and what services are available. They generally cost somewhere between $30,000 and $40,000 a year, but they can go much higher. Medicare and Medi-gap may pick up part of this expense, but the bulk of the cost is usually paid out of your pocket or through long-term-care insurance.

Who exactly lives in a nursing home?

The typical resident is an 80-year-old widow with several chronic conditions. She's probably been in the home for at least 18 months, and before that lived in another type of health-care facility.

You breathe a sigh of relief and say, that's not me!

True, but time passes. And the thing to remember about nursing homes is that most people are admitted into them in an emergency or crisis situation, before they've had a chance to investigate. So keep this list of things to consider at the back of your mind as you encounter different housing options for your retirement years. You'll sleep easier if you've located a good nursing home long before you ever need it.

The list of items to check out for a CCRC also applies to a nursing home. Other things you should be on the lookout for when scouting a prospective nursing home:

• Study the physical surroundings. Be alert to signs of disrepair or danger, such as loose carpeting or obstacles in the halls. Make sure it doesn't smell of foul odors, a sign of neglected patients.

• Find out about the food. Make sure meals are nutritious and special diets are available.

• Beware of indications that there is wide use of restraints or calming drugs.

• Be sensitive to the attitudes and compassion of the staff. Their treatment of patients greatly affects the patients' quality of life.

• Make sure that residents' money is secure.

• Ask about "extras" in the basic cost, such as fees for physical therapy and laundry.

• Make sure residents have access to a telephone, and social activities. Visit the residents' lounge and be wary if it's empty; residents may not be able to walk to the lounge or may not want to—in either case, it doesn't reflect well on the home.

DETOURING TO ASSISTED LIVING

Say you don't need a nursing home but can't afford or, because of your health, can't qualify for a continuing-care residential community. You have another choice, what's loosely called "assisted living."

These are homes that offer a spectrum of services and care on a monthly basis. No entrance fee, no contract, no guarantees. Think of them as a fully furnished apartment for elders.

So what do you get? A relatively inexpensive home in Maryland, for example, offers room and board, daily living assistance, and an entire rec hall of amenities, including exercise classes, parties, concerts, library, beauty parlor, and laundry for $1,500 to $2,000 a month.

At the other end of the shopping mall, so to speak, a full-service Maryland residence provides room and board, room service, housekeeping and linen service daily, round-the-clock nursing, transportation, movies, music, exercise, religious meetings, group discussions, crafts, and games. It charges $3,100 to $3,600 a month.

Prices rise and fall with the available amenities somewhat, but a high-priced assisted-living facility is not necessarily the cushiest. For instance, away from major urban centers, costs will be lower and amenities comparable.

Assisted living can be grouped into two categories:

"Board-and-care" programs are managed by an overseer who cares for up to six people in a setup similar to a boarding house. Meals and housekeeping are attended to, as are low-level health-care concerns like bathing and medication. Care varies to reflect the residents' needs, as does the price. The other benefits offered in the home also affect the price, which can range from $200 to $1,000 a month.

"**Assisted-living centers**" are larger facilities—similar to nursing homes except with a more homey atmosphere. Residents live in private or shared units and are offered regular meals and a variety of care depending on what they need. A wide range of services and conveniences are available; the price swings accordingly. Full-care assisted-living centers are generally more expensive because they are more inclusive, between $300 and $2,000 a month.

FINAL CHECKLIST

Regardless of where you lay your head at night, most, if not all, retirement communities require you to sign an agreement or contract. Before you do, be cautious and thorough.

- Read over the contract carefully with the assistance of a lawyer.
- Inspect the facility at various times of the day and week, for a full picture of what it's like to live there.
- Insist on seeing the certification and registration of the home and the qualifications of the staff.
- Talk to residents for a candid version of life in the community, and an honest assessment of its pros and cons.
- Review the facility's financial records.
- Check its reputation with local authorities or monitoring organizations such as the Better Business Bureau and state Office on Aging.

GETTING IN GEAR

hile writing this book, I took a couple of steps to get my own retirement plan in gear. I moved investments that were wasting away in a money-market fund to a tax-deferred retirement growth fund. Already I can see a difference—the fund grew 14 percent last year. I also tightened up my savings habits, tucking away a little more than before. But money wasn't the only thing on my mind. I had a serious talk with my family about where we're going to live when we get old, and I updated my will. The best part was that I finally got certified as a scuba diver!

Thinking about retirement can be daunting, and now that you've read this book, it may seem even more formidable. But it need not be. You probably have years to put the pieces in place. What's required is regular attention to your plans so that when you hit age 65, or whatever age you decide to retire at, your new life is ready.

The important thing is to start now. You can start small, the way I did: nothing complicated, nothing time-consuming, but thoughtful and earmarked for retirement. You shouldn't do exactly what I did—your retirement is going to be unique. Just don't lose sight of your goals, and keep at them.

One last thing: Don't forget the fun stuff. Now that I can dive the Red Sea in my senior years, I've got my eye on helicopter skiing. So, what are *you* going to do once you have the time to do it?

Glossary

Accelerated depreciation: An accounting method that allows deducting the cost of a business asset over a shorter period of time than the regular straight-line method.

Accidental death benefit (also known as *double indemnity*): An additional benefit on a life insurance policy that is paid off in the case of an accidental death.

Accredited Personal Financial Specialist (APFS): A financial planner who is also a certified public accountant.

Accrued benefit: The amount of benefit earned by contributions to a retirement plan.

Accrued vested benefit: The accrued benefit that an employee is entitled to withdraw on retirement or when leaving an employer.

Actuary: A professional whose work includes making calculations and analyses for insurance estimates.

Adjustable-rate mortgage (ARM) (also known as a *variable mortgage*): Mortgage with an interest rate that is adjusted every one, three, five, or seven years.

Adjusted gross income (AGI): The IRS term for an individual's gross income less certain deductions.

Alternative minimum tax (AMT): A tax calculation that is used when certain deductions reduce a taxpayer's income below a certain level.

AMEX: American Stock Exchange.

Angina pectoris: A condition resulting from the narrowing of coronary arteries that causes tightness or pain in the middle of the chest, extending sometimes to the neck, jaw, and arms.

Annuitize: To arrange for a gradual payout, for instance monthly or semi-annually, of an investment, such as a pension or annuity contract, over a stated number of years or your life expectancy (or joint life expectancy with your beneficiary), instead of taking it in one single sum.

Annuity: An investment that promises regular payments over a certain period of time.

Asset: Something owned by an individual or company, with monetary value.

Asset allocation: Acquiring investments or assets that have different degrees of risk and that are influenced by different economic conditions.

Assignment: Doctors who agree to limit their charges to Medicare's federal fee scales are said to accept "assignment." Doctors who don't accept assignment usually charge a higher amount than Medicare allows and the patient pays the difference.

Atherosclerosis: A hardening of the arteries as the inner walls become thick from deposits of fatty substances, such as cholesterol.

Backup trustee: See *Successor trustee.*

Balloon mortgage: A short-term fixed-rate mortgage. Initial payments are for interest only and are relatively low; all principal and interest come due in about five years.

Bank Investment Contract (BIC): Notes managed by banks with federal insurance backing their deposits.

Base amount: An income level fixed by the IRS beyond which an elderly and/or disabled taxpayer qualifies for tax credits. For head of household or single filers, the base amount is $5,000; for joint filers with one spouse eligible, $5,000; for joint filers if both spouses are eligible, $7,500; for married couples filing separate returns, $3,750. Social Security has fixed another base amount, an income level beyond which benefits are taxed. For single filers, this base amount is $25,000; for joint filers, $32,000.

Basis: The original cost of a purchase with certain adjustments. For example, basis is reduced by the item's depreciation.

Bear market: A market that is dropping in value.

Beneficiary: (1) Someone who receives Social Security or Medicare benefits. (2) The person(s) or organization(s) named to receive property under a will or trust.

Bequeath: To leave an asset to a person or organization as part of an inheritance.

Big Board: A term for the New York Stock Exchange.

Blood pressure: The force generated by the heart as it pumps blood through the circulatory system; measured in the arteries.

Blue chip: A large company with a long history of rising earnings, steady dividends, sound finances, and established brands or reputation. A known market leader.

Bond: A debt instrument issued by companies and governments that promises to pay interest and return the principal to an investor within a specified period of time.

Bond fund: A collection of bonds issued by different companies or government agencies that is managed and traded as a single security by an investment company.

Bottom fishing: Slang for an investment strategy that concentrates on companies that are out of favor or in financial difficulty.

Breaks in service: Times when a pension plan participant is not working for the company sponsoring the plan, which may affect vesting or pension distribution schedules.

Broker/dealer: A registered stockbroker who sells stocks to clients and acts as a dealer between a client buying stock and a brokerage firm that is selling stock.

Bull market: A market that is rising in value.

Bypass trust: See *Credit shelter trust.*

Calling a bond: Paying off the principal of a bond before the maturity date in order to cease paying an interest rate that is higher than prevailing rates.

Cap: The ceiling or level at which certain taxes or benefits stop.

Capital appreciation (gains): An increase in value of an investment from the basis or original cost.

Capital loss: The decrease in the value of an investment from the basis or original cost.

Captives: Insurance agents who sell mainly for one company.

Carcinogens: Cancer-causing agents.

Career-average formula: The method of determining the amount of a defined-benefit pension by multiplying a percentage of the employee's average salary over the years of employment by the number of years of service to the company.

Cash profit-sharing plan: A plan that pays employees a portion of its profits in cash or stock.

Cash refund annuity: An immediate annuity wherein a beneficiary receives the remainder of a policyholder's payments in a lump sum.

Cash value (also known as *cash surrender value*): The amount of money an insurance policy pays to a policyholder or beneficiary before it expires or pays death benefits.

Cash-value insurance: See *Whole life insurance*.

Certificate of Deposit (CD): An investment instrument available from financial institutions that pays a fixed rate of return, or interest, for a specified period of time.

Certified Financial Planner (CFP): A financial planner who has completed courses and exams administered by the Institute of Certified Financial Planners, Denver, Colorado.

Charitable remainder trust: A trust created in order to leave assets to a charity at some time in the future. Usually a person receives income from the trust while alive. The trust principal goes to the charity upon his or her death.

Chartered Financial Analyst (CFA): An analyst who has completed the courses and exams given by the Financial Analysts Federation and who is a specialist in analyzing companies for investment purposes.

Chartered Financial Consultant (ChFC): A financial professional who has completed courses and exams administered by The American College, Bryn Mawr, Pennsylvania.

Chartered Life Underwriter (CLU): An insurance agent who has completed courses and exams administered by the American College, Bryn Mawr, Pennsylvania.

Chartered Property/Casualty Underwriter (CPCU): An insurance agent who has completed courses and exams administered by The American College, Bryn Mawr, Pennsylvania, and who specializes in property and life insurance.

Churning: Excessive buying and selling by a stockbroker in order to generate commissions.

Cliff vesting: Awarding full benefits to an employee after a certain number of years of service (maximum 5) in a company.

COLA: See *Cost-of-Living Adjustment.*

Collagen: Protein in the skin that is a primary component of connective tissue; changes in this protein that come with aging cause the skin to be less pliable.

Collateral bond: A bond backed by securities that the company owns.

Collateralized Mortgage Obligation (CMO): A bondlike investment consisting of mortgaged-backed securities issued by government agencies and sold by investment companies.

Collateralized Mortgage Obligation REIT (CMO REIT): A real estate investment trust comprised of pools of collateralized mortgages.

Combination profit-sharing plan: A plan that offers immediate cash or stock as well as deferred profit sharing.

Commission-only planner: A financial planner who is compensated through commissions on investments sold to his or her planning clients.

Common stock: Shares of stock that are created when a company incorporates and are sold to the general public. Each shareholder then owns a percentage of the corporation.

Competitive Medical Plan (CMP): A network of health-care providers who have contracted with Medicare to offer a full range of services to patients in exchange for a flat monthly fee that is generally paid by Medicare. In addition, some plans charge patients small monthly premiums and co-payments.

Compounding: The growth of principal left undisturbed as it gathers interest and interest on the interest.

Congestive heart failure: A condition marked by the heart muscle's inability to pump efficiently because it has weakened or stiffened.

Connie Lee: An acronym for securities pooled together by the College Construction Loan Insurance Association.

Conservator: A person or institution appointed by a court to handle the financial affairs of a person.

Consumer Price Index (CPI): The official inflation rate compiled monthly and annually by the government. It reflects changes in prices in the general economy.

Conversion ratio: A formula for determining the number of convertible preferred stock or bond shares that can be traded for one share of common stock.

Convertible ARM: An adjustable-rate mortgage that allows a borrower to decide at any time between the second and fifth year whether to convert to a fixed rate.

Convertible bond: A bond that can be traded for a company's common stock.

Convertible preferred stock: A special class of stock that can be traded for a company's common stock.

Coordinated-care plan: A network of health-care providers—usually doctors, hospitals, and nursing facilities—that coordinate medical care to plan members on a prepaid basis. CMPs and HMOs are coordinated-care plans.

Co-payment or **Co-insurance payment:** What a patient pays in addition to Medicare's reimbursement for medical services.

Coronary arteries: Vessels that bring blood freshened with oxygen and nutrients from the lungs to the heart.

Corporate bond fund: A collection of company bonds managed as a single investment.

Cost: The original purchase price, with adjustments; same as *basis*.

Cost-of-living adjustment (COLA): An annual adjustment on wages or other regular payments (e.g. Social Security) that is in line with the Consumer Price Index or some other rate of inflation.

Coupon rate: The fixed dollar amount received annually from a bond.

Coupon yield: The declared percentage paid of a bond's face value.

Credit shelter trust: A will under which a person divides his or her estate into two parts. The first part passes directly to the spouse. The second part goes into a trust for children or other beneficiaries, but the spouse receives the interest. Upon the death of the spouse, the trust is distributed to the heirs. Also known as a *bypass trust.*

Credited service: The number of years of employment that count toward earning pension benefits.

Current yield: The annual percentage paid by a bond, determined by a bond's coupon rate and its market value.

Custodial care: Help with bathing, dressing, eating, taking medication, and other personal needs.

Cyclical stock: A stock that fluctuates according to the economic climate.

Debenture: A bond backed by a company's good faith and credit.

Deductible: A fee a patient must pay before Medicare or another insurance carrier contributes its portion. For Medicare Part A, the deductible was $652 in 1992; for Part B, the deductible was $100.

Deep-discount broker: An individual or company that processes stock trades and offers few, if any, other services. As a result, the trading fee is less than what a full-service or discount broker charges.

Default: The status of a company or other bond issuer that fails to make payments on its debts, including bonds and loans.

Deferred fixed annuity: An annuity that pays a fixed rate of return over a set period of time.

Deferred income: Income that is due an individual but has not been actually received by that individual and is usually not taxed until it has been.

Deferred profit-sharing plan: A plan that pays employees in cash or stock according to company profits, but withholds actual payment until the employee retires.

Defined-benefit plan: An employer pension plan that pays a fixed annual amount to employees at retirement and is guaranteed by the Pension Benefit Guarantee Corporation, a U.S. government agency.

Defined-contribution plan: An employer pension plan offering annual payments to employees at retirement that vary according to employee and employer contributions and the fund's performance. Payments are not government guaranteed.

Dementia: Irreversible mental deterioration.

Depreciation: An accounting method that allows a taxpayer to deduct a portion of the original cost of an asset. The amount of the deduction depends on the estimated life of the asset. The most common type of depreciation is straight-line, which allows for an equal portion of the asset to be deducted every year.

Diastolic pressure: The blood pressure in the arteries when the heart relaxes; it is the second number in a blood pressure reading; for example, in 120/80 (a healthy reading), 80 is the diastolic pressure.

Digitalis: A heart stimulant and diuretic.

Discount broker: An individual or company that processes stock trades for commissions and charges additional fees for other investment services, such as research reports.

Discretionary account: An account that authorizes a stockbroker to make trades in a client's name without first notifying the client.

Distressed stock: Stock of a company in a precarious financial condition, perhaps even on the verge of bankruptcy or in bankruptcy.

Diuretic: A substance that increases the flow of urine.

Dividend: A periodic payment made by a company to stockholders. The amount of the dividend is determined by the company's board of directors.

Dividend reinvesting: An investment strategy that uses dividend income to purchase more of the same stock or fund.

Dollar-cost averaging: An investment strategy of purchasing stocks, bonds, or funds at regular intervals, thus averaging the cost.

Double indemnity: See *Accidental death benefit.*

Due diligence: A thorough review of an investment or investment manager that includes background, performance, and intended use of funds.

Durable health-care power of attorney: A legal document by which a person grants another person authority to act in cases involving medical decisions after the principal has become incapacitated.

Early retirement: Although the majority of workers retire before the full retirement age of 65, Social Security allows early retirement from age 62 on, with reduced benefits.

Earned income: Generally, income from work performed either in a self-employed capacity or for a company or another employer. It doesn't include income from investments, capital gains, or pensions.

Earnings and benefit statement: The work sheet supplied by Social Security to provide an estimate of your future retirement benefits.

Earnings limitation test: A ceiling on earnings set by the Social Security Administration. There's a penalty for continuing to earn income while receiving Social Security benefits. If you earn more than the allowed amount, benefits will be reduced. This doesn't apply to people over 70 years old.

Earnings test: Income amounts from various sources that Social Security uses to determine whether benefits will be reduced.

Edema: Swelling.

Effective tax rate: The actual percentage of adjusted gross income paid in taxes.

Elimination period: The period between the time a policyholder becomes disabled and the date when payments from disability insurance begin.

Employee Stock Ownership Plan (ESOP): Profit-sharing plans that offer primarily a company's own stock, but not for immediate trading or selling.

Employment Retirement Security Income Act (ERISA): A federal law that contains guidelines for the operation of pension plans.

Endometrium: The mucous membrane that lines the uterus.

Equipment trust bond: A bond backed by a company's equipment.

Equity: The net value of a company that may be traded in the form of stock.

Equity REIT: A real estate investment trust that invests in and actively manages property.

Estate: All assets, including but not limited to personal property, real estate, and investments, left by a person at death.

Estate tax: A tax levied on the estate of the deceased and not on the heir receiving the property.

Estrogen: One of several female sex hormones.

Excess distributions: Payments from a pension in excess of $750,000 (lump sum) or $150,000 (an annual annuity) and subject to a 15 percent penalty tax.

Excess interest whole life insurance: A variety of universal life insurance that has a cash value that grows at a rate similar to market-sensitive instruments while other parts of the policy, premium payments and death benefits, generate returns set at fixed amounts.

Executor: A person or institution named to carry out a will's instructions.

Exemptions: An amount a taxpayer is allowed to subtract from adjusted gross income. Specific personal exemptions exist for yourself and your dependents.

Explanation of Medicare Benefits: Every time Medicare is billed for a procedure, it sends this form to the patient to explain what has been paid to whom.

Face amount: The stated value of a life insurance policy that is paid at maturity or on death.

Face value: The amount or value of a bond that the issuer promises to repay.

Fannie Mae: An acronym for mortgage-backed securities issued by the Federal National Mortgage Association.

Fee/commission combination planner: A financial planner who is compensated through a fixed fee and through commissions on financial products purchased by clients. Sometimes called a *fee-based planner*.

Fee-offset planner: A financial planner who charges a single fee for a plan, then reduces this amount by commissions from investments purchased by the client.

Fee-only planner: A financial planner compensated only by a flat fee calculated either on an hourly basis or as a percentage of the assets invested or managed.

FICA: The Federal Insurance Contributions Act and a tax on income that ensures eligibility for Social Security payments and Medicare.

Fiduciary: An individual or institution responsible for holding and managing someone else's property, which can be benefits, assets, or money.

Finite life-equity REIT (FREIT): A real estate investment trust that buys and sells properties with time-limited mortgages, generally five to fifteen years.

Flat-benefits formula: A method of determining a defined-benefits pension that awards all employees a pension based on length of service, regardless of earnings.

Flexible-premium deferred-variable annuity: A type of variable annuity that offers choices regarding premium payments, rates of return, and when to begin receiving payments.

Flexible-premium variable life insurance: A variable life insurance policy that offers choices regarding premium payments and when payments begin. The rate of return is fixed.

Forward averaging: An accounting method for calculating and reducing taxes on lump sum distributions.

401(k): An employee investment and retirement plan that allows contributions from employees and employers to be invested and grow tax-free until withdrawal.

403(b): An investment and retirement plan for employees of nonprofit organizations and public agencies that allows contributions to be invested and grow tax-free until withdrawal.

Franchise stock: Stock issued by a company that is a market or brand leader.

Freddie Mac: An acronym for mortgage-backed securities issued by the Federal Home Loan Mortgage Corporation.

Full retirement: The Social Security Administration considers 65 to be full retirement age. If you retire before this age, your benefits will be lower. This benchmark is set to rise to 67 for those born after 1960.

General obligation bond (GO): A municipal bond backed by an authority's power to impose and collect taxes.

Gift-tax exemption: The federal tax code allowing a person to give cash or assets worth $10,000 annually tax-free to an unlimited number of individuals. There is no limit to the number of gifts allowed per year.

Ginnie Mae: An acronym for securities issued by the Government National Mortgage Association.

Going public: A company goes public when it first offers its stock for sale to the general public.

Government bond fund: A collection of bonds issued by the federal government with varying interest rates and maturity dates.

Government-plus fund: A federal government bond fund that pays generally higher interest rates because the fund, in addition to holding government bonds, also trades in options that add to the fund's income.

Graded vesting: Method of vesting which makes available no less than 20 percent of an employee's benefits at 3 years and all benefits available at 7 years, or other similarly phased vesting.

Graduated Payment Mortgage (GPM): Mortgage with low initial interest rate that gradually rises on an agreed timetable.

Grantor: The person who establishes a trust. Also known as a *settlor* or *trustor*.

Grantor Retained Income Trust (GRIT): A trust in which the grantor transfers title (generally to a personal residence) to the trust for a specified number of years. GRITs are structured so that the grantor outlives the contract, allowing for estate tax breaks.

Gray Lobby: The term that applies to senior citizens organizations in Washington, D.C., that push for legislation that helps the elderly.

Growth stock: Stock with a record of consistent, steady financial growth.

Guaranteed annuity: An annuity with an initial fixed rate for a period of one to three years. After this time, the rate is reset according to prevailing rates.

Guaranteed Investment Contracts (GICs): Fixed-interest-bearing notes issued by insurance companies and banks.

Guaranteed renewable and noncancelable policy: Disability insurance coverage guaranteed to be renewable and not canceled because of a policyholder's health. The premium rates of this type of policy cannot be raised beyond the initial rate.

Guardian: An individual appointed by a court to make personal and financial decisions on behalf of someone who is incapacitated.

Head of household: A category of taxpayer who is unmarried and maintains a household for dependent(s).

Health Care Financing Administration (HCFA, pronounced "Hick-Fa"): This government agency, a branch of the Department of Health and Human Services, oversees Medicare and Medicaid programs.

Health Maintenance Organization (HMO): A network of health-care providers, often housed under one roof, that provide all medical care for a fixed monthly sum.

Heart attack: A disease that results in the death of heart muscle cells when the blood supply is cut off from the heart, usually because of a blood clot formed in a coronary artery that has been hardened by fatty deposits such as cholesterol.

Heir: Technically, a person who, under state law, is entitled to inherit from an individual who dies without a will. The term is commonly used to refer to anyone who stands to inherit from another, whether by state decree or any other means, such as a will.

High-yield stock: A stock that pays dividends higher than prevailing rates.

Home equity: The value you actually hold in your home. If your home is worth $150,000 (what you can sell it for) and you still owe $70,000 on your mortgage, your home equity is $80,000.

Home equity loan: A loan on the equity in your home (also called a second mortgage if an initial mortgage is still outstanding).

Home health service agencies: Agencies that provide nurses or physical therapists to administer medical services in the patient's home.

Hormones: Substances the body produces to control the functions of its organs.

Hospice: Organization that helps manage the health care and provides support services for terminally ill patients and their families.

Hybrid REIT: A real estate investment trust that combines equity- and mortgage-type REITs.

Hypertension: High blood pressure.

Immediate annuity: An annuity that immediately begins to make payments to a policyholder. The opposite of a ''deferred'' annuity.

Immune system: A complex group of cells and organs that defend the body from foreign substances that might cause disease.

Incapacitated: The state of a person unable to manage his or her own affairs, either temporarily or permanently, because of physical or mental illness.

Income stock: A stock that generates immediate and regular payments to stockholders through dividends.

Income threshold: The income level at which Social Security stops taking FICA taxes out of your paycheck. In 1992 the income threshold for Social Security was $57,600. It extended to $135,000 for the Medicare tax.

Individual Retirement Account (IRA): A retirement fund set up with a maximum annual contribution of $2,000 ($2,250 for a spousal IRA), which grows tax-deferred until withdrawal.

Informal probate: An expedited probate process adopted by many states for estates that are uncomplicated and uncontested. It's less costly and time-consuming than normal probate.

Initial Public Offering (IPO): A new issue of stock available to the public.

Installment refund annuity: An immediate annuity that pays the original investment to a beneficiary if the policyholder dies.

Insurance adviser: An insurance professional who provides potential policyholders with information and policy evaluations.

Integration: The calculation of a pension benefit that reflects the amount due an employee from Social Security; also known as *permitted disparity*.

Intestate: The legal term for the status of an estate when a person dies without a will or other legal method of distributing assets.

Irrevocable trust: A type of trust that cannot be modified or canceled after its creation.

Joint-and-survivor annuity: An annuity that makes payments until both the policyholder and the designated beneficiary die.

Joint-and-survivor pension: A plan that offers monthly payments lower than a single-life pension, but the payments extend beyond the death of the employee through the spouse's lifetime.

Joint filers: A married couple who combine their tax reporting into one return.

Joint tenancy (with right of survivorship): A type of ownership in which two or more people own the same property—for example, a home owned by a husband and wife. When one owner dies, the ownership automatically passes to the surviving joint owner. Property in joint tenancy does not pass through probate.

Junk bond: A corporate bond with a low rating that pays higher-than-average interest rates.

Keogh: A retirement plan for self-employed people that allows pre-tax contributions to be invested and grow tax-deferred until withdrawal, after age 59½.

Laddering: An investment strategy of purchasing bonds with staggered maturity dates.

LEAPS: An acronym for long-term equity anticipation securities, which are options to buy a share of stock in the future at a set price.

Leukemia: Cancer of the blood-forming organs, the bone marrow and spleen.

Leveraged ESOP: A type of profit-sharing plan that borrows money to purchase stock from a company; the loan is repaid by the company.

Life-and-certain-period annuity: An immediate annuity that pays for a specified period of time, for example 10, 15, or 20 years. If the policyholder dies before the end of the specified number of years, it pays a beneficiary until the end of that period.

Life insurance trust: A combination of life insurance with an irrevocable trust. Used for estate planning.

Life-support systems: Medical technology that keeps a person alive through artificial means, such as a respirator.

Life tenure reverse mortgage: A reverse mortgage with a payment schedule that runs for the rest of your life.

Lifetime-only annuity: See *Straight life annuity*.

Limited-payment whole life insurance: Whole life insurance offering coverage for an entire life, but with premium payments for a limited number of years.

Liquidity: The ease and speed with which an investor can convert an investment into cash.

Living trust: A trust that becomes effective during the holder's lifetime. A living trust is an alternative to a will. It does not pass through probate when the holder dies.

Living will: A legal document that states a person's views about artificial life-support decisions should he or she become terminally ill and unable to voice an opinion.

Load: A sales commission on the purchase or sale of mutual fund shares.

Long-term: With regard to investing and computing taxes, long-term means over a year.

Long-term care: The continuous care required by individuals who need help with daily activities such as bathing, eating, and walking, as well as possibly needing medical or nursing attention. One in four Americans need this kind of care (usually provided in a nursing home) at some point in their life.

Loss ratio: A ratio that compares the amount an insurance company pays out in claims to the sum it receives in premiums.

Lump sum annuity: An annuity paid to a policyholder in one large amount.

Lymphoma: A type of cancer that begins in the lymphatic system, which produces, stores, and channels infection-fighting cells.

Margin account: An account with a brokerage firm that allows a client to buy stock "on margin," that is, by putting up only a percentage of the total value of the purchase.

Marginal rate: The highest rate at which a taxpayer's earnings are taxed.

Maturity date: The year the issuing company promises to buy back its bonds.

Maximum benefits: Most insurance policies, including Medicare, have a limit on benefits, which may restrict either the dollar amount that will be paid for treatment or the number of days of care for which payment will be made.

Maximum family benefit: The highest amount of money per family that the Social Security retirement, disability, and survivors benefits will pay, generally less than about 175 percent of what the covered worker would receive. This level applies no matter how large the family and how many dependents qualify for coverage.

Medicaid: State-run health-care programs for the poor or disabled, jointly financed by federal and state funds.

Medicare: The federal health insurance program for individuals 65 and over, and for those who qualify under Disability rules. There are two parts; see *Part A* and *Part B*.

Medigap: Private commercial insurance that covers some of the gaps in Medicare coverage.

Melanin: Pigment in the skin.

Melanoma: A cancer of the pigment-producing cells that usually starts in the skin and, unlike common skin cancers, tends to spread to internal organs.

Menopause: The time in a woman's life when regular menstruation stops, usually between ages 45 and 55.

Metastasize: To spread by metastasis (the movement of tumor-forming cancer cells to other parts of the body).

Modified life insurance: Whole life coverage with premium costs that are modified to be less in early years and larger later on.

Money market account: A deposit with a bank or mutual fund company that guarantees the safety of the principal, a variable interest rate, and immediate access.

Money-purchase Keogh: A retirement plan that requires a self-employed person to contribute a certain percentage of income each year.

Mortgage-backed security: A security issued by an agency of the government that has as collateral the principal and interest payments from a large pool of home mortgages.

Mortgage bond: A bond backed by company buildings or property.

Mortgage REIT: A real estate investment trust that holds mortgages, like a bank or savings and loan, rather than managing the property.

Multi-employer pension plan: Pension plans for specific trade or craft industries, and which cover employees from different companies. Typically offered to union members.

Municipal bond (muni): A bond issued by a state or local government or agency. Interest payments from munis are exempt from federal income tax.

Municipal bond fund: A collection of munis managed by an investment company.

Mutual fund: A portfolio of securities acquired by an investment company and sold to investors as shares.

NASDAQ: See *Over-the-counter.*

Net worth: The sum total of all an individual's or company's assets minus the value of any debts or other liabilities.

No-load: A fund that can be bought and sold without an investor paying a sales commission.

Nonprobate property: Property and assets that aren't subject to probate, such as life insurance benefits, retirement plans, trusts, and property held in joint tenancy.

Nonforfeiture value: The cash or value in terms of insurance coverage a policy pays when premium payments have stopped.

Normal Retirement Age: The age the Social Security Administration uses to define when a person can claim full retirement benefits. The normal retirement age is currently 65; the age will rise to 67 in years to come.

Over-the-counter: A stock market trading exchange. The National Association of Securities Dealers Automated Quotations system (NASDAQ).

Paid-up insurance: A policy on which premium payments are up-to-date or are paid off for the life of the policy.

Par value: A value assigned to shares of stock created when a company incorporates.

Part A: One part of Medicare's two-part program, Part A provides Hospital Insurance, including skilled nursing care, home health services, and hospice care.

Part B: The second part of Medicare, Part B is Medical Insurance and covers doctors' fees, outpatient services, and other medical care.

Participating physician: A doctor who always accepts *assignment* for Medicare patients.

Passive income: Income generated by investments in which a taxpayer doesn't play an active role. This usually includes money from rentals, royalties, dividends, interest, and annuities.

Penny stock: Stock usually valued at less than a dollar and traded through local brokerages or over-the-counter, usually not national exchanges.

Pension Benefits Guaranty Corporation (PBGC): The federal agency that insures defined-benefit pension benefits if a plan becomes insolvent.

Pension maximization proposal (pension max): An option at retirement, pension max is a single-life pension combined with life insurance to provide spousal protection.

Permanent life insurance: See *Whole life insurance*.

Permitted disparity: See *Integration*.

Pickup tax: A portion of the federal estate tax claimed by an individual state. The tax burden on the individual stays the same: Only the apportionment between the federal government and the state varies.

Pink sheets: A source of information about securities not traded on national or major over-the-counter markets but through individual market makers, such as local brokerage firms.

Placebo: An inert substance prescribed in lieu of medication.

Policy dividend: A financial payment to an insurance policyholder as a regular declared payout or when premium amounts have been overestimated.

Pour-over will: A supplement to a living trust. A pour-over will directs that any property or asset left out of the trust be placed into it when the owner dies.

Power of attorney: A written document in which a mentally competent adult appoints another person or institution to handle decisions should he or she become incapacitated.

Pre-existing conditions: Generally, health problems identified by a physician within about six months before an insurance policy went into effect. Most private insurance will not cover pre-existing conditions, which they carefully define in every policy.

Preferred stock: A class of stock issued by a company that entitles the stockholder to preferred treatment over owners of common stock should the company be liquidated.

Premium: The regular payment a policyholder must make to keep an insurance policy in force.

Price-to-earnings ratio: The current market price of a share divided by the company's annual earnings per share. The higher the ratio, the more demand there is for the stock.

Prime rate: The interest rate charged by banks and other lending institutions to their most creditworthy borrowers.

Probate: The state court process a will must pass through before it can be completed and the assets dispersed to beneficiaries.

Profit-sharing Keogh: A retirement plan that allows a self-employed person to contribute up to 15 percent of taxable business income. It grows tax-deferred until withdrawal at age $59\frac{1}{2}$.

Prospectus: A legal document that is supposed to contain all relevant information about an investment offering. It is sent to prospective investors.

Prostate: The male organ that secretes semen, a fluid that contains sperm.

Qualified joint-and-survivor annuity: An instrument that requires employers to pay an employee's pension; after the employee dies, his or her spouse receives benefits.

Qualified plan: A pension or retirement plan that meets certain IRS standards and so can shelter some contributions and earnings from taxes until retirement.

"Qualified" retirement plan: A plan designed to meet tax code requirements so that contributions will be exempt from certain taxes until withdrawal.

Qualified Terminal Interest Property (QTIP): A type of trust popular with people who are in a second marriage and have children from a prior marriage. A QTIP trust instructs how the proceeds are to be distributed upon the death of the second spouse.

Quarterly estimated taxes: Taxes paid to the IRS and to the state on April 15, June 15, September 15, and January 15 for income that has not been subject to withholding tax.

Rate of return: How much an investment generates, expressed as a percentage of the total investment.

Real estate annuity: A variable annuity that invests in real estate.

Real estate investment trust (REIT): A professionally managed fund that owns or invests in property. An individual invests in a REIT by buying its stock, which is traded on the major exchanges.

Real estate limited partnership: A partnership that sells units to individual investors (the limited partners) and is managed by a professional investment company (the general manager).

Receivables: Cash or other items of value owed by one party and due to be received by another party.

Refinancing: Paying off an existing mortgage and arranging for another one on the same property at a lower interest rate.

Revenue bond: A municipal bond backed by revenue generated by the project for which the bond was issued.

Reverse mortgage: A mortgage that reverses the normal flow of money in a home loan, with the lending company making payments to the homeowner based on the value of the home and the length of time payments will extend.

Revocable trust: Another term for a living trust that can be amended, modified, or canceled at any time.

Riders: With regard to insurance, riders are additions to the terms of an insurance policy that extend or limit the coverage.

Risk classification: See *Underwriting*.

Rollover IRA: An IRA account opened with funds from a qualified retirement plan.

Roll-up: A collection of real estate partnerships combined into one entity and sold on the open market.

Sallie Mae: An acronym for securities issued by the Student Loan Marketing Association.

Scheduled-premium variable life insurance: Variable life insurance that has a fixed schedule of payments for a set amount.

Sector fund: A mutual fund that invests in a single industry, such as electronics manufacturers.

Secured cards: Credit cards aimed at high-risk users that require them to keep a minimum deposit with the issuing institution and which may earn a low rate of return.

Settlor: See *Grantor*.

Short-term: In tax and investment activities, one year or less.

Short-term bond funds: Funds which consist of government or corporate bonds that expire within a year.

Simple will: A will that leaves everything to the spouse, children, charity, or other persons.

Simplified Employee Pension (SEP-IRA): A self-directed pension plan designed for the self-employed or small companies; an IRA with extended capacity.

Single filer: A tax category for someone who is not married and not head of household.

Single-life pension: A plan consisting of maximum monthly payments to an employee upon retirement and until his or her death.

Single-premium deferred annuity: A variable annuity established by a lump sum payment that pays to the beneficiary at some future date.

Single-premium whole life insurance: Whole life insurance that consists of one large payment for complete coverage.

Skilled-nursing care: Health care that requires the supervision of medically trained staff. An aide who helps an individual with bathing, eating, or daily activities doesn't count as skilled nursing care.

Skilled-nursing facility: A nursing home that provides medical care to patients who no longer need to be in the hospital but still need daily supervised medical treatment or physical therapy.

Social Security Administration (SSA): The branch of the Department of Health and Human Services that runs the Social Security program.

Social Security Disability Insurance: One of the key components of the Social Security system, it supplies benefits to workers and families whose breadwinner can no longer work because of a medical disability.

Source tax on pensions: A state tax imposed on pension payments made to former residents.

Spousal benefits: Social Security benefits for a spouse who works in the home, based on the outside-the-home working partner's employment record. They generally total 50 percent of the working spouse's benefit.

Spread: In the context of mortgages, the number of percentage points an adjustable-rate mortgage differs from a fixed-rate mortgage.

Stable loan: An adjustable-rate mortgage with a portion at a fixed rate and a portion at an adjustable rate.

Standard deduction: A fixed amount allowed every taxpayer who does not itemize deductions when figuring income tax.

Step-up: A method of increasing the cost basis of an heir's inheritance to the fair market value of the property as of the date of the decedent's death. Thus, when these assets are sold by heirs, they are taxed on the gain between the stepped-up value (not the original value) and current market value. Generally, the difference is less and so taxes are less.

Straight life annuity (also known as *lifetime only*): An immediate annuity that pays until death.

Straight life insurance: See *Whole life insurance.*

Street name: The name of the brokerage company or investment firm that maintains physical possession of its clients' stock certificates.

STRIPS: An acronym for separate trading of registered interest and principal of securities, which is a high-yield hybrid of Treasury bonds.

Stroke: A medical condition triggered when blood fails to reach brain cells because of a blood clot or hemorrhaging.

Successor trustee: A person or institution named in a trust agreement who handles the trust's affairs when the first trustee dies or is incapacitated. Also called a *backup trustee.*

Summary plan description: A description of the terms and operation of an employee's pension plan and the benefit formula, as required by ERISA (Employee Retirement Income Security Act).

Supplementary Security Income (SSI): A program that provides poor retirees, the blind, and the disabled with supplemental income.

Surrender fee: A penalty charge, usually set at 1 percent a year, assessed an annuity holder if a policy is redeemed before a certain number of years, usually seven to ten.

Survivors insurance: The part of the Social Security system that pays benefits to families and dependents if the main wage-earner dies.

Survivorship contract: An insurance policy that pays off after the death of more than one person.

Systematic withdrawal: The withdrawal of money at regular intervals by an annuity customer who has ceased investing in a policy.

Systolic pressure: The pressure in arteries when the heart contracts; the first number in a blood pressure reading; for example in 120/80, a healthy reading, 120 is the systolic pressure.

Tax bracket: A percentage that represents the amount of tax an individual pays on his or her last dollar of income.

Tax credits: Dollar amounts that reduce an individual's tax liability dollar-for-dollar.

Tax rate: A percentage of income paid in taxes; same as *tax bracket*.

Tax shelter: An investment that reduces taxable income through deductions or credits.

Term insurance: A type of life insurance that provides only death benefits.

Tiered rate: The two levels of interest rates offered by an insurer on an annuity. The higher rate applies only after premiums have accumulated and the contract is annuitized.

Timesharing: Sharing ownership on a vacation property. Ownership is usually sold in terms of specific weeks when each timeshare owner can use the property.

Total and residual policy: A type of disability insurance that pays if a person is either partially or totally disabled.

Trading down: Selling a larger home and purchasing a smaller one.

Trustee: A person or institution named to manage, administer, and distribute a trust's assets according to the instructions in the trust agreement.

Trustor: See *Grantor*.

Underwriter: An investment company, such as a brokerage firm, that acts as an intermediary between a stock-issuing company and the buying public.

Underwriting (also called *risk classification*): Classifying and grouping people according to various insurance risk characteristics, such as age, sex, health, occupation, and smoking habits.

Unearned income: Income generated by investments, as opposed to salary and wages.

Unit trust: A collection of securities (bonds, munis, Ginnie Maes, even common stock) similar to a mutual fund but with a specific expiration date for its holdings and distribution of its income and gains.

Universal life insurance: A type of whole life insurance that offers choices, such as the size of the premiums, the payment schedule, the size of the death benefits, and the portion of payments that go toward the insurance and the cash value.

Unleveraged ESOP: A type of profit-sharing plan where the company creates an ESOP trust fund and periodically gives it money or stock to purchase stock.

Unlimited marital deduction: The federal government permits a spouse to inherit an entire estate, free of estate taxes, no matter how large.

Urethra: The canal through which urine is discharged from the bladder; in men, also the duct through which semen flows.

U.S. Treasury bills (T-bills): Government debt notes that expire in three months, six months, or one year. They are sold at a discount to face value, without a stated interest rate.

U.S. Treasury bonds (Treasuries): Government debt notes that expire in ten to thirty years.

U.S. Treasury notes (T-notes): Government debt notes that expire in one to ten years.

Variable annuity: An annuity that enables a policyholder to choose where premiums are invested. Rate of return on this annuity varies with the investment performance.

Variable mortgage: See *Adjustable-rate mortgage*.

Vasodilator: An agent that widens the cavity of the blood vessels.

Vesting: The amount of time an employee must work for a company before he or she has unforfeitable rights to accrued benefits.

Whole life insurance (also known as *straight life, permanent life,* and *cash-value insurance*): Insurance that offers death benefits for an entire lifetime and also includes a savings or investment feature.

Will: A legal document setting out a person's wishes as to the manner in which he or she wants property distributed after death.

Wrap account: An account that consolidates an investor's holdings and places them in the hands of a professional money manager.

Yield to maturity: How much interest a bond generates over its lifetime, calculated by figuring its change in market price and yield.

Zero-coupon bond: A bond sold at a discount or for less than its face value. At maturity it is redeemed for its full face value plus accumulated interest.

Appendix A

NORTH AMERICAN SECURITIES ADMINISTRATORS

Alabama
Securities Commission: 205/242-2984

Alaska
Department of Commerce & Economic Development, Division of Banking, Securities & Corporations: 907/465-2521

Arizona
Corporation Commission, Securities Division: 602/542-4242

Arkansas
Securities Department: 501/324-9260

California
Department of Corporations: 213/736-2741

Colorado
Division of Securities: 303/894-2320

Connecticut
Department of Banking, Securities & Business Investments Division: 203/566-4560

Delaware
Department of Justice, Division of Securities: 302/577-2515

District of Columbia
Securities Commission: 202/626-5105

Florida
Office of Comptroller, Department of Banking and Finance: 904/488-9805

Georgia
Division of Business Services and Regulation: 404/656-2894

Hawaii
Department of Commerce and Consumer Affairs: 808/586-2744

Idaho
Department of Finance, Securities Bureau: 208/334-3684

Illinois
Office of the Secretary of State, Securities Department: 217/782-2256

Indiana
Office of the Secretary of State, Securities Division: 317/232-6681

Iowa
Insurance Division, Securities Bureau: 515/281-4441

Kansas
Office of Securities Commissioner: 913/296-3307

Kentucky
Department of Financial Institutions, Division of Securities: 502/564-3390

Louisiana
Securities Commission: 504/568-5515

Maine
Department of Professional and Financial Regulation, Bureau of Banking, Securities Division: 207/582-8760

Maryland
Office of the Attorney General, Division of Securities: 410/576-6360

Massachusetts
Secretary of the Commonwealth,
Securities Division: 617/727-3548

Michigan
Department of Commerce,
Corporation and Securities Bureau:
517/334-6212

Minnesota
Commissioner of Commerce,
Department of Commerce: 612/296-2488

Mississippi
Office of the Secretary of State,
Securities Division: 601/359-6364

Missouri
Office of the Secretary of State: 314/751-4136

Montana
Office of the State Auditor: 406/444-2040

Nebraska
Department of Banking and
Finance, Bureau of Securities: 402/471-3445

Nevada
Office of the Secretary of State,
Securities Division: 702/486-6440

New Hampshire
Bureau of Securities Regulation:
603/271-1463

New Jersey
Department of Law & Public
Safety, Bureau of Securities: 201/648-2040

New Mexico
Regulation and Licensing
Department, Securities Division:
505/827-7140

New York
Bureau of Investor Protection and
Securities: 212/341-2186, 2984

North Carolina
Office of the Secretary of State,
Securities Division: 919/733-3924

North Dakota
Office of the Securities
Commissioner: 701/224-2910

Ohio
Division of Securities: 614/644-7381

Oklahoma
Securities Commission, Department
of Securities: 405/521-2451

Oregon
Department of Insurance and
Finance, Securities Section: 503/378-4387

Pennsylvania
Securities Commission: 717/787-8061

Rhode Island
Department of Business Regulation,
Securities Division: 401/277-3048

South Carolina
Department of State, Securities ·
Division: 803/734-1087

South Dakota
Division of Securities: 605/773-4823

Tennessee
Department of Commerce and
Insurance, Securities Division: 615/741-5911

Texas
State Securities Board: 512/474-2233

Utah
Department of Commerce,
Securities Division: 801/530-6955

Vermont
Department of Banking, Insurance
and Securities, Securities Division:
802/828-3420

Virginia
State Corporation Commission,
Division of Securities and Retail
Franchising: 804/786-7751

Washington
Department of Licensing, Securities
Division: 206/753-6928

West Virginia
State Auditor's Office, Securities
Division: 304/348-2257

Wisconsin
Office of the Commissioner of
Securities: 608/266-3431

Wyoming
Secretary of State, Securities
Division: 307/777-7370

Appendix B

FIELD OFFICES OF THE PENSION AND WELFARE BENEFITS ADMINISTRATION

Atlanta Area
(Tennessee, North Carolina, South
Carolina, Georgia, Alabama, Puerto
Rico, Mississippi, Florida)
Room 205, 1371 Peachtree
    Street, NE
Atlanta, GA 30367
404/347-4090

Boston Area
(Rhode Island, Vermont, Maine,
New Hampshire, most of
Connecticut, Massachusetts, central
and western New York)
JW McCormack Poch Building,
    Suite L-2
Boston, MA 02109
617/223-9837

Chicago Area
(northern Illinois, northern Indiana,
Wisconsin)
401 S. State Street
Suite 840
Chicago, IL 60605
312/353-0900

Cincinnati Area
(Michigan, Kentucky, Ohio,
southern Indiana)
1885 Dixie Highway, Suite 210
Ft. Wright, KY 41011
606/292-3121

Dallas Area
(Arkansas, Louisiana, New Mexico,
Oklahoma, Texas)
525 Griffin Street, Room 707
Dallas, TX 75202
214/757-6831

Kansas City Area
(Colorado, southern Illinois, Iowa,
Kansas, Minnesota, Missouri,
Montana, Nebraska, North Dakota,
South Dakota, Wyoming)
911 Walnut Street, Room 2200
Kansas City, MO 64106
816/426-5131

Los Angeles Area
(American Samoa, Arizona, Guam,
Hawaii, southern California, Wake
Island)
3660 Wilshire Boulevard, Room 718
Los Angeles, CA 90010
213/252-7556

New York Area
(eastern New York, southern
Connecticut, northern New Jersey)
1633 Broadway, Room 226
New York, NY 10019
212/399-5191

Philadelphia Area
(Delaware, Washington, DC,
Maryland, southern New Jersey,
Pennsylvania, Virginia, West
Virginia)
3535 Market Street, Room M300
Philadelphia, PA 19104
215/596-1134

San Francisco Area
(Alaska, northern California, Idaho,
Nevada, Oregon, Utah,
Washington)
71 Stevenson Street, Suite 915
P.O. Box 190250
San Francisco, CA 94119
415/744-6700

Appendix C

STATE INSURANCE COMMISSIONERS

Life insurance is regulated by states, not the federal government, and every state has an insurance commissioner to enforce licensing and regulatory standards, monitor insurance company practices, and handle consumer complaints. These offices will provide inquirers information about the ratings and financial solvency of companies operating in their states. Direct inquiries to your State Insurance Office, care of the commissioner or director.

Alabama
Commissioner
135 S. Union Street
Montgomery, AL 36104
205/269-3550

Alaska
Director
P.O. Box 110805
333 Willoughby Avenue
Juneau, AK 99801
907/465-2515

Arizona
Director
3030 North 3rd Street, Suite 1100
Phoenix, AZ 85012
602/255-5400

Arkansas
Commissioner
400 University Tower Building
1123 So. University Street
Little Rock, AR 72204
501/686-2900

California
Commissioner
One City Center Building,
 Suite 1120
770 L Street
Sacramento, CA 95814
916/445-5544

Colorado
Commissioner
1560 Broadway, Suite 850
Denver, CO 80202
303/894-7499

Connecticut
Commissioner
P.O. Box 816
Hartford, CT 06142
203/297-3802

Delaware
Commissioner
Rodney Building
841 Silver Lake Boulevard
Dover, DE 19901
302/736-4251

District of Columbia
Superintendent
613 G Street, NW
Washington, DC 20001
202/727-7424

Florida
Commissioner
State Capitol, Plaza Level Eleven
Tallahassee, FL 32399
904/922-3100

Georgia
Commissioner
2 Martin Luther King, Jr., Drive
704 West Tower
Atlanta, GA 30334
404/656-2056

Hawaii
Commissioner
250 S. King Street, 5th Floor
Honolulu, HI 96813
808/586-2790

Idaho
Director
500 S. 10th Street
Boise, ID 83720
208/334-2250

Illinois
Director
320 West Washington Street,
    4th floor
Springfield, IL 62767
217/782-4515

Indiana
Commissioner
311 West Washington Street,
    Suite 300
Indianapolis, IN 46204
317/232-2385

Iowa
Commissioner
Lucas State Office Building,
    6th floor
Des Moines, IA 50319
515/281-5705

Kansas
Commissioner
420 S.W. 9th Street
Topeka, KS 66612
913/296-7801

Kentucky
Commissioner
229 West Main Street
Frankfort, KY 40602
502/564-3630

Louisiana
Commissioner
950 North 5th Street
Baton Rouge, LA 70801
504/342-5900

Maine
Superintendent
State Office Building
State House, Station 34
Augusta, ME 04333
207/582-8707

Maryland
Commissioner
501 St. Paul Place, 7th floor south
Baltimore, MD 21202
410/333-2520

Massachusetts
Commissioner
280 Friend Street
Boston, MA 02114
617/727-7189

Michigan
Commissioner
611 West Ottawa Street,
    2nd floor north
Lansing, MI 48933
517/373-9273

Minnesota
Commissioner
133 East 7th Street
St. Paul, MN 55101
612/296-6848

Mississippi
Commissioner
1804 Walter Sillers Building
Jackson, MS 39205
601/359-3569

Missouri
Director
301 West High Street, 6 north
Jefferson City, MO 65102
314/751-4126

Montana
Commissioner
126 North Sanders
Mitchell Building, Room 270
Helena, MT 59601
406/444-2040

Nebraska
Director
Terminal Building
941 O Street, Suite 400
Lincoln, NE 68508
402/471-2201

Nevada
Commissioner
1665 Hot Springs Road
Carson City, NV 89710
702/687-4270

New Hampshire
Commissioner
169 Manchester Street
Concord, NH 03301
603/271-2261

New Jersey
Commissioner
20 West State Street CN325
Trenton, NJ 08625
609/292-5363

New Mexico
Superintendent
P.O. Drawer 1269
Santa Fe, NM 87504
505/827-4500

New York
Superintendent
State of New York
160 West Broadway
New York, NY 10013
212/602-0429

North Carolina
Commissioner
Dobbs Building
430 North Salisbury Street
Raleigh, NC 27611
919/733-7349

North Dakota
Commissioner
600 E. Boulevard
Bismarck, ND 58505
701/224-2440

Ohio
Director
2100 Stella Court
Columbus, OH 43266
614/644-2658

Oklahoma
Commissioner
1901 North Walnut
Oklahoma City, OK 73105
405/521-2828

Oregon
Commissioner
21 Labor and Industries Building
Salem, OR 97310
503/378-4271

Pennsylvania
Commissioner
Strawberry Square, 13th floor
Harrisburg, PA 17120
717/787-5173

Rhode Island
Commissioner
233 Richmond Street, Suite 237
Providence, RI 02903
401/277-2223

South Carolina
Commissioner
1612 Marion Street
Columbia, SC 29201
803/737-6117

South Dakota
Director
Insurance Building
910 E. Sioux Avenue
Pierre, SD 57501
605/773-3563

Tennessee
Commissioner
Volunteer Plaza
500 James Robertson Parkway
Nashville, TN 37243
615/741-2241

Texas
Chairman
State Board
333 Guadalupe Street
P.O. Box 149104
Austin, TX 78714
512/463-6169

Utah
Commissioner
3110 State Office Building
Salt Lake City, UT 84114
801/538-3800

Vermont
Commissioner
120 State Street
Montpelier, VT 05602
802/828-3301

Virginia
Commissioner
1200 Jefferson Building
1220 Bank Street
Richmond, VA 23219
804/786-7694

Washington
Commissioner
Insurance Building
P.O. Box 40255
Olympia, WA 98504
206/753-7301

West Virginia
Commissioner
2019 Washington Street East
Charleston, WV 25305
304/348-3394

Wisconsin
Commissioner
121 E. Wilson
Madison, WI 53702
608/266-0102

Wyoming
Commissioner
Herschler Building
122 West 25th Street
Cheyenne, WY 82002
307/777-7401

Appendix D

REGIONAL OFFICES OF THE SOCIAL SECURITY ADMINISTRATION

Region I
(Connecticut, Maine,
Massachusetts, New Hampshire,
Rhode Island, Vermont)
John F. Kennedy Federal Building,
   Room 1100
Boston, MA 02203
617/835-2870

Region II
(New Jersey, New York, Puerto
Rico, Virgin Islands)
26 Federal Plaza
New York, NY 10278
212/264-3915

Region III
(Delaware, District of Columbia,
Maryland, Pennsylvania, Virginia,
West Virginia)
3535 Market Street
Philadelphia, PA 19101
215/596-6941

Region IV
(Alabama, Florida, Georgia,
Kentucky, Mississippi, North
Carolina, South Carolina,
Tennessee)
101 Marietta Tower Building
Atlanta, GA 30301
404/331-0612

Region V
(Illinois, Indiana, Michigan,
Minnesota, Ohio, Wisconsin)
300 S. Wacker Drive
Chicago, IL 60606
312/353-8277

Region VI
(Arkansas, Louisiana, New Mexico,
Oklahoma, Texas)
1200 Main Tower Building,
   Room 1440
Dallas, TX 75202
214/729-4210

Region VII
(Iowa, Kansas, Missouri, Nebraska)
601 E. 12st Street
Kansas City, MO 64106
816/867-3701

Region VIII
(Colorado, Montana, North Dakota,
South Dakota, Utah, Wyoming)
1961 Stout Street, Room 1185
Denver,CO 80294
303/564-2388

Region IX
(American Samoa, Arizona,
California, Guam, Hawaii, Nevada)
10 United Nations Plaza, 5th floor
San Francisco, CA 94102
415/556-3226

Region X
(Alaska, Idaho, Oregon,
Washington)
2001 Sixth Avenue, M/S RX-50
Seattle, WA 98121
206/399-0417

Appendix E

STATE AGENCIES ON AGING

Alabama
Commission on Aging
770 Washington Avenue, Suite 470
Montgomery, AL 36130
205/242-5743

Alaska
Older Alaskans Commission
Department of Administration
Pouch C–Mail Station 0209
Juneau, AK 99811
907/465-3250

Arizona
Aging and Adult Administration
Department of Economic Security
1789 W. Jefferson Street
Phoenix, AZ 85007
602/542-4446

Arkansas
Office of Aging and Adult Services
Department of Human Services
P.O. Box 1437, Slot 1412
7th and Main Streets
Little Rock, AR 77201
501/682-2441

California
Department of Aging
1600 K Street
Sacramento, CA 95814
916/322-5290

Colorado
Aging and Adult Service
Department of Social Services
1575 Sherman Street, 4th floor
Denver, CO 80203
303/866-3851

Connecticut
Department on Aging
175 Main Street
Hartford, CT 06106
203/566-3238

Delaware
Division on Aging
Department of Health and
    Social Services
Administration Building,
    Annex 2nd floor
1909 North DuPont Highway
New Castle, DE 19720
302/577-4791

District of Columbia
Office on Aging
1424 K Street, NW, 2nd floor
Washington, DC 20005
202/724-5626

Florida
Department of Elder Affairs
Building I, Room 317
1317 Winewood Boulevard
Tallahassee, FL 32399
904/922-5297

Georgia
Office of Aging
878 Peachtree Street, NE,
    Room 632
Atlanta, GA 30309
404/894-5333

Hawaii
Executive Office on Aging
Office of the Governor
335 Merchant Street, Room 241
Honolulu, HI 96813
808/586-0100

Idaho
Office on Aging
Statehouse, Room 108
Boise, ID 83720
208/334-3833

Illinois
Department on Aging
421 East Capitol Avenue
Springfield, IL 62701
217/785-2870

Indiana
Choice/Home Care Services
Department of Human Services
251 North Illinois Street
P.O. Box 7083
Indianapolis, IN 46207
317/232-7020

Iowa
Department of Elder Affairs
Jewett Building, Suite 236
914 Grand Avenue
Des Moines, IA 50319
515/281-5187

Kansas
Department on Aging
Docking State Office Building,
    122-S
915 S.W. Harrison
Topeka, KA 66612
913/296-4986

Kentucky
Division of Aging Services
Cabinet for Human Resources
CHR Building, 6th West
275 East Main Street
Frankfort, KY 40621
502/564-6930

Louisiana
Office of Elderly Affairs
4550 N. Boulevard, 2nd floor
P.O. Box 80374
Baton Rouge, LA 70806
504/925-1700

Maine
Bureau of Elder & Adult Service
Department of Human Services
State House, Station 11
Augusta, ME 04333
207/626-5335

Maryland
Office on Aging
State Office Building
301 West Preston Street, Room 1004
Baltimore, MD 21201
301/225-1100

Massachusetts
Executive Office of Elder Affairs
38 Chauncey Street
Boston, MA 02111
617/727-7750

Michigan
Office of Services to the Aging
P.O. Box 30026
Lansing, MI 48909
517/373-8230

Minnesota
Board on Aging
444 Lafayette Road
St. Paul, MN 55155
612/296-2770

Mississippi
Council on Aging
Division of Aging and Adult
    Services
421 West Pascagoula Street
Jackson, MS 39203
601/949-2070

Missouri
Division on Aging
Department of Social Services
P.O. Box 1337
615 Howerton Court
Jefferson City, MO 65102
314/751-3082

Montana
Governor's Office on Aging
State Capitol Building
Capitol Station, Room 219
Helena, MT 59620
406/444-3111

Nebraska
Department on Aging
P.O. Box 95044
301 Centennial Mall, South
Lincoln, NE 68509
402/471-2306

Nevada
Division for Aging Services
Department of Human Resources
340 North 11th Street, Suite 114
Las Vegas, NV 89101
702/486-3545

New Hampshire
Division of Elderly and Adult
  Services
6 Hazen Drive
Concord, NH 03301
603/271-4680

New Jersey
Division on Aging
Department of Community Affairs,
  CN807
South Broad and Front Streets
Trenton, NJ 08625
609/292-4833

New Mexico
State Agency on Aging
224 East Palace Ave, 4th floor
La Villa Rivera Building
Santa Fe, NM 87501
505/827-7640

New York
Office for the Aging
New York State Plaza
Agency Building 2
Albany, NY 12223
518/474-4425

North Carolina
Division of Aging
CB 29531
693 Palmer Drive
Raleigh, NC 27626
919/733-3983

North Dakota
Aging Services Division
Department of Human Services
P.O. Box 7070
Northbrook Shopping Center
North Washington Street
Bismarck, ND 58507
701/224-2577

Ohio
Department of Aging
50 West Broad Street, 9th floor
Columbus, OH 43266
614/466-5500

Oklahoma
Aging Services Division
Department of Human Services
P.O. Box 25352
Oklahoma City, OK 73125
405/521-2327

Oregon
Senior and Disabled Services
  Division
313 Public Service Building
Salem, OR 97310
503/378-4728

Pennsylvania
Department of Aging
231 State Street
Harrisburg, PA 17101
717/783-1550

Rhode Island
Department of Elderly Affairs
160 Pine Street
Providence, RI 02903
401/277-2858

South Carolina
Commission on Aging
400 Arbor Lake Drive, Suite B-500
Columbia, SC 29223
803/735-0210

South Dakota
Office of Adult Services and Aging
700 N. Illinois Street
Kneip Building
Pierre, SD 57501
605/773-3656

Tennessee
Commission on Aging
706 Church Street, Suite 201
Nashville, TN 37243
615/741-2056

Texas
Department on Aging
P.O. Box 12786 Capitol Station
1949 IH 35 South
Austin, TX 78741
512/444-2727

Utah
Division of Aging and Adult
    Services
Department of Social Services
120 North–200 West
Box 45500
Salt Lake City, UT 84145
801/538-3910

Vermont
Aging and Disabilities
103 South Main Street
Waterbury, VT 05676
802/241-2400

Virginia
Department for the Aging
700 Center, 10th floor
700 East Franklin Street
Richmond, VA 23219
804/225-2271

Washington
Aging and Adult Services
Administration Department of
Social and Health Services
P.O. Box 45050
Olympia, WA 98504
206/586-3768

West Virginia
Commission on Aging
Holly Grove–State Capitol
Charleston, WV 25305
304/348-3317

Wisconsin
Bureau of Aging
Division of Community Services
217 South Hamilton Street,
    Suite 300
Madison, WI 53707
608/266-2536

Wyoming
Commission on Aging
Hathaway Building, Room 139
Cheyenne, WY 82002
307/777-7986

Sources and Resources

CHAPTER 1

Publications

Aging in America: Trends and Projections. Washington, DC: Senate Special Committee on Aging, American Association of Retired Persons, Federal Council on the Aging, and U.S. Administration on Aging, 1991.

Andresky, J. "When I'm 65." *Financial World*, January 10, 1989: 40.

Barnes, R. "Planning For Your Golden Years." *Black Enterprise*, April 1990: 64.

"Changes in Family Finances 1983 to 1989." *Federal Reserve Bulletin* Vol. 78, No. 1 (January 1992).

Dychtwald, K. *Age Wave*. New York: Bantam, 1990.

Eargle, J. "Household Wealth and Asset Ownership: 1988." Washington, DC: U.S. Commerce Department, Bureau of the Census, 1988.

"Employee Benefits Survey." Washington, DC: U.S. Department of Labor, Bureau of Labor Statistics.

Facts About Financial Planners. Washington, DC: American Association of Retired Persons, 1990.

Fierman, J. "How Secure Is Your Nest Egg?" *Fortune*, August 12, 1991: 50.

Fritz, M. "Marriage of Convenience." *Forbes*, October 15, 1990: 224.

Gottschalk, E., Jr. "CPAs Find Investment Role Too Taxing." *Wall Street Journal*, January 16, 1991: C1.

Hayes, C. "Women and Retirement: The Harsh Realities." *Best's Review*, July 1991: 71.

"How to Afford Retirement." *U.S. News & World Report*, August 14, 1989: 55.

"How to Build Your Future." *U.S. News & World Report*, July 30, 1990: 54.

Investment Advisers Act of 1940. Washington, DC: U.S. Securities and Exchange Commission, 1991.

Kirkpatrick, D. "Will You be Able to Retire?" *Fortune*, July 31, 1989: 56.

Koren, E. F. *Estate & Personal Financial Planning*, Deerfield, IL: Calaghan & Co., 1992.

Lavine, A. "How to Retire with Financial Security." *Consumers Digest*, March/April 1991: 54.

Luciano, L., and Fenner, E. "Having to Play Catch-Up." *Money*, June 1991: 101.

Luxenberg, S. "Choosing a Financial Planner." *New Choices*, July/August 1991: 96.

Managing Your Personal Finances, Coping with Change. Washington, DC: U.S.

Department of Agriculture, Extension Service, 1986.

Merrill, Lynch, Pierce, Fenner & Smith, Inc. "The Future Doesn't Add Up." 1991.

"Money Guide Round Table." *U.S. News and World Report*, July 15, 1991: 76.

Morgenson, G. "Meaningless Label." *Forbes*, June 25, 1990: 254.

NASAA State-by-State Summary: Recent Financial Planning– Related Enforcement Developments. North American Securities Administrators Association, 1985.

Raphaelson, E., and Raphaelson West, C. *How To Be Your Own Financial Planner*. Glenview, IL: Scott Foresman, 1990.

Regan, J. J. *Tax, Estate, & Financial Planning for the Elderly*. New York: Matthew Bender/Times Mirror Books, 1991.

Rock, A. "Financial Advice You Can Trust." *Money*, November 1989: 80.

Ruhm, C. "Why Older Americans Stop Working." *The Gerontologist* Vol. 29, No. 3 June 1989: 294.

Salwen, K. "The SEC Proposes Tightening Reins on 17,000 Advisers." *Wall Street Journal*, January 24, 1991: C1.

Schultz, E. "Financial Planners Blur Their Price Tags." *Wall Street Journal*, May 29, 1991: C1.

————. "Is a Financial Planner Really Necessary?" *Wall Street Journal*, May 13, 1991: C1.

————. "Retirement Planners Try to Scare Up Business." *Wall Street Journal*, June 22, 1992: C1.

Shilling, D. "Retirement Early, Normal, Late or Never." *Sylvia Porter's Personal Finance*, April 1989: 66.

Slater, K. "Conflict Issues Cloud Financial Planning." *Wall Street Journal*, March 22, 1990: C1.

Sloane, L. "Accountants as Financial Planners." *New York Times*, January 19,1991: A54.

Veninga, R. L. *The Renaissance Years*. Boston: Little, Brown, 1991.

Watterson, T. "Regulating Financial Planners." *Boston Globe*, July 26, 1990: 33.

Companies / Organizations / Government

The American College, Bryn Mawr, PA

American Institute of Certified Public Accountants, Personal Financial Planning Division, New York, NY

Armstrong, Welch & MacIntyre, Inc., Washington, DC

Cook & Franke, Milwaukee, WI, Thomas Draught, attorney

Institute of Certified Financial Planners, Denver, CO

International Association for Financial Planning, Atlanta, GA

International Board of Standards and Practices for Certified Financial Planners, Inc., Denver, CO

Malgoire Drucker, Inc., Personal Financial Advisors, Bethesda, MD

National Association of Personal Financial Advisors, Buffalo Grove, IL

New Mexico (state) Regulation & Licensing Department, Securities Division, Albuquerque, NM

North American Securities Administrators Association, Inc., Washington, DC

T. Rowe Price Investment Services, Inc., Baltimore, MD

U.S. Securities and Exchange Commission, Office of Filings, Information and Consumer Services, Office of Disclosure, Washington, DC

Westbrook Financial Advisors, Inc., Watchung, NJ

William M. Mercer, Inc. Compensation and Benefits Consultants, Louisville, KY

CHAPTER 2

Publications

Asinof, L. "Taking Early Profits on Bonds May Add Up to Losses." *Wall Street Journal,* February 13, 1992: C1.

Bary, A. "Ginnie, Fannie and Freddie." *Barron's,* May 5, 1991: 24.

Clements, J. "How to Bet on Recovery With Mutual Funds." *Wall Street Journal,* January 27, 1992: C1.

———. "Sooner Is Better When Starting With Funds." *Wall Street Journal,* September 25, 1991: C1.

———. "Too Many Bonds Can Squeeze Retiree Income." *Wall Street Journal,* September 27, 1991: C1.

———. "Why It's Risky Not to Invest More in Stocks." *Wall Street Journal,* February 11, 1992: C1.

Consumers' Financial Guide. Washington, DC: U.S. Securities and Exchange Commission, 1992.

CreditReview: Mutual Funds, Bond Funds. New York: Standard & Poor's, June 1991.

Donnelly, B. "CMOs May Promise Big Fat Yields, But Investors Should Know the Risks." *Wall Street Journal,* November 12, 1991: C1.

———. "Weighing Muni Bonds Vs. Treasurys," *Wall Street Journal,* January 27, 1992: C1.

Droms, William G., ed. Homewood, IL: Dow Jones Irwin, 1986.

Fact Book For The Year 1992. New York: New York Stock Exchange, 1992.

Faltermayer, E. "How to Juice Up Your Retirement Income." *Fortune,* November 4, 1991: 28.

"Financial Planning." *Fortune 1992 Investor's Guide,* January 1992.

Fixed Income Investments, A Personal Seminar. New York: New York Institute of Finance, 1989.

Ginnie Mae Investment Facts. Washington, DC: U.S. Department of Housing and Urban Development, Government National Mortgage Association, 1991.

Gottschalk, E., Jr. "Franchise Stocks May Be Worth the Premium for the Risk Averse." *Wall Street Journal,* October 9, 1991: C1.

Gould, C. "The Investor's Typical Mistakes." *New York Times,* September 8, 1991: F16.

Graham, B. *The Intelligent Investor.* New York: Harper & Row, 1973.

Halverson, G. "Choosing the Right Certificates." *Christian Science Monitor,* April 12, 1989: 9.

Jasen, G., and Gottschalk, E., Jr. "Low Rates Prompt Individual Investors to Rethink Strategies." *Wall Street Journal,* February 5, 1991: A1.

Levine, Sumner N., ed. *The 1992 Business One Irwin Business and Investment Almanac.* Homewood, IL: Business One Irwin, 1992.

Loeb, M. *Marshall Loeb's 1992 Money Guide.* Boston: Little Brown, 1992.

Lowenstein, R., and Donnelly, B. "Hot IPOs Best Played by Those With Cool Heads." *Wall Street Journal,* May 10, 1991: C1.

Mendes, J. "Getting the Most From Brokers." *Fortune's 1992 Investor's Guide,* January 1992: 183.

Meyer, M. "The Best Bonds." *Money,* November 1991: 112.

Mitchell, C., and Torres, C. "Rushing to Buy Convertibles? Slow Down." *Wall Street Journal,* January 29, 1992: C1.

"New Penny Stock Cold Calling Rule." *Consumers' Research,* November 1990: 30.

1993–94 Directory of Mutual Funds. Washington, DC: Investment Company Institute, 1993.

Quinn, J. *Making the Most of Your Money.* New York: Simon & Schuster, 1991.

Risky Investments. Santa Fe, New Mexico: State of New Mexico, Regulation and Licensing Department, Securities Division.

Rosen, J. "Raising Returns With Less Risk." *New York Times,* May 18, 1991: A36.

Schultz, E. "Climbing High With Discount Brokers." *Fortune 1990 Investor's Guide,* January 1990: 219.

———. "Failing to Consider Commission Can Be Costly Error." *Wall Street Journal,* June 25, 1991: C1.

———. "Reaching for Higher Yields With Bond Funds." *Wall Street Journal,* August 6, 1991: C1.

Serwer, A. "Stocks, Bonds, or Cash?" *Fortune,* June 18, 1990: 27.

Shareownership 1990. New York: New York Stock Exchange.

Siegel, J., and Shim, J. *Accounting Handbook*. New York: Barron's, 1990.

Slater, K. "Time For Short-Term Bond Funds Overlooked, May Be Here." *Wall Street Journal,* April 19, 1990: C1.

Srodes, J. "New Dollars For Scholars." *Financial World,* February 4, 1991: 20.

Thompson, T. "Time For Another Date With Ginnie Mae?" *U.S. News & World Report,* October 9, 1989: 77.

Veale, Stuart R., ed. *Stocks, Bonds, Options Futures.* New York Institute of Finance. New York: Prentice-Hall, 1987.

Weberman, B. "Back to Basics." *Forbes,* May 1, 1989: 405.

———. "Pitfalls in GNMAs." *Forbes,* July 9, 1990: 113.

What Every Investor Should Know. Washington, DC: U.S. Securities and Exchange Commission, 1990.

"What Type of Investor Are You?" *Donoghue's Moneyletter,* 1990.

"Will You Save Money With a Discount Broker?" Reprinted from "Investor Advisory: Discount Brokers," Better Business Bureau of Metropolitan New York. *Consumers' Research,* March 1989.

Yoshihashi, P., and Pae, P. "A Retirement Haven Struggles With Curse of Low Interest Rates." *Wall Street Journal,* January 29, 1992: A1.

Companies / Organizations / Government

Dennis M. Gurtz and Associates, Washington, DC

The Donoghue Organization, Inc., Holliston, MA

Federal Deposit Insurance Corporation, Washington, DC

Federal Home Loan Mortgage Association, Washington, DC

Federal National Mortgage Association, Washington, DC

Government National Mortgage Association, Washington, DC

Investment Company Institute, Washington, DC

National Association of Securities Dealers, Washington, DC

New York Stock Exchange, Inc., Washington, DC

North American States Securities Agencies, Washington, DC

Securities and Exchange Commission, Washington, DC

Securities Investor Protection Corporation, Washington, DC

Standard & Poor's Ratings Group, New York, NY

Student Loan Marketing Association, Washington, DC

U.S. Department of the Treasury, Bureau of Public Debt, Washington, DC

U.S. Savings Bonds Division, Department of the Treasury, Washington, DC

Veribanc, Inc., Wakefield, MA

CHAPTER 3

Publications

Asinof, L. "If Ax Falls, Know Your Benefits, Rights, and Don't Forget the Art of Negotiation." *Wall Street Journal,* January 17, 1992: C1.

Bucci, M. "Contributions to Savings and Thrift Plans." *Monthly Labor Review,* November 1990: 28.

Castro, J. "Is Your Pension Safe?" *Time,* June 3, 1991: 42.

Crooks, L. "Women and Pensions: Inequities for Older Women." *Vital Speeches of the Day,* February 15, 1991: 283.

Delfico, J. "Defined Benefit Pensions: Hidden Liabilities From Underfunded Plans." *General Accounting Office Testimony.* Washington, DC: Subcommittee on Employment and Housing, October 1991.

Deutschman, A. "The Great Pension Robbery." *Fortune,* January 13, 1992: 76.

EBRI Databook on Employee Benefits. Washington, DC: Employee Benefit Research Institute, 1992.

Emering, E. "Defined Benefits Are in Jeopardy." *Personnel Journal,* April 1991: 104.

Employer's Pension Guide. Washington, DC: U.S. Department of Labor, Pension and Welfare Benefits Administration.

Evans, M. "Nest-Egg Alert!" *GQ,* October 1991: 158.

Fundamentals of Employee Benefit Programs. Washington, DC: Employee Benefit Research Institute, 1990.

Gottlich, V. *Lay Person's Guide to Private Employer-Sponsored Health and Pension Benefits After Retirement.* Washington, DC: National Senior Citizens Law Center, October 1989.

Gould, C. "Packing Up Retirement Funds." *New York Times,* November 17, 1991: C16.

Gross, A. "Survivor Benefit Election: Not as Tough as You Think." *Government Executive,* September 1991: 44.

Guide to Summary Plan Description Requirements. Washington, DC: U.S. Department of Labor, Pension and Welfare Benefits Administration, 1991.

A Guide to Understanding Your Pension Plan. Washington, DC: Pension Rights Center and American Association of Retired Persons, 1989.

Hughes, W. "Your Pension: Danger Ahead?" *USA Today,* July 1991: 40.

Kirkpatrick, D. "Retirement: Save Until It's Painful." *Fortune,* February 25, 1991: 121.

Kleiman, C. "Firms Shifting Retirement Planning, Risk to Workers." *Chicago Tribune,* January 19, 1992: 8

Kobliner, B. "Avoiding a Pension Plan Rip-Off." *Money,* November 1991: 96.

———. "Seeding, Feeding and Weeding Your IRA." *Money,* March 1990: 138.

Kosnett, J. "Time to Wake up Your IRA." *Kiplinger's Personal Finance Magazine,* October 1991: 53.

Leonard, F., and Loeb, L. "Heading for Hardship: The Future of Older Women in America." *USA Today,* January 1992: 19.

Loomis, C. "The Hidden Risks in Your 401(k)." *Fortune,* February 12, 1990: 107.

Morgan, J. "More Women Delaying Retirement, Even if Husbands Don't." *Washington Post,* December 15, 1991.

Nasar, S. "Pensions Covering Lowering Percentage of U.S. Work Force." *New York Times,* April 13, 1991: A1.

Pae, P., and Jasen, G. "Where to Find Lower Credit Card Rates." *Wall Street Journal,* November 14, 1991: C1.

Pension and Annuity Income. Washington, DC: Internal Revenue Service, 1991.

Quinn, J. "Taking Stock of 401(k)s." *Washington Post,* June 9, 1991: H3.

Reporting and Disclosure Guide for Employee Benefit Plans. Washington, DC: U.S. Department of Labor, Pension and Welfare Benefits Administration, 1992.

Retirement Plans for the Self-Employed. Washington, DC: Internal Revenue Service, 1991.

Rowland, M. "How Secure Is Your Pension." *New Choices,* September 1991: 40.

———. "Sweeteners in Lieu of More Pay." *New York Times,* December 29, 1991: C16.

———. "When Facing Retirement at 50." *New York Times,* March 15, 1992.

Santelmann, N. "The Long Strings on Pension Plans." *Forbes,* May 1, 1989: 145.

Seburn, P. "Evolution of Employer-Provided Defined Benefit Pensions." *Monthly Labor Review,* December 1991: 16.

Sege, I. "Old Age Seen Erasing Any Gains for Women." *Boston Globe,* April 10, 1990: 1.

Smith, C. "Investor Control of Retirement Funds Is Rising." *Wall Street Journal,* January 31, 1992: B4.

"Spread the Risk." *Wall Street Journal,* January 7, 1991: A1.

Stern, L. "Ten Basics About Keogh and SEP-IRA Retirement Plans." *Home Office Computing,* February 1991: 26.

Thomas, R. "Saving: Not the American Way." *Newsweek,* January 8, 1990: 44.

Thompson, T. "Watchdogging Your Pension." *U.S. News & World Report,* July 30, 1990: 64.

Topolnicki, D. "What You Should Know If Your Pension Plan Gets Shut Down." *Money,* June 1989: 187.

Watterson, T. "How $30 a Week Becomes $258,000 by

Retirement." *Boston Globe,* March 14, 1991: 60.

————. "Use a Keogh Account to Cut Tax Bill the Easy Way." *Boston Globe,* April 1, 1991: 35.

————. "When Early IRA Withdrawals Aren't Penalized." *Boston Globe,* December 23, 1991.

What You Should Know About the Pension Law. Washington, DC: U.S. Department of Labor, Pension and Welfare Benefits Administration, May 1988.

White, J. "As ESOPs Become Victims of 90s Bankruptcies, Workers Are Watching Their Nest Eggs Vanish." *Wall Street Journal,* January 25, 1991: C1.

Wiatrowski, W. "New Survey Data on Pension Benefits." *Monthly Labor Review,* August 1991: 8.

————. "Supplementing Retirement Until Social Security Begins." *Monthly Labor Review,* February 1990: 25.

Wilcox, D. "Household Spending and Saving: Measure, Trends, and Analysis." *Federal Reserve Bulletin,* January 1991: 1.

Willis, C. "How To Protect Your Retirement Money." *Money,* November 1991: 90.

A Woman's Guide to Pension Rights. Washington, DC: American Association of Retired Persons.

Woolley, S. "Pension Plans Pay Off for Small Businesses, Too." *Business Week,* January 29, 1990: 98.

Companies / Government / Organizations

American Association of Retired Persons, Washington, DC

Bankcard Holders of America, Herndon, VA

Citibank Mastercard and Visa, Consumer Education, New York, NY

Employee Benefit Research Institute, Washington, DC

Fidelity Investments Retirement Products, Boston, MA

Hewitt Associates, Consultants and Actuaries, Lincolnshire, IL

MassMutual, Pension Management, Springfield, MA

National Center for Employee Ownership, Oakland, CA

National Coalition on Older Women's Issues, Washington, DC

National Senior Citizens Law Center, Washington, DC

Pension Benefit Guaranty Corporation, Public Affairs, Washington, DC

Pension Rights Center, Washington, DC

Pension and Welfare Benefits Administration, U.S. Department of Labor, Washington, DC

The Vanguard Group of Investment Companies, Valley Forge, PA

The Wyatt Company, Washington, DC

CHAPTER 4
Publications

Anthony, J. "Retirement and Real Estate." *Consumers Digest,* March/April 1991: 62.

Berg, E. "The Bad Boy of Insurance Ratings." *New York Times,* January 5, 1992.

Building Your Future with Annuities: A Consumer's Guide. Washington, DC: U.S. Department of Agriculture, Fidelity Investments Insurance and Annuity Group, 1991.

Canellos, P., and Chafetz, G. "Home Equity Lenders Under Fire Across US." *Boston Globe,* May 26, 1991: A1.

Canner, G., Luckette, C., and Durkin, T. "Mortgage Refinancing." *Federal Reserve Bulletin* Vol. 76, No. 8 (August 1990): 604.

Chambliss, L. "A Buyer's Guide to REITs." *Financial World,* June 13, 1989: 81.

Delfico, J. "Private Pensions: Risks to Retirees Posed by Insurance Annuities." Washington, DC: Testimony Before the Select Committee on Aging, April 1991.

Dorning, M. "Home Equity a Ready Source of Money—and Debt." *Chicago Tribune,* February 24, 1991: 19.

Evans, M. "Oops! We Added Wrong . . ." *GQ,* August 1991: 102.

Fink, R. "Rollup Roundup." *Financial World,* March 31, 1992: 100.

Giese, W. "Vacation Property For 40 Cents on the Dollar." *Changing Times,* August 1990: 41.

Gottschalk, E., Jr. "Life Insurance Trusts Become Popular Way to Transfer Wealth." *Wall Street Journal,* November 6, 1991: C1.

Harney, K. "Bloom is Back on the Adjustable Rate Mortgage." *Washington Post,* April 28, 1990: F20.

Home-Made Money: Consumer's Guide to Home Equity Conversion. Washington, DC: American Association of Retired Persons, July 1991.

How To Buy Real Estate. Jacksonville, FL: Resolution Trust Corporation Sales Center, 1992.

"Is It Time to Refinance Your Mortgage?" *Home Mechanix,* June 1991: 10.

Jasen, G. "Fixed-Rate Mortgages May Be No Bargain." *Wall Street Journal,* September 9, 1991: C1.

Jereski, L., Light, L., and Kelly, K. "Real Estate Partnerships Are Sinking, With No Lifeboats in Sight." *Business Week,* July 3, 1989: 74.

Kosnett, J. "Annuities: What's in 'Em For You?" *Changing Times,* February 1990: 65.

Lalli, F. "The Empty Promise of Annuities." *Money,* April 1992: 7.

Lehman, H. "The Loan Arrangers: Creating Financing." *Washington Post,* March 17, 1990: F1.

Light, L., and Farrell, C. "Are You Really Insured?" *Business Week,* May 5, 1991: 42.

McCleary, E. "Are Timeshare Vacations Worth the Money?" *Consumers Digest,* November/ December 1991: 22.

Miller, A., et al. "Time to Refinance?" *Newsweek,* September 30, 1991: 44.

O'Donnell, A. "Memorandum to Republican Members of the Select Committee on Aging Re Subcommittee Hearings on Annuities." Washington, DC: U.S. House of Representatives, April 1991.

Options for Elderly Homeowners: A Guide to Reverse Mortgages and Their Alternatives. Washington, DC: U.S. Department of Housing and Urban Development, 1989.

O'Reilly, B. "How To Make The Most of Annuities." *Fortune 1992 Investor's Guide,* January 1990: 109.

Paulson, M. "What If You Couldn't Work Anymore?" *Changing Times,* August 1990: 53.

Pension and Annuity Income. Washington, DC: Internal Revenue Service, 1991.

Peterson, I. "Most Buyers Are Choosing Fixed-Rate Mortgages." *New York Times,* September 9, 1990: 10.

Product Report: Life Insurance for Older Adults. Washington, DC: American Association of Retired Persons, 1990.

Quinn, J. "The Boom in Annuities." *Newsweek,* March 9, 1992: 57.

Rappaport, E. *Life Insurer Insolvency.* Washington, DC: Congressional Research Service, February 1992.

Rock, A. "Top Yields and Prospects of Gains Make REITs Right." *Money,* June 1989: 159.

Rowland, M. "Benefiting From Reverse Equity." *New York Times,* October 13, 1991.

———. "Changing the Insurance Game." *New York Times,* June 10, 1990: 16.

———. "Preparing for Disability." *New York Times,* April 29, 1990: C17.

Schiffres, M. "Winning Big With Variable Annuities." *Kiplinger's Personal Finance Magazine,* April 1992: 49.

Schultz, E. "An Annuity by Any Other Name May Sell Better, Some Firms Hope." *Wall Street Journal,* February 27, 1991: C1.

———. "Help For Confused Insurance Purchasers." *Wall Street Journal,* September 11, 1991: C1.

———. "Real Estate Annuity: Mutant Investment With Pitfalls." *Wall Street Journal,* February 22, 1990: C1.

———. "Variable Annuities Offer High Yields, A Smaller Tax

Bite and Pitfalls, Too.'' *Wall Street Journal,* December 11, 1992: C1.

———and Slater, K. "Buyers Guide: This May be Last Chance to Purchase Annuities But Use Caution." *Wall Street Journal,* February 5, 1992.

Segal, T. "Steady Income, Low Risk. This Can't Be Real Estate." *Business Week,* May 1, 1989: 142.

———. "When Limited Partnerships Get Lumped Together." *Business Week,* February 11, 1991: 88.

Sichelman, L. "Refinancing For Lower Interest." *Homeowner,* June 1991: 10.

Simmons, M., and Thompson, C. "Life Insurance Benefits for Retired Workers." *Monthly Labor Review,* September 1990: 17.

Slater, K. "Shop Around for a Fatter Annuity Payoff." *Wall Street Journal,* April 1990: C1.

———. "Stockbrokers Dress Up Life Insurance for New Pitch." *Wall Street Journal,* February 2, 1989: C1.

Sloane, L. "Buying Life Insurance: Where to Start." *New York Times,* March 2, 1991: A48.

Updegrave, W. "Cashing In On Your Big Blue Chip." *Money Guide,* Fall 1989: 83.

———. "Getting Past the Hype of Annuities." *Money,* September 1991: 118.

VA-Guaranteed Home Loans for Veterans. Washington, DC:

Veterans Benefits Administration, 1989.

Vinocur, B. "Billions Down the Drain." *Barron's,* September 4, 1989: 17.

Watterson, T. "On The Rocks With Your Life Insurer." *Boston Globe,* July 18, 1991: 47.

Companies / Organizations / Government

A.M. Best Company, Oldwick, NJ

American Association of Retired Persons, Consumer Affairs, Washington, DC

American Council of Life Insurance, Washington, DC

Annuity & Life Insurance Shopper, Englishtown, NJ

Comparative Annuity Reports, Albuquerque, NM

Fidelty Investments, Boston, MA

House of Representatives Select Committee on Aging, Washington, DC

Insurance Information, Inc., South Dennis, MA

Life Insurance Advisers Association, W. Bloomfield, MI

Lipper Analytical Services, New York, NY

Merrill Lynch, Life/Health Insurance Services, Plainsboro, NJ

Mortgage Bankers Association of America, Washington, DC

National Association of Life Underwriters, Washington, DC

National Association of Real Estate Investment Trusts, Inc., Washington, DC

National Consumer Law Center, Boston, MA

National Partnership Exchange, Tampa, FL

Resolution Trust Corporation, Washington, DC

Sills & Brodsky, Washington, DC

SelectQuote Insurance Services, San Francisco, CA

U.S. Senate Select Committee on Aging, Washington, DC

Standard & Poor's Insurance Rating Services, New York, NY

The Stanger Report, Shrewsbury, NJ

U.S. Department of Housing and Urban Affairs, Federal Housing Administration, Washington, DC

U.S. General Accounting Office (Testimony), Washington, DC

Weiss Research, Inc., West Palm Beach, FL

CHAPTER 5

Publications

Brown, D. "Social Security." *New Choices,* April 1991: 84.

Buying Your Medigap Policy. 1992 Edition. Washington, DC: National Committee to Preserve Social Security and Medicare, 1992.

"Con Games That Target the Elderly." *Consumers' Research,* September, 1991: 30

Conklin, J. "Medicare Made Easy." *New Choices,* September 1991: 37.

Detlefs, D., and Myers, R. *1992 Medicare.* Louisville, KY: William M. Mercer, 1991.

——. *1992 Mercer Guide to Social Security & Medicare.* Louisville, KY: William M. Mercer, December 1991.

——. *1992 Social Security and Medicare, A Plan Administrator's Reference.* Louisville, KY: William M. Mercer, 1991.

Dietz, J. "Know Your Social Security Rights." *Boston Globe,* February 6, 1991: 32.

Fast Facts & Figures About Social Security. Washington, DC: U.S. Department of Health and Human Services, Social Security Administration, 1990.

Hardy, D., and Hardy, C. *Social Insecurity: The Crisis in America's Social Security System and How to Plan Now for Your Own Financial Survival.* New York: Villard Books, 1991.

Hodge, M., and Blyskal, J. "Coping With Medicare." *New Choices,* January 1990: 56.

How Work Affects Your Social Security Benefits. Washington, DC: Social Security Administration, 1991.

"Inside Social Security." *Consumer Reports,* June 1991: 474.

Medicare Employer Health Plans 1991. Washington, DC: Department of Health and Human Services, Health Care Financing Administration, 1991.

The Medicare 1992 Handbook. Washington, DC: U.S. Department of Health and Human Services, Health Care Financing Administration, 1992.

Medicare Q & A. Washington, DC: U.S. Department of Health and Human Services, Health Care Financing Administration, 1991.

An NCSC Guide to Social Security for Women. Washington, DC: National Council of Senior Citizens.

"New Insurance Rules Regarding Medigap Insurance." *Consumers' Research,* January 1991.

"The New Medigap Plans." *Consumer Reports,* September 1991: 616.

1991 NTUF Chartbook, Entitlements and the Aging of America. Washington, DC: National Taxpayers Union Foundation, 1990.

1992 Annual Report of the Board of Trustees of the Federal Old-Age and Survivors Insurance Trust Fund. Washington, DC: Committee on Ways and Means, 1992.

1992 Guide to Health Insurance For People With Medicare. Washington, DC: National Association of Insurance Commissioners and Health Care Financing Administration, U.S. Department of Health and Human Services, 1992.

Peak, R. "Despite 1991 Law, Many on Medicare Are Overcharged." *New York Times,* February 29, 1992: A1.

"Perils of Procrastination." *Changing Times,* June 1989: 94.

Quinn, J. "Getting Your Due From Social Security." *Washington Post,* June 30, 1991: H3.

Retirement. Washington, DC: U.S. Department of Health and Human Services, Social Security Administration, 1991.

Schaeffer, C. "Help With Medicare Forms." *Changing Times,* July 1989: 76.

Sing, B. "How to Avoid Getting Stung on Medigap Policy." *Los Angeles Times,* May 6, 1990: D4.

Sloane, L. "Going Beyond Social Security." *New York Times,* March 9, 1991: 28.

Smith, L. "The Tyranny of America's Old." *Fortune,* January 13, 1992: 67.

Terrell, P. "Social Security: The Search For Fairness." *Congressional Quarterly,* April 5, 1991: 190.

Tritch, T. "Get Yourself a Social Security Checkup." *Money,* April 1990: 21.

Understanding Social Security. Washington, DC: U.S. Department of Health and Human Services, Social Security Administration, 1992.

Walsh, J. "Bridging Those Medicare Gaps." *Barron's,* July 30, 1990: 28.

Wasik, J. "No Miracle Medigap." *Barron's,* January 22, 1990: 38.

When You Get Social Security Retirement Or Survivors Benefits. Washington, DC: U.S. Department of Health and Human Services, Social Security Administration, 1991.

Wilcox, M. "Fundamentals." *Changing Times,* January 1991: 22.

Companies/Organizations/Government

National Committee to Preserve Social Security and Medicare, Washington, DC

National Council of Senior Citizens, Washington, DC

Social Security Administration, Press Office, Baltimore, MD

William M. Mercer, Inc., Louisville, KY

CHAPTER 6
Publications

Barrett, W. "IBM, Esq." *Forbes,* July 22, 1991: 308.

Birenbaum, A. "The Right To Die in America." *USA Today,* January 1992: 28.

Bove, A. *The Complete Book of Wills and Estates.* New York: Henry Holt, 1989.

———. "Uncoordinated Estate Plan Just Doesn't Make the Right Moves." *Boston Globe,* October 31, 1991: 58.

Budish, A. "The Multipurpose Trust." *Modern Maturity,* August/September 1991: 44.

Bulkeley, W. "Software Programs Help Non-Lawyers Prepare Wills, Other Legal Documents." *Wall Street Journal,* July 22, 1991: B1.

A Consumer's Guide to Probate. Washington, DC: American Association of Retired Persons, 1989.

Davies, P. "Where There's a Will." *Mpls/St. Paul,* March 1991: 46.

"Death Erases Taxes." *Changing Times,* November 1990: 98.

Dunn, D. "First Things First: A Last Will and Testament." *Business Week,* December 9, 1991: 108.

Ellentuck, A. "Insurance Trusts." *Nation's Business,* December 1991: 51.

Estate Planning: A Guide for the Days After a Loved One Dies. Hartford, CT: Aetna Insurance Company, 1989.

Faltermayer, E. "The (Financially) Perfect Death." *Fortune,* February 25, 1991: 131.

Fisher, A. "Keeping Down Estate Taxes." *Fortune 1990 Investor's Guide* (Fall 1989): 189.

Gottschalk, E., Jr. "Beware of Tax Traps While Giving Away Assets." *Wall Street Journal,* September 17, 1991: C1.

"Help With Probate." *Changing Times,* June 1990: 104.

Jasen, G. "Give It Away While You're Alive . . . Just Don't Give 'Til It Hurts." *Wall Street Journal,* April 22, 1991: C1.

Klug, M. *Living Trusts and Wills.* Washington, DC: American Association of Retired Persons, 1991.

Lamaute, D. "Where There's a Will." *Black Enterprise,* June 1990: 263.

Lavine, A. "Minimizing Estate and Gift Taxes." *Financial World,* December 12, 1990: 66.

Life and Death Choices. Gloucester, VA: National Resource Center for Consumers of Legal Services.

Murphy, C. "Great Expectations." *Atlantic,* December 1990: 24.

Myers, W., Jr. "Tend Your Estate Before You Buy the Farm." *Wall Street Journal,* June 10, 1991: A10.

The Next Step. State Farm Insurance Companies.

Nigito, D. *Avoiding the Estate Tax Trap.* Chicago: Contemporary Books, 1991.

Okie, S. "Living Will No Assurance Patient's Wishes Will be Followed, Study Finds." *Washington Post,* March 28, 1991: A8.

"Protection for Your Heirs When You're Terminally Ill." *Nation's Business,* October 1990: 66.

Ravo, N. "A Windfall Nears in Inheritances From the Richest Generation." *New York Times,* July 22, 1990: 4.

Roha, R. "Seven Reasons to Change Your Will." *Kiplinger's Personal Finance Magazine,* February 1992: 61.

Rosch, W. "Legal Software Offers Help With Preparing Wills and Other Documents." *PC Magazine,* August 1990: 537.

Rosenthal, E. "Filling the Gap Where a Living Will Won't Do." *New York Times,* January 17, 1991.

Rowland, M. "Estates: Foiling the Tax Man." *New York Times,* August 12, 1990.

Schultz, E. "In Preparing for Your Heirs, A Will Isn't Sole Consideration." *Wall Street Journal,* January 2, 1991: C1.

Significant Features of Fiscal Federalism, Budget Processes and Tax Systems. Washington, DC: Advisory Commission on Intergovernmental Relations, February 1993.

Silver, M. "Confronting the Death of a Parent." *U.S. News & World Report,* May 22, 1989: 74.

Simon, R. "How to Talk to Your Parents About Money." *Money,* December 1991: 145.

Tellalian, C., and Rosen, W. *Retirement and Estate Planning Handbook.* Grants Pass, OR: Oasis Press/PSI Research, 1991.

Tritch, T. "Tax-Cutting Ways to Give To Your Kids." *Money,* November 1991: 129.

What Type of Will is Best for You? Hartford, CT: Aetna Life

Insurance and Annuity Company, 1990.

Wiener, L. "Tapping the Gifts of a Lifetime." *U.S. News & World Report,* July 30, 1990: 67.

"Will Builder." *Compute,* September 1991: 130.

Zabel, W. "Thy Will Be Done?" *Town & Country,* May 1991: 123, June 1991: 111.

Companies /Organizations / Government

Aetna Life Insurance Company, Hartford, CT

American Association of Retired Persons, Washington, DC

Cook & Franke, Milwaukee, WI

Council on Foundations, Washington, DC

National Academy of Elder Law Attorneys, Inc., Tucson, AZ

National Funeral Directors Association, Milwaukee, WI

National Resource Center for Consumers of Legal Services, Gloucester, VA

U.S. Advisory Commission on Intergovernmental Relations, Washington, DC

CHAPTER 7

Publications

Crenshaw, A. "Calculating Mutual Fund Gains, Losses." *Washington Post,* March 8, 1992: H3.

————. "Good Financial Records Pay Economic Dividends." *Washington Post,* January 12, 1992: H3.

Dingle, D. "How To Cut All of Your Taxes." *Money,* January 1992: 68.

Donnelly, B. "Beware Tax Consequences of Mutual Funds." *Wall Street Journal,* February 20, 1992: C1.

Faltermayer, E. "Ready to Retire: Decisions Galore." *Fortune,* Fall 1991: 137.

"Federal Individual Income Tax (Average and Marginal Tax Rates), Selected Income Groups and Years, 1954–1990." *Fiscal Federalism.* Washington, DC: Advisory Commission on Intergovernmental Relations, 1991.

Gottschalk, E., Jr. "Across the Country, Increased State Levies Hit Incomes Harder." *Wall Street Journal,* November 20, 1991: C1.

————. "Retiree's Woe: Tax Man Haunts Your Place in the Sun." *Wall Street Journal,* April 17, 1992: C1.

Harris, M. "Is a Nondeductible IRA Worth the Record-Keeping Hassles? *Money,* December 1991: 41.

Herman, T. "After the Gain Comes the Taxing Pain of Figuring Your Mutual-Fund Return." *Wall Street Journal,* February 26, 1992: C1.

Investment Income and Expenses. Washington, DC: Internal Revenue Service, 1991.

Jasen, G. "A Secure Retirement Takes Long Years of Sound Planning, Even After It Begins." *Wall Street Journal,* May 29, 1992: C1.

Lasser, J. K. *J. K. Lasser's Your Income Tax 1992.* New York: Prentice-Hall, 1991.

Leong, G. *Special Report: State Rates and Collections, Fiscal Year 1990.* Washington, DC: Tax Foundation, 1991.

Lohse, D. "Where Retirees Save —And Where They Get Whacked." *Money,* July 1992: 146.

Nastas, G., and Moore, S. *A Consumer's Guide to Taxes: How Much Do You Really Pay in Taxes?* Washington, DC: CATO Institute, April 1992.

Pension and Annuity Income. Washington, DC: Internal Revenue Service, 1991.

"Property Tax Rates, Selected Cities, 1990." *Fiscal Federalism.* Washington, DC: Advisory Commission on Inter-governmental Relations, 1992.

Relocation Tax Guide: State Tax Information for Relocation Decisions. Washington, DC: American Association of Retired Persons, 1991.

Retirement Plans for the Self-Employed. Washington, DC: Internal Revenue Service, 1991.

Robbins, A., and Robbins, G. "Will IRA's Pay Off in the End?" *Consumers' Research,* January 1990: 29.

Rowland, M. "The Lump-Sum Pension Payout." *New Choices,* September 1990: 62.

Saunders, L. "Death, Taxes, and IRAs." *Forbes,* November 12, 1990: 132.

Schultz, E. "Pension Payouts Will Face a New Tax Trap." *Wall Street Journal,* July 13, 1992: C1.

Significant Features of Fiscal Federalism, Budget Processes and Tax Systems. Washington, DC: Advisory Commission on Intergovernmental Relations, 1992.

Tax Guide for U.S. Citizens and Resident Aliens Abroad. Washington, DC: Internal Revenue Service, 1991.

Tax Information for Older Americans. Washington, DC: Internal Revenue Service, 1991.

U.S. Tax Treaties. Washington, DC: Internal Revenue Service, 1991.

Your Social Security Checks While You Are Outside the United States. Washington, DC: Social Security Administration, 1990.

Companies / Government / Organizations

CATO Institute, Washington, DC

O'Connor & Desmarias, McLean, VA

Internal Revenue Service, Washington, DC

RESIST (Retirees to Eliminate State Income Source Tax) of America, Carson City, NV

National Conference of State Legislatures, Washington, DC

Tax Foundation, Washington, DC

U.S. Advisory Commission on Intergovernmental Relations, Washington, DC

CHAPTER 8

Publications

Allison, M. "Aging and Exercise: Improving the Odds." *Harvard Health Letter,* February 1991: 4.

Anderson, K. "Retirees' Health Plans Get the Ax." *USA Today,* November 14, 1991: B1.

Andres, R., et al. "Impact of Age on Weight Goals." *Annals of Internal Medicine* Vol. 103, December 1985: 1030.

Barinaga, M. "How Long is the Human Life-Span?" *Science* Vol. 254, November 1991: 936.

Bechtel, S., and Waggoner, G. "How Old Are You Really?" *Esquire,* May 1990.

Bound for Good Health: A Collection of Age Pages. Bethesda, MD: National Institute on Aging, 1991.

Boyer, P. "Nonsurgical Wrinkle Reducers." *Prevention,* March 1991: 45.

Choosing an HMO: An Evaluation Checklist. Washington, DC: American Association of Retired Persons, 1986.

"Diet Breakthroughs to Keep You Younger, Longer." *Prevention,* March 1991: 34.

Dolnick, E. "Why Do Women Outlive Men?" *Washington Post,* August 13, 1991: WH10.

Doress, Paula B., Siegal, Diana L., and the Midlife and Older Women Book Project, with the Boston Women's Health Book Collective. *Ourselves, Growing Older.* New York: Simon & Schuster, 1987.

Evans, W., and Rosenberg, I. "Boosting Your Biomarkers of Youth." *Prevention,* March 1991: 120.

Fries, J. *Aging Well: A Guide for Successful Seniors.* Menlo Park, CA: Addison Wesley, 1989.

Gallagher-Allred, C. "Nutrition and the Elderly." *Caring Magazine,* May 1991: 68.

Health Benefits Under the Consolidated Omnibus Budget Reconciliation Act. Washington, DC: U.S. Department of Labor, Pension and Welfare Benefits Administration, 1990.

Henig, R. "Collagen Risks: Still Unknown." *Washington Post,* May 26, 1992: H7.

Hermann, M., and Sheinman, A. "Vitamins: The ABCs of Good Health." *New Choices,* April 1991: 46.

Katahn, M. "A Diet That Fights Aging and Illness." *New Choices,* December 1991/January 1992: 77.

Kolata, G. "Alzheimer's Disease: Dangers and Trials of Denial." *New York Times,* February 28, 1991: B15.

Krucoff, C. "The Elderly Who Don't Take Aging Sitting Down." *Washington Post,* July 2, 1991: 9.

———. "Exercise and Menopause." *Washington Post,* June 30, 1992: H16.

Laufer, M. B. *Have You Heard? Hearing Loss and Aging.* Washington, DC: American Association of Retired Persons, 1984

Main, J. "The Battle Over Benefits." *Fortune,* December 16, 1991: 91.

Marmot, M., and Poulter, N. "Primary Prevention of Stroke." *The Lancet* Vol. 339, February 8, 1992: 344.

Myers, T. *How To Keep Control of Your Life After 50.* Lexington, MA: Lexington Books, 1990.

O'Brien, S., and Vertinsky, P. "Unfit Survivors: Exercise as a Resource for Aging Women." *The Gerontologist* Vol. 31, No. 3 (1991): 347.

Perl, R. "Finding The Fountain of Youth Through Exercise." *Atlanta Journal/Atlanta Constitution,* July 18, 1991: K7.

Perry, P. "Fitness Report." *American Health,* October 1990: 26.

Squires, S. "What to Eat After 60." *Washington Post,* January 14, 1992: H8.

Stevens, C. "Staying Young." *Washingtonian,* February 1991: 85.

Sugarman, C. "Dietary Fat and Longevity: What the New Study Means." *Washington Post,* July 2, 1991: 16.

Rauch, K. "Sexuality in Later Years." *Washington Post,* April 29, 1992: H8.

Rovner, S. "When Anger Is a Mask for Depression." *Washington Post,* May 26, 1992.

Wasik, J. "Planning For Medical Costs." *Consumers Digest,* March/April 1991: 65.

Who? What? Where? Resources for Women's Health & Aging. Bethesda, Md.: National Institute on Aging, 1992.

Wood, P. "Exercise!" *World Health,* May/June 1991: 25.

Organizations / Companies / Government

Alcohol, Drug Abuse, and Mental Health Administration, U.S. Department of Health and Human Services, Washington, DC

Alzheimer's Association, Chicago, IL

Alzheimer's Disease Education and Referral Center, Silver Spring, MD

American Academy of Dermatology, Evanston, IL

American Academy of Facial Plastic and Reconstructive Surgery, Inc., Washington, DC

American Association of Homes for the Aging, Washington, DC

American Academy of Orthopaedic Surgeons, Park Ridge, IL

American Association of Retired Persons, Washington, DC

The American College of Obstetricians and Gynecologists, Washington, DC

American Heart Association, National Center, Dallas, TX

Arthritis Foundation, Atlanta, GA

Beverly Foundation, Pasadena, CA

Depression Awareness, Recognition, and Treatment Program, National Institute of Mental Health, Rockville, MD

Employee Benefit Research Institute, Washington, DC

Gerontology Research Center, Baltimore, MD

Health Insurance Association of America, Washington, DC

Healthtrac, Inc., Blue Shield of California, San Francisco, CA

Help for Incontinent People, Union, SC

Metropolitan Life Insurance Company, New York, NY

National Academy of Elder Law Attorneys, Tucson, AZ

National Cancer Institute, Bethesda, MD

The National Council on the Aging, Washington, DC

National Heart, Lung, and Blood Institute, Bethesda, MD

National Institute of Arthritis and Musculoskeletal and Skin Diseases, Bethesda, MD

National Institute of Diabetes and Digestive and Kidney Diseases, Bethesda, MD

National Institute on Aging, Gaithersburg, MD

National Osteoporosis Foundation, Washington, DC

President's Council on Physical Fitness and Sports, Washington, DC

The Skin Cancer Foundation, New York, NY

United Seniors Health Cooperative, Washington, DC

CHAPTER 9

Publications

Aging America: Trends and Projections. 1991 Edition. Washington, DC: U.S. Senate Special Committee on Aging, 1992.

"Attitudes on Aging." *Current Health*, February 1990: 22

Benzaia, D. "Complete Guide to Quality Long-Term Health Care." *Consumers Digest*, November 1990: 22.

Brown, A. "How Old Is Old?" *Current Health*, December 1991: 2.

Checklist For Choosing a Nursing Home. Hartford, CT: Aetna Life and Casualty, 1987.

Christian, S. "Volunteerism." *Los Angeles Times*, May 4, 1989: 10.

Collins, C. "Retirees in Search of the Perfect Fit." *New York Times*, August 8, 1991: C1.

"Communities for the Elderly." *Consumer Reports*, February 1990: 123.

The Continuing Care Retirement Community. Washington, DC: American Association of Homes for the Aging.

Dickinson, P. "Best Places to Retire in the U.S." *Consumers Digest,* May/June 1992: 73.

Dietz, J. "Fighting Age Bias on the Job." *Boston Globe,* January 20, 1990: A25.

Directory of Centers for Older Learners. Washington DC: American Association of Retired Persons.

Dychtwald, K., and Flower, J. *Age Wave.* New York: Bantam, 1990.

Employing Older Americans: Opportunities and Constraints. Racine, WI: The Conference Board, 1987.

Fischer, R. "Higher Education Confronts the Age Wave." *Education Record,* Winter 1991: 14.

Garland, S. "Before You Settle on a Retirement Community." *Business Week,* May 20, 1991: 150.

Glazer, S. "Anywhere But Florida?" *Washington Post,* April 29, 1992: 12.

Guide to Choosing a Nursing Home. Washington, DC: U.S. Department of Health and Human Services, Health Care Financing Administration, 1991.

"A Guide to Long-Term Care Insurance." *Consumers' Research,* June 1991: 25.

Knierim, H. "International Elderhostel Programs: A Look to the Future." *Journal of Physical Education, Recreation & Dance,* May 1991: 58.

Larsen, D. "The Endless Autumn." *Los Angeles Times,* February 26, 1989: VI1.

———. "For Better or Worse, Many Retirees Say Bye Bye, Miss American Pie." *Los Angeles Times,* June 23, 1989: VI1.

The Mature Traveler. Special Report. Reno, NV: The Mature Traveler, 1992.

McManus, K. "Homes Across the Sea." *Changing Times,* March 1989: 98.

Moloney, T., and Paul, B. "The Workplace Needs Older Americans." *USA Today,* January 1992: 16.

New, A. "Elder Care Alternatives to the Nursing Home." *Better Homes and Gardens,* September 1991: 56.

Nursing Home Life: A Guide for Residents and Families. Washington, DC: American Association of Retired Persons, 1991.

Palder, E. *The Retirement Sourcebook.* Silver Spring, MD: Woodbine House, 1989.

"Remarkable Senior Performances." *Senior Patient,* July/August 1989: 61.

Roark, A. "The Special Years: Busy, Active, Happy." *Los Angeles Times,* May 4, 1989: SS1.

Robinson, J. "Quitting Time."
American Demographics, May
1991: 34.

Rock, A. "The Truth About Post-
Job Jobs." *Money Guide,* Fall
1989: 73.

Salmen, J. *The Do-Able
Renewable Home.* Washington,
DC: American Association of
Retired Persons, 1991.

*A Shopper's Guide to Long-Term
Care Insurance.* Kansas City,
MO: National Association of
Insurance Commissioners, 1990.

*Statistical Abstract of the United
States, 1991: The National Data
Book.* Washington, DC: U.S.
Department of Commerce, 1991.

Taylor, S. "Talents, Tools; and
Time." *Modern Maturity,* April/
May 1990: 79.

Thompson, T. "Jobs That Will
Keep You Working Happily Ever
After." *U.S. News & World
Report,* August 14, 1989: 64.

*Tomorrow's Choices: Preparing
Now for Future Legal, Financial
and Health Care Decisions.*
Washington, DC: American
Association of Retired Persons,
1991.

Wilcox, M. "Life Care That
Won't Cost Your Life Savings."
*Kiplinger's Personal Finance
Magazine,* January 1992: 59.

Organizations/Companies/Government

Action, The Federal Domestic
Volunteer Agency, Washington,
DC

American Association of Homes
for the Aging, Washington, DC

American Bar Association,
Commission on Legal Problems of
the Elderly, Washington, DC

American Express/The AARP
Travel Experience, New York,
NY

Bureau of Consular Affairs, U.S.
Department of State, Washington,
DC

Continuing Care Accreditation
Commission, Washington, DC

Family Caregivers of the Aging,
Washington, DC

Forty Plus, Washington, DC

Grand Circle Travel, Boston, MA

Health Insurance Association of
America, Washington, DC

National Academy of Elder Law
Attorneys, Inc., Tucson, AZ

National Alliance of Senior
Citizens, Washington, DC

National Association of Area
Agencies on Aging, Washington,
DC

National Citizens Coalition for
Nursing Home Reform,
Washington, DC

National Consumers League,
Washington, DC

National Executive Service
Corps, New York, NY

National League for Nursing,
New York, NY

National Park Service, U.S.
Department of the Interior,
Washington, DC

Older Women's League, Washington, DC

Operation ABLE, Chicago, IL

Retired Senior Volunteer Program, Washington, DC

Senior Community Service Employment Program, U.S.

Department of Labor, Washington, DC

Service Corps of Retired Executives Association, Washington, DC

United Seniors Health Cooperative, Washington, DC

U.S. Tour Operators Association, New York, NY

Index

Q

R